MACBETH AND THE PLAYERS

MACBETH
AND THE PLAYERS

DENNIS BARTHOLOMEUSZ
Lecturer in English, Monash University
Victoria, Australia

CAMBRIDGE
AT THE UNIVERSITY PRESS
1969

Published by the Syndics of the Cambridge University Press
Bentley House, 200 Euston Road, London N.W.1
American Branch: 32 East 57th Street, New York, N.Y.10022

Library of Congress Catalogue Card Number: 69–10270
Standard Book Number: 521 06925 4

Printed in Great Britain
at the University Printing House, Cambridge
(Brooke Crutchley, University Printer)

CONTENTS

82017

PLATES

(BETWEEN PAGES 96 AND 97)

Photographs for the text figures in appendix II by Moreton-Pritchard

vii

PREFACE

In this task of reconstructing and evaluating players' interpretations of Macbeth and Lady Macbeth I have been assisted by the players themselves. Sir Lewis Casson, Dame Sybil Thorndike, Dame Flora Robson, Miss Beatrix Lehmann and Mr Eric Porter talked of productions of *Macbeth* and gave me much valuable information. For this I am grateful. I wish to thank Mr Byam Shaw, who put his notes and his director's copy of *Macbeth* at my disposal, Mr Robert Speaight who discussed several productions of *Macbeth* with me, Sir Alec Guinness and Sir John Gielgud for their letters, which helped to answer some of my questions.

A study of this kind necessarily owes much to the work of scholars in many fields. I found the scholarly excavations of Professor A. C. Sprague, Professor Alan Downer, Dr Bertram Joseph and Dr Kalman Burnim in my own field indispensable. Mr Nash of the Gabrielle Enthoven Collection and his staff, the staff of the British Museum, the staff of the Shakespeare Memorial Library at Stratford, Miss J. Aylmer of the British Theatre Museum, Mrs Jane Nicholas of the British Council, Mrs Mary Salas and Mrs Norma Bolton of the English Department of Monash University helped to make my way smoother.

I must record a special though not fully definable debt of gratitude to Professor Geoffrey Bullough of King's College, University of London. To Professor W. A. Armstrong, whose help cannot be measured, and whose suggestions were of the greatest value when this book was being written as a Doctoral thesis at King's, I am particularly indebted. To the editors of the Cambridge University Press, who presided over the transformation of *Macbeth and the Players* from thesis to book, and Dr Geoffrey Hiller of Monash, I owe much again.

To my wife, who helped to keep the book alive at all times, I dedicate *Macbeth and the Players*.

D. B.

Melbourne
1967

INTRODUCTION

I have tried in this book to test the proposition that players achieve special insights into a text, insights not normally available to critics and scholars, in rehearsal and during performance, as musicians perceive the richness of the music they play in the very act of playing. Scholars have supported the proposition. In the eighteenth century, Steevens wrote that to Garrick, a single glance of whose eye had long been the best expositor of Shakespeare's meaning, the cold annotations of the scholars must appear tedious.[1] And Professor Brander Matthews wrote early in our century of the importance of the tones of a player's voice, movements, gestures, subtle, creative, seemingly unpremeditated, which give life and body to character and illuminate a text. Brander Matthews thought that no commentary on *Hamlet*, of all the countless hundreds that had been written, would be a more useful aid to a larger understanding of the text than a detailed record of the readings, the gestures, the business employed in the successive performances of the part by Burbage and by Betterton, by Garrick, Kemble, Macready and Irving.[2]

Players themselves have believed in the truth of the proposition examined in this book, and some have been strong-minded enough to assert it. Macready wrote in 1844 that neither Goethe, Schlegel, nor Coleridge had revealed in all their elaborate remarks the 'exquisite artistical effects' he could see in *Hamlet*. Long meditation over *Hamlet*, like long straining after sight, had brought forth the 'minutest portion of its excellence' to his view.[3] When, a few weeks after seeing his particularly expressive and illuminating interpretation of Marlowe's Jew in *The Jew of Malta* at Stratford-upon-Avon, I suggested to Eric Porter that actors achieve specific and particular insights into a text, the idea was so obvious to him it hardly needed asserting.

Yet while good actors certainly do reveal a text, bad ones

[1] See chapter 4, pp. 58–9.
[2] *Shakespearean Studies*, ed. Brander Matthews and Ashley H. Thorndike (1916), p. 6.
[3] See chapter 8, pp. 156–7.

obscure it. If players' interpretations of character on the stage have been creative and illuminating, they have also been unintelligent, unsubtle and purely external. The idea needed to be tested. A single text—*Macbeth*—was chosen to test it. Interpretations of the two principal characters in the play were singled out because it was the only way in which this study could be kept within manageable bounds.

As this book begins with the earliest known description of a performance of *Macbeth*, on April 20, 1611, the first task was one of reclamation and reconstruction. As I had to consider players' interpretations of character not merely in terms of ideas but in terms of concrete realities of expression, of speech, of make-up and costume, of gesture and movement as well, the task of reclamation was both laborious and exciting. The evidence, slight but important in the age of Burbage, grew in volume as the centuries rolled by. It was sometimes necessary to consider lighting, for make-up, costume and lighting are interrelated. At other times it was useful to consider décor, for properties and objects on the stage can affect gesture and movement. Evidence relating to the way in which actors spoke the words in *Macbeth* led to an investigation of the nature of the stage, for the structure of the stage and the size of the theatre affect the speech of the actor. The English stage itself, like other social institutions, has responded to the movement of history.

As the task of reclamation and evaluation went on, this study began to throw some light on the implications of old disputes. What, for example, was the style of acting at the Globe? Professor Alfred Harbage has expressed the view that the style of acting in Shakespeare's day, like the stage on which the actors worked, was non-realistic, 'formal' and not 'natural'.[1] It seemed to follow that, ideally, interpretations of Shakespeare's characters could not be subject to variation but would be fixed in an immutable, formal pattern. More recently, in *Acting Shakespeare* (1960), Dr Bertram Joseph has shown that while Shakespeare's art had formal elements, these elements had to be approached creatively by the actor: they had to be re-lived and re-created afresh. Dr Marvin Rosenberg, totally dissenting from any formalist view of Elizabethan acting, has attempted to show from internal evidence and descriptions of performances in Shakespeare's day that the

[1] See *Theatre for Shakespeare* (1955), p. 92.

more skilled players at the Globe were not 'marionettes', but essentially natural and creative in their approach.[1]

A great deal, of course, depends on the meanings we give to the words 'formal' and 'natural'; their meanings alter from one period to another and from one culture to another; and they may become interchangeable. What is natural in one age may appear to be formal in another.

While these words may contain an intensely subjective element, at given periods in the history of the English theatre they have been used to describe different ways of interpreting Shakespeare on the stage. Quin's approach to Macbeth was formal without success, while Cooke was thought to be natural, though not successful either. The great interpreters of Macbeth and Lady Macbeth appear to have combined formal and natural elements in their art. Garrick, as Macbeth, cut Duncan's throat with dignity,[2] and Byron, writing of Mrs Siddons, reports that among the actors he knew, Cooke was the most natural, Kemble the most supernatural, Kean the medium between the two. But Mrs Siddons was worth them all put together.[3] Players like Garrick and Mrs Siddons were equally responsive to naturalistic and formal elements in Shakespeare's art, while players like Quin or Cooke stressed one element at the expense of the other.

Shakespeare's own language shows that a balanced approach would be most effective. Macbeth does at times speak a language removed from ordinary conversation, a language mysteriously grand and powerful:

> ...this my hand will rather
> The multitudinous seas incarnadine,
> Making the green one red.   (II. ii. 61–3)

But there are occasions when Macbeth speaks colloquially:

> I'll put it on.
> Send out moe horses, skirr the country round;
> Hang those that talk of fear. Give me mine armour.
> How does your patient, doctor?   (v. iii. 34–7)

Yet at all times his language seems in character, natural to him and fully alive.

[1] 'Elizabethan Actors: Men or Marionettes', *PMLA*, LXIX (1954), 919.
[2] See chapter 4, p. 80.
[3] See chapter 6, p. 103.

While writing this book, I have not at any point wished to dismiss 'business' and 'spectacle' from the Shakespearean stage altogether. Business can be functional and organic, as in the arming of Macbeth, or irrelevant and distracting, as when Rossi, playing Macbeth in Paris, confronted by the ghost of Banquo in the banquet scene, tripped over his cloak and somersaulted.[1] Spectacle has been associated with the commercial impulse, with the irrelevant and the decorative, taking our attention away from Shakespeare's words. But it can in his own hands become dramatic and relevant. The stage blood in *Macbeth* is spectacular and yet profoundly functional.

The use of spectacle and business in Shakespearean production demands tact and discrimination and some idea of the total rhythm of the play. If one outlawed them, as John Wain clearly wishes to,[2] this would only impoverish Shakespeare's plays on the stage and deprive them of necessary acts and rituals. The notion that Shakespeare's words alone can speak for themselves on the stage is a notion that ought to be entertained only by those who see drama not as a thing done but as a thing read. When an actor speaks he uses tones of one kind or another, and tones imply an interpretation. It is impossible to speak Shakespeare's lines intelligently and not interpret them.

What this study investigates is another approach to Shakespeare—the player's. At a time when critics like Derek Traversi and John Holloway offer their different approaches to Shakespeare with little or no thought of the stage, it seems useful, if only as a mild corrective, to suggest that there is, and has been yet another approach to Shakespeare, one which could not help but keep the stage in mind.

[1] See chapter 10, p. 209.
[2] See *Encounter*, xxii (1964), 59.

ABBREVIATIONS

MLR   *The Modern Language Review.*

N & Q   *Notes and Queries.*

PMLA *Publications of the Modern Language Association of
          America.*

RES   *The Review of English Studies.*

SP   *Studies in Philology.*

TN   *Theatre Notebook.*

Note   Unless otherwise stated, the place of publication of
          works referred to in this book is London.

Texts References are to Peter Alexander's *Tudor* edition of
          The Complete Works of Shakespeare (1951), unless
          otherwise stated.

CHAPTER I

MACBETH AT THE GLOBE

In the first years of the seventeenth century, when Shakespeare and Jonson were writing for the theatre, the English actor was a serious craftsman. In his Preface to *Speculum Aestheticum*, dated 1613, the German writer Johannes Rhenanus reports that English actors believed in constant rehearsal—they were 'instructed daily'. To Rhenanus this approach to the actor's craft gave 'life' to well-written plays, and made English players the best in Europe. The players had a rare advantage. According to Rhenanus, even the most eminent actors allowed themselves to be 'instructed' by the playwright.[1]

Richard Flecknoe confirms this in 'A Short Discourse of the English Stage' (1664). Talking about Shakespeare, Jonson, Beaumont and Fletcher, Flecknoe tells us that they 'instructed'— the word today would be 'directed'—their own actors. The best of these actors, players like Nathan Field and Burbage, appear to have been both 'docile and excellent'.[2] John Downes, who attended the rehearsals of Sir William Davenant's company after the Restoration, observed that the part of Henry VIII was 'rightly and justly done by Mr Betterton, he being instructed in it by Sir William, who had it from Old Mr Lowen, that had his instructions from Mr Shakespeare himself'. The instructions seem to have been remembered long after Shakespeare's death: surviving the

[1] Quoted in David Klein, 'Did Shakespeare Produce his own Plays?', *MLR*, LVII (1962), 556: 'Was aber die actores antrifft, werden solche (wie ich in England in acht genommen) gleichsam in einer schule täglich instituiret, dass auch die vornembsten actores deren orter sich von den Poeten müssen underwaysson lassen, welches dann einer walgeschriebenen Comoedien das leben vnd zierde gibt vnd bringet. Dass also kein wunder ist, warum die Englandische *Comoedianten* (Ich rede von geübten) andern vorgehen vnd den Vorzug haben'—'So far as actors are concerned, they, as I noticed in England, are daily instructed, as it were in a school so that even the most eminent actors have to allow themselves to be instructed by the Dramatists, which arrangement gives life and ornament to a well-written play, so that it is no wonder that the English players (I speak of the skilled ones) surpass and have the advantage of others.' Translation by J. Isaacs. See 'Shakespeare as a Man of the Theatre', in *Shakespeare Criticism*, 1919–35, ed. Anne Bradby (1936), p. 302.
[2] See *Critical Essays of the Seventeenth Century*, ed. J. E. Spingarn (3 vols. 1908), II, 94–5.

vicissitudes of the Civil War, they seem to have passed down from Lowin to Davenant, and from Davenant to Betterton. They must have had extraordinary vitality, rightness and sustaining power to survive in this way. When Betterton played Hamlet, Downes tells us that 'Sir William (having seen Mr Taylor of the Black-Fryars Company Act it, who being Instructed by the author Mr Shakespeare) taught Mr Betterton in every particle of it'.[1] As Professor Armstrong has remarked, Shakespeare apparently made it his business to establish in detail the lines along which his leading roles were to be interpreted.[2]

The Folio text of *Macbeth* (1623) certainly suggests that Shakespeare was interested in details of interpretation. As an actor, he seems to have appreciated the importance of stage business. During the arming of Macbeth in v. iii. of the play, the stage business becomes relevant and dramatic—an actor's fumbling serves a definite purpose; the business on-stage becomes as it were the objective correlative of Macbeth's insecurity. When the news of the arrival of Malcolm's army is confirmed, Macbeth calls for his armour, though Seyton does not think that there is an immediate need for it. Macbeth repeats his request for armour three times, and the poetry helps us to visualise the stage business when Seyton with some reluctance brings his armour on. Macbeth speaks alternately to the Doctor and Seyton as he dons his armour:

> Throw Physicke to the Dogs, Ile none of it.
> Come, put mine Armour on; give me my Staffe:
> Seyton, send out: Doctor, the Thanes flye from me:
> Come sir, dispatch. If thou could'st Doctor, cast
> The Water of my Land, finde her Disease,
> And purge it to a sound and pristine Health,
> I would applaud thee to the very Eccho,
> That should applaud again. Pull't off I say,
> What Rhubarb, Cyme or what purgative drugge
> Would scowre these English hence? Hear'st thou of them?[3]

'Pull't off I say' seems to be addressed to Seyton, 'who while busily untying some band or other is commanded to break it off instead'.[4] 'Pull't off I say' has no meaning in isolation. Business

---

[1] *Roscius Anglicanus* (1708), pp. 21, 24.
[2] 'Actors and Theatres', *Shakespeare Survey*, 17 (1964), p. 197.
[3] First Folio, Actus Quintus, Scena Tertia, p. 149.
[4] See *Macbeth*, ed. H. H. Furness (1963), p. 323, n. 65.

must accompany it if its meaning is to be grasped at all. The stage
business is of the kind that a good actor or director discovers
spontaneously during rehearsal. It is realistic and seems entirely
right. But naturalistic though it is on one level, on another it is
symbolic. One recalls the comment made by Caithness about
Macbeth in the previous scene:

> He cannot buckle his distempered cause
> Within the belt of Rule.[1]

There is a visual commentary on this remark in the 'Pull't off'
business. The stage business in the arming of Macbeth does not
veil Shakespeare's words but gives them greater immediacy and
power.

It seems very likely that Shakespeare had instructed the actors
in *Macbeth* when Simon Forman saw them playing in a production
at the Globe on April 20, 1611. While we have no record of
Shakespeare's 'instructions' in *Macbeth*, Forman's account gives
us glimpses of what possibly was the result of creative collabora-
tion between actor and playwright. Forman left a record of his
impressions, brief but significant, to be found in his *Bocke of
Plaies* (1611), a manuscript in the Bodleian Library.[2] The evidence
he provides is slender, but rich in implication. It sheds some light
on the ways in which the Elizabethan actor interpreted Macbeth
and Lady Macbeth at the Globe. Forman's comments on the first
entrance of Macbeth, the murder of Duncan, the second appearance of Banquo's ghost, and the sleep-walking scene are revealing.

Describing the entrance of Macbeth, Forman recorded a bit of
dramatic stage business which tells us a great deal about the way
in which the actors at the Globe approached their task in 1611:

In Mackbeth at the Glob, 1610 [1611],[3] the 20 of Aprill [Saturday],
ther was to be obserued, firste, howe Mackbeth and Bancko, 2 noble

[1] First Folio, Actus Quintus, Scena Secunda, p. 148.
[2] Bodl. Ashm. MS. 208, fos. 200–13. The note on *Macbeth* occupies 207 and 207 v.
See 'Authenticity of Simon Forman's Bocke of Plaies', in *RES*, xxiii (July 1947),
by John Dover Wilson and R. W. Hunt. Professor Wilson and Dr R. W. Hunt,
Keeper of the Western MSS. at the Bodleian, after considering the evidence,
conclude that the *Bocke of Plaies* is genuine; not a forgery as Dr Samuel A. Tannen-
baum thought.
[3] Saturday fell on April 20 in 1611, not in 1610. Forman seems to have mistakenly
written 1610. See E. K. Chambers, *William Shakespeare* (2 vols. 1930), ii, 337.

men of Scotland, Ridinge thorowe a wod, the[r] stode before them 3
women feiries or Nimphes, And saluted Mackbeth, sayinge, 3 tyms
vnto him, haille Mackbeth, king of Codon...

The observation made by Forman is, if true, slightly startling in
its implications. The actor playing Macbeth appears to have made
his first entrance at the Globe on horseback.

It was possible for actors to enter riding, on the large open
stages in London in Shakespeare's day. At the Fortune Theatre,
the open stage was 43 ft. wide by 27½ ft. deep, and the Fortune
was built by Peter Street on much the same lines as those on
which he built the Globe.[1] The open stage was 'adapted to large
and mobile casts, often grouped in opposing factions or massed in
scenes of pageantry'.[2] Besides, there was a long tradition of
entrances on horseback, which began with the mystery plays of
the Middle Ages and continued through Tudor and Stuart times.[3]
In June 1522, the Spanish ambassador saw a French play at court
in which a horse was imaginatively used to suggest changes of
mood, from wild ferocity to quiet obedience. As the ambassador
described the scene:

A man came on the stage with a great horse, very wild and ferocious.
Friendship, Prudence and Might asked him what he wanted. He
answered that that horse belonged to him, but that it was so wild and
untamable that he could not make any use of him. Friendship said...
they knew how to manage an unruly horse.... They made a bridle, and
bridled the horse with it. That done, they asked the master of the horse
to mount him. At first the master was afraid, but when he mounted the
horse he found he was quiet and obedient, although he raised his head
very high. Friendship said they would make him lower his head. A
curb (Barbado) was attached to the horse, which directly lowered his
head. Without being led, the horse followed his master wherever he
went.[4]

The horse is a symbol of passion. At first wild and uncontrollable,
disciplined by Prudence, Friendship and Might, he lowers his
head in quiet obedience.

Horses continued to appear on the stage in the last quarter of

[1] See J. P. Collier, *The History of English Dramatic Poetry* (3 vols. 1831), III, 297; and
contract for building the Fortune Theatre, quoted in J. Dover Wilson, *Life in
Shakespeare's England* (1944), pp. 208–10.
[2] Harbage, *Theatre for Shakespeare*, p. 24.
[3] Louis B. Wright, 'Animal Actors on the English Stage before 1642', *PMLA*,
XLII (1927), 656.   [4] *Ibid.* 658–9.

the sixteenth century, in the first half of the seventeenth century and during the Restoration. A horse was used in the anonymous pre-Shakespearean tragedy *Woodstock*, which was staged around the year 1597. Thomas Woodstock, Duke of Gloucester, a plainly dressed Duke, is mistaken for a groom by a 'Spruce Courtier on horseback' and instructed to walk his horse. Without disclosing his identity Thomas Woodstock accepts the task, and talks to the horse as he leads him over the stage:

...you're a very indifferent beast, you'll follow any man that will lead you...[1]

In 1633, *Late Lancashire Witches*[2] was staged at the Globe and Act IV has a direction beginning: 'Enter drum (beating before) a Skimmington and his wife on a horse'. The two are pulled off the horse at once and beaten. The tradition went on into the Restoration. On Saturday, July 11, 1668, Pepys went to the Theatre Royal 'to see an old play of Shirley's called Hide Parke; the first day acted where horses are brought upon the stage'. These instances of the presence of horses on the stage in Tudor and Stuart times indicate that Macbeth could have made his first entrance in this way.

Of course one may protest that there is no supporting stage direction in the Folio text for the stage business observed by Simon Forman. But stage business in the theatre frequently goes unrecorded because it is often the result of creative, spontaneous discoveries made during rehearsals. While there is no explicit stage direction in the Folio, it is possible to argue that the rhythm of the scene and the imagery of the play justify an entrance on horseback, that it is theatrically arresting and is dramatically right.

Horses play an important role in the rhythm and imagery of the play. They are restless, move fast, suggest nightmare and chaos and mirror Macbeth's state of mind. Dr Caroline Spurgeon observed the 'rapid riding' which 'emphasises a certain sense of rushing, relentless and goaded motion', the swift journey of the messenger on horseback who arrives 'almost dead for breath',[3]

[1] III. ii. 162; ed. A. P. Rossiter (1946). III. ii. has a stage direction: 'Enter a Spruce Courtier on horseback.'

[2] Thomas Heywood and Richard Brome (1634).

[3] See 'Leading Motives in the Imagery of Shakespeare's Tragedies', in *Shakespeare Criticism*, ed. Bradby, p. 42.

ahead of Macbeth. Macbeth himself outrides Duncan. The king remarks with unconscious irony,

> ...but he rides well,
> And his great love, sharp as his spur, hath holp him
> To his home before us. (i. vi. 22–4)

Images of riding crowd into Macbeth's brain: the new-born babe

> Striding the blast, or heaven's cherubin hors'd
> Upon the sightless couriers of the air... (i. vii. 22–3)

Macbeth, speaking of his 'intent', thinks of a horse lacking sufficient spur to action, and the image then dissolves into a picture of a horse that 'o'er-leaps itself', and falls on the farther side. As rehearsals progressed and the players at the Globe began to sense the movement of the play, the entrance of Macbeth on horseback perhaps became necessary.

But the horse could well have performed another function. Actors know how an object can assist in the interpretation of character, in the definition of feeling, the communication of a state of mind. The 'nice conduct of a clouded cane' can reveal and define character on the stage. Actors are careful about the objects they choose because objects possess connotations which can assist them in living their parts.

The horse used by the actor at the Globe could have helped him to make several points about the character. It could have helped to define Macbeth's class and station—Forman noted that Macbeth was 'noble'—and fleetingly to suggest the soldier married to war, 'Bellona's bridegroom' as Ross describes him, the man interested in power.

One can accept in its literal sense Forman's statement that Macbeth entered riding. But one cannot afford to take literally his remark that Macbeth and Lady Macbeth could not, after the murder of Duncan, wash the blood off their hands 'by any means': 'And when Mack Beth had murdred the kinge, the blod on his handes could not be washed of by Any meanes, nor from his wiues handes, which handled the bloddi daggers in hiding them, By which means they became both moch amazed and Affronted.' Commentators from Collier onwards have argued that Forman's account of Duncan's murder points to a scene which the Folio omits, because they have taken his statement that the blood

6

could not be washed off by any means in its literal sense. If we accept their view, then on April 20, 1611, Shakespeare and his actors were using spectacle of an unbelievably sensational kind.

We don't, however, have to accept the literal view. J. M. Nosworthy, who is not happy with Collier's interpretation and writes that Forman's description of the scene may only suggest 'a bowl of water and a towel' or 'ablutions accompanying the dialogue',[1] does not himself escape a disturbing literalness. Forman appears to have been thinking and writing metaphorically and his remarks need not imply properties or business so obvious and so literal. Simon Forman could not have read the play before he saw the production of *Macbeth* at the Globe, but the actors seem to have communicated one of Shakespeare's themes to him: the sensitiveness of the murderers to the evil in which they are caught. This, one suspects, is the real significance of his remark that the blood could not be washed off their hands by any means. Forman understood that Lady Macbeth's Pilate-like desire

> A little water clears us of this deed (II. ii. 67)

could not be achieved. The sense of terrible violations appears to have come through.

Forman's description of the third episode he remembered, the second appearance of Banquo's ghost, throws some light again on the depth and range of the actor's art in Shakespeare's day:

The next night, beinge at supper with his noble men whom he had bid to a feaste to the which also Banco should haue com, he began to speake of Noble Banco, and to wish that he wer ther. And as he thus did, standing vp to drincke a Carouse to him, the ghoste of Banco came and sate down in his cheier behind him. And he turninge About to sit down Again sawe the goste of Banco, which fronted him so, that he fell into a great passion of fear and fury . . .

Forman registers the shock as Macbeth drinks to Banquo, turns to sit down and finds the ghost behind him seated in his own chair. The audience at the Globe saw Banquo's ghost before Macbeth saw him, and possibly appreciated the ironic contrast between the figure of the ghost of Banquo, with his blood-soaked hair and eyes without 'speculation' in them, and Macbeth unaware, drinking a 'carouse' to him. Once again this must have

---

[1] 'Macbeth at the Globe', *The Library*, II (1947–8), 113.

been business worked out during rehearsals, for the written text does not tell us where the ghost entered or what he did. All the Folio text has is a brief stage direction: 'Enter Ghost', as Macbeth fills his cup and drinks 'to the general joy o' th' whole table', and 'our dear friend Banquo, whom we miss'.[1] Shakespeare and his actors must have worked out Banquo's movements in detail as they rehearsed.

Forman described the way in which the Elizabethan actor interpreted the character of Macbeth when he turned round and discovered the ghost. Forman remembered that Macbeth 'fell into a great passion of fear and fury'. The reactions observed, fear, the impulse to retreat, and fury, the impulse to attack, indicate that the Elizabethan actor was bringing complex feelings to the surface.

What seems like a possible reference to *Macbeth* in *The Knight of the Burning Pestle*, a contemporary play by Beaumont, completes the picture we have in this scene, of the complexity and range of the art involved in the Elizabethan actor's interpretation of the character of Macbeth:

> When thou art at thy table with thy friends,
> Merry in heart, and filled with swelling wine,
> I'll come in midst of all thy pride and mirth,
> Invisible to all men but thy self,
> And whisper such a sad tale in thine ear
> Shall make thee let the cup fall from thy hand,
> And stand as mute and pale as death itself.[2]

Both J. Q. Adams[3] and C. B. Young suggest that this is an 'obvious' reference to the second appearance of Banquo's ghost. C. B. Young writes:

These lines, spoken by Jasper 'with his face mealed', were clearly intended to recall the apparition of Banquo on the stage, and suggest that the stage business of dropping the cup, mentioned by Garrick, and used by Charles Kemble and many others, goes back to the original staging at the Globe.[4]

The line
> And stand as mute and pale as death itself

---

[1] III. iv. 88–9.
[2] (1613), Actus Quintus, Scena Prima.
[3] *Macbeth*, ed. J. Q. Adams (1931), p. 297.
[4] See *Macbeth*, ed. J. Dover Wilson (1947), p. lxix.

certainly does recall Macbeth's remark to his wife after the ghost leaves:

> You make me strange
> Even to the disposition that I owe,
> When now I think you can behold such sights
> And keep the natural ruby of your cheeks,
> When mine is blanch'd with fear.   (III. iv. 112–16)

If Adams and Young are right, then Beaumont had seen *Macbeth* and observed the swift transition of feeling from 'mirth' to paralysed fear as the cup clattered down, the fear revealed in the face of the actor, 'as pale as death itself.'

Forman leaves us with the impression that he had seen a skilled actor play Macbeth; and if we accept the reference in *The Knight of the Burning Pestle* as well, the impression of an actor who attempted to achieve a complete identity with the character is unavoidable. It is more than probable that Forman has afforded us glimpses of Richard Burbage—Burbage who allowed himself to be 'possessed' by Shakespeare's great tragic figures, as all the surviving evidence about him suggests.

Burbage was known for his concentration and his 'action'. Richard Flecknoe wrote that Burbage had the capacity for 'so wholly transforming himself into his Part, and putting off himself with his Cloathes, as he never (not so much as in the Tyring-house) assum'd himself again until the Play was done'.[1] Flecknoe tells us that Burbage could 'transform himself into what shape he would' and praises him for his 'action':

> we may say
> 'Twas only he who gave life unto a play
> Which was but dead, as twas by the author writ,
> Till he by action animated it.[2]

Cicero defined action, and this sense of the word was understood in Shakespeare's day as the 'language and the eloquence of the body'.[3] The body of the actor playing Macbeth would have been eloquent when he grew 'as pale as death itself'. We could say of him that his 'body thought'.

---

[1] *Critical Essays*, ed. Spingarn, II, 95.
[2] 'The Praises of Richard Burbage', in Edwin Nungezer, *A Dictionary of Actors* (1929), p. 78.
[3] See *Actors on Acting*, ed. T. Cole and H. K. Chinoy (1949), p. 26.

Action could and did include pronunciation, the eloquence of the voice, as well as of the eyes or hands: Burbage had the capacity to speak expressively and could change tone successfully, one of the most important means of dramatic effect in the theatre. Flecknoe writes that Burbage could 'artfully vary and modulate his Voice, even to know how much breath he is to give to every syllable...animating his words with speaking, and Speech with Action'.[1]

Burbage allowed himself to be so possessed with his characters that members of his audience sometimes found it difficult to disentangle the actor from the characters he played. Richard Corbet, Bishop of Oxford, tells the story of 'mine host...full of ale and history', for whom the figure of Richard III gradually transformed itself as he spoke of 'the inch where Richmond stood, where Richard fell', into that of Richard Burbage:

> ...he mistooke a player for a King
> For when he would have sayd, King Richard dyed
> And call'd—A horse—he, Burbidge cry'de.[2]

When Burbage died in March 1618, the writer of *A Funerall Elegye on ye Death of the famous Actor Richard Burbedg* believed that Shakespeare's tragic heroes had died with him. The writer of the elegy felt that neither 'young Hamlet', nor 'ould Heiroymoe' and 'moe beside' would be played satisfactorily again:

> No more young Hamlet, ould Heiroymoe
> King Lear, the Greued Moore, and moe beside,
> That lived in him; have now forever dy'd.[3]

Around 1611, however, when Forman saw *Macbeth*, Burbage was still very much alive and at the height of his powers, as surviving actors' lists tell us, and playing the principal tragic roles at the Globe. In 1610, on May 31, Burbage took part in a city pageant with the boy-actor John Rice. Burbage played 'Amphion, the Father of hermonie or Music, a grave and iudicious Prophetlike personage, attyred in his apte habits, every way answerable to his state and profession'.[4] During the first half of the year

---

[1] *Critical Essays*, II, 95.
[2] See Nungezer, *Dictionary of Actors*, p. 77.
[3] *Ibid.* p. 76.
[4] See *The Athenaeum* (May 19, 1888), p. 641.

1611, Burbage played in Jonson's *Catiline*[1] and his name headed a list of 'principall Tragoedians'[2] published by Jonson. In the same year he played Ferdinand in *The Duchess of Malfi*.[3] It was a very busy year, and it seems very likely that when Simon Forman visited the Globe on April 20, 1611, it was Burbage who played Macbeth.

It is probable though less certain that on April 20, 1611, John Rice, the boy-actor, played Lady Macbeth. In 1607, as 'a very proper Child well spoken, being clothed like an angell of gladness with a Taper of Frankincense burning in his hand',[4] Rice had delivered an eighteen-verse speech by Ben Jonson to King James, for the Merchant Taylors. He took part in the pageant of May 31, 1610, with Burbage. On this occasion Burbage and Rice were described as 'two absolute actors even the verie best our instant time can yield'. Rice was Corinea of Cornwall 'a very fayre and beautiful Nimphe, representing the Genius of olde Corineus Quene of the Province Cornwall, suited in her watrie habit yet rich and costly, with a Coronet of Pearles and Cockle Shells on her head'.[5] As Rice, trained by Heminge, was the principal boy-actor in Shakespeare's company between 1607 and August 1611, and an excellent actor of the regal line, it is possible that he played Lady Macbeth on April 20, 1611. If he did, Lady Macbeth must have been 'very fayre and beautiful'.

Margaret Webster, commenting on the work of the Chinese boy-actor Mei-Lan-Fang, recalls the exquisite grace of his playing, and observes that he was entirely convincing in women's roles, whether he portrayed seductiveness, ardour, simplicity or passion—so convincing that an 'Occidental actress' could respect the truth of his playing.[6]

The tradition that boys should play women's roles has persisted in the Chinese theatre, while the Elizabethan tradition died during the Restoration. But as long as the tradition was alive in England, Elizabethan boy-actors were, like Mei-Lan-Fang, convincing. Certainly Simon Forman seems to have been con-

[1] *Ben Jonson*, ed. C. H. Herford and Percy and Evelyn Simpson (10 vols. 1925–50), IX, 240.
[2] *Ibid.*
[3] See Nungezer, *Dictionary of Actors*, p. 74.
[4] See T. W. Baldwin, *The Organization and Personnel of the Shakespearean Company* (1927), p. 227.
[5] *Athenaeum* (May 19, 1888), p. 641.
[6] *Shakespeare Today* (1957), p. 106.

vinced by the new identity the boy-actor had achieved as Lady Macbeth: 'Mackbetes quen did Rise in the night in her slepe, and walke and talked and confessed all, and the docter noted her wordes...'

The actors at the Globe carried conviction on April 20, 1611, but their interpretation of the characters of Macbeth and Lady Macbeth was not achieved in isolation from the stage on which they worked and the audience before which they acted. Burbage and Rice had the advantage of working in a fine acting tradition. They had, as well, a theatre in which there was intimate contact between actors and audience. Shakespeare's *Macbeth* is built around dramatic soliloquies, explicit and implicit. Macbeth and Lady Macbeth are not so much heard as overheard. If the inner world of Macbeth and Lady Macbeth was communicated vividly to Simon Forman, it was no doubt in part due to the special immediacy of effect obtainable on the apron-stage.

The second obvious advantage that the actors at the Globe naturally had over actors of later generations was that they were playing for the audience which Shakespeare had in mind when he wrote *Macbeth*. As L. A. Cormican has shown, Shakespeare was using a number of folk beliefs, medieval convictions and attitudes in *Macbeth*.[1] The actors at the Globe had an audience that was responsive to the language of metaphor in *Macbeth* and to Shakespeare's tragic themes. The audience Burbage acted for was relatively unburdened by the scientific rationalism which in the later years of the seventeenth century began to regard metaphor as delusive and fictitious, and by the scepticism which in the age of Betterton was already preparing to dismiss the supernatural from nature and from the stage.

In the second half of the seventeenth century, when Betterton came to act Macbeth, the picture had changed. When Davenant, addressing Hobbes in the Preface to *Gondibert* (1650), wrote that 'the elder Poets...fed the world with supernaturall Tales' and that 'a Christian Poet, whose Religion little needs the aids of Invention, hath less occasion to imitate such Fables as meanly illustrate a probable Heaven by the fashion and dignity of Courts, and make a resemblance of Hell out of the Dreams of frighted Women, by which they continue and increase the melancholy mistakes of the People',[2] he was reflecting a change in taste. When

---

[1] See 'Medieval Idiom in Shakespeare', *Scrutiny*, XVII (1950), 186. [2] P. 7.

Betterton came to act Macbeth, the audience that Burbage played for no longer existed. After seeing a performance of *Hamlet*, John Evelyn wrote in his *Diary* on November 26, 1661: 'I saw Hamlet, Prince of Denmark played, but now the old plays begin to disgust this refined age, since his Majesties' being so long abroad.' The actors playing Macbeth and Lady Macbeth had changes in taste and new problems to grapple with in the age of Betterton.

CHAPTER 2

THE AGE OF BETTERTON

Colley Cibber, who had worked with Betterton, wrote: 'Should I therefore tell you, that all the Othellos, Hamlets, Hotspurs, Macbeths and Brutus's whom you may have seen since his Time, have fallen far short of him; this still should give you no Idea of his particular Excellence.'[1]

Cibber gives us no idea of Betterton's 'particular excellence' in *Macbeth*, though he describes Betterton's playing of Hamlet and the way in which he 'could vary his spirit to the different characters he acted'.[2] Cibber tells us that Betterton had the 'requisite Variation of Voice' that made every line he spoke 'seem his own, natural, self-delivered Sentiment'.[3] Betterton had an expressive voice and a capacity for identifying himself with Shakespearean characters as different as Brutus and Hotspur, Falstaff and Othello, Hamlet and King Henry VIII. A Restoration gentleman who had frequently seen Betterton play Hamlet told the author of *The Laureat* that in the Closet Scene he had observed Betterton's face, 'which was Naturally ruddy and sanguin...turn instantly on the Sight of his Father's Spirit as pale as his Neckcloath when every Article of his Body seem'd to be affected with a Tremor inexpressible...'[4] Betterton was known for his power as well as his fine restraint[5] in Shakespearean roles. Pope[6] and Dryden[7] acknowledged his stature as an actor, and men of such different tastes

[1] *An Apology for the Life of Mr Colley Cibber, Comedian* (1740), ed. R. W. Lowe (2 vols. 1889), I, 100.
[2] *Ibid.* 103.
[3] *Ibid.* 241.
[4] *The Laureat: or, the Right Side of Colley Cibber, Esq.* (1740), pp. 31, 32.
[5] For a description of the restraint that Betterton showed when, as Hamlet, he encountered his father's ghost, see Cibber, *Apology*, I, 101.
[6] Thomas Davies, in his *Dramatic Miscellanies* (3 vols. 1784), III, 399, tells us that Pope when young was charmed by Betterton, 'and when he died would have a sentence of Tully for his epitaph: "Vitae bene actae jucundissima est recordatio."'
[7] Downes, in his *Roscius Anglicanus*, p. 52, quotes Dryden's tribute to Betterton: 'He like the setting Sun, still shoots a Glimmering Ray, Like Ancient Rome Majestic in decay.'

and outlook as Richard Steele, Colley Cibber, Anthony Aston, and Samuel Pepys[1] were in agreement about his excellence.

Nicholas Rowe, in the introduction to his edition of Shakespeare, writes of Betterton: 'No man is better acquainted with Shakespeare's manner of Expression, and indeed he has study'd him so well, and is so much a Master of him, that whatever Part of his he performs, he does it as if it had been written on purpose for him, and that the Author had exactly conceiv'd it as he plays it.'[2] Yet, when he came to play Macbeth, Betterton used a text which would hardly have pleased Shakespeare if he had lived to see it. The text he used was *Macbeth* rewritten by Sir William Davenant for the Restoration stage, in response to new tastes. One of the disillusioning facts about the stage-history of *Macbeth* during the Restoration is that, even after Davenant died in 1668, Betterton continued to use his version of the play in preference to Shakespeare's.

Downes tells us that 'The Tragedy of *Macbeth*, alter'd by Sir William Davenant' and staged at the Dorset Garden Theatre in 1672, was a success,

being drest in all it's Finery, as new Cloaths, new Scenes, Machines, as flyings for the Witches, with all the Singing, and Dancing in it: The first composed by Mr Lock, the other by Mr Channel and Mr Joseph Priest; it being all Excellently performed, being in the nature of an Opera, it Recompenc'd double the Expence...[3]

Betterton seems to have continued to stage Davenant's *Macbeth* because it was popular.

In the production of *Macbeth* at the Globe, the actors, concentrating on dramatic essentials, like the sensitiveness of Macbeth and Lady Macbeth to the evil in which they are caught, captured Forman's imagination. Davenant, in an attempt to capture the Restoration imagination, shifted the emphasis to spectacle.

[1] For further comments on Betterton see Pepys's *Diary*, ed. Richard, Lord Braybrooke (2 vols. 1825), I, October 16, 1667, November 6, 1667.
[2] *The Works of Mr William Shakespeare* (6 vols. 1709), I, xxxiii–xxxiv.
[3] *Roscius Anglicanus*, p. 33. Dryden, in the Preface to *Albion and Albanius* (1685), defines Opera as a 'musical drama' and tells us that an 'Opera is a poetical tale or Fiction, represented by Vocal and Instrumental Music, adorn'd with Scenes, Machines and Dancing'. Clearly, Downes was not thinking of the Italian opera with its continuous succession of recitation and chorus, which was later to become very popular in London.

During the Restoration the witches flew, they danced, sang, and provided comic interest, while instrumental music filled the theatre.

Pepys, who saw the play in the 1660s at Lincoln's Inn Fields, found it 'a most excellent play in all respects, but especially in divertisement'.[1] When he saw the play again on April 19, 1667, he wrote: 'Here we saw Macbeth, which though I have seen it often, yet it is one of the best plays for a stage, and variety of dancing and musique, that ever I saw.' Drama in the case of Pepys began in delight but did not necessarily end in wisdom. In this he was representative, very much the average Restoration man. What Pepys enjoyed was likely to be popular. Dryden, in contrast to Pepys, was critical of the new *Macbeth* but he belonged to a dissident minority. In an *Epilogue to the University of Oxford*, Dryden glanced ironically at the Davenant version:

> But when all fail'd, to strike the Stage quite Dumb,
> Those wicked Engines call'd Machines are come.
> Thunder and Lightning now for Wit are Play'd
> And shortly Scenes in Lapland will be Lay'd:
> Art Magique is for Poetry profest,
> And cats and Dogs, and each obscener Beast
> To which Aegyptian Dotards once did bow,
> Upon our English stage are worshipd now.
> Witchcraft reigns there, and raises to Renown
> Macbeth, the Simon Magus of the Town.[2]

In spite of Dryden, Davenant's *Macbeth* continued triumphantly into the eighteenth century, as an advertisement in the *Daily Courant*, which appeared on Monday, December 29, 1707, shows:

At the Queen's Theatre in the Hay-Market, this present Monday being the 29th December will be Reviv'd The Tragedy of Mackbeth. The part of Mackbeth to be perform'd by Mr Betterton, And the Parts of the King by Mr Keene, Macduff by Mr Wilks, Banquo by Mr Mills, Lenox by Mr Booth...Hecate by Mr Johnson, 1 Witch by Mr Norris, 2 Witch by Mr Bullock, 3 Witch by Mr Bowan, Lady Mackbeth by Mrs Barry, Lady Macduff by Mrs Rogers. And all the other Parts to the best advantage. With the addition of several Scenes proper to the

[1] *Diary*, II, January 7, 1667.
[2] *The Works of John Dryden*, ed. E. N. Hooker and H. T. Swedenberg (2 vols. 1956), I, 148.

Play With the last New Vocal Epilogue, Composed and perform'd by the famous Signior Cibberini, after the newest English, French, Dutch and Italian Manner.[1]

The cast on December 29 was one of the finest to play *Macbeth* in the eighteenth century. All the resources of the theatre were once again dedicated to producing the new version of *Macbeth*.

Thomas Davies, who was sharply critical of Davenant's *Macbeth*, acknowledged in his *Life of Garrick* that many in the theatre found it enjoyable:

Locke's excellent music had given the managers an opportunity of adding a variety of songs and dances, suitable in some measure to the play, but more agreeable to the taste of the audience, who were pleased with the comic dress which the actors gave to the witches, contrary in the opinion of every person of taste to the original design of the author.[2]

Necessity probably was the mother of Davenant's invention. As remarks made by John Evelyn and Pepys show, Shakespeare, undiluted, could be unpopular. Pepys thought *A Midsummer Night's Dream* an 'insipid and ridiculous play'[3] and in comparison with *The Adventures of Five Hours*, he felt *Othello* was 'a mean thing'.[4] An anonymous writer of the period tells us that 'Shakespeare himself revived, finds no success'.[5]

As we read Downes and Davies, it becomes clear that one of the first things Davenant did to Shakespeare's play was to change the function and purpose of the witches. Forman describes the witches at the Globe as 'feiries'; this indicates that they were mysterious, other-worldly figures. There is nothing in Forman's description to suggest that the witches at the Globe were comic. In Shakespeare's play the witches are 'secret, black and midnight' creatures of chaos and evil. Shakespeare takes them seriously as symbols. Davenant did not. He used the witches to achieve operatic and comic effects. The actors who played the witches in the 1707 production with Betterton were comedians. Johnson

---

[1] Burney Collection of newspapers (1707): British Museum, 1831.
[2] Thomas Davies, *Memoirs of the Life of David Garrick, Esq.* (2 vols. 1780), I, 114, 115.
[3] *Diary*, II, September 29, 1668.
[4] *Ibid.* August 20, 1666.
[5] *Circa* 1684–5. See *More Seventeenth Century Allusions to Shakespeare*, ed. George Thorn-Drury (1924), p. 20.

and Bullock in particular were comedians well known for their skill.[1]

The Restoration audience does not seem to have been seriously interested in Shakespeare's treatment of evil. Davenant himself, one suspects, would have associated the supernatural in *Macbeth* with 'the frightened dreams of old women'. In Shakespeare's *Macbeth* evil is palpable; yet it leads man to emptiness, to disillusionment, to 'nothing' as Macbeth finds out; the powers of darkness have an endless capacity to delude and deceive—the devil is a liar. But the Restoration did not seem capable of understanding Shakespeare's conception of evil. Pope's lines seem to fit the new mood:

> To rest, the Cushion and soft Dean invite,
> Who never mentions Hell to ears polite.[2]

Davenant's alteration of the function and purpose of the witches, who now sang and danced and flew, while in perfect harmony with the scepticism and the triviality of the Restoration, was bound to affect the play as a whole and the other characters in it.

Minor characters can affect principals. Witches in comic dress who sing and dance to entertain an audience, could make Macbeth's first soliloquy:

> This supernatural soliciting
> Cannot be ill; cannot be good... (I. iii. 130–1)

seem part of the comedy too. The tastes of an audience, and a director's wish to entertain them with spectacular effects, must modify the performance of an actor, however skilled he is. Davenant probably nursed a hope that he could serve Shakespeare and Mammon at the same time, but Betterton's first soliloquy, as Shakespeare had written it, would have been ill served by witches who had lost their mysterious flavour and become vaudevillians.

As if aware that the atmosphere established by the singing and dancing witches, who made their first entrance flying, would

---

[1] Davies, in *Dramatic Miscellanies*, III, 493, says that 'Bullock was an actor of great glee and much comic vivacity...The comic ability of Bullock was confirmed to me by Mr Macklin, who assured me, very lately, that he was, in his department, a true genius of the stage'. In his *Life of Garrick*, I, 30, Davies describes Johnson's powers as a comedian.

[2] Epistle IV, To Richard Boyle, Earl of Burlington, 'Of the Use of Riches', in *Epistles to Several Persons*, ed. F. W. Bateson (1951), pp. 151–2.

clash with Shakespeare's poetry, Davenant substantially altered the language of the play, removing from it much of its depth of feeling and its intellectual force. As Betterton's interpretation of the character of Macbeth would have been conditioned by the words he had to speak, it is useful to examine the way in which Davenant's alterations of rhythm, tone and image radically altered character as well. A comparison between the two texts helps to bring out the nature of the change.

In Shakespeare we first see Macbeth through the eyes of the 'bleeding Sergeant'. He reports that Macbeth having 'carved out' his passage to reach Macdonwald,

> ...unseam'd him from the nave to th' chaps,
> And fix'd his head upon our battlements.   (I. ii. 22–3)

The description indicates that there is something of the 'butcher' in Macbeth's character. In a sense, Malcolm's description of Macbeth at the end of the play as the 'dead butcher',[1] and the bringing of his head on to the stage,[2] are anticipated by the Sergeant's report. In Davenant we see Macbeth through the eyes of Seyton, who is not bloody. This removes one of a sequence of images of blood, almost all of which Davenant changed or eliminated. Duncan observes that Seyton is old—

> What aged man is that?[3]

says the king. The aged Seyton's description of Macbeth's encounter with Macdonwald is more decorous than the bleeding Sergeant's:

> Then having conquered him with single force
> He fix'd his head upon our Battlements.[4]

The suggestion of violent, cold brutality in the character of Macbeth comes through vividly in Shakespeare. In Davenant, Macbeth is more restrained. He is less of a butcher.

The logic of Davenant's strategy becomes clearer when Macbeth speaks his first soliloquy after the first encounter with the witches. We are given the impression of a seventeenth-century

---

[1] v. viii. 69.
[2] *Ibid.* See stage direction: 'Enter Macduff with Macbeth's head', in the First Folio, Actus Quintus, Scena Septima, p. 151.
[3] Davenant, *Macbeth* (1674), I. i. p. 1.
[4] *Ibid.* p. 2.

aristocrat and gentleman reflecting on a rather unusual event in a reasonable, slightly detached way. Davenant's Macbeth regards the prophecy of the witches as 'strange'.

> This strange prediction in as strange a manner
> Deliver'd; neither can be good nor ill.[1]

The costume Betterton wore is likely to have reinforced the Restoration colouring. Downes tells us that Macbeth was staged with 'new Cloaths'. The new costumes were probably rich but contemporary. Betterton, as Macbeth, would have worn the full bottomed wig, coat, suit, lace cravat and buckled shoes of the later seventeenth-century aristocrat. Macbeth is dressed in this fashion in the frontispiece to Rowe's edition of the play, published in 1709 (see Plate 1). It shows Macbeth in the witches' cave, and obviously reflects what was going on in the theatres.[2]

Macbeth, in the Davenant version, considers the prophecy of the witches 'not dogmatically but deliberately':

> If ill; 'twould give no earnest of success
> Beginning in a truth: I'm Thane of Cawdor;
> If good? why am I then perplext with doubt.[3]

He is 'perplext'. After the vision of evil in the shape of flying, singing and dancing witches, objects of amusement, it is understandable that he tends to dismiss them from his mind:

> Duncan does appear
> Clouded by my increasing Glories: but
> These are but dreames.[4]

In Shakespeare Macbeth does not have a 'strange prediction': he is 'supernaturally solicited'. Macbeth sways between alternatives; he is cruelly disturbed. The 'sickening see-saw rhythm'[5] helps to bring out the tension within him. When he begins to yield to the temptation of murder he is much more than 'perplext'. Listening to the witches he becomes vulnerable:

[1] Davenant, *Macbeth* (1674), p. 7.
[2] See also *Roscius Anglicanus*, p. 21. Downes writes that when Davenant's *Love and Honour* was acted in 1661, it was 'Richly Cloathed; The King giving Mr Betterton his Coronation Suit...the Duke of York giving Mr Harris his...And my Lord of Oxford gave Mr Joseph Price his'.
[3] I. i. p. 7.   [4] *Ibid.*
[5] L. C. Knights, *Explorations* (1951), p. 20.

My thought, whose murder yet is but fantastical,
Shakes so my single state of man
That function is smother'd in surmise,
And nothing is but what is not. (I. iii. 139–42)

Unreality takes over. The final line of the soliloquy anticipates
Macbeth's last extremity of boredom, emptiness and impotence at
the end of the play, the 'sound and fury, signifying nothing'. The
last four significant lines of the soliloquy are omitted in Davenant,
and Macbeth's encounter with the witches loses much of its
meaning though, considering the way in which the witches
initially behaved in Davenant, this was probably just as well.
Comparing the two versions, one appreciates anew the Cole-
ridgean idea that Shakespeare's plays have an 'organic form'.
Making an alteration in a Shakespeare play is like throwing a
stone into a pool—the repercussions are felt throughout the text.

Davenant's *Macbeth* was composed for a Restoration audience. In
the Davenant version Macbeth's conversation has been refined
and made rational. 'Now if any ask me', says Dryden, 'whence it
is that our conversation is so much refin'd? I must freely, and
without flattery, ascribe it to the Court.'[1] Shakespeare's *Macbeth*
is less refined though not less sensitive and imaginative. One feels
that Eliot's objection to the eighteenth century applies in some
measure to the Restoration. They cultivated their formal garden
quite well, he pointed out, while rather restricting the area under
cultivation.[2]

Macbeth in Shakespeare is composed of 'mighty opposites';
but Davenant attempted to iron them out. Shakespeare's hero is
both more sensitive (though not more refined) and more brutal
than Davenant's. 'It is not permissible', Dryden declares, 'to set
up a character as composed of mighty opposites...A character
...is a composition of qualities which are not contrary to one
another in the same person. Thus the same man may be liberal
and valiant, but not liberal and covetous.'[3] Shakespeare's attitude
to character is more like Brecht's than Dryden's. What Brecht
observed about Shaw's technique of characterisation is true of

[1] 'Defence of the Epilogue', in *The Essays of John Dryden*, ed. W. P. Ker (2 vols.
1926), I, 176.
[2] T. S. Eliot, *What is a Classic?* (1955), p. 18.
[3] 'Preface to "Troilus and Cressida"', *Essays of Dryden*, ed. Ker, I, 215.

Shakespeare's as well: 'We picture a usurer as cowardly, furtive, and brutal. Not for a moment do we allow him to be in any way courageous...Shaw does.'[1] After the murder of Duncan, Macbeth, in Shakespeare, is sensitive to the evil in which he is caught. Shakespeare expresses this sensitiveness in poetry of astonishing emotional power:

> Will all great Neptune's ocean wash this blood
> Clean from my hand? No; this my hand will rather
> The multitudinous seas incarnadine,
> Making the green one red. (II. ii. 60–3)

Macbeth's tones in Davenant are in contrast clinical:

> What hands are here! can the Sea afford
> Water enough to wash away the stain?
> No, they would add a tincture to
> The Sea, and turn the green into a red.[2]

Davenant's image has a special kind of neatness. 'Tincture' is almost meticulous and it is obviously colder than Shakespeare's 'incarnadine'. Certainly Davenant's figure of speech quite alters the character of Macbeth.

When the Messenger arrives in Act v, pale, frightened and inarticulate, with the news that the 'English force' is close to Dunsinane, Davenant's Macbeth is polite:

> Now Friend, what means thy change of Countenance?[3]

Shakespeare's Macbeth is brutal:

> The devil damn thee black, thou cream-fac'd loon!
> Where got'st thou that goose look? (v. iii. 11–12)

Betterton's projection of the character of Macbeth must clearly have been conditioned by the text he used and the audience he acted for. If Davenant kept attempting to clarify Shakespeare's metaphors, it was, no doubt, because the Restoration audience could no longer respond to the dramatic life implicit in them. Shakespeare's

> Sleep that knits up the ravell'd sleave of care, (II. ii. 37)

---

[1] *Brecht on Theatre*, translated by John Willett (1964), p. 11.
[2] II. i. p. 20.   [3] v. iii. p. 58.

with its dramatic energy and fine definition of feeling becomes Davenant's

> Sleep that locks up the senses from their care...[1]

Macbeth's invocation to night in Shakespeare's text, with its dramatic evocation of evil and its metaphors imbued with life:

> Come, seeling night,
> Scarf up the tender eye of pitiful day,
> And with thy bloody and invisible hand
> Cancel and tear to pieces that great bond
> Which keeps me pale. Light thickens, and the crow
> Makes wing to th' rooky wood;
> Good things of day begin to droop and drowse,
> Whiles night's black agents to their preys do rouse...
>
> (III. ii. 46–53)

becomes in Davenant's hands formal and descriptive. The crow 'makes wing' not to a 'rooky' wood but to a 'shady Grove', while the 'seeling night' becomes 'dismal'. Macbeth is once more made less sensitive when Davenant, clarifying Shakespeare's metaphors, substitutes 'Close' for 'Scarf' and omits 'tender' and 'pitiful' in his description of the 'Day':

> Come dismal Night
> Close up the Eye of the quick sighted Day
> With thy invisible and bloody hand.
> The Crow makes wing to the thick shady Grove,
> Good things of day grow dark and overcast,
> Whilst Night's black Agents to their Preys make hast...[2]

The frightening line which makes Macbeth's commitment to evil quite clear, with its brutal resolution,

> Cancel and tear to pieces that great bond
> Which keeps me pale...   (III. ii. 49–50)

is completely omitted. The word 'bond', so central in Shakespeare's thought, implying rights, duties, affections—an important word in *King Lear*[3] as well—is dropped.

It seems clear that given the conditions under which Betterton played the poetry he had to speak, he could not have created a

[1] II. i. p. 19.   [2] III. i. p. 37.
[3] I. i. 91–3: *Cor.* I love your majesty/According to my bond; nor more nor less.

fully tragic Macbeth. Betterton, playing Macbeth, would have died with a moral on his lips:

> Farewell, vain world,
> And what's most vain in it, Ambition...[1]

The lines drive the moral home but not the tragedy.

In Shakespeare the poetry is central. The 'overpowering intensity' of Macbeth's despair 'comes not from the unforgettable fact of a terrible or hideous situation (as it frequently does in Greek tragedy) but from the sheer weight of the phrasing'.[2] But if Shakespeare's language is to achieve its purpose, the actor playing Macbeth has to be in intimate contact with his audience in some way (not necessarily physical), as was suggested in the last chapter. Davenant's alterations result in a language less subtle, more obvious and more explicit, making things less complex for the Restoration actors and the Restoration audiences, in the theatres in which *Macbeth* was staged. Restoration theatres tended to encourage a drama of spectacle and statement rather than a drama of suggestion.

Betterton played Macbeth at Lincoln's Inn Fields, Drury Lane, Dorset Garden and the Queen's Theatre, Haymarket. At Lincoln's Inn Fields, where Betterton played Macbeth in the 1660s, though the theatre was probably less ornate than either Dorset Garden or the Haymarket, drama was often replaced by spectacle. Drury Lane by 1700 was so 'improved' by Christopher Rich that there was less, not more, intimate contact between actors and audience.[3] Rich shortened the stage at Drury Lane, reducing the size of the old apron by adding boxes at the sides and enlarging the pit. One result of these changes was that the actors were forced about ten feet further back from the audience. Neither Drury Lane nor Lincoln's Inn Fields escaped the demand for spectacle. Tom Brown writes to George Moult in 1699:

In short, for Thunder and Lightning, for Songs and Dances, for Sublime Fustian and magnificent Nonsense, it [Bartholomew Fair] comes not short of Drury Lane or Lincoln's Inn-field...One would almost swear, that Smithfield had removed into Drury Lane and Lincoln's

---

[1] Davenant, v. vi. p. 65.
[2] Hazelton Spencer, *Shakespeare Improved* (1927), p. 172.
[3] Cibber, *Apology*, II, 84–6.

Inn-fields, since they set so small a Value on good Sense, and so great a one on Trifles that have no relation to the Play.[1]

Dorset Garden, where Betterton played Macbeth between 1672 and 1673 amidst scenes of operatic splendour,[2] was better suited to spectacular scenic effects[3] than to the kind of intimate dramatic revelation which Shakespeare's language demands. The Queen's Theatre, Haymarket, was built for impressive spectacles and, initially, Cibber tells us, the actors could not be heard there.[4] The acoustics of the theatre were subsequently improved[5] but shortly after Betterton had played in his last production of *Macbeth* at the Haymarket in 1709, the theatre, better suited for song, was used exclusively for the staging of operas.[6]

To say that *Macbeth* was one of the great spectacles of the Restoration, and to admit that Betterton's Macbeth could not have been a fully tragic figure, is not to deny that he probably achieved some distinction in the part. Pepys missed Betterton in the part when he fell ill and was replaced by an actor called Young. On October 16, 1667, Pepys writes petulantly that he went to Lincoln's Inn Fields and was 'vexed to see Young (who is but a bad actor at best) act Macbeth'. Pepys was disappointed again on November 6 at Lincoln's Inn Fields: 'To a play..."Macbeth", which we still like mightily, though mighty short of the content we used to have when Betterton acted, who is still sick.'

Betterton's acting made a difference to Davenant's text; so apparently did Mrs Betterton's. Cibber spoke of her naturalness as Lady Macbeth, her capacity to create awe and terror. Cibber could be describing the sleep-walking scene when he talks of the way she could 'throw out those quick and careless strokes of terror, from the disorders of a guilty mind'.[7] If Cibber is describing the sleep-walking scene, then Mrs Betterton interpreted the character at this point not in the stiff, slow, stately manner of the conventional stage sleep-walker, but more naturally, as Mrs Siddons was to do at the end of the eighteenth century. Mrs Betterton seems to have been able to create awe without being unnatural. Cibber spoke of her as both 'tremendous and delight-

---

[1] Quoted in Staring B. Wells, *A Comparison between the Two Stages* (1942), p. 149.
[2] Downes, *Roscius Anglicanus*, p. 33.
[3] See *The London Stage*, part 2, ed. Emmet L. Avery (1960), p. xxiii.
[4] *Apology*, I, 321. [5] Cibber, *Apology*, II, 87.
[6] *London Stage*, ed. Avery, p. 153. [7] *Apology*, I, 162.

ful', and added that 'she was to the last the admiration of all true lovers of nature and Shakespeare'.[1]

Mrs Betterton was succeeded in the role of Lady Macbeth by Mrs Elizabeth Barry, who played opposite Betterton at Drury Lane and at the Queen's Theatre, Haymarket. Anthony Aston writes that Mrs Barry 'was solemn and august', and Cibber confirms Aston's impression but adds that her voice 'was full, clear and strong so that no Violence of Passion could be too much for her'.[2] Mrs Barry had the capacity to experience fully what she acted.[3] If Cibber preferred Mrs Betterton to Mrs Barry in the role, this only says a great deal for Mrs Betterton's powers. Comparing their performances, Cibber writes:

Mrs Betterton, tho' far advanc'd in Years, was so great a Mistress of Nature, that even Mrs Barry, who acted the Lady Macbeth after her, could not in that Part, with all her superior Strength, and Melody of Voice, throw out those quick and careless Strokes of Terror...[4]

Yet the interpretations of Lady Macbeth by both Mrs Betterton and Mrs Barry must have been limited by the text they used. While Davenant tampered less with Lady Macbeth's words than he had with Macbeth's in the first three acts, he had made drastic changes in the fourth act, when he gave Lady Macbeth's character a sentimental and moralistic dimension. Duncan's ghost appeared twice to Lady Macbeth in this act:

> His fatal Ghost is now my shadow and pursues me
> Where e're I go.[5]

She becomes didactic:

> Resign your Kingdom now,
> And with your crown put off your Guilt...[6]

and makes an explicit act of repentance:

> See me no more
> As King your Crown sits heavy on your Head
> But heavier on my Heart: I have had too much
> Of Kings already. See the Ghost again.[7]

---

[1] *Apology*, I, 162.
[2] 'A Brief Supplement to Colley Cibber, Esq.' (1748): reprinted in Cibber, *Apology*, II—see 303; *Apology*, I, 160.
[3] Aston, 'Brief Supplement', *Apology*, II, 302–3.
[4] *Apology*, I, 161–2.   [5] IV. i. p. 52.
[6] *Ibid.* p. 53.   [7] *Ibid.*

It was fortunate that neither Mrs Betterton nor Mrs Barry were exponents of the 'rant', 'cant' and 'tone'[1] of the Restoration stage, which made tragedy dull; and though Davenant's text would have imposed limits on what they could do, their acting may have to some extent relieved the moralistic element in his version of *Macbeth*.

In the years between Betterton's death in 1710 and Garrick's first performance as Macbeth, players less skilled succeeded in making the Davenant text less stage-worthy. With the solitary exception of Mrs Porter, the stage-history of *Macbeth* between 1710 and 1744 serves to confirm Pope's feeling in *The Dunciad* that art after art was going out, while dullness reigned.

[1] See John Harold Wilson, 'Rant, Cant and Tone on the Restoration Stage', *SP*, III (1955), 598; Alan S. Downer, 'Nature to Advantage Dressed', *PMLA*, I (1943), LVIII, 1002; and A. C. Sprague, 'Did Betterton Chant?' *TN*, I (1946), 54–5.

CHAPTER 3

POWELL AND MILLS:
QUIN AND MRS PORTER

The French actor Jean-Louis Barrault defines the problem that faces the actor when he has to speak verse. Verse, Barrault observes, demands an entrance into a specifically poetic world, a 'state of awakening', a condition of 'extra-lucidity' experienced in those moments 'when the creature is near ecstacy'.[1] The condition of extra-lucidity occurs during a moment of heightened consciousness when the actor so lives the verse he speaks that he enchants his audience.

In the seventeenth century Burbage seems to have had this gift of extra-lucidity. The writer of his *Funerall Elegye* felt that Burbage could have charmed Death away with his 'Inchaunting toung':

> Had'st thou but spoake to death, and us'd thy power
> Of thy Inchaunting toung, att that first hower
> Of his assault, he had lett fall his Dart
> And quite been Charmed, by thy all Charming Art.[2]

The state of the actor speaking verse is lyrical (as Barrault points out), analogous to the state of the singer, but it is a state which involves identification with character and takes in the dramatic. The lyrical state of the actor speaking verse admits dramatic variety. Flecknoe uses the analogy from music when he describes the way in which Burbage spoke verse, but he associates it closely with the principle of identification. Burbage, as Flecknoe observed, was

a delightful Proteus, so wholly transforming himself into his Part... as he never (not so much as in the Tyring-house) assum'd himself again until the Play was done; there being as much difference betwixt him and one of our common Actors, as between a Ballad-singer who onely mouths it, and an excellent singer, who knows all his Graces, and can artfully vary and modulate his Voice, even to know how much breath he is to give to every syllable.[3]

---

[1] See *Nouvelles Réflexions sur le théâtre* (1959), p. 65.
[2] See Nungezer, *Dictionary of Actors*, p. 75.
[3] *Critical Essays*, ed. Spingarn, II, 95.

Shakespeare's verse is not identical with colloquial speech, though it does not exclude it. Certain passages in *Macbeth* are colloquial; others clearly are not. A heightened consciousness—the state of extra-lucidity—and the perception of dramatic variety would be demanded of the actor speaking the poetry of Macbeth, and Burbage seems to have had both the lyrical impulse and the dramatic imagination.

Betterton probably inherited the Burbage tradition of verse-speaking from contemporary players like Hart, Lowin and Taylor, who acted before 1642. Thomas Davies relates that when Betterton was rehearsing the part of Alexander in *The Rival Queens*, he was dissatisfied with his own interpretation of a line and enquired whether anyone could remember how Charles Hart had dealt with it: 'At last, one of the lowest of the company repeated the line exactly in Hart's key. Betterton thanked him heartily, and put a piece of money in his hand as a reward for so acceptable a service.'[1] Betterton was a careful craftsman, concerned with the inscape of the single line. It is significant that Cibber uses the analogy from music when he describes Betterton's speaking of verse:

In the just Delivery of Poetical Numbers, particularly where the Sentiments are pathetic, it is scarcely credible upon how minute an Article of Sound depends their greatest Beauty or Inaffection. The voice of a Singer is not more strictly tied to time and tune, than that of an Actor in Theatrical Elocution: the least Syllable too long or too slightly dwelt upon in a Period, depreciates it to nothing; which very syllable, if rightly touched shall, like the heightening Stroke of Light from a Master's pencil, give Life and Spirit to the whole. I never heard a line in Tragedy come from Betterton, wherein my Judgement, my Ear and my Imagination, were not fully satisfied.[2]

Burbage and Betterton, Mrs Barry and Mrs Betterton, appear to have possessed the lyrical as well as the dramatic impulse. Mrs Barry's voice was so expressive that 'no Violence of Passion could be too much for her'. Yet, says Cibber, even 'while she was impetuous and terrible she pour'd out the Sentiment with enchanting Harmony'.[3]

To speak verse as these distinguished performers of the seventeenth century spoke it must have required individual genius

---

[1] *Dramatic Miscellanies*, III, 271, 272.
[2] *Apology*, I, 110–11. [3] *Ibid.* 160.

as well as a fine sense of the actor's craft. But towards the end of
Betterton's career his sense of the actor's craft was less in evidence.
Rehearsals were approached with less concentration. Betterton
told Gildon: 'When I was a Young Player under Sir William
Davenant, we were under a much better Discipline, we were
obliged to make our Study our Business, which our young Men
do not think it their duty now to do.'[1] The actors and actresses
who played Macbeth and Lady Macbeth immediately after Betterton and Mrs Barry lacked their craftsmanship. With the solitary
exception of Mrs Porter, they failed to achieve identification with
even Davenant's less complex re-creations, and the verse of
Macbeth became a positive obstacle to the creation of character.
Betterton was succeeded in the role of Macbeth by George
Powell, who indulged in 'rants', and John Mills, who suffered
from the 'affectation of the monotone'.[2]

George Powell succeeded Betterton on November 28, 1707 at
Drury Lane, in the Davenant version of *Macbeth*, the music 'being
all new set and performed by Leveridge, Ramondon, Hughes,
Lawrence and others', the dancing by 'Mr Evans, de la Garde
and Miss Norris', with the 'Scenes, Machines, Flyings and other
Decorations in the same order they were originally'.[3] Spectacle
went on being an embellishment; the choreography and music
once again appear to have been used as ends in themselves.

As if in revolt against the restraint and discipline of Betterton's
art, Powell indulged in sensational excesses and, often inspired by
Nantz-brandy,[4] enjoyed making his own contribution to the
spectacular productions which audiences at Drury Lane demanded. Aston tells us that

Powell attempted several of Betterton's Parts, as Alexander, Jaffier,
etc., but lost his Credit; as in Alexander, he maintained not the Dignity
of a King, but out-Heroded Herod; and in his poison'd mad Scene,
out-rav'd all Probability; while Betterton kept his Passion under, and
shew'd it most (as Fume smoaks most, when stifled).[5]

When Powell spoke the verse of tragedy he would indulge in
sudden bursts of violence where quietness and restraint were more

---

[1] Charles Gildon, *The Life of Mr Thomas Betterton* (1710), p. 15.
[2] See Cibber, *Apology*, I, 103. Cf. Aston, 'Brief Supplement', *Apology*, II, 301, and
Davies, *Dramatic Miscellanies*, II, 132.
[3] See *London Stage*, ed. Avery, p. 159.
[4] Davies, *Dramatic Miscellanies*, III, 416.
[5] 'Brief Supplement', *Apology*, II, 301.

relevant. 'I have seen Powell very often raise himself a loud clap by this Artifice', says Addison.[1] Powell seems to have believed that the road of excess led to the palace of art.

If Powell out-raved all probability, John Mills's sobriety had a soporific effect. Mills seems to have first played Macbeth on November 18, 1710, at the Queen's, Haymarket, in the Davenant version, with 'all the Musick composed by Mr Leveridge and sung by Renton, Mrs Mills, Mrs Willis, the dancing by Mrs Santlow, Prince and Mrs Bicknell',[2] and he went on playing the role for twenty-six years. He played Macbeth for the last time on November 18, 1736.[3] But despite the efforts of twenty-six years, the verse in *Macbeth* seems to have remained, for him, an obstacle to the creation of character. Davies, who remembered Mills's performance as Macbeth, writes:

Mills was deficient in genius to display the various passions and turbulent scenes of the character, his voice was manly and powerful but not flexible; his action and deportment decent. I have seen him in *Macbeth*; but neither his manner of speaking, nor his deportment made an impression on my mind greatly to his advantage. He spoke, indeed, the celebrated soliloquy on the progress of time, beginning with 'To-morrow! tomorrow! and tomorrow!' with propriety and feeling, and it produced considerable effect on the audience... [4]

But if Mills gave the impression that the soliloquy 'To-morrow, and to-morrow, and to-morrow' (v. v. 19) was on 'the progress of time', then even Davies's qualifying praise of Mills's acting of Macbeth must be called into question. For the soliloquy is only secondarily about the progress of time. It is primarily an expression of Macbeth's tragic disillusionment, his bitter desolation. Mills was capable of propriety and feeling, virtues which indicate the nature of his strength, but 'useful actor' though he was in less demanding roles, it seems clear that he lacked the imagination and craftsmanship so essential for the tragic actor playing Macbeth. As his voice lacked flexibility, Mills seems to have made the verse of *Macbeth* sound monotonous. Davies tells the story of the squire who found Mills's propriety in Macbeth unbearably dull—the incident described illustrates Mills's par-

---

[1] *The Spectator*, ed. G. Gregory Smith (8 vols. 1907), iv, 122.
[2] *London Stage*, ed. Avery, p. 325.
[3] Charles Beecher Hogan, *Shakespeare in the Theatre* (2 vols. 1951), i, 286.
[4] *Dramatic Miscellanies*, ii, 133.

ticular flaw. Seeing *Macbeth* one evening, the squire was so wearied by Mills's monotonous elocution that when Powell, an old boon companion of his, came on the stage, he exclaimed, so that the whole audience heard him: 'For God's sake, George, give us a speech and let me go home.'[1]

Powell and Mills failed as Macbeth where Betterton succeeded. They clearly lacked his ability. Had Booth or Wilks attempted Macbeth the change would not have been so marked. But Wilks, who played Macduff with fine imagination, avoided the role, and Booth played Banquo. The atmosphere in the theatres, which had been changing in Betterton's time, changed even more sharply after his death. Audiences wanted light entertainment and spectacle, and the actor's art, as Betterton had conceived it, seemed threatened with extinction.

The 'most applauded Pieces for some Years past in our Theatres', said a writer in the *Universal Spectator* of April 10, 1731, 'have not been the Composition of Poets, but of Dancing Masters'.[2] The rage was for 'operas, rope-dancing, Italian farces and pantomimes'.[3] Spectacular theatrical effects were introduced on the stage and 'frequented by persons of the first quality in England to the twentieth and thirtieth time'.[4] After the death of Betterton, the theatres, though structurally unaltered, became imbued with a new spirit—the spirit of John Rich, who sought spectacle as an end in itself. The kind of effect Rich preferred on the stage at Covent Garden, where Quin played Macbeth before he succeeded Mills at Drury Lane in 1736, was not the kind of effect Betterton was known for. Pope in *The Dunciad*, Book III, defines the kind of atmosphere generated by Rich:

> [He] look'd, and saw a sable Sorc'rer rise,
> Swift to whose hand a winged volume flies:
> All sudden, Gorgons hiss, and Dragons glare,
> And ten-horn'd fiends and Giants rush to war.
> Hell rises, Heav'n descends, and dance on Earth:
> Gods, imps, and monsters, music, rage, and mirth,
> A fire, a jig, a battle, and a ball,
> 'Till one wide conflagration swallows all.[5]

---

[1] *Dramatic Miscellanies*, II, 132.
[2] *London Stage*, ed. Avery, p. clxxv.
[3] *Mist's Weekly Journal*, January 14, 1727, quoted in *London Stage*, p. clxxv.
[4] See *The Dunciad*, ed. James R. Sutherland (1943), book III, p. 176, n. to l. 229.
[5] *Ibid.* pp. 176, 177.

James Quin began playing Macbeth at Lincoln's Inn Fields on November 13, 1718, and succeeded Mills in the role at Drury Lane on December 23, 1736.[1] Quin, who played a memorable Falstaff, and was evidently not embarrassed by Shakespeare's verse when satiric or comic effects were called for, seems to have been uncomfortable with the poetry of the tragedies. In his serious moments, Quin found the solemnity of Milton more congenial than the seriousness of Shakespeare. When he spoke 'The Star that bids the Shepherd fold', with its grave, Miltonic grandeur, in *Comus*, he 'made darkness', says John Hill. Later, when Quin came to

> The Sounds, and Seas with all their finny drove
> Now to the Moon in wavering Morrice move,

the audience in the theatre 'saw the curled waves break in upon the calm repose of night, and the peaceful fishes rising and falling under their indented motion'.[2] Quin seems to have been more at home in the solemn, magical land of *Comus* than in the tragic world of Macbeth.

The complex variety of Shakespeare's verse eluded Quin, even though a great deal of that variety had been filed away in the Davenant version of *Macbeth*, which was still used in his time. As Macbeth, Quin 'was deficient in animated utterance and wanted flexibility of tone'.[3] Thomas Davies connects Quin's failure to speak the verse of Macbeth satisfactorily with his inability to identify himself with the character:

He could neither assume the strong agitation of mind before the murder of the king, nor the remorse and anguish in consequence of it —much less could he put on that mixture of despair, rage and frenzy that mark the last scenes of Macbeth. During the whole representation he scarcely ever deviated from a dull, heavy monotony.[4]

Milton's distinctive virtues, his formal grace and solemnity are not Shakespearean in their force. Keats' reaction to Milton comes to mind: 'Life to him would be death to me.'

[1] Hogan, *Shakespeare in the Theatre*, I, 273, 286. Several actors attempted Macbeth after John Mills and before Garrick in 1744, but none had achieved the eminence of Quin, and their performances do not appear to have excited comment, favourable or otherwise.
[2] *The Actor* (1755), p. 235.
[3] Davies, *Dramatic Miscellanies*, II, 133.   [4] *Ibid.*

In No. 92 of the *Prompter*, Aaron Hill imagined Shakespeare addressing the players of the period. Quin is described as 'Mr All-Weight' and warned that he has lost the advantage of his 'pausing solemn significance' because he is always solemn: 'though dignity is finely maintained by the weight of majestic composure, yet there are scenes in your parts where the voice should be sharp and impatient, the look disordered and agonised, the action precipitate and turbulent'.[1] The dignity was in the voice and this appears to have remained unvaried throughout *Macbeth*, but Quin did attempt at some stage to look 'disordered' and make his action 'precipitate and turbulent'. Garrick's ironic description of Quin's interpretation of Macbeth indicates that Quin attempted to be 'precipitate and turbulent' though not very successfully.[2] What he did finally offer was a caricature of precipitancy and turbulence. The gestures he used lacked restraint. Quin's lack of restraint in his use of the language of gesture is made very clear in Garrick's description of the scene with the imaginary dagger. Quin's performance seems to have been dangerously close to comic hysteria—Garrick says with delighted irony:

Come let me clutch thee is not to be done by one Motion only, but by several successful Catches at it, first with one Hand, and then with the other, preserving the same Motion at the same Time with his Feet, like a Man out of his Depth, and half drowned in his Struggles, catches at Air for Substance. This would make the Spectator's Blood run cold and he would feel the Agonies of the Murderer himself.

During the second appearance of Banquo's ghost Quin seems to have tried to make his whole body express fear. Quin believed, according to Garrick, that Macbeth at this point 'should sink into himself...imitate the contracting power of a Snail...his Mind should...denote its strong Workings and Convulsions at his Eyes...'[3] Quin's use of 'the language and eloquence of the body' may have been an attempt to meet the criticism of Aaron Hill. But with the exit of Banquo's ghost, when Macbeth shows courage in the face of the supernatural, Quin's acting tipped over into undeniable excess: 'Then at the...words, Dare me to the Desart

---

[1] Reprinted in *The Gentleman's Magazine* (1784), p. 571.
[2] See 'Supplementary Appendix to "An Essay on Acting",' *Tracts Relating to Shakespeare* (1779), p. 18.
[3] *Ibid.* p. 21.

with thy Sword, Macbeth should draw his Sword, and put him-self in a posture of Defense; and when he comes to Hence horrid Shadow! he should make a home Thrust at him, and keep passing at him till he has got him quite out of the Room.' Quin seems to have had his reasons for duelling with a ghost in this fashion. '...if any Objection is made that Macbeth should know that Ghosts are not vulnerable, I answer Macbeth's Horror confounds him...'[1]

In the scene with the imaginary dagger, and in the banquet scene, Quin seems to have over-stepped 'the modesty of nature'. Quin's excesses do not suggest that he was in the restrained yet passionate Bettertonian tradition of acting. It was not merely Quin's solemn declamation that was against him.

There was only one really restrained moment in Quin's per-formance during the scene with Banquo's ghost—when Macbeth dropped the glass of wine in his hand: 'the Glass of Wine in his Hand should not be dash'd upon the Ground, but should fall gently from him, and he should not discover the least Conscious-ness of having such a Vehicle in his hand, his Memory being quite lost in the present Guilt and Horror of his Imagination.'[2]

The business used by Quin at this point was probably tradi-tional. It resembles Beaumont's description of this particular detail in *The Knight of the Burning Pestle*. The fact, however, that Quin used a traditional bit of business once does not prove that he had the capacity to inherit what was left of the Shakespearean acting tradition that came down through Lowin and Taylor to Betterton. Francis Gentleman's comments on Quin's Macbeth suggest that much of what he said and did was outside that tradition. Gentleman found him 'undescribably cumbersome as Macbeth...His face which had no possible variation from natural grace, except sternness and festivity, could not be ex-pected to exhibit the acute sensations of the character; his figure was void of the essential spirit, and his voice far too monotonous for transitions which so frequently occur.'[3] It is not irrelevant that Quin played in Davenant's *Macbeth* for several years without knowing that it was an adaptation of the original.[4]

Tradition cannot be mechanically transmitted. Betterton was

[1] *Ibid.* p. 19. [2] *Ibid.* p. 21.
[3] *The Dramatic Censor* (2 vols. 1770), I, 108.
[4] See Margaret Barton, *David Garrick* (1948), p. 73.

able to possess a major part of the tradition passed down to him by Shakespeare's actors, Lowin and Taylor, because he had a sympathy with that tradition and the capacity to possess it. During the years after Betterton's death, in productions of *Macbeth*, it was not Quin who seems to have inherited the great tradition through Betterton but Mrs Porter. 'Mrs Porter always spoke of Betterton', says Davies, 'with great respect and veneration. She was so little when first under his tuition, that he threatened her, if she did not speak and act as he would have her, to put her into a fruit-woman's basket and cover her with a vine-leaf...'[1]

In spite of her early training and experience, Mrs Porter tended to be 'cold and ineffectual in comedy'[2] but tragedy set her imagination ablaze. Here the tradition passed down to her by Betterton and Mrs Barry assumed a new and brilliant life. Davies writes:

when the passions predominated, she exerted her powers to a supreme degree; she seemed then to be another person, and to be informed with that noble and enthusiastic ardour which was capable of rousing the coldest auditor to an equal animation. Her deportment was dignified with graceful ease, and her action the result of the passion she felt.[3]

Mrs Porter was restrained yet passionate, and succeeded in achieving identity with the character of Lady Macbeth from within as Chetwood observed:

...if an Actor of good understanding is truly possessed with his Character the true Action will involuntarily occur. I remember Mrs Porter to whom Nature had been niggard in Voice and Face for great in many Parts, as Lady Macbeth, Alicia in Jane Shore...her just Action, Eloquence of Look and Gesture, moved Astonishment! and yet I have heard her declare, she left the Action to the possession of the Sentiments in the Part she performed.[4]

Mrs Porter kept the Bettertonian tradition of disciplined yet vividly expressive acting alive at a time when audiences seemed insensitive to genuine dramatic values. She acted in the Davenant version of *Macbeth*. Within this already limited frame, she seems to have been confined still further, as the century advanced to its

---

[1] *Dramatic Miscellanies*, III, 464.
[2] *Ibid.* 467.   [3] *Ibid.*
[4] William Rufus Chetwood, *A General History of the Stage* (1749), p. 29.

close, by the insatiable demands of an audience in harmony with the spirit of John Rich. When Mrs Porter played *Macbeth* at Drury Lane on November 18, 1736, before 'Their Royal Highnesses the Prince and Princess of Wales', there was 'Dancing between the Acts by Mons. Muliment (lately arriv'd from Paris) being the first time of his performance in England...'[1]

Given these conditions, it is astonishing that Mrs Porter played as effectively as she did. Macklin preferred her performance as Lady Macbeth to that of Mrs Pritchard, who played with Garrick. 'And when I say that,' added Macklin, 'I say a bold word, but she had more consciousness of what she was about than Pritchard, and looked more like a queen.'[2] Mrs Pritchard did not carry out Shakespeare's original intention in the scene after Duncan's death —she did not faint as the text demands: she did not make her entrance at all. It was believed in the eighteenth century that no audience would stomach 'the hypocrisy of such a scene'. 'Mr Garrick thought', writes Davies, 'that even so favourite an actress as Mrs Pritchard would not in that situation, escape derision from the gentlemen in the upper regions. Mr Macklin is of the opinion that Mrs Porter alone could have credit with an audience to induce them to endure the hypocrisy of Lady Macbeth.'[3] Before an audience dangerously naive in its outlook, Mrs Porter continued to play Lady Macbeth, opposite Mills and then Quin, with distinction.[4] Her individual talent and the tradition inherited from the days of Betterton seem to have sustained her.

[1] See manuscript transcriptions of newspaper bills made in the 1880s by Frederick Latreille (British Museum Add. MSS. 32249–52, 4 vols.), III, 314.
[2] William Cooke, *Memoirs of Charles Macklin, Comedian* (1804), p. 26.
[3] *Dramatic Miscellanies*, II, 152–3.
[4] For dates of her performances see Hogan, *Shakespeare in the Theatre*, I, 272–92. Several other actresses attempted the part during the period but not, apparently, with the same distinction. They seem to have provoked no comment.

CHAPTER 4

GARRICK AND MRS PRITCHARD

Mrs Porter, who had worked with Betterton, was 'much charm-ed'[1] by Garrick when she saw him play. Mrs Porter's response to Garrick suggests continuity with the tradition of acting estab-lished by Betterton. If Betterton was praised for his naturalness, so was Garrick. Every utterance of Betterton's 'seemed his own natural self-delivered sentiment'.[2] And the Earl of Chatham singled out Garrick's convincing naturalness for comment: '. . . Inimitable Shakespeare! but more matchless Garrick! always as deep in Nature as the Poet, but never (what the Poet is too often) out of it. . .'[3]

Garrick's art did not, of course, correspond at every point with Betterton's. While there were important similarities between Betterton's art and Garrick's, there were significant differences. Betterton's voice was an expressive instrument and his appeal seems to have been first to the ear. Garrick appealed strongly to both ear and eye. When a celebrated performer was once acting a drunken character, Garrick called to him: 'Your feet are sober.'[4] Garrick brought to Shakespearean tragic acting elements of an art familiar to actors like Burbage and Alleyn—the ancient art of mime. 'Betterton', says Aston, 'could not dance a step.'[5] The Elizabethan actor could. So indeed could Garrick, who held his body like a dancer.

Pope, who had seen Betterton play, went to Goodman's Fields to see Garrick in *Richard III*. Garrick reports that when he became aware of Pope 'dressed in black, seated in a side-box near the stage' viewing him 'with a serious and earnest attention', he 'had some hesitation in proceeding from anxiety and from joy', but as Richard 'gradually blazed forth, the conspiring hand of Pope shadowed him with laurels'. Pope, who had liked Better-

---

[1] Davies, *Dramatic Miscellanies*, III, 469.
[2] Cibber, *Apology*, II, 241.
[3] See *The Private Correspondence of David Garrick*, ed. James Boaden (2 vols. 1831–2), II, 364.
[4] *The Monthly Mirror*, VII (1799), 103.
[5] 'Brief Supplement', *Apology*, II, 300.

ton's achieved dignity, after he had seen Garrick's Richard III, told Lord Orrery: 'that young man never had his equal as an actor, and he will never have a rival'.[1]

Garrick was an original actor. Originality meant a return at times to the beginning, as it did when Garrick announced that he was going to play Macbeth, 'as written by Shakespeare'.[2] Davenant's *Macbeth* had received something like two hundred performances during the first forty-three years of the eighteenth century.[3] Eighteenth-century audiences knew no other version. Quin, who had been playing Macbeth for over twenty years, expressed surprise when Garrick made his announcement. 'Don't I play Macbeth as Shakespeare wrote it?' asked Quin.[4]

When Garrick made an attempt to go back to the text of *Macbeth* as it existed in the First Folio, he appeared to be doing something unacceptably original. He met with immediate and widespread opposition. The press could not see why any change had to be made, as the Davenant version had given satisfaction for eighty years. Dr Johnson's law, the force of which Garrick was to feel throughout his career, began to operate:

> The drama's laws the drama's patrons give,
> For we that live to please must please to live.[5]

Garrick 'took fright...When he staged *Macbeth* on the 7th January, 1744, the play was not exactly as written by Shakespeare.'[6]

While it is true that Garrick did not remain completely faithful to *Macbeth* as written by Shakespeare, in many scenes he restored Shakespeare's original words. Garrick had a respect for Shakespeare's language as Davenant evidently had not. And it can be claimed that, after a considerable lapse of time, Shakespeare's distinctive tones, metaphors and rhythms were heard again in Garrick's production. How far his respect for Shakespeare's language extended can be assessed by comparing the Folio of 1623 with Davenant's *Macbeth* (1674) and Garrick's version of

---

[1] See *Correspondence of Garrick*, ed. Boaden, I, vii.
[2] Barton, *Garrick*, p. 73.
[3] Kalman Burnim, *David Garrick, Director* (1961), p. 103.
[4] Barton, *Garrick*, p. 73. Cf. Davies, *Life of Garrick*, I, 116–17.
[5] 'Prologue, Spoken by Mr Garrick, At the Opening of the Theatre in Drury Lane' (1747). See *The Works of Samuel Johnson*, ed. Robert Lynam (6 vols. 1825), VI, 325.
[6] Barton, *Garrick*, p. 73.

the play.[1] As what a character says is the basis on which an actor constructs an interpretation, such a comparison throws some light on Garrick's intentions. Garrick's interpretation of Macbeth began when he began meditating on the text he was to use.

Davenant's opening, the prelude to Macbeth's entrance, was spectacular and diverting. The witches emerged through trap-doors and made spectacular exits, flying. In Garrick's production, the witches were grounded and, instead of flying out, disappeared through trap-doors. In the 1774 Bell edition (1. p. 4) the witches 'sink'. The witches retained something of their comic character primarily because the convention established by Davenant still retained its hold on the popular imagination, though Garrick seems to have controlled the comedy.[2] Garrick himself seems to have favoured the proposition that the witches should be creatures of an exclusively tragic world, but did not carry out the idea because he felt the audiences at Drury Lane were not ready for it.[3]

In Davenant's version the witches make their second appearance flying, just before the entrance of Macbeth. In the Bell edition the witches 'rise from under the stage', though in the prompt copy used in the 1770s at Drury Lane, Garrick's prompter, Hopkins, has crossed this direction out and substituted 'OP & PS'.[4] This suggests that Garrick may have had the witches enter from stage left and right—the least spectacular of the alternatives.

For Macbeth's entrance Garrick retained a line which is in the Davenant version and not in the Folio of 1623:

Command they make a halt upon the heath[5]

a line which suggests the presence of an army; and added one of his own, so that the illusion of a waiting army was more securely established. Macbeth's command was carried down the ranks:

Halt, Halt, Halt.[6]

[1] Garrick's version of *Macbeth* is to be found in Bell's editions of Shakespeare's plays 'as they are now performed at the Theatres Royal in London, Regulated from the Prompt Book of each Theatre' (1773; 2nd ed. 1774).
[2] Davies, *Dramatic Miscellanies*, II, 119.
[3] See Robert Wyndham Ketton-Cremer, *Early Life and Diaries of William Windham* (1930), p. 30.
[4] The prompt book, now at the Folger Library, is made on a 1773 edition of the play. It is examined by Burnim in *Garrick, Director*, p. 108.
[5] Bell (1774—all subsequent references are to this edition), 1. p. 8. There are no numbered scene divisions in the Bell text.
[6] *Ibid.* Cf. Davenant, 1. i. p. 4.

The atmosphere established by Garrick before Macbeth's entrance and immediately after it would appear to have been, on the whole, more realistic than the atmosphere established by Davenant. Downes, it will be remembered, spoke of Davenant's *Macbeth* as 'being in the nature of an Opera'.[1] The cries of 'Halt' were heard off-stage. Garrick, unlike Macklin some years later, did not let the visible presence of an army dissipate interest in 'all that passed between Macbeth and the witches'.[2] It would appear that Garrick's realism was more subtle than Macklin's.

In his interpretation of Macbeth's character, as revealed in the encounter with the witches, Garrick seems to have followed up directions embodied in Shakespeare's original text. Garrick reacted to the prophetic greeting of the witches with 'Astonishment...highly wrought'. He reacted in the way Shakespeare may have wanted Macbeth to react. Banquo's comment:

> Good sir, why do you start, and seem to feare
> Things that do sound so faire?   (I. iii. 51–2)

contains the suggestion. Astonishment followed by the gradual revelation of ambition were the two salient features in Garrick's interpretation of Macbeth's first scene with the witches. 'How his ambition kindles', wrote Thomas Wilkes, 'at the distant prospect of a crown when the witches prophesy.'[3]

The witches have hardly 'vanished' when Ross arrives to announce that Macbeth has been made Thane of Cawdor, confirming the prophecy of the second witch. Garrick's direction at this point, his grouping of the characters so as to isolate Macbeth, was considered satisfactory in his day. Garrick began his first soliloquy ruminatingly, as Banquo conferred apart with the messengers.[4]

In the adaptation by Davenant, Macbeth begins his first soliloquy like a sceptical, reasonable Restoration man. Macbeth in the Folio of 1623 is more imaginative—'present fears', he tells himself, 'are less than horrible imaginings'—and therefore more disturbed. Garrick chose the Folio of 1623, though at two points he altered the way in which the original words had been arranged on the page. In Garrick's version of the soliloquy, an attempt was

---

[1] *Roscius Anglicanus*, p. 33.
[2] See *The St. James's Chronicle*, October 28–30, 1773.
[3] *A General View of the Stage* (1759), p. 248.
[4] See editor's note, Bell, p. 71.

made to smooth down what appeared to be metrical irregularities in Folio I.

Where the Folio has a regular pentameter line:

> This supernatural soliciting

followed by two irregular lines, one of four beats—a see-sawing tetrameter:

> Cannot be ill; cannot be good.

and one of six:

> If ill why hath it given me earnest of successe[1]

in the Garrick version a formal order has been imposed on the second two lines by attaching 'If ill' to the end of 'Cannot be ill; cannot be good.'[2] An attempt to make Shakespeare's words look metrically respectable is made again at the end of the soliloquy. In the First Folio the soliloquy concludes with one fairly regular line:

> My Thought whose murther yet is but fantastical

followed by three unmistakably irregular ones:

> Shakes so my single state of man
> That Function is smothered in surmise,
> And nothing is, but what is not.

In the Garrick stage version the last three lines are regularised by attaching 'that function' to 'Shakes so my single state of man', 'and nothing is' to 'smothered in surmise' while a half line 'But what is not' brings the soliloquy to its close. An attempt has been made, in eighteenth-century terms, to make Macbeth's modulation perfect. The pauses which suggest in the First Folio that Macbeth's 'single state of man' is indeed shaken, have been blurred. In the Folio the line:

> Shakes so my single state of man,

with its four stressed accents and its soft, alliterative sibilants, moves slowly. There is a moment's pause at the end of the line as indicated by the comma in the Folio. In the lines:

> That Function is smothered in surmise,
> And nothing is, but what is not

Actus Primus, Scena Tertia, p. 133.   [2] Bell, I. p. 11.

we have commas after 'surmise' and 'is'; which may show how Shakespeare wished the lines to be spoken—the first distinctly brought to its end, the last divided into halves.

Garrick's version of Macbeth's first soliloquy is an improvement on Davenant but it is not identical with the First Folio. In refining the words on the page metrically, Garrick was influenced by Theobald and Johnson and possibly Rowe and Pope as well. But, as Richard Flatter has shown, when eighteenth-century editors interfered with the line divisions in the First Folio, cutting off part of a verse here and pasting it to another verse there, they spoiled the rhythm of the passages affected and made unrecognizable what might be called implied stage directions.[1]

Fortunately, when Garrick came to interpret the first soliloquy on the stage, he realised that he could not afford to make Macbeth's modulation perfect when his 'single state of man' is shaken and his mind is full of 'horrible imaginings'. On the stage, Garrick rebelled against the regularity of his own text. His act of rebellion did not escape criticism. On January 22, 1762, a correspondent who signed himself H.H., wrote to Garrick:

Early in the play, speaking the following lines,
    'My thought, whose murder yet is but fantastical,
    Shakes so my single state of man', &c.

you stop at the adjective *single*, which has a very bad effect, as the phrase of 'single state of man' which is a very quaint, forced one, can be only understood by collecting the whole passage closely together in speaking. I am sure your good sense will readily subscribe to the propriety of this observation.[2]

Garrick said in his reply that if he stopped at the word 'single', it would be a 'glaring fault, for the sense would then be imperfect', but he added:

...my idea of that passage is this: Macbeth is absorbed in thought, and struck with the horror of the murder, though but in idea (fantasticall,) and it naturally gives him a slow tremulous under-tone of voice; and though it might appear that I stopped at every word in the line more than usual, yet my intention was far from dividing the substantive from its adjective, but to paint the horror of Macbeth's mind, and keep the voice suspended a little which it will naturally be in such a situation.

---

[1] *Shakespeare's Producing Hand* (1948), pp. 10–11.
[2] *Correspondence of Garrick*, ed. Boaden, I, 133.

Garrick proceeds to explain what he means by 'the voice suspended a little':

I have been frequently abused by the gentlemen of the pen for false stops; and one in particular wrote against me for stopping injudiciously at this line in Hamlet:

'I think it was to see—my mother's wedding.'

I certainly never *stop* there, (that is close the *sense*), but as certainly suspend my voice, by which your ear must know that the sense is suspended too; for Hamlet's grief causes the break, and with a sigh, he finishes the sentence—'my mother's wedding'. I really could not from my feelings act it otherwise.[1]

In shaking off what he called the 'fetters of numbers',[2] Garrick the actor was fighting an eighteenth-century belief in rigid correctness which led actors to speak 'like the Minute hand of a Clock, that measures Time not meaning'.[3] It is significant that when Garrick gave his reasons for interpreting the soliloquy as he did, H.H. confessed in his reply:

I am myself of a profession which has made it necessary for me to study oratory; but indeed that species of it which being rather inanimate, attended with but little action, and scarce requiring more than bare propriety of elocution, may mislead in judging of stage declamation, which being impassioned, frequently to a degree of enthusiasm, does not admit of rigid correctness.[4]

Garrick spoke the first soliloquy absorbed in thought, with a 'tremulous undertone of voice'. Drury Lane, which was still a small theatre with an apron-stage, making for intimate contact between actor and audience, made Garrick's approach to the soliloquy technically possible and his voice, which could be heard clearly even when it dropped to a whisper, was an ideal instrument for his purposes. Garrick's whole conception of the passage was dramatic. He saw Macbeth as a sensitive murderer and believed that his interpretation of the soliloquy was the best way of realising that conception. By paying attention to passion and

---

[1] *Correspondence of Garrick*, ed. Boaden, I, 135–6.
[2] R. J. Smith, *A Collection of Material Towards an History of the English Stage* (British Museum 11826, r.s. 2 vols. n.d.): see F. G. Waldron, 'Appendix to Downes's "Roscius Anglicanus"' (1829), II, 25, and Garrick's letter to Peter Whalley, II, 23.
[3] Hill, *The Prompter*, No. 92.
[4] *Correspondence of Garrick*, ed. Boaden, I, 138.

meaning he came close to using the broken, disturbed rhythms which Shakespeare had created. Quin's reaction to Garrick's dramatic approach to Shakespeare's verse indicates the real nature of his achievement: 'If this young fellow is right', commented Quin, 'then we must be all wrong'.[1]

Garrick was alive to the importance of the decisive passages in the Folio. When the king names Malcolm heir to the throne, Prince of Cumberland, Davies writes that Garrick revealed the 'tumult' in Macbeth's mind to his audience.

In the Folio of 1623, the tumult in Macbeth's mind comes through:

> The Prince of Cumberland: that is a step,
> On which I must fall downe, or else o'er-leape,
> For in my way it lyes. Starres hide your fires,
> Let not Light see my black and deepe desires:
> The Eye winke at the Hande; yet let that bee,
> Which the Eye feares, when it is done to see.[2]

Davenant rewrote the passage, making distracting alterations in punctuation and metaphor, and adding two lines of his own:

> The Prince of Cumberland: that is a step,
> On which I must fall downe, or else o'er-leap;
> For in my way it lies. Stars! hide your fires,
> Let no light see my black and deep desires,
> The strange Idea of a bloudy act
> Does into doubt all my resolves distract.
> My eye shall at my hand connive, the Sun
> Himself should wink when such a deed is done...[3]

Davenant's mark of exclamation after 'Stars' makes Macbeth's address to the stars a self-conscious flight of rhetoric. The direct address to the stars, natural for Shakespeare's day, had become a matter for rhetorical emphasis in Davenant's time. Davenant brings in a distracting image of the sun, making vague and diffuse the morally tragic implication of a man resolved to destroy his own integrity by dividing hand from eye. He retained the idea of connivance between hand and eye, but removed the idea of dissociation that followed it. Davenant's closing rhythms are smooth and regular and lack the harsh intensity of the rhythms of the Folio of 1623.

---

[1] Davies, *Life of Garrick*, I, 44.
[2] Actus Primus, Scena Quarta, pp. 133–4.　　　　[3] I. i. p. 9.

Garrick restored the language of the First Folio which Davenant had altered, though he made revealing changes in punctuation:

> The Prince of Cumberland!...that is a Step,
> On which I must fall down, or else o'erleap;
> For in my way it lies. Stars, hide your fires!
> Let not light see my black and deep desires;
> The eye wink at the hand! yet let that be,
> Which the eye fears, when it is done, to see.[1]

Following Rowe[2] and Theobald,[3] Garrick introduced the mark of exclamation and the ominous pause after 'Cumberland'. He introduced a comma after 'stars', influenced by Theobald. The alterations, with the exception of the slightly self-conscious comma after 'stars', help to sharpen and clarify the sense of the original lines. Garrick understood the importance of the final image; the mark of exclamation introduced after 'hand' (the Folio has a semi-colon) may provide a clue to the way in which Garrick spoke the lines:

> The eye wink at the hand! yet let that be
> Which the eye fears, when it is done, to see.

In the image of connivance and dissociation, Macbeth accurately forecasts his own state of mind after the murder. Describing the actor's task after the murder, Garrick wrote: 'the murderer should be seen in every Limb, and yet every Member, at that instant should seem separated from his Body and his Body from his Soul'.[4]

While Macbeth's words explicitly indicate murderous resolve, the images of darkness and of the offending hand and averted eye which he uses to express this resolve, with their biblical echoes, indicate the presence of a moral imagination. Garrick perceived the 'innately ambitious' streak in Macbeth's character, but reminds us that Macbeth could be 'religiously humane'. Garrick believed that Macbeth's character grew and developed in the play. He saw Macbeth as

an experienc'd General, crown'd with Conquest, ambitious and humane, spurred on by *metaphysical* Prophecies, and the *unconquerable*

---

[1] Bell, 1. pp. 13–14.
[2] *Works of Shakespear*, v, 2309.
[3] *The Works of Shakespeare*, ed. Lewis Theobald (8 vols. 1740), vi, 280.
[4] 'Essay on Acting', *Tracts Relating to Shakespeare*, p. 9.

Pride of his *Wife*, to a Deed, *horrid* in *itself*, and *repugnant* to his Nature
...his *Milk* soon becomes *Gall*, imbitters his whole Disposition, and
the Consequence is the *Murder* of *Duncan*, the *taking off of Banquo*, and
his own *Coronation*.[1]

The phrase, 'religiously humane' and the statement, 'his Milk
soon becomes Gall', show that Garrick had Lady Macbeth's
description of Macbeth, in the Folio of 1623, in his mind:

> yet doe I feare thy Nature,
> It is too full o' th' Milke of humane kindnesse...[2]

'Humane' was a common earlier spelling of 'human' which
became restricted to a particular group of scenes in the eighteenth
century. This would account for the fact that Garrick used 'human'
in his stage text of *Macbeth*. Kindness, in Shakespeare's day, still
retained its root meaning of 'naturalness'. Murphy sees this description of Macbeth by his wife as central to any conception of
Macbeth's character,[3] as Garrick obviously did. In his performance
at Drury Lane in 1744, it was this aspect of Garrick's Macbeth that
observers like Aaron Hill most vividly remembered—the naturalness 'untouched by affectation', the 'pensively preparatory
attitudes', the 'soft falls of sorrow, terror and compassion'.[4]

But not every observer approved of Garrick's idea of Macbeth,
or the way in which he attempted to realise the idea, at least in the
first three acts. On January 17, 1743 [1744][5] Garrick received an
unsigned letter, which he preserved. The writer of the letter was
critical of Garrick's interpretation of Macbeth in the first three
acts:

I saw you last week act Macbeth, and was very well pleased with your
performance in the fourth and fifth Acts; but can't say the same of the
three first. You did not seem to me to hit the character of the man; for
you almost everywhere discovered an excessive dejectedness of the
mind, whereas Shakespeare represents him as a very odd and daring
fellow. I'll grant you that, as he is not naturally malicious, and as he
bears no hatred to the man he kills, and is excited by his ambition only,
the stings of conscience fill him with horror, and he appears greatly

[1] 'Appendix to "Essay"', *Tracts*, p. 13.
[2] Actus Primus, Scena Quinta, p. 134.
[3] Arthur Murphy, *Life of David Garrick Esq.* (2 vols. 1801), i, 73.
[4] See *Works* (4 vols. 1753), ii, 34—Letter to Mr Mallet, April 20, 1744.
[5] The letter is mistakenly dated 1743, the result possibly of a copyist's error, for
Garrick's first performance as Macbeth was in 1744.

disturbed. But the passion, as you managed it, had more the appearance of grief than horror: and all those long pauses, those heart-heavings, and that melancholy countenance and slack carriage of body, were by no means proper to express remorse in a man so warm and full of courage. Macbeth being by nature intrepid and seeming born to command, his behaviour ought to have something great, even when he is most stung with his guilt; and therefore the sorrowful face and lowly gesture of a penitent, which have even a mean and pitiful look, however commendable the temper of mind from which they proceed, are quite incompatible with his character.[1]

Garrick's correspondent seems to have failed to sympathise with, or perhaps even to fully understand, what Garrick was about. His own interpretation of Macbeth—'Shakespeare represents him as a very odd and daring fellow'—suggests obvious limitations of outlook.

Lady Macbeth attempts to extinguish the natural instinctive impulses in herself, and she helps to turn 'the milk of human kindness' in Macbeth to gall. Davenant had tampered with the language in which she expresses this resolve. The alterations Davenant made in Lady Macbeth's speeches were not as extensive as those he made to Macbeth's, but changes there were, and Garrick restored to the speeches of Lady Macbeth nearly all their original power. In Lady Macbeth's first soliloquy, Davenant sacrificed the dominant metaphor of the 'golden round',[2] to which all her references point in the Folio of 1623. Garrick restored the metaphor and made only two minor alterations.[3] As character and poetry are inseparable in Shakespeare, the restoration meant that the eighteenth-century actresses who played with Garrick had the basic elements—the words—with which to project character as Shakespeare had originally conceived it. The language in Davenant's version, spoken by Mrs Betterton, Mrs Barry and Mrs Porter when they played Lady Macbeth, may be usefully compared with the language spoken by Mrs Giffard and then Mrs Pritchard, who played Lady Macbeth in Garrick's stage version. Mrs Giffard, who first played Lady Macbeth opposite Garrick, appears to have lacked the kind of sensibility and skill

[1] *Correspondence of Garrick*, ed. Boaden, I, 19.
[2] I. i. p. 11.
[3] Bell, I. p. 14. Influenced by Johnson, he substituted 'me' for 'it' in: 'Thus thou must do, if thou have it'. 'Human' was substituted for 'humane'.

that would make Shakespeare's character believable, while Mrs Pritchard, who played the role later, appears to have projected an entirely believable character. As a correspondent in the *Universal Museum* of April 1768, pointed out: 'Her powers were so great, that the deception was hardly perceived, and Lady Macbeth, not the actress seemed to appear before us...the audience felt at once the powers of the writer combined with those of the actress.'[1] Mrs Pritchard appears to have had an instinctive sympathy with the natural rhythms of Shakespeare's poetry and her identification with Lady Macbeth's character was probably so complete because the verse held no real terrors for her. Genest writes that Mrs Pritchard 'had an uncommon method of pleasing the ear, she uttered her words, as the great poet advises the actor, smoothly and trippingly from the tongue; and however voluble in enunciation her part might require her to be, yet by her exact articulation not a syllable was lost'.[2] Mrs Pritchard before and after the murder of Duncan, wrote Davies, presented the image of a mind 'insensible to compunction and inflexibly bent to cruelty'.[3]

In Davenant the coldness and wintry harshness of Lady Macbeth's words are reduced somewhat by the substitution of smooth metres and refined images. In Davenant the raven's voice is musical, not harsh, and heaven perhaps peeps through 'the Curtains of the dark'.[4]

In Garrick's stage version the 'hoarse raven' returns, and with it 'the blanket of the dark':

> ...Come, thick night!
> And pall thee in the dunnest smoke of hell
> That my keen knife see not the wound it makes;
> Nor heav'n peep through the *blanket* of the dark,
> To cry, hold, hold!...

> *Enter Macbeth*
> Great Glamis! worthy Cawdor! (*Embracing him*)[5]

The stage direction 'Embracing him' is not found in either the Folio or in Davenant. We are not told how Garrick and Mrs Pritchard embraced, but it does not appear to have interfered

---

[1] P. 163.
[2] John Genest, *Some Account of the English Stage, 1660 to 1830* (10 vols. 1832), V, 173.
[3] *Life of Garrick*, II, 182.
[4] I. i. p. 12. [5] Bell, I. p. 15.

with the striking contrast of character established by them in the first three acts.

Macbeth's sensitiveness to evil makes him retreat momentarily from the decision to murder the king, when he has a vision of the judgements of various kinds that may follow his crime. The vision of judgement occurs in the soliloquy which precedes the banquet prepared for Duncan. In the Folio, Macbeth's soliloquy before the banquet has an inward quality. When Davenant re-wrote it, he altered its rhythms and excluded Shakespeare's most evocative metaphors. The language became colder, more rational, less imaginative:

> If it were well when done; then it were well
> It were done quickly; if his Death might be
> Without the Death of nature in my self,
> And killing my own rest; it wou'd suffice;
> But deeds of this complexion still return
> To plague the doer, and destroy his peace:
> Yet let me think; he's here in double trust.
> First, as I am his Kinsman, and his Subject,
> Strong both against the Deed: then as his Host,
> Who should against his murderer shut the door,
> Not bear the sword myself. Besides, this Duncan
> Has born his faculties so meek, and been
> So clear in his great Office; that his Vertues,
> Like Angels, plead against so black a deed;
> Vaulting Ambition! thou o're-leap'st thyself
> To fall upon another: now, what news?[1]

In his stage version Garrick almost entirely restored the inward-ness, the warmth, the rhythms and images of the Folio:

> If it were *done*, when 'tis done, then 'twere well
> It were done quickly; if that but this blow
> Might be the be-all and end-all...*Here.*
> But *here*, upon this bank and shoal of time,
> We'd jump the life to come....But in these cases,
> We still have judgement *here*, that we but teach
> Bloody instructions; which being taught, return
> To plague th' inventor. Even-handed Justice
> Returns th' ingredients of our poison'd chalice,

[1] I. i. p. 11.

To our own lips. He's here in double trust;
First as I am his kinsman and his subject,
Strong both against the deed; then as his host,
Who should against his murd'rer shut the door,
Nor bear the knife myself. Besides, this Duncan
Hath borne his faculties so meek, hath been
So clear in his great office, that his virtues
Will plead, like angels, trumpet-tongu'd against
The deep damnation of his taking off:
And Pity, like a naked new-born babe,
Striding the blast, or heav'ns cherubin hors'd
Upon the sightless couriers of the air:
Shall blow the horrid deed in ev'ry eye.
That tears shall drown the wind. I have no spur
To prick the sides of my intent, but only
Vaulting Ambition, which o'erleaps itself
And falls on the other...

Enter Lady Macbeth
How now! What news.[1]

Garrick regrettably omitted the comma after the first line in the soliloquy, as it is found in the First Folio. The comma indicates a pause after 'well', both in the rhythm and the sense of the line. Shakespeare's meaning seems to have been: 'If it were done (ended) when 'tis done (performed) then it would be well. It were done (ended) quickly if the assassination could clear itself from all consequences.' What Macbeth fears is the possibility that the consequences of Duncan's assassination might be endless. As R. G. White points out, the consequence of the omission of the comma in the First Folio has been a misapprehension of the significance of these lines, even among actors, by whom they are generally read as if they meant, 'if the murder is to be done, when I do it I had better do it quickly'.[2]

Garrick omitted, as well, Shakespeare's image of the net (trammel) which indicates Macbeth's fear that some consequences might escape the net. Macbeth's imagination is still circling round his initial idea, 'if it were done, when 'tis done, then 'twere well'.

Fortunately, Garrick's third significant alteration of the Folio text, following Theobald, was not an omission but a clarification of the earlier image, 'bank and Schoole of Time' in the Folio.

[1] Bell, I. p. 18. [2] See *Macbeth*, ed. Furness, p. 94, nn. 5–7.

Theobald had substituted 'shoal' for 'Schoole', finding 'bank and Schoole' 'a monstrous complement of heterogeneous ideas'. Theobald suggests that Shakespeare had used 'shoal', meaning: 'this Shallow, this narrow Ford of human life, opposed to the great Abyss of Eternity'.[1] Garrick adopted 'shoal' and, for eighteenth-century audiences, possibly made Shakespeare's original meaning clearer, because 'schoole' could well have been an earlier spelling of 'shoal'.

To Shakespeare's final images of judgement Garrick's responsiveness was acute enough, even if critics like Francis Gentleman felt that the images of pity, heaven's cherubin, and ambition 'all upon the full gallop' were 'strained figures' and 'not at all adapted to a man deliberating upon one of the foulest most important murthers he could commit'. Gentleman was speaking in the name of a conventional eighteenth-century decorum and sense, but Garrick accepted the imaginative logic in the metaphors that Gentleman rejected.

The anonymous observer H.H. had some reservations about Garrick's delivery of the soliloquy on the stage, and his objections centre upon Garrick's interpretation of one of the figures that Gentleman felt were strained, and another related figure. Garrick's reply to H.H. makes the vividness and precision of his response to Shakespeare's poetry quite clear, and indicates that he had a clear sense of the depth and range of Macbeth's moral awareness. Garrick had paused slightly at 'angels' and unaccountably at 'hors'd'. H.H. wrote:

In speaking the passage, viz.

> 'That his virtues
> Will plead like angels trumpet tongued against,' &c.

you make a stop at *angels*, which I suppose wrong, as you by this manner transfer the epithet *trumpet-tongu'd* from *angels* to *virtues* which, with great deference to your opinion, I do not take to be the idea of Shakespeare who meant to describe angels under the usual representation of them, which is generally with trumpets.[2]

Garrick, defending his use of a pause after 'angels', argued that Macbeth had conceived of Duncan's virtues (not the angels only) as 'trumpet-tongu'd':

[1] *Works of Shakespeare*, VI, 284.
[2] *Correspondence of Garrick*, ed. Boaden, I, 133.

I am sorry to differ with you about the joining 'angels' and 'trumpet-tongu'd' together. I really think the force of those exquisite four lines and a half would be shortly lost for want of a small aspiration at *angels* —the epithet may agree with either of the substantives, but I think it more elegant to give it to the *virtues* and the sense is the same; for if his *virtues* are like *angels*, they are *trumpet-tongu'd* and may be spoke justly either way.

For the pause he had made after 'hors'd', Garrick offered no defence:

'Heaven's cherubim hors'd' with a stop, is certainly wrong, and was not so intended to be spoken; but when the mind is agitated it is impossible to guard against these slips...'[1]

The last admission is of some interest. It suggests that Garrick, in the effort to achieve identification, could be carried away. Garrick believed that some of an actor's best insights were not calculated and arose from giving himself completely to the feelings of a character at a given moment. But if H.H. is right, Garrick's doctrine of total engagement had its dangers.

When Macbeth, momentarily altered by his sensitiveness to the evil which has attracted him, changes his mind, Lady Macbeth's role in the action of the play becomes decisive. When it would appear that Macbeth has decided against the murder of the king, she persuades him that the assassination of Duncan would be an act of courage. She works out the details of the assassination and convinces Macbeth of its practicability. Davenant made some changes from the Folio in this scene which Garrick rejected, returning to Shakespeare's original phrasing. Where the possibility of assassination hangs in the balance, Davenant, among other changes, altered the tone, rhythm and connotations of the line which Johnson considered to be one of the finest in Shakespeare. When Macbeth replies to Lady Macbeth's charge of cowardice and indecision, Davenant's altered version reads:

> I prithee peace: I dare do all that may
> Become a man; he who dares more, is none.[2]

Garrick restored the line, maintaining the tone of Folio 1:

> Prythee peace.
> I dare do all that may become a man;
> Who dares do more, is none.[3]

[1] *Ibid.* 136.　　　[2] I. i. p. 15.　　　[3] Bell, I. p. 19.

53

This is stronger. In Act I, before the decision to murder Duncan is finally taken, Garrick seems to have stressed the sensitiveness of Macbeth to the evil in which he is caught. In Act II when preparations for the murder get under way, Garrick began to stress other aspects of Macbeth's character as well.

In II. i., while Duncan sleeps after the banquet, Macbeth and Banquo meet unexpectedly in the dark. Davenant's alterations make what is subtle and barely hinted at in Macbeth's remarks to Banquo painfully over-explicit. In the First Folio, Macbeth's comments on Banquo's remark that the 'three weyward Sisters' had shown 'some truth', are casual, dissembling and then plainly ambiguous:

> *Banq*. All's well.
>   I dreamt last Night of the three weyward Sisters:
>   To you they have shew'd some truth.
>
> *Macb*. I thinke not of them:
>   Yet when we can entreat an houre to serve
>   We would spend it in some words upon that Businesse,
>   If you would graunt the time.
>
> *Banq*. At your kind'st leysure.
>
> *Macb*. If you shall cleave to my consent,
>   When 'tis, it shall make Honor for you.
>
> *Banq*. So I lose none,
>   In seeking to augment it, but still keepe
>   My Bosome franchis'd, and Allegeance cleare,
>   I shall be counsail'd.
>
> *Macb*. Good repose the while.[1]

Macbeth is at first casual, then elaborately courteous. The courtesy is followed by what Dr Johnson called, 'the affected obscurity'[2] of:

> If you shall cleave to my consent.

As Johnson observes, Macbeth does not mention the crown, though it lurks behind the obscure implications of his words.

Davenant, with his passion for rewriting Shakespeare, intro-

---

[1] Actus Secundus, Scena Prima, p. 136.
[2] See *The Plays of William Shakespeare*, ed. Samuel Johnson and George Steevens (2nd ed., 10 vols. 1778), IV, 435.

duced clarity where obscurity seems more dramatic. To Banquo's 'At your kindest leisure', in Davenant, Macbeth replies:

> If when the Prophesie begins to look like truth
> You will adhere to me, it shall make honour for you.[1]

Garrick restored the dramatic subtlety of the scene by restoring the original language of the First Folio.

On the stage and at his best, Garrick re-created the 'forced, dissembling gaiety' implicit in the text, adding a few touches of his own to suggest that Macbeth was not able to forget the murder he was about to commit. Arthur Murphy, describing Garrick 'as a little too disengaged, too free, and too much at ease', when he played this scene in 1768, recalls an earlier, more successful interpretation:

I will tell you how I have seen you do it:—you dissembled indeed, but dissembled with difficulty. Upon the first entrance the eye glanced at the door; the gaiety was forced, and at intervals the eye gave a momentary look towards the door, and turned away in a moment. This was but a fair contrast to the acted cheerfulness with which this disconcerted behaviour was intermixed. After saying, 'Good, repose the while'; the eye then fixed on the door, there after a pause in a broken tone, 'Go, bid thy mistress' &c....Pray observe, that as you assume a freedom and a gaiety here, it will be also a contrast to the fine disturbance of mind and behaviour, in the night gown, after the murder is committed, when no cheerfulness is affected. I am sure this was the way formerly, and I own it strikes me most. If I am wrong, you must thank yourself for it.[2]

The scene with Banquo, as Garrick played it, provided a sharp contrast to the scene with the imaginary dagger as well. The dagger scene, which follows immediately, presents an actor with the problem of making unreality real; the scene must be treated 'judicially', says Francis Gentleman or, he adds, 'as we have sometimes seen, it may take a ludicrous turn'.[3] The language Shakespeare chose for Macbeth was vividly evocative without being melodramatic. The hallucinated vision demands and gets the most delicately poised rhythms and images. When Davenant introduced smooth, regular metres where Shakespeare's original rhythms were uncertain and halting, he obscured the elusive

---

[1] II. i. p. 17. [2] *Correspondence of Garrick*, ed. Boaden, II, 363.
[3] *Dramatic Censor*, I, 107.

feelings which they had helped to express. Davenant's changes in this soliloquy are particularly unfortunate:

> ...now, to half the world
> Nature seems dead, and wicked dreams infect
> The health of sleep; now witchcraft celebrates
> Pale *Heccate*'s Offerings; now murder is
> Alarm'd by his nights Centinel: the wolf,
> Whose howling seems the watch-word to the dead:
> But whilst I talk, he lives: hark, I am summon'd
> O *Duncan*, hear it not, for 'tis a bell
> That rings my Coronation and thy Knell.
>   *Exit.*[1]

The concluding lines of the soliloquy are robbed of all their power. 'Now' thrice repeated has a melodramatic ring; 'O Duncan' is weakly rhetorical; and the substitution of 'infect' for 'abuse' and 'The health of sleep' for 'The curtain'd sleep' negates the effect of the original description of 'dead nature' described by Johnson: 'He that pursues Shakespeare looks round alarmed, and starts to find himself alone.'

Garrick almost entirely restored the language of the First Folio. He omitted two lines in which Macbeth comments on his own volubility:

> Whiles I threat, he lives:
> Words to the heat of deedes too cold breath gives...[2]

accepted Davenant's second 'now' but not his third; substituted 'sound' for 'sure' in 'sure and firm-set Earth', and introduced pauses which he could have deduced from colons and full stops in the Folio, and may have used to make Macbeth's vision of the dagger convincing on the stage. Apart from these changes the poetry of the First Folio remains almost intact:

> Go, bid thy mistress, when my drink is ready,
> She strike upon the bell. Get thee to bed.
> Is this a dagger which I see before me,
> The handle tow'rd my hand? Come, let me clutch thee.
> I have thee not, and yet I see thee still;
> Art thou not, fatal vision, sensible
> To feeling as to sight? or art thou but

---

[1] II. i. p. 18.   [2] Actus Secundus, Scena Prima, p. 136.

A Dagger of the Minde, a false Creation,
Proceeding from the heat-oppressed brain?
I see thee yet, in form as palpable,
As this which now I draw...
Thou marshal'st me the way that I was going;
And such an instrument I was to use...
Mine eyes are made the fools o' th'other senses,
Or else worth all the rest...I see thee still;
And on the blade o' th' dudgeon gouts of blood,
Which was not so before...There's no such thing...
It is the bloody business which informs
Thus to mine eyes...Now o'er one half the world,
Nature seems dead, and wicked dreams abuse
The curtain'd sleep; now witchcraft celebrates
Pale Hecate's offerings: and wither'd murder,
(Alarmed by his sentinel, the wolf,
Whose howl's his watch) thus with his stealthy pace,
With Tarquin's ravishing strides, tow'rds his design
Moves like a ghost...Thou sound and firm-set earth,
Hear not my steps, which way they walk, for fear
The very stones prate of my where-about;
And take the present horror from the time,
Which now suits with it...
I go, and it is done: the bell invites me.
Hear it not, *Duncan*, for it is a knell
That summons thee to heav'n, or to hell.[1]

The Bell text provides possible hints of the way in which Garrick spoke the lines. The pauses seem to indicate necessary changes of tone. But besides the hints provided in the text itself there are several descriptions of the way in which Garrick interpreted the scene with the imaginary dagger.

H.H. in 1762 objected to Garrick's interpretation of a particular line: 'In the air-drawn dagger scene, you lay a prodigious strong emphasis on *was*, in this line, "And such an instrument I was to use," which I do not see the reason of, and rather think that *use* is the word to be marked.'[2] In his reply Garrick argued that both *was* and *use* should be equally, though slightly impressed '...and if you please to consider the passage, you will find that they are both emphatical. The vision represents what *was* to be *done*, not what is doing, or what had been done: but in many passages like

---

[1] Bell, II. p. 22.   [2] *Correspondence of Garrick*, ed. Boaden, I, 134.

this, the propriety will depend wholly upon the manner of the actor.'[1]

Garrick's manner, on which, as he argued, the propriety of his interpretation depended, has been described by Francis Gentleman: '...who ever saw the *immortal actor* start at, and trace the imaginary dagger previous to Duncan's murder, without embodying, by sympathy, unsubstantial air into the alarming shape of such a weapon?'[2] One of the common symptoms associated with 'Satanic possession' is to visualise objects which are not there—at such times the imagination is feverish and 'nothing is but what is not'. Garrick seems to have understood this and entered fully into Macbeth's mind. As Davies's account indicates, Garrick seems to have lived through the transitions of feeling in the dagger soliloquy. 'The sudden start on seeing the dagger in the air—the endeavour of the actor to seize it,—the disappointment—the suggestion of its being only a vision of the disturbed fancy,—the seeing it still in form most palpable, with the reasoning upon it,—these are difficulties which the mind of Garrick was capable of encountering and subduing.'[3]

Excellent mime that he was, Garrick achieved the maximum effect with economy of means. His own satirical description of Quin's playing of the line,

Come let me clutch thee

suggests that Garrick used 'one Motion only' when he attempted to clutch the dagger.[4] That single gesture was not mechanical but lived. A writer in the *Monthly Mirror* describes the effect it had on a responsive spectator:

What he is able to effect without speaking, I lately witnessed in Macbeth; when he with the satanic look of a man resolved on murder, fancies he sees a dagger and (as if snatching the crown itself) grasps at the handle; a foreigner, in the same box with myself, who was totally ignorant of the piece, for he did not understand a word of English, sunk, overpowered with horror, at my feet.[5]

When one reads this description one understands what Steevens meant when he wrote that: 'To Mr Garrick, a single glance of

[1] *Correspondence of Garrick*, ed. Boaden, I, 136.   [2] *Dramatic Censor*, I, 107.
[3] *Dramatic Miscellanies*, II, 88.
[4] 'Appendix to "Essay"', *Tracts Relating to Shakespeare*, p. 17.
[5] VII (1799), 103.

whose eye has long been the best expositor of Shakespeare's meaning, our cold annotations must appear tedious.'[1] Baron Grimm's description of Garrick's playing of the dagger scene in a drawing-room in Paris, without the usual aids of theatrical illusion, shows that he secured conviction by following the dagger through the air with his eyes.[2]

In the dagger scene Garrick appears to have successfully relived the sensations of a man resolved on murder. In Act I he made Macbeth a potential murderer capable of arousing pity. In the dagger scene in Act II he made him capable of arousing exactly the opposite emotion—of terror.

In the murder scene which followed, Davenant had made alterations in Shakespeare's language which Garrick could not accept. Where Davenant had written:

> Macbeth has murdered sleep, the innocent sleep,
> Sleep that locks up the senses from their care.[3]

Garrick restored the original metaphor:

> Macbeth doth murder sleep; the innocent sleep,
> Sleep, that knits up the ravell'd sleeve of care.[4]

For Davenant's clinical:

> What hands are here! can the Sea afford
> Water enough to wash away the stains?
> No, they would sooner add a tincture to
> The Sea, and turn the green into a red.[5]

Garrick substituted the more abrupt, powerful Folio rhythms which are on the edge of reason:

> What hands are here? hah! they pluck out mine eyes.
> Will all great Neptune's Ocean wash this blood,
> Clean from my hand? No, this my hand will rather
> The multitudinous Sea incarnadine,
> Making the green one, red.[6]

---

[1] *Correspondence of Garrick*, ed. Boaden, I, 581.
[2] *Correspondence Littéraire*, 1 juillet 1765. Quoted in F. A. Hedgcock, *David Garrick et ses Amis français* (1911), p. 25: 'Nous lui avons vu jouer la scène du poignard dans la tragédie de *Macbeth*, en chambre, dans son habit ordinaire, sans aucun secours de l'illusion théâtrale; et à mesure qu'il suivait des yeux ce poignard suspendu et marchant dans l'air, il devenait si *beau* qu'il arrachait un cri général d'admiration à toute l'assemblée.'
[3] II. i. p. 20.   [4] Bell, II. p. 24.
[5] II. i. p. 20.   [6] Bell, II. p. 25.

Initially, Garrick adopted the comma in the Folio after 'green one'. Later he adopted the alteration proposed by Murphy in the *Gray's Inn Journal*, dropped the comma after 'one' and spoke the line as most modern editors of *Macbeth* believe it should be spoken: 'Making the green one red.'[1] One can make a case for both readings. The other interesting alteration was the substitution of the singular 'sea' for 'seas' in the First Folio.

In the scene after the murder Garrick and Mrs Pritchard began with an initial advantage over their predecessors. If their performance was memorable, part of their success must be attributed to the fact that they were using Shakespeare's remarkable original script. Though Davies, in his account of the performance, holds that 'the poet here gives only an outline to the consummate actor',[2] one can hardly think of a better outline, and Garrick and Mrs Pritchard brought out the suggestions implicit in the text. The silence and the agonized horror reported by Davies are there from the outset:

> *Lady M.* My husband?
> *Macb.* I have done the deed. Didst thou not hear a noise?
> *Lady M.* I heard the owl scream and the crickets cry...[3]

Davies noted the finely contrasted interpretation of character: 'His distraction of mind and agonizing horrors were finely contrasted by her seeming apathy...and confidence'; and he describes the way in which Garrick and Mrs Pritchard heightened the tension:

The beginning of the scene after the murder was conducted in terrifying whispers. You heard what they spoke, but you learned more from the agitation of mind displayed in their action and deportment...the dark colouring given by the actor to these abrupt speeches makes the scene awful and tremendous to the auditors.[4]

The stage-whispering appears to have been perfect, technically. 'You heard what they spoke', says Davies, and Francis Gentleman remembered the pitch and quality of Garrick's voice. 'Whoever heard', wrote Gentleman, 'the low but piercing notes of his voice when the deed is done, repeating those inimitable passages which mention the sleeping grooms, and murder of sleep, without feeling a vibration of the nerves?'[5]

---

[1] *Life of Garrick*, I, 82. [2] *Dramatic Miscellanies*, II, 149.
[3] Bell, II. p. 23. [4] *Dramatic Miscellanies*, II, 148–9.
[5] *Dramatic Censor*, I, 108.

Garrick interpreted character with his body as well as his voice: feet, hands, eyes, face came into play. 'The wonderful expression of heartfelt horror when he showed his bloody hands, can only be conceived and described by those who saw him',[1] writes Davies. Murphy tells us that Garrick's 'complexion grew whiter every moment till at length...he said in a tone of wild despair:

> Will all great Neptune's ocean wash this blood
> Clean from my hand?'[2]

The *Connoisseur*, September 1, 1754, suggests that he merely wiped the make-up from his face before entering,[3] but whatever means Garrick used to achieve the effect, he seems to have been remarkably convincing.

It is true that, on his first night, he appears to have over-stepped the bounds of his own imaginative logic. When he entered the stage after the murder of Duncan, he had his wig in disorder and the buttons of his coat and waistcoat undone. John Hill approved, and regretted that Garrick had omitted these signs of disorder in subsequent performances:

The first time that Mr *Garrick* played *Macbeth* he took occasion in one of his scenes of greatest confusion, to enter upon the stage with his coat and waistcoat both unbutton'd, and with some other discomposures in his dress, that added greatly to the resemblance of nature in that part of his character. He did this however only the first night and lost, by the omitting it afterwards, all the merit of having done it at all.[4]

One feels more inclined to agree, however, with the *Connoisseur*'s ironic comment. Garrick, the *Connoisseur* writes, without directly naming him,

after having acted that noble scene in the second act of Macbeth, in so fine a manner, that one would almost imagine both the poet and the player must have been murderers to represent one so well, goes out to execute the supposed murder. After a short space he returns as from the fact; but though the expression in his face is still remarkably excellent, one cannot but smile to observe, that he has been employing himself behind the scenes in putting his wig awry and untying one of the ties to it. This doubtless is designed to raise terror; but to every discerning spectator it must appear most absurdly ridiculous: for who

[1] *Dramatic Miscellanies*, II, 149.   [2] *Life of Garrick*, I, 82.
[3] Quoted in Burnim, *Garrick, Director*, p. 113.   [4] *The Actor* (1750), p. 226.

can forbear laughing, when he finds that the player would have us imagine, that the same deed, which has thrown all that horror and confusion into his countenance, had also untwisted one of the tails of his periwig?[1]

Unless Macbeth grappled with Duncan, it is difficult to see how his wig and buttons could have come undone. Duncan, we know, was asleep. After his first performance Garrick removed the deficiencies in this scene and the total effect of his playing had an almost physical impact. Robert Lloyd in the *Actor* testifies to the effect of Garrick's playing in this scene:

> Through ev'ry Vein I feel a Chilness creep,
> When Horrors such as thine *have murder'd Sleep.*[2]

Mrs Pritchard's interpretation of Lady Macbeth and Garrick's interpretation of Macbeth in this scene inspired a minor poet and critics as well as painters to comment upon it. Painters as different as Zoffany and Fuseli attempted to re-create the scene after the murder, as Garrick and Mrs Pritchard had played it at Drury Lane.

Fuseli saw Garrick play in *Macbeth* with Mrs Pritchard during his first visit to London in the 1760s. The scene following the murder of Duncan appears to have haunted his imagination for many years afterwards. In the painting of this scene at the Art Gallery in Zürich,[3] which has Lady Macbeth's 'My husband!' and Macbeth's reply, 'I have done the deed', inscribed on it by Fuseli, the whispered exchanges described by Davies are suggested by a single detail. Mrs Pritchard stands with the forefinger of her left hand to her lips, her right hand outstretched towards Macbeth. Garrick and Mrs Pritchard wear contemporary costume but Garrick's costume seems to be in some disarray; and as he holds the daggers in his hands, the eyes suggest panic. In his second version, Fuseli has stripped Garrick of his garments, though Lady Macbeth remains clothed. Macbeth's ribs are outlined and his whole body suggests pain and tension. Fuseli has defined his own sensations and feelings for us. He saw Garrick's art in emotional terms as 'a blow struck for Romanticism, part of

---

[1] No. 34 (September 19, 1754), p. 60.
[2] (1760), p. 2.
[3] Reproduced in Paul Ganz, *The Drawings of Henry Fuseli* (1949), p. 16.

a new appreciation of Shakespeare'.[1] At the same time his paintings suggest that Garrick had transcended the limitations of contemporary costume and touched the human substance.

That Fuseli's paintings were not purely fanciful constructions is supported by two further pieces of evidence. In Fuseli's imaginative reconstructions Garrick carries a dagger in each hand, and so he bears them in the frontispiece to Bell's edition of 1774. Cooper's description of this scene reads like an interpretation of Fuseli. Cooper had not seen Garrick play, but he had seen Sheridan, Mossop, Reddish and Henderson, and he suggests that, with 'more or less success', they followed the strategy planned and carried out brilliantly by Garrick in this scene: 'The noise of a hasty foot was heard within' and as Lady Macbeth said, after a pause,

Had he not resembled
My father as he slept, I had done't.

the door opened and Macbeth appeared, a frightful figure of horror, rushing out sideways with one dagger, and his face in consternation, presented to the door, as if he were pursued, and the other dagger lifted up as if prepared for action. Thus he stood as if transfixed, seeming insensible to everything but the chamber, unconscious of any presence else, and even to his wife's address of 'my husband'.[2]

Zoffany illustrated the moment which follows the entrance of Macbeth with the daggers in his hand, when Lady Macbeth saying, 'Give me the daggers', takes them from him, to return them to the room where Duncan's body lies. In the painting by Zoffany in the possession of the Gaekwar of Baroda, of which there is a mezzotint by Green, dated 1775 (see Plate 2), forked lightning crosses the sky, seen through a great window at the back, as Lady Macbeth turns away with the daggers in her hand. Garrick and Mrs Pritchard, in scarlet and black, stand in a flood of light which comes through an open door, while candles, on Gothic pillars, burn in a darkened hall.

Zoffany has painted details of costume with some fidelity. It is possible, though not certain, that he was faithful in other details as well. Kalman Burnim suggests that the large window at the back would have offered no technical problem at Drury Lane.[3] In November 1762, a correspondent signing his letter J.H., told

---

[1] Michael Levey, *From Giotto to Cézanne* (1962), p. 259.
[2] See A. C. Sprague, *Shakespeare and the Actors* (1945), p. 241.
[3] *Garrick, Director*, p. 98.

Garrick about a new window technique, which the manager 'undoubtedly was already aware of':

A few Months ago I happened to be at one of ye Portuguese Theatres in Lisbon, where I saw a little Improvement in point of Scenery that had a pretty Effect. The Intention of it was to give a View of a number of Gallants passing before a Window of a Lady; for this purpose there was two Large Windows made in ye Scene in ye Venetian taste, & covered with white Gauze, which besides its transparency & resemblance to Glass, has an air of elegance that the latter can not come up to. There are likewise a number of cross Barrs in imitation of Casement, which is the fashion in those Countrys. I imagine this hint might be made use of in ye Last Scene of y 2nd Act of the Wonder; and if on that or any other occasion you find it of service, it will give me great pleasure.[1]

In Drury Lane's production of *King Arthur* (December 13, 1770) a Gothic stained-glass window was part of the set. The effect of stained glass was achieved by lighting from behind. Horace Walpole confirms the fact: 'This scene which should be a barbarous temple of Woden, is a perfect cathedral, and the devil officiates at a kind of high mass. I never saw greater absurdities.'[2]

The Gothic pillars and the large double doors shown on stage right in the painting by Zoffany, would have presented no technical problems either. During Garrick's management at Drury Lane the action, supported by new lighting techniques, withdrew more and more into the frame of the proscenium, and more natural means of entrance were required 'if the correctness of the illusion was to be maintained'.[3] If Zoffany was painting what actually took place, then Garrick used Gothic décor and lighting effects—the lightning in the window, the darkened hall, a shaft of light coming through an open door—to heighten the tension established by himself and Mrs Pritchard after the murder of Duncan.[4]

---

[1] MS. in Harvard Theatre Collection, TS 116.255. 3. Quoted in *Garrick, Director*, p. 101.

[2] *The Letters of Horace Walpole*, ed. Paget Toynbee (16 vols. 1903–5), VII, 429–30.

[3] Burnim, *Garrick, Director*, pp. 97–8.

[4] It is possible, though not certain, that Garrick used the Gothic décor and all the lighting effects painted by Zoffany, at some time. In the painting of the same scene by Fuseli at the Zürich Kunsthaus, there is only a faint suggestion of folding screens and nothing else. In the other version of this scene by Fuseli, the folding screens have disappeared and there is no suggestion of a set at all. Fuseli's interest may have been primarily in the characters and the emotions engendered by them. He was not a believer in photographic realism.

The murder of Duncan appears to have been the climactic point of Garrick's production of *Macbeth*. Obviously nervous about upsetting an atmosphere so carefully established, and probably failing to understand his real function, Garrick, following Davenant, omitted the Porter, who enters after Macbeth and Lady Macbeth leave the stage in the First Folio. Francis Gentleman supported the omission.[1] As a result of the deletion Garrick introduced nine lines to allow Macbeth time to change swiftly into the costume of a man who was supposed to have been sleeping all night. Quin evidently re-entered the scene during which the murder is discovered in a nightgown of 'red damask', but Garrick seems to have used a flowered gown.[2] One is tempted to speculate that this may have been the result of an unconscious association of ideas, for it does recall Lady Macbeth's advice earlier in the play:

> ...looke like th' innocent flower
> But be the Serpent under't.[3]

Garrick played the serpent under his flowered gown. As Davies tells us, during the scene of discovery, Garrick, 'struggling to assume the appearance of innocence and deep concern', dared not meet the eye of anyone on stage.[4]

In Garrick's stage version of *Macbeth*, Lady Macbeth did not enter the action at this point. In the First Folio she faints as Macbeth ends his elaborate speech explaining why he killed the grooms:

> ...who could refraine
> That had a heart to love; and in that heart
> Courage, to make's love knowne.[5]

Garrick omitted this arresting and dramatic piece of business in his production. Davies tells us that the audience was responsible for the omission. In an earlier production when Lady Macbeth entered and did faint, as the Folio of 1623 specifies, she was hooted off by the upper gallery. Although Garrick once made an effort to restore the business, Mrs Pritchard failed to execute it to the satisfaction of her eighteenth-century audience.[6] But there

---

[1] *Dramatic Censor*, I, 90.
[2] See 'Appendix to "Essay"', *Tracts Relating to Shakespeare*, p. 18.
[3] First Folio, Actus Primus, Scena Quinta, p. 134.
[4] *Dramatic Miscellanies*, II, 99.
[5] Actus Secundus, Scena Tertia, p. 138.
[6] Cooke, *Macklin*, p. 27.

may have been a further reason for the omission. As Kalman Burnim observes, Mrs Pritchard may have been occupied backstage, dressing for her regal appearance as queen in Act III.[1]

After the discovery of the murder of Duncan, Garrick moved away again, in quite a radical fashion, from the Folio text. Influenced by Davenant, he introduced a choric commentary on the death of the king, sung by the witches:

> 1 *Witch*. Speak, sister.—is the deed done?
> 2 *Witch*. Long ago, long ago;
> About twelve glasses since have run...
> 4 *Witch*. He will spill much more blood,
> And become worse, to make his title good.
> *Chor*. He will, he will spill much more blood,
> And become worse, to make his title good.[2]

The music for the choral song was probably composed by Leveridge and the music for the 'Witches Dance' probably by Locke.[3] Of the *Macbeth* music Burney wrote that its 'rude, wild excellence cannot be surpassed'.[4] The song of the witches prepared the audience for Macbeth's scene with Banquo in the third act.

Macbeth's casual remarks to Banquo—'Ride you this afternoon? ...Is it far you ride?'—conceal a murderous intent. A note by Francis Gentleman in the Bell edition provides a possible clue to Garrick's interpretation of the scene.[5] Gentleman writes: 'Macbeth should here put on a most fair-faced affability; for a designing villain most particularly seems what he is not.' In Macbeth's scene with Banquo's murderers, which follows immediately, the relevance of the witches' song becomes much clearer.

Though the murderers have been described, accounts of the way in which Garrick interpreted his scene with them do not appear to have been unearthed. The exchange between Macbeth and the murderers was curtailed in the text used by Garrick. But in Macbeth's next scene with Lady Macbeth, Garrick restored the words of the Folio text, including the powerful invocation to

[1] *Garrick, Director*, p. 116. Burnim refers to *Tit For Tat*, p. 25; and *St. James's Chronicle* (October 28–30, 1773).
[2] Bell, II. p. 29.
[3] See Roger Fiske, 'The Macbeth Music', *Music and Letters*, XLV (April 1964), 122–3.
[4] *Ibid.* p. 117.   [5] Bell, III. p. 33.

night. Yet though we know what Garrick and Mrs Pritchard said in III. ii., we do not know how they said it and what they did. It is when we arrive at the banquet scene that the evidence helps us to see and hear again their interpretation of character on the stage.

In the Bell text, which differs slightly from the Folio at this point, the first murderer enters during Macbeth's speech of welcome, not before it, and a stage direction indicates that Macbeth, as he finished speaking, moved away from his guests to a door where the murderer stood.[1]

The ghost of Banquo enters after the first murderer leaves. Garrick's interpretation of Macbeth's reactions to Banquo's ghost changed through the years. In the early years at Drury Lane he brought out Macbeth's terror during both the first and the second appearance of Banquo's ghost. Garrick's unknown correspondent of January 17, 1744, found his interpretation of the scene indefensible:

...as to the general behaviour of Macbeth, I think his pronunciation should be more loud and quick, especially in the speech that begins— 'Avaunt and quit my sight!'—for a man who is naturally very bold, does not speak in a faint manner, when he is frightened...Banquo, who performed his part very poorly, should have stepped back much quicker at last; such excessively slow motions are preposterous and unnatural, and keep the spectator in painful suspense. Macbeth should likewise have followed him step for step. I remember to have seen it acted in that manner, and it had a very good effect.[2]

The criticism of his performance may have helped Garrick to change his mind, even though he could not have agreed with it at every point. Eighteen years later his interpretation had changed, for, in January 1762, H.H. objected to the fact that Macbeth was not 'totally overpowered' by the 'super-natural appearance of Banquo'.

Garrick's reply to H.H. shows that his interpretation of the scene had changed since 1744. He now felt that Macbeth's first response to the appearance of Banquo's ghost should be distinguished from his response to the ghost when it appeared for the second time:

...the first appearance of the Spirit overpowers him more than the second; but even before it vanishes at first, Macbeth gains strength:

---

[1] III. p. 39.   [2] *Correspondence of Garrick*, ed. Boaden, I, 20.

'If thou canst nod, speak too'—must be spoke with horror, but with a recovering mind: and in the next speech with him, he cannot pronounce 'Avaunt and quit my sight!' without a stronger execution of his powers, under the circumstances of horror: the—'Why so—being gone,' &c. means in my opinion—I am a man again, or returning to my senses, which were before mad and inflamed with what I had seen. I make a great difference between a mind sunk by guilt into cowardice, and one rising with horror to acts of madness and desperation...

Garrick admitted a 'degree of resolution' in *Macbeth* during the second appearance of Banquo's ghost, but denied that he had advanced on the ghost, as actors like Quin had done.

Garrick's mature interpretation of Macbeth's scene with the ghost of Banquo brings to mind Forman's description of the actor, who was almost certainly Richard Burbage, playing Macbeth at the Globe in 1611. At the Globe, Macbeth broke out into 'a great passion of fear and fury' when Banquo's ghost appeared for the second time. That there was an element of 'fury' as well as 'fear' in Garrick's performance is proved by the way in which he transformed the traditional business with the cup used by Macbeth to drink Banquo's health.

It would appear from what may be a reference to the scene in *The Knight of the Burning Pestle* that Macbeth at the Globe turned round and, seeing Banquo's ghost, let the cup fall from a nerveless hand.[1] The business possibly became traditional. Quin dropped the cup in this way, letting it fall gently from him without 'the least Consciousness of having such a Vehicle in his hand'.[2] Garrick adopted a different strategy. He flung the cup away in a great passion of fear and fury. Sprague quotes Smollett attacking Garrick seven years later for doing this:

At a juncture when his whole soul ought to be alarmed with terror and amazement, and all his attention engrossed by the dreadful object in view...he expresses no passion but that of indignation against a drinking glass, which he violently dashes in pieces on the floor, as if he had perceived a spider in his wine.[3]

Smollett's description recalls the image of the 'poison'd chalice' in the 'If it were done' soliloquy:

[1] See above, pp. 8–9. [2] See above, p. 35.
[3] See *The Stage Business in Shakespeare's Plays: A Postscript*, The Society for Theatre Research; Pamphlet Series no. 3 (1953), p. 26; and H. S. Buck, *A Study in Smollett* (1925), p. 155.

This even-handed justice
Commends th' ingredience of our poison'd chalice
To our own lips.   (I. vii. 10–12)

Garrick's mature interpretation of the line 'Avaunt, and quit my sight' would have suited the new business better than it did in 1744. In 1744 he appears to have spoken the line 'in a faint manner'. In 1762 Garrick told H.H. that Macbeth could not pronounce '"Avaunt, and quit my sight" without a stronger execution of his powers'.

While Macbeth lost control of himself, Mrs Pritchard as Lady Macbeth tried to retain some measure of control. As in the scene after Duncan's murder, Garrick and Mrs Pritchard presented characters in sharp contrast. Davies writes:

This admirable scene was greatly supported by the speaking terrors of Garrick's look and action. Mrs Pritchard showed admirable art in endeavouring to hide Macbeth's frenzy from the observation of the guests and drawing their attention to conviviality. She smiled on one, whispered to another, and distantly saluted a third; in short she practised every possible artifice to hide the transaction that passed between her husband and the vision his disturbed imagination had raised. Her reproving and angry looks, which glanced towards Macbeth, at the same time were mixed with marks of inward vexation and uneasiness. When at last, as if unable to support her feelings any longer, she rose from her seat, and seized his arm, and with a half-whisper of terror, said, 'Are you a man!' she assumed a look of such anger, indignation and contempt as cannot be surpassed.[1]

Davies is referring to the first appearance of Banquo's ghost. The passage Mrs Pritchard based her interpretation on was this:

Sit worthy Friends: my Lord is often thus,
And hath been from his youth. Pray you keep Seat,
The fit is momentary, upon a thought
He will again be well. If much you note him
You shall offend him, and extend his Passion
Feed, and regard him not. Are you a man?[2]

Garrick and Mrs Pritchard appear to have done well in the banquet scene. Their exceptional success must have been in some measure due to the fact that they were using Shakespeare's language for the most part, and not Davenant's. The difference

[1] *Dramatic Miscellanies*, II, 166.   [2] Bell, III. p. 40.

between Davenant's language and Shakespeare's in the banquet scene can be illustrated by a single example. Talking of his network of spies, after the ghost and the guests have gone, in the Davenant version, Macbeth says:

> There's not one great *Thane* in all Scotland,
> But in his house I keep a Servant.[1]

In the Folio and the Bell edition the same idea is expressed with much greater immediacy:

> There's not one of them but in his house
> I keep a Servant Feed.[2]

Garrick and Mrs Pritchard had a better script to work with than their predecessors, even though he made some changes in the original. Garrick possessed a copy of the First Folio (now at Queen's College, Oxford), and some of his best effects come from following it.

At the end of the third act Garrick unfortunately departed from the text of the Folio, and used the business contrived for Hecate by Davenant, at the end of the third act. In the Bell edition, the witches meet Hecate and there is a 'Symphony whilst Hecate places herself in the machine to exit'.[3] The fourth act commences, however, with the cavern scene as it is in the Folio. Garrick restored the 'bloody child' and the 'child crowned, with a tree in his hand'—symbols of suffering and mysterious regeneration—and the apparition of the 'armed head', examples of Shakespearean spectacle, dramatic rather than theatrical, which Davenant had rejected.

The writer in *St. James's Chronicle* (October 28–30, 1773) who at this point preferred Macklin's interpretation, felt that Garrick's entrance in the cavern scene lacked solemnity, that he came down the steps of the cavern too swiftly and seemed to be inadequately 'moved at the Preparations for a Deed on which the Witches themselves declare their inability to bestow a Name'. Macklin by contrast had evidently paused in 'silent wonder' before he descended. The writer in *St. James's Chronicle* felt that Garrick's manner of entering and his modern dress created altogether the wrong sort of expectation.

[1] III. i. p. 41.
[2] Bell, III. p. 43. Cf. First Folio, Actus Tertius, Scena Quarta, p. 142.
[3] III. p. 44.

The last Dress in which you played Macbeth was that of a *modern fine Gentleman*; so that when you came among the Witches in the 4th Act, you looked like a Beau, who had unfortunately slipped his Foot and tumbled into a Night Cellar, where a Parcel of old Women were boiling Tripe for their Supper. The very Door in the Rock by which you enter, like the Gates of Hell in *Milton* ought to fly open

> 'With impetuous Recoil and jarring Sound
> ...and on its Hinges grate
> Harsh Thunder'.

I am convinced that a greater Dignity of Habit, and a Little more Attention to Decorations, would effectually enhance the Terrors of this powerful Scene.

Garrick evidently had his reasons for interpreting the character of Macbeth in the cavern scene as he did. When Macklin's solemn interpretation was preferred to Garrick's, Eumenes wrote in *St. James's Chronicle* (November 2–4, 1773):

A Pause and a Start from Mr Garrick, in the 4th Act, would certainly please because gracefully performed; but I question whether they are necessary in this Place. The Witches were Macbeth's Acquaintances, therefore why this Ceremony among old Friends?...Macbeth is impatient to know his Destiny and therefore conjures his Oracle immediately to answer his Question. A Pause and a Start would take off from the abrupt and Disordered State of the Speaker's Mind. The modern Dress is justly condemned. I am credibly informed, that Mr Garrick has long since provided such Habits and Decorations as he believed to be most suitable to this great Drama, and very different from any that have been yet exhibited. But as it would look invidious to endeavour to stop the Run of Mr Macklin's Macbeth, he puts off the Representation till some future Time.

Influenced by the new convention of historic realism argued for by Aaron Hill as early as 1731,[1] and experimented with by Macklin, Garrick clearly did have some idea of playing Macbeth in the 'ancient dresses'. Writing to Sir William Young on January 10, 1773, he suggests in a postscript: 'I shall play Lear next week, & Macbeth (perhaps) in the old Dress with New Scenes the week after that & then exit Roscius...'[2] A remark he made to Luke Gardiner, written on December 13, 1777, indicates

---

[1] See A. M. Nagler, *Sources of Theatrical History* (1952), p. 391.
[2] *The Letters of David Garrick*, ed. David M. Little and George M. Karhl (3 vols. 1963), II, 854.

that Garrick regarded the new convention as being more suitable for *Macbeth* than the older convention of dressing the actors in contemporary costume: 'The Ancient Dresses', he wrote to Gardiner, 'are certainly preferable to any Modern ones.'[1] But he left the stage without proving the usefulness of the new convention in practice.

To a modern eye, the incongruity of Garrick's eighteenth-century dress is not as disturbing as one might expect. Garrick substituted naturalistic for formal elements in his approach to eighteenth-century dress, taking into account fine details like the crease in his French coat that Lichtenberg noticed, when Hamlet stood with his back to the audience on first seeing the ghost.[2] It was worth the play of facial expression twice over. Clothes on Garrick, whether contemporary or not, had character, and his approach to the eighteenth-century clothes he used was functional. This was possibly why he preferred the short Tye-wig[3] he wore as Macbeth to the elaborate 'tragical flows' previously worn. His eighteenth-century clothes in the engraving of Macbeth in the witches' cave, made by Bannerman after a painting by Dawes and dating from 1763, seem natural enough and functional.[4] In Garrick's version of *Macbeth*, the cavern scene occupied the major part of the fourth act. Most of the scene that followed, between Lady Macduff and her son, was omitted, and their murder was not enacted on the stage. Ross reports it later (Bell, IV. 57). Eighty lines of Malcolm's description of his own intemperance in the Folio version of *Macbeth* were cut, being considered 'unsuitable for refined taste'. The sleep-walking scene followed swiftly on the nightmare visions of the cavern scene.

In the sleep-walking scene Garrick returned to the text of the Folio. Francis Gentleman seems to have had Mrs Pritchard's interpretation of the scene in mind when he commented, in a note, on the stage direction—*Enter Lady Macbeth, with a Taper*, in the fifth act of the Bell edition.[5] Lord Harcourt's description of

[1] *Letters of Garrick*, ed. Little and Karhl, III, 1204.
[2] Georg Christoph Lichtenberg, *Briefe aus England* (1776–8), ed. W. Grenzmann (3 vols. 1953), I, 990. See also translation by M. L. Mare and W. H. Quarrell, *Lichtenberg's Visits to England* (1 vol. 1938), pp. 22 ff.
[3] See 'Appendix to "Essay"', *Tracts Relating to Shakespeare*, p. 15.
[4] See Burnim, *Garrick, Director*, p. 122.
[5] P. 59.

Mrs Pritchard's performance certainly gives the impression that Mrs Pritchard brought out the nightmare horror of the scene. Dr Doran writes that Lord Harcourt, 'no lukewarm friend of Mrs Siddons', missed in her Lady Macbeth 'the unequalled compass and melody of Mrs Pritchard'. In the famous sleep-walking scene, Lord Harcourt still held Mrs Siddons to be inferior—'there was not the horror in the sigh, nor the sleepiness in the tone, nor the articulation in the voice'.[1] The sigh referred to by Lord Harcourt is in the text:

> *Lady.* Here's the smell of the blood still: all the perfumes of
> *Arabia* will not sweeten this little hand. Oh! Oh! Oh!
> *Doct.* What a sigh is there? The heart is sorely charg'd.[2]

Gentleman comments in a note: 'This deep sigh is highly in nature. Those who experienced oppressive dreams, have felt such without waking.'[3] Davies writes that during the sleep-walking scene, when the terrors of a guilty conscience keep the mind awake while the body sleeps, Mrs Pritchard's acting resembled sudden flashes of lightning 'which more accurately discover the horrors of the surrounding darkness'.[4]

The second scene in the fifth act of the Folio was dropped in Garrick's production. This was unfortunate, because it contained two revealing comments on Macbeth's character: Caithness comments:

> Great Dunsinane he strongly Fortifies:
> Some say hee's mad: Others, that lesser hate him,
> Do call it valiant Fury, but for certaine
> He cannot buckle his distemper'd cause
> Within the belt of Rule.[5]

Angus is not quite so gentle:

> Now do's he feele his Title
> Hang loose about him, like a Giants Robe
> Upon a dwarfish Theefe.[6]

Garrick omitted this scene and went straight to v. iii. which enacts Macbeth's sense of insecurity. Davies writes that Garrick

---

[1] J. Doran, *Annals of the English Stage, from Betterton to Kean* (2 vols. 1864), II, 287; revised ed. R. W. Lowe (3 vols. 1888), III, 173.
[2] Bell, v. p. 60.   [3] *Ibid.*
[4] *Life of Garrick*, II, 183–4.   [5] Actus Quintus, Scena Secunda, p. 148.
[6] *Ibid.* p. 149.

brought back to the stage the language given to Macbeth in its original form in v. iii. and that when he first acted Macbeth

So little did the players know of Shakespeare's text that Quin, after he had seen Garrick in this character, asked him where he got such a strange and out of the way expressions, as

'The devil damn thee black, thou cream fac'd loon
Where gott'st thou that goose look?'

Mr Garrick advised him to consult the original, and not borrow his knowledge of Shakespeare from the altered copies of his plays.[1]

In fact, the Bell edition suggests that Garrick dropped 'The devil damn thee black', though he retained

Thou cream fac'd loon
Where got'st thou that goose look?[2]

This certainly was an improvement on Davenant's

Now Friend what means thy change of countenance?[3]

if less expressive than the original line.

Later on, in v. iii., Garrick made another minor alteration in the Folio text, influenced by Johnson. He substituted 'May of life' for 'way of life' in the well-known passage, which now ran:

I have liv'd long enough—my May of life
Is fall'n into the sear, the yellow leaf...[4]

Garrick's interpretation of the passage on the stage made Dr Scrope accept the 'restoration'. On April 19, 1769, Dr Scrope wrote to Garrick:

Your judicious emphasis on the word *May* struck me, and upon reflection I was convinced this must be the right reading. It is Shakespeare's way of saying, My Spring is declined to Autumn; and it is confirmed beyond dispute by another passage of the same author. For in 'Much Ado about Nothing', one of the old men tells Claudio he is resolved to be revenged on him notwithstanding his 'May of youth and bloom of lustihood...'[5]

As the passage expressing Macbeth's disillusionment in terms of a fading autumn comes to its close, Seyton enters, and Macbeth begins to call for his armour. He speaks alternately to Seyton and

---

[1] *Life of Garrick*, II, 183–4.   [2] v. p. 61.
[3] v. iii. p. 58.   [4] Bell, v. p. 62.
[5] *Correspondence of Garrick*, ed. Boaden, I, 342.

the Doctor; at one point in this exchange Murphy preferred Garrick's earlier interpretation to his mature approach in 1768. Speaking of Garrick's rendering of the passage beginning, 'Doctor, the Thanes fly from me', Murphy wrote in a letter: '. . . it used to be a strong involuntary burst of melancholy, and the other night I thought it sounded very differently'.[1] Garrick, in his reply, denied that he had once interpreted the passage in the way described but, as Boaden points out, Garrick did not seem to grasp the full complexity of Murphy's description of his own earlier performance. Garrick said in his reply:

You are certainly right in your account of my speaking—'Doctor, the Thanes fly from me'—but I differ a little with you in opinion, that I formerly spoke it in 'a burst of melancholy'.—Macbeth is greatly heated and agitated with the news of the English force coming upon him; his mind runs from one thing to another, all in hurry and confusion; would not his speaking in a melancholy manner in the midst of his distraction be too calm? 'Come, put my armour on'—'Give me my staff—Seyton, send out'—'Doctor, the Thanes fly from me!'— 'come, Sir, despatch'—'pluck it off'—'bring it after me' &c.[2]

As Boaden comments, however:

It should be remembered that Murphy's expression is 'a *strong*, involuntary, *burst* of melancholy'—it is a varied emotion, but has no calmness surely about it, and I think is finely descriptive of the deserted tyrant's condition. Mr Garrick forgot that Macbeth, who had received no fresh news since, in the very speech preceding puts to this same doctor the most truly *melancholy* question that human misery ever articulated into language.

> 'Canst thou not minister to a mind diseased,
> Pluck from the memory a rooted sorrow?'

In hurry itself, he sees and feels *all* his wretchedness.[3]

In the closing scenes of the play Garrick appears to have brought out Macbeth's feeling of desolation and loss. In the last scene, during which Macbeth receives news of his wife's death, Garrick restored the poetry of disillusionment which Davenant had tampered with. Where Davenant had written:

> To Morrow, to Morrow, and to Morrow,
> Creeps in a stealing pace from Day to Day,

[1] *Ibid.* II, 363.　　　　[2] *Ibid.* 364.　　　　[3] *Ibid.*

> To the last Minute of recorded Time
> And all our yesterdays have lighted Fools
> The way to dusty death. Out, out, that candle...[1]

Garrick brought back the original words of the Folio:

> To morrow, and to morrow, and to morrow
> Creeps in this petty pace from day to day,
> To the last Syllable of recorded Time:
> And all our yesterdays have lighted Fools
> The way to dusty death. Out, out, brief Candle...[2]

The exchange of letters between H.H. and Garrick gives us some idea of the way in which Garrick may have interpreted the original lines on the stage. H.H. wrote:

When you come to the 'Out, out, brief candle!' you give two starts, and accompany each word with a strong action of both hands: is not this wrong? I should suspect it is; for the whole train of Macbeth's reasoning tends to enforce the insignificance of life, which he slights as of little value...

The candle stands for 'our yesterdays' and Macbeth's own past as well, lighting the way for fools, and he wants it swiftly snuffed out—hence possibly the strong action of both hands on 'Out, out...' Garrick clearly did not take happily to the thought that he had not communicated the meaning of the lines: 'I quite agree with you about—"Out, out, brief candle"—but surely I must have spoken these words quite the reverse of my own ideas, if I did not express with them the most contemptuous indifference of life.'[3] What Garrick certainly succeeded in arousing was the feeling of pity. Pity was the emotion experienced by the Rev. S. Nott—

Macbeth's comparison of life to

> ...'A poor player,
> That struts and frets his hour upon the stage,
> And then is heard no more,'

pronounced by the softest voice that ever drew pity from the heart of man, I well remember to have affected me beyond expression.[4]

In the early years Garrick seems to have made Macbeth move abruptly from a mood of quiet desolation to a mood of physical

---

[1] v. iv. p. 61.   [2] Bell, v. p. 65.
[3] *Correspondence of Garrick*, ed. Boaden, I, 137.   [4] *Ibid.* 377.

violence. When the Messenger entered to announce that Birnam
Wood had begun to move, Garrick used to strike the helpless
man with a truncheon, shouting 'Liar, and slave' (*St. James's
Chronicle*, October 28–30, 1773). But Eumenes, in a letter published in the November 2–4 issue of *St. James's Chronicle*, points
out that Garrick had changed his strategy over the years:

The gentleman has surely not seen Mr Garrick act Macbeth these ten
Years, else he could not have charged him with breaking a Truncheon
upon a Messenger's Arm. This absurd Practice was humourously
ridiculed by Mr Murphy, in his Farce of the Apprentice...There can
be no doubt that Garrick took the Hint from the Farce; for in his late
Representation of that Character, when the Messenger informed him
of the Marching of Birnam Wood, he put his Hand upon his Sword
and with a look of Terror mixed with Despondency pronounced his
Threat to him.

The 'despondency' and 'terror' were a preparation for the
closing moments of the play. In Garrick's production at Drury
Lane, the tragic carpet had been placed on the stage floor[1] before
the act began and Macbeth died on-stage not off, as he does in the
Folio. Garrick wrote additional lines for Macduff and Macbeth.
In the Folio, Macbeth says:

> Lay on Macduff,
> And damned be him that first cries hold, enough.[2]

and they exit 'fighting'. In the Bell edition they do not exit and
Macduff replies, drawing blood. When 'Macbeth falls', Macduff
goes out, leaving him to die alone on the stage. Garrick wrote a
dying speech for Macbeth, based on what is hinted at in his last
words in the Folio:

> And damned be him that first cries hold, enough.

The echoes of Faustus are made explicit in Garrick's version:

> 'Tis done! the scene of life will quickly close.
> Ambition's vain, delusive dreams are fled,
> And now I wake to darkness, guilt and horror.
> I cannot bear it! let me shake it off—
> Two' not be; my soul is clogg'd with blood—
> I cannot rise! I dare not ask for mercy—

---

[1] See Burnim, *Garrick, Director*, p. 124.
[2] Actus Quintus, Scena Septima, p. 151.

It is too late, hell drags me down. I sink,
I sink—Oh!—my soul is lost for ever!
Oh![1]

The force and brilliance of Garrick's art as an actor appear to have
made his audience disregard the overblown rhetoric of the dying
speech. Noverre, in his account of Macbeth's death, tells us that
Garrick sent a 'shudder' through his audience:

I have seen him represent a tyrant who, appalled at the enormity of his
crime, dies torn with remorse. The last act was given up to regrets and
grief, humanity triumphed over murder and barbarism: the tyrant
obedient to the voice of conscience, denounced his crimes aloud; they
gradually became his judges and his executioners; the approach of
death showed each instant on his face; his eyes became dim; his voice
could not support the effort he made to speak his thoughts. His
gestures, without losing their expression, revealed the approach of his
last moment; his legs gave way under him, his face lengthened, his
pale and livid features bore the signs of suffering and repentance. At
last, he fell; at that moment his crimes peopled his thoughts with the
most horrible forms; terrified at the hideous pictures which his past
acts revealed to him, he struggled against death; nature seemed to make
one supreme effort. His plight made the audience shudder, he clawed
the ground and seemed to be digging his own grave, but the dread
moment was nigh, one saw death in reality, everything expressed that
instant that makes all equal. In the end he expired. The death rattle and
the convulsive movements of the features, arms and breast, gave the
final touch to this terrible picture.[2]

---

[1] Bell, v. p. 69.
[2] *Letters on Dancing and Ballet*, trans. Cyril W. Beaumont (1951), pp. 84–5; Jean
Georges Noverre, *Lettres sur la Danse et sur les Ballets* (1783), p. 163: 'Je lui ai vu,
dis-je, jouer un tyran, qui, effrayé de l'énormité de ses crimes, meurt déchiré de
ses remords. Le dernier acte n'étoit employé qu'aux regrets & à la douleur;
l'humanité triomphoit des meurtes & de la barbarie; le tyran sensible à sa voix
détestoit ses crimes; ils devenoint par gradation ses juges & ses bourreaux; la
mort à chaque instant s'imprimoit sur son visage; ses yeux s'obscureissoiet; sa
voix se prêtoit à peine aux efforts qu'il fasoit pour articuler sa pensée: ses gestes,
sans perdre de leur expression, caractérisoeint les approches du dernier instant;
ses jambes se déroboient sous lui, ses traits s'alongeoient; son teint pâle & livide
portroit l'empreinte de la douleur & du repentir; il tomboit enfin: dans cet
instant ses crimes se retracoient à son imagination sous des formes horribles;
"effrayé" des tableaux hideux que ses forfaits lui présentoient, il luttoit contre la
mort; la nature sembloit faire un dernier effort. Cette situation fasoit frémir: il
grattoit la terre, il creusoit en quelque façon son tombeau; mais le moment
approchoit on voyoit réellement la mort; tout peignoit cet instant y qui ramène
a l'égalité; il expiroit enfin: le hoquet de la mort & les mouvemins convulsifs de
la physionomie, des bras & de la poitrine, donnoient le dernier coup à ce tableau
terrible.'

Francis Gentleman felt that Macbeth's death on-stage was a justifiable change from the Folio:

If deaths upon the stage are justifiable, none can be more so than that of *Macbeth*. Shakespeare's idea of having his head brought on by Macduff, is either ludicrous or horrid, therefore commendably changed to visible punishment—a dying speech and a very good one has been furnished by Mr Garrick, to give the actor more éclat.[1]

It is interesting to compare this view of the way Macbeth should die with a twentieth-century opinion, expressed by Kenneth Tynan when he reviewed a production in which Sir Michael Redgrave played Macbeth: '...heads on pikes, by an odd veering of taste, are now ludicrous where they were once horrifying'. '*Macbeth*', Tynan goes on to suggest, rather inaccurately, 'has never been the most effective of Shakespeare's plays in our theatres; nobody is remembered for having played it; and it fails in the last analysis, as a tragedy for this very reason—that tragic heroes do not die off-stage in battle.'[2]

Dr Johnson had some harsh things to say about Mrs Pritchard, and claimed that she never read the whole of *Macbeth*. What we do know with greater certainty is that she achieved identification with the character of Lady Macbeth so completely that Garrick does not seem to have wished to play Macbeth without her. When she left the stage in 1768, Garrick, who went on playing the taxing role of Lear, did not play Macbeth again. They had worked together, and Mrs Pritchard's interpretation of Lady Macbeth was necessary if his own conception of the reluctant sensitive murderer was to be fully realised. Together Garrick and Mrs Pritchard achieved a balance of contrasts. Mrs Pritchard's approach helped Garrick to bring out Macbeth's 'kindness'.

Garrick, as Professor Stone has demonstrated, helped to inspire a new criticism of Shakespeare in terms of character.[3] Johnson, speaking of Garrick, acknowledged what came to be generally recognised: 'He was the only actor I ever saw, whom I could call a master both in tragedy and comedy...A true conception of

---

[1] See note in Bell, v. p. 69.
[2] See Kenneth Tynan, *He that Plays the King* (1950), p. 81.
[3] See 'David Garrick's Significance in the History of Shakespearean Criticism', *PMLA*, XLV (1950), 183–97.

character and natural expression of it were his distinguished excellence.'[1]

Garrick was not responsible for the excesses of the new criticism. He did not harbour the illusion that Shakespeare's play consisted of one or two significant characters only. At Drury Lane he took special pains, as director, with minor characters, and wanted to achieve a satisfying total effect. He saw each play, as well as his own role, in terms of naturalness. To Peter Garrick, he wrote, after seeing a group of strolling actors at Lichfield:

I don't know how it is, but the Strollers are a hundred years behind—we in Town are Endeavouring to bring the Sock and Buskin down to Nature, but *they* still keep to their strutting, Bouncing and Mouthing, that with whiskers on, they put me in mind of y late Czar of Russia who was both an Idiot & a Madman.[2]

Garrick enriched the idea of naturalness which had survived from Betterton's time, though subjected to many attacks, and extended its range. The Earl of Chatham's view that Garrick was supremely natural in his art is relevant to his success in *Macbeth*, where his interpretation of character secured conviction and compelled imaginative belief. The great revolution which Garrick introduced in the theatre by changing an elevated tone of voice, a mechanical depression of tones, and a formal measured step in traversing the stage into an easy, familiar manner of speaking and acting, gave at first some encouragement to the players (who inwardly felt his superiority) to view the revolution as a dangerous novelty which threatened the dignity of theatrical enunciation. Yet Garrick was natural without being prosaic. When Macklin played Macbeth in 1773, he seemed, in comparison with Garrick, to lack essential dignity. A wit wrote on the occasion of Macklin's performance:

> Tis somewhere old *Dryden* has said or has sung,
> That *Vergil* with Majesty tosses his dung,
> And now if alive, he might sing or might say
> That with dignity *Garrick cuts throats* in a play:
> But Macklin appears so ungrateful a wretch
> His murders are done in the stile of Jack Ketch.[3]

[1] James Boswell, *The Life of Samuel Johnson, LL.D.*, ed. G. B. Hill, revised and enlarged by L. F. Powell (6 vols. 1934–40), IV, 243.
[2] Cited by Burnim, *Garrick, Director*, p. 59.
[3] See *The London Chronicle* (October 26–8, 1773).

Francis Gentleman, describing Garrick's art in *Macbeth*, tells us that it was cultivated and civilised though an organic thing, seeming spontaneous to the beholder, and connected to the deep unconscious springs of the imagination:

Theatrical performance to most spectators appears a mechanical disposition of limbs, and a parrotted mode of speech; so indeed it really is too often, but intrinsic merit soars far beyond such narrow, barren limits, she traces nature through her various windings, dives into her deepest recesses and snatches ten thousand beauties which plodding method can never display; the dullest comprehension may be taught to enter on this side or that; to stand on a particular board, to raise the voice here and fall it there; but unless motion and utterance are regulated by a cultivated knowledge of life, and self-born intelligent feelings, no greater degree of excellence can be attained than unaffecting propriety; like a fair field whose native fertility of soil produces a beauteous luxuriant crop of spontaneous vegetation which art can regulate, not enrich; Mr Garrick's genius not only captivates our sportive senses, he furnishes high relished substantial food for our mind to strengthen by.[1]

To Garrick's credit it must be said that when the drama's patrons were flocking to the 'commercials' of John Rich at Covent Garden, he tried at Drury Lane to maintain a Shakespearean tradition that was both serious and alive. When one reads Gentleman's account of Garrick's art, the word that immediately springs to mind is Coleridge's word 'Imagination'. The word 'imaginative'—with its many possible meanings—best describes Garrick's interpretation of Macbeth. He brought together the sensitive and the satanic elements in the character. The ability to understand how these opposites could exist in the same person was an imaginative act. Quite unlike the reasonable decorous character created by Davenant, Garrick's Macbeth was an imaginative rather than a reasonable man. All that Garrick perceived was rooted in Shakespeare's text—the 'human tenderness' and the brutality, the melancholy and the violence. Reconciling opposite and discordant qualities, he created an imaginatively consistent character. 'Garrick alone', says Davies, 'could comprehend and execute the complicated passions of Macbeth. From the first scene in which he was accosted by the witches to the end of the part he was animated and consistent.'[2]

---

[1] *Dramatic Censor*, I, 108. [2] *Dramatic Miscellanies*, II, 133.

CHAPTER 5

INTERPRETATIONS FROM MOSSOP
TO HENDERSON

Garrick was so good as Macbeth that he established a standard by which actors who succeeded him in the role were judged. The actors who played the role after him in the eighteenth century offered imperfect substitutes and pale shadows of his Macbeth, or attempted to rebel against his conception. Mossop, Barry, Sheridan, Powell, Holland and Henderson appear to have followed the main lines of interpretation laid down by Garrick, but without the same success. Macklin and Kemble attempted a fresh interpretation.

Macklin belonged to the natural school as Garrick did. He tried to make the tones and rhythms of tragic poetry approximate to the language of ordinary life. 'It was his manner', says John Hill, 'to check all the cant and cadence of tragedy; he would bid his pupil first speak the passage as he would in common life, if he had occasion to pronounce the same words; and then giving them more force but preserving the same accent, to deliver them on the stage.'[1] Yet there was a difference between Macklin's natural method and Garrick's. Macklin's conception of truth was distinctively his own. 'The world', he wrote, 'is tired of truth; it is so plain, so obvious, so simple and so old.'[2] The words 'plain' and 'chaste' were often used to describe Macklin's style. His Iago set forth the plot against Cassio plainly and without ornament, and had nothing of the conventional stage villain about him.[3] And though Garrick followed Macklin successfully in Iago,[4] his conception of naturalism was richer and more inclusive. Macklin's idea of truth, plain and chaste, worked well when he played Shylock and Iago. In 1773 it did not work quite so well when he played Macbeth, partly because he could not consistently live up to his own principles, and partly because his principles were clearly inadequate to the full range of expression and feeling in *Macbeth*.

[1] *The Actor* (1755), pp. 239, 240.
[2] See E. A. Parry, *Charles Macklin* (1891), p. 146.
[3] *Actor* (1755), pp. 274, 275.   [4] *Ibid.*

As Macbeth Garrick had succeeded in reconciling naturalness with dignity, while in 1773 Macklin's plain style too often excluded it. At Covent Garden the dignity that goes with Macbeth's rank and station was missed when Macklin made his first entrance, despite the careful preparation for it.

Macbeth's entrance was prepared for by the Coldstream March which John Taylor thought 'the most delightful music' he had ever heard.[1] Macklin appears to have made his entrance up-stage, Garrick further down and obviously from the wings. Touchstone, writing in the *Morning Chronicle* (October 30, 1773), preferred Macklin's point of entrance: 'The march over the blasted heath at the first appearance of Macbeth has more dignity than the Drury Lane manner of entering at the side-scene, without showing that Macbeth is then at the head of his army.' Yet the martial bearing—the dignity—that appears to have been initially there was swiftly dissipated by the costume Macklin wore and the way he moved. William Cooke reports that he looked 'more like a Scotch Piper, than a General and Prince of the Blood' as he advanced 'stumping down the stage'.[2] Macklin's choice of the 'old' Scottish dress for Macbeth's entrance—he was using the convention of historical realism, the outcome of a conception of naturalism—however important it may be in the history of costume and the history of Shakespearean tragedy, was not dramatically right.

While it seems very likely that Macklin used the 'old' Scottish dress in *Macbeth* on the English stage for the first time,[3] one has to remember that West Digges had done this sixteen years before him on the Scottish stage. In 1757 Digges produced *Macbeth* in Edinburgh 'new dress'd after the manner of the Ancient Scots'.[4] Garrick anticipated Macklin in theory, in his letters to Sir Grey Cooper (December 1772), and Sir William Young (January 10, 1773).[5] He had thought of staging *Macbeth* in the 'old dresses' a good nine months before the Covent Garden production of October 1773. Macklin rushed in where Garrick had evidently feared to tread.

[1] *Personal Reminiscences*, ed. R. H. Stoddard (1875), p. 290.
[2] *Macklin*, p. 284.
[3] See M. St Clare Byrne, 'The Stage Costuming of Macbeth in the Eighteenth Century', *Studies in English Theatre History* (1952), p. 59.
[4] See James Dibdin, *The Annals of the Edinburgh Stage* (1888), p. 95.
[5] *Letters of Garrick*, ed. Little and Karhl, II, 837-8; II, 845-6.

6-2

The convention of historical realism had been in the air for many years before Macklin experimented with *Macbeth*. The first intelligent statement of the convention came from Aaron Hill in 1731, when his play *The Generous Traitor, or Aethelwold*, set in Anglo-Saxon Britain, was about to be staged. Hill wrote to Wilks at Drury Lane, on October 28, 1731, making detailed suggestions about the old Saxon costumes to be used. The letter makes it clear that the new convention was to be used with dramatic rather than scientific precision: 'The *Furrs* which you will observe pretty frequent, in the figures, are a prime *distinction*, in the *old Saxon* habits; and will have something of a *grandeur* not without *beauty*: but they need not be *real* furrs...' Aaron Hill did not wish to sacrifice all colour, form and grace to the demands of historical realism. His aim was to strike a nice balance between realism and the demands of form: 'I had regard to a *contrast* of colours, in the several parts of each person's dress.' He was aware that the new convention could be dangerous for tragedy as he conceived it: 'It weakens *probability*...it relaxes the pomp of Tragedy, and the generality, being led, by the *eye*, can conceive nothing extraordinary, where they see nothing uncommon.' Aware of the problem of fitting clothes to actors, he points out another difficulty that might arise with the new convention: 'A fine, natural *shape* receives great *advantage* from a well-imagined turn of *habit*, and an awkward, unnatural one has an *air*, that *burlesques* dignity without it.'[1]

Macklin was much less scrupulous than Aaron Hill. Historically his costumes were inaccurate. They were not consistent with each other, nor theatrically satisfying. The events in *Macbeth* take place before the Norman conquest, but the long plaid, the tartan stockings and the tunic (rather like the 'leine croich', or saffron linen shirt) worn by Macklin for his first entrance, resembled the dress worn in the highlands of Scotland in the late sixteenth century.[2] For his second costume, Macklin wore breeches. The second costume (sketched from the life in the *London Magazine* of November 1773—see Plate 3) resembled very closely 'a Scottish innovation dating from the time of the Forty-Five' used by the Scottish nobility.[3] While Macklin experimented with two

[1] *Works*, I, 89–91.
[2] See Denis Donoghue, 'Macklin's Shylock and Macbeth', *Studies: An Irish Quarterly Review*, XLIII (1954), 426. Cf. J. Laver, *Costume in the Theatre* (1964), p. 98.
[3] See Byrne, *English Theatre History*, p. 63.

costumes, quite different in time, for himself, Mrs Hartley as Lady Macbeth wore fashionable contemporary dress which by 'no means accorded with the habits of the other personages'.[1]

Eumenes in a later issue of *St. James's Chronicle* (November 2–4, 1773) tells us that, when Garrick heard *Macbeth* was going to be staged at Covent Garden, he declared that Macklin's performance 'would give a good lesson to the best Actor of that difficult Part'. And so it did. But Garrick's remark did not merely have an ironic application. In his interpretation of individual lines and passages Macklin did at times offer the most searching and minute criticism of Garrick's interpretation of Macbeth that had yet been made.

As Touchstone wrote in the *Morning Chronicle* (October 30, 1773):

...the reading of Macbeth is in many passages improved by Mr Macklin...Garrick says

'*Time* and the *hour* runs through the roughest day...'

This is flat tautology. Macklin reads,

'Time,—and the hour (i.e. opportunity)
runs through the roughest day.'

In the former, the line is of no import; in the latter, it is characteristic, and marks a mind intensely bent upon the idea of murder which had already engrossed the imagination.

Macklin's interpretation of the line (i. iii. 147) finds support in the First Folio, which has a comma after 'Time', indicating a pause, and a comma after 'hour':

Time, and the Houre, runs through the roughest Day.[2]

At the end of the first act, Macklin conceived the idea of sitting down during the 'If it were done' soliloquy. Macklin's production notes indicate how he intended to improve on Garrick: 'Scene the last of the first act—If it were done,—In this scene should be table and chairs, Macbeth should sit down sometimes in this soliloquy,—then start up—traverse—it would diversifie the actor's position—better mark his perturbation.'[3] Macklin's manuscript notes contain impulsive fresh thoughts. They are not

---

[1] *London Chronicle* (October 23–6).
[2] Actus Primus, Scena Tertia, p. 133.
[3] See manuscript notes made by Macklin in extra-illustrated copy of Kirkman's *Life of Macklin*, quoted in Sprague, *Shakespeare and the Actors*, p. 235.

reflected in his production at every point—he does not seem to have worn the 'pistols' mentioned in his notes when he made his first entrance. And the many letters provoked by reviews of Macklin's production of *Macbeth* do not tell us whether he did sit down during the soliloquy on judgement or not; but if he did, it would have been an innovation. Sprague points out that 'standing during the speaking of soliloquies was well nigh obligatory' as late as the middle of the nineteenth century. Macklin seems to have anticipated the realism of nineteenth-century actors like Fechter and Booth.

The realistic principle seems to have dictated the logic of Macklin's innovations in the scene with the imaginary dagger immediately before the murder of Duncan.[1] Touchstone describes Macklin's interpretation of this scene in the *Morning Chronicle*. Macklin first took the dagger 'for reality' at 'let me clutch thee': but, suspecting that the dagger was 'the effect of a troubled imagination, of the heat-oppressed brain, he closed his eyes, turned his head away, holding his forehead in his hand'. At 'Thou marshall'st me the way that I was going' Touchstone's description suggests a swift change of tone: 'Lightning itself is not so swift as an overheated imagination; and the military term "marshall" which the poet has chosen implies fiery expedition...' Judgement asserted itself again at 'Mine eyes are made the fools o' th' other senses Or else worth all the rest'. But Macklin looked up once more and seeing the dagger with 'gouts of blood,' turned away his eyes. At 'There's no such thing: /It is the bloody business which informs/ Thus to mine eyes', imagination tired, and judgement prevailed.

As Macbeth ends his soliloquy, Lady Macbeth rings the bell in the interior of the castle. The sound of the bell tells Macbeth that the stage is set for murder. Macklin used a 'single stroke upon the bell' which was 'more awful than the tingle-tingle of the modern chamber'. Defending the innovation, Touchstone writes: 'It has been objected that the sound of a loud bell might rouse the family: yes, if rung like an alarum bell but not being repeated, no bustle is like to ensue...Mr Macklin's plan is not only impressive of terror but consonant to the poet's idea.' Concluding his de-

---

[1] As Sprague has shown (*ibid.* p. 237), at 'I see thee yet, in forme as palpable, / as this which now I draw', Macklin, with concern for realistic effects, substituted a dagger for the long Toledo conventionally used.

scription of the dagger scene, and comparing Macklin's interpretation with Garrick's, Touchstone concludes that Macklin was more natural in the dagger scene:

From the moment he [Garrick] sees a dagger in the air, till he says 'There's no such thing', the eye is constantly fixed on the vision of his mind...Is his execution in this scene natural? When judgement begins to stir, and enquire 'Art thou a dagger of the mind proceeding from the heat-oppressed brain?' would not Macbeth endeavour to convince himself by closing his eyes and applying the hand to the forehead?... When he says, '*Thou marshal'st me the way*' would the phantom of an over-heated imagination move slowly before him, and for a tedious length of time, when the nature of the mind, and the force of the words import, that it should pass with the most rapid celerity?

Touchstone does not seem to have responded adequately to Garrick's playing in the dagger scene—we know that it was one of Garrick's most expressive and dramatic moments. Judging by other descriptions of Garrick's playing in the dagger scene, it would seem more accurate to say that Macklin's interpretation of the scene was rational, Garrick's intuitive.

Macklin's rational realism is illustrated in his production notes on the décor and the lighting for ii. i. Macklin queries, 'should not this scene be dark?'[1] He evidently had Banquo's

> There's husbandry in heaven;
> Their candles are all out   (ii. i. 4–5)

in mind, and eventually staged the scene in the 'inward quadrangle of an old Gothic castle' because 'Banquo sees the sky'.[2] A comment in the notes on the traditional business with the servant, who leaves Macbeth in the dark, illustrates Macklin's pervasive rationality:

In this scene, the Servant comes on with two candles, he goes off & leaves his master in the dark that is a breach of manners even to absurdity, to remedy this the scene must lie in a Hall, or anti-chamber, in which there must be a Table in the apartment and when the Servant goes off he must leave the candles on the Table, on which I think Macbeth must put them out.

This scene [sic] reconsidered, for the absurdity must not remain.[3]

---

[1] This note from Kirkman's *Life of Macklin* is quoted in Donoghue, *Studies*, XLIII, 427.
[2] See Touchstone, *Morning Chronicle* (October 29, 1773).
[3] See manuscript notes quoted in Sprague, *Shakespeare and the Actors*, p. 237.

Touchstone does not tell us whether Macklin carried out this strategy.

Macklin's realistic treatment of the scene with the imaginary dagger earned him praise from at least one critic. But after the murder of Duncan Macklin appears to have violated the tragic dignity of Macbeth. And, unlike Garrick after the murder, he does not seem to have been concerned with bringing out the real sensitiveness of Macbeth to the evil in which he is caught. We are told in the *Morning Chronicle* of October 26 that Macklin, after Duncan's murder, did not modulate his voice 'in some fear of being overheard'. He did instead 'so bellow and roar, that it was not only likely to wake the sleeping, but also to fright the waking *audience* and almost raise the dead'.

Tragic dignity, which involves sensitiveness, was missed again in the banquet scene, by the writer of the letter to Garrick in *St. James's Chronicle* (October 28–30, 1773). Macklin's banquet, he reports, was 'more magnificent' than Garrick's, but a single unfortunate gesture seems to have dissipated some of the grandeur. Macklin did not give any 'additional Dignity' to Macbeth, says the writer of the letter to Garrick, when he pulled up 'the waistband of his Breeches' as he came forward to invite his nobles to the banquet.

When Macklin did appear dignified, in the cavern scene, his dignity was portentous rather than sensitive. Macklin's conception of the cavern scene, both in his notes and in the way it was staged, suggests that he wanted to create an atmosphere of solemnity and awe. In his notes Macklin writes: 'Cave scene in the 4th act. there must be high rocks All round so as to form the stage into a deep cave and down the back part must be a winding way for Macbeth to come down to the Wetches.'[1] When Macklin entered, the door in the rock seemed to fly open 'like the Gates of Hell' in Milton:

> With impetuous Recoil and jarring Sound...

He appears to have 'paused in silent wonder' before descending, 'struck with the solemnity' of the scene.[2] Macklin's interpretation, though slightly theatrical and perhaps a little too reminiscent of the terror novel, was probably intended to harmonise with his

---

[1] Quoted in Donoghue, *Studies*, XLIII, 428.
[2] *St. James's Chronicle* (October 28–30, 1773).

conception of the witches. In his production of *Macbeth* the 'witches were represented seriously'.[1]

In the final scenes of *Macbeth*, Macklin produced 'little more than ineffectual Fire' and 'seemed determined to find Gold in a Mine' which Garrick 'had already exhausted',[2] with the possible exception of his interpretation of Macbeth's reply to the Messenger who brought the news that Birnam Wood was moving to Dunsinane:

> If thou speak'st false,
> Upon the next tree shalt thou hang alive
> 'Til famine cling thee: if thy speech be true,
> I care not if thou dost for me as much.[3] (v. v. 38–40)

William Cooke tells us that Macklin caught the change of tone in the lines and communicated it to his audience: 'The first part of this speech was delivered in a tone and look of such terrible menace as almost petrified the audience; while in the last line he fell into such an air of despondency, as showed the effect of contrast in a most masterly manner...'[4] Macklin altered the business once used by Garrick, of beating the Messenger with 'a sawed off truncheon'. He seized the Messenger's arm instead and bent him to the ground.[5]

During his best moments Macklin's interpretation of Macbeth had obvious qualities of 'intelligence' and 'precision'.[6] He seems to have transmitted these qualities to Mrs Hartley, who played Lady Macbeth in his production at Covent Garden. A writer in the *London Evening Post* observed 'the improvement of Mrs Hartley's *thinking in Lady Macbeth*' and felt that it was the result of 'some intelligence she had received from Mr Macklin'.[7] Macklin's ideas for *Macbeth* if not, as the *Morning Chronicle* of October 25, 1773, claimed, 'visibly chaste,[8] natural and perfect', had the

---

[1] *Ibid.*

[2] *St. James's Chronicle* (October 28–30, 1773).

[3] The passage runs as quoted in Cooke, *Macklin*, p. 285. 'True' has been substituted for 'sooth' in 'if thy speech be sooth' (First Folio, p. 150).

[4] *Ibid.* pp. 285–6.

[5] *St. James's Chronicle* (October 28–30, 1773).

[6] *Morning Chronicle* (October 30, 1773).

[7] See Macklin, *An Apology for the Conduct of Mr Charles Macklin, Comedian* (1773), p. 6.

[8] The word 'chaste' meant the absence of declamation, and implied a certain purity and control. See the *Morning Post* (February 3, 1785), quoted in chapter 6, pp. 102–3, on Mrs Siddons's acting.

quality of genuine innovations. This probably was the real reason for the claim made by the dramatic critic of the *Morning Chronicle* on October 25, that 'in some parts of the play' Macklin was 'superior to almost every contemporary'. The dramatic critic of the *London Chronicle*[1] thought that Macklin's innovations would be 'of great use to some future young actor'—as indeed they were. Henderson, Kemble, Macready and Charles Kean were influenced by Macklin's experimental use of historical costume and décor at Covent Garden. Macklin's reason, as much as Garrick's imagination, had its impact on nineteenth-century interpretations of Macbeth.

But not even Macklin's most sympathetic critics could claim that his production of *Macbeth* was a satisfying whole. While many of Macklin's decisions were sensible, there were occasions when his good sense seemed to desert him. Feeling that in Davenant's version of *Macbeth* Lady Macduff usurped too much attention, he eliminated her altogether; though the text he finally adopted was closer to Shakespeare than Davenant's version.[2] There were times when the realism, both in conception and execution, was not 'chaste' enough. A note provided by Macklin on the décor of *Macbeth* shows a tendency to crowd his set with realistic objects: 'Inside of the Castle—every room should be full of bad pictures of warriors, sword, helmet, target and dirk—Escutchions—and the Hall, bores stufft, wolves—and full of Pikes and broadswords'.[3] This tendency to crowd his stage was doubtless responsible for the disturbing presence of the soldiers during Macbeth's encounter with the witches. Eumenes, writing in *St. James's Chronicle* (November 2–4, 1773), thought that 'the soldiers by a single Word or Action, should have been dismissed, and the scene left to be occupied only by the Witches, Macbeth and Banquo'. Macklin's excesses in the murder scene were clearly not 'chaste'. At such times he did not live up to his own principles.

At other times his principles seem to have been inadequate to deal with the full range of expression and feeling in *Macbeth*. There was a limiting cerebral quality in Macklin's playing. As William Cooke remarked: 'His performance on the whole,

[1] October 23–6.
[2] See William Appleton, *Charles Macklin* (1962), p. 173.
[3] Quoted in Donoghue, *Studies*, XLIII, 428.

though there were passages that shewed the force of observation and a sound judgement, may be classed more under the head of a *lecture on the part* than a *theatrical representation*. The scene demanded the embodying of the character'.[1] Cooke's statement contains the main distinction to be drawn between Macklin's interpretation of Macbeth and Garrick's. Garrick 'embodied' the character of Macbeth.

Macklin's interpretation of Macbeth was experimental rather than satisfying. The performance that came closest to being satisfying after Garrick's was Mossop's. Mossop played Macbeth at Drury Lane during Garrick's management. He used Garrick's text and Mrs Pritchard played Lady Macbeth opposite him. He attempted to follow the main lines of interpretation laid down by Garrick.

A review by the dramatic critic of the *London Chronicle* (April 14–15, 1757) shows that Mossop successfully re-created Macbeth's melancholy intensity which Garrick had earlier drawn so well:

...a melancholy Gloom overcasts the Mind of Macbeth; but this is by slow and imperceptible Degrees, till at length it settles into a Kind of determined Despondency, that makes him *grow a weary of the sun*, and therefore resolved desperately to hazard every Thing. We think this Performer very just in his Execution of this difficult Part of the Character; in him we perceive the strong Brilliancy of the Colouring fade away by proper Gradations till it finally ends in the darkest shade.

Mossop's performance had a consistent, imaginative logic, nor was it based on a static conception of Macbeth. Like Garrick, Mossop saw Macbeth's character in terms of growth and development.

Mossop's playing, when gloom shrouded Macbeth, had a quality of imaginative intensity which was moving. The dramatic critic of the *London Chronicle* felt that Mossop achieved complete identification with the character of Macbeth in the scene with the imaginary dagger—the prelude to Duncan's murder:

...the Poet does not here so much help the Actor, as in other passages, but on the contrary he requires great Aid from the Performer, to give as it were, Reality to airy nothing, and terrify the audience against the testimony of the faithful Eyes, As Horace calls them. The Effect in this

[1] *Macklin*, p. 286.

case must proceed from the strong Tokens the Player gives of his being possessed with the Idea, and the Idea cannot be excited but by a strong and creative Imagination.

Mossop needed to have his effects carefully planned. While this is done by all actors who take their profession seriously, in Mossop's case there were, unfortunately, times when the element of calculation tended to reveal itself in performance. During Macbeth's scene with Banquo's ghost, in the 1757 production, Mossop's pauses were felt to be too long. The dramatic critic of the *London Chronicle*, reviewing Mossop's performance, uses an analogy from music to illustrate the danger of the long pause in acting: 'In Musick a sudden Cessation of the whole Band has a fine Effect, because it breaks out again very quickly into a full Tumult of Harmony, which would be greatly hurt, if the Pauses were allowed to be too long.'

Mossop's voice 'could rise from the lowest note to the highest pitch of sound'. 'It was indeed a voice,' says Davies, 'the most comprehensive I have ever heard.'[1] And yet despite the superiority of his voice, Mossop seems to have managed it with less skill than Garrick. What Churchill calls the 'studied impropriety'[2] of Mossop's speech appears to have occasionally revealed itself in his interpretation of Macbeth.

Mossop found it difficult at times to make calculation seem wholly spontaneous. The dramatic critic of the *London Chronicle* felt that his performance suffered by comparison with Garrick's for this reason. Garrick as Macbeth had fire and grace. The critic felt that in comparison, Mossop's playing was 'constrained'.

...if Mossop will resolve to play this Part more carelessly, he will play it better; because, while he is over studious to please, his Deportment becomes constrained, whereas every attitude of Macbeth requires Boldness and Freedom; and indeed in the last Circumstance consisted the superior Merit of Mr Garrick, who supported this extra hard part with such a commanding Air in every movement, and such a graceful Horror, if we may so express it, as has hardly been equalled even by himself in any other Performance.

Davies confirms the truth of this description of Mossop's playing in *Macbeth*. 'Mossop's power of expression, in several situations of Macbeth commanded attention and applause', writes Davies.

[1] *Life of Garrick*, I, 196.　　　　[2] *The Rosciad* (1761), p. 20.

'Had he been acquainted with variety of action and easy deportment, he would have been justly admired in it.'[1]

If Mossop suffered by comparison with Garrick, so did Barry. The 'silver tones' of Barry's voice—the phrase is Macklin's[2]— his characteristic ease and grace, his tall 'manliness and sweetness'[3] were not entirely adequate for Macbeth. Barry understood the sensitiveness of Macbeth, which Garrick had projected so vividly, but not his tortured violence.

At Covent Garden he used Davenant's watered-down text: this may have been partly responsible for the impression received by Francis Gentleman that Barry 'made but a luke-warm affair of Macbeth'.[4] Within the narrow dimensions of Davenant's text Barry succeeded in arousing pity for Macbeth's condition. In the second act he brought out 'a mixture of remorse and generosity' in the character which made his audience 'rather pity than abhor him'.[5] An illustration in the Enthoven collection shows Barry after the murder of the king, with a dagger in each hand, glancing back over his shoulder to the door of Duncan's chamber. It was in the last two acts that Barry failed to satisfy even his most enthusiastic supporters. Here he clearly suffered most by comparison with Garrick. The tortured violence of Macbeth eluded Barry. Davies felt that he should not have attempted a role 'so opposite to his natural manner...He was not formed', writes Davies, 'to represent the terrible agonies of Macbeth.' Garrick alone could 'comprehend and execute the complicated passions of this character'.[6]

At Covent Garden on March 17, 1752, Barry's interpretation of Macbeth led to unexpected disaster in the last scene of the tragedy. On that night, Barry seems to have thought a full-bottomed peruke necessary to his interpretation of Macbeth. Rejecting Garrick's idea of a short tie-wig, he resurrected an old convention which rested on the belief that a full-bottomed wig, whose bushy expanse spread over the whole back of its wearer, conferred a special kind of heroic dignity. Bonnell Thornton tells us how the wig, in the last scene, ironically had an effect quite opposite to that which Barry must have intended:

[1] *Dramatic Miscellanies*, II, 133.   [2] Cooke, *Macklin*, pp. 160 ff.
[3] Bertram Joseph, *The Tragic Actor* (1959), p. 137.
[4] *Dramatic Censor*, I, 109.
[5] *An Estimate of the Theatrical Merits of the Two Tragedians of Crow Street* (1760), p. 16.
[6] *Dramatic Miscellanies*, II, 133.

Mr Barry this night chose to appear in one most curiously frizzled out and of the fullest tragical flow I ever saw: When in the last act it was our hero's turn to be kill'd, honest Ryan, being eager to despatch him, just as he was to plump down upon the carpet, entangled his hand in the vast profusion of Macbeth's hair; and by jerking back his sword after the concluding stab, away came poor perriwig along with it, while our hero was left expos'd in the last agonies of death,—bareheaded. Ryan in the meanwhile with some confusion contemplated Full-bottom which he held dangling in his hand, but badly tumbled and out of curl: at length he good naturedly adjusted it on the bald pate of the tyrant, who was then enabled to make his dying speech with proper regularity and decorum.[1]

Neither Barry's wig, nor personality, nor Davenant's text were well chosen for Macbeth. Barry was excellent as Macduff: he brought out Macduff's tenderness and affection for his wife and children, but as Macbeth, with the shadow of Garrick falling over him, he seemed limited. As Thomas Wilkes wrote:

...tho' Barry chose to play Macbeth 'the murderous savageness' of the character becomes him not near so well...Garrick exhibits this Play as it was written. Barry performs it with Betterton's alterations, which I cannot think any ornament to the piece. They put us in mind of German money, wherin we find copper and silver intermixed.[2]

On the night of March 17, Mrs Cibber played opposite Barry. Of the many performers who played opposite him, Mrs Cibber earned the most exact praise for her interpretation of Lady Macbeth, despite the disastrous conclusion to the production. On that night she acted effectively with her face. As Bonnell Thornton wrote:

The muscles of Mrs Cibber's face are so finely form'd by nature to answer the emotions of every passion which agitates the heart, that the effect is most strongly enforc'd upon the audience. Nothing could be equal to the amazement which dwelt upon her brow just before and immediately after *Macbeth* had *done the deed*; and the contrition she shew'd, when in her sleep she seem'd to smell to her fingers, was painted on her countenance beyond the faint colouring of the most masterly artist.[3]

After Mossop and Barry, most interpretations of Macbeth until the arrival of Kemble—Macklin excepted—appear to have been

---

[1] *Have at You All: Or, The Drury Lane Journal* (March 13, 1752), p. 230.
[2] *General View of the Stage*, pp. 294-5.   [3] *Drury Lane Journal*, p. 228.

like familiar variations on a theme by Garrick. Sheridan had the good fortune to play Macbeth with Mrs Pritchard as Lady Macbeth, on April 29, 1761, at Drury Lane. Of Sheridan's interpretation, Gentleman writes: 'Without any exaggeration of compliment to that gentleman, we must place him in a very reputable degree of competition with Mr Garrick, in the dagger scene; and at the same time confess a doubt, whether any performer ever spoke the words, "this is a sorry sight", better.'[1] But after the second act Sheridan's performance seems to have collapsed: 'As to the third, fourth and fifth acts,' writes Gentleman, 'his meaning well, was all we could perceive to recommend him.'[2]

At Covent Garden on January 20, 1768, Powell played Macbeth with Mrs Yates as Lady Macbeth. A couplet:

> In Yates another Cibber greets our Eyes
> In Powell see another Garrick rise

and a favourable review by Duns Scotus in *St. James's Chronicle* (January 19–21) greeted the performance. The production was important in one respect. The witches were portrayed seriously— an innovation which Macklin was to adopt—and their traditional comic folk dress abandoned. Duns Scotus observed a new 'solemnity' in the witches that 'gave the Horror to the scene which now suits with it'. D. T. Mackintosh has argued in *The Times Literary Supplement* (August 25, 1927) that the actors in this production may have worn 'ancient Scots' dresses, providing the inspiration for Macklin's production at Covent Garden in 1773. But his case rests on uncertain foundations. A surviving illustration, dated 1769–73, shows Mrs Yates as Lady Macbeth, wearing a rather extravagant eighteenth-century dress with excessively circumambient skirts, in the scene after the murder of Duncan.[3]

Though Duns Scotus wrote that both Powell and Mrs Yates were effective, Gentleman tells us that Powell was not generally considered to be successful as Macbeth.[4] Some of Powell's interpretations of particular moments appear to have been unusual, but not successful, variations on Garrick's Macbeth: 'After the murder, his feelings dwindled into a kind of boyish whimpering, and his countenance rather described bodily than mental pain.'[5]

---

[1] *Dramatic Censor*, I, 109.   [2] *Ibid.*
[3] See G. C. D. Odell, *Shakespeare from Betterton to Irving* (2 vols. 1921), I, plate facing 448.
[4] *Dramatic Censor*, I, 110.   [5] *Ibid.*

Gentleman felt that in the soliloquies Powell was 'too sententiously heavy'; in the third act 'he seemed unequal to the arduous task of describing extreme horror'; in the fifth 'Macbeth's weight of desperation bore him down'.[1]

At Drury Lane, after Sheridan, Holland first attempted the role of Macbeth on February 28, 1764, opposite Mrs Pritchard. Garrick still played Macbeth at Drury Lane when the mood was on him, and his shadow fell across Holland, who offered a mechanical imitation of Garrick. As Gentleman writes:

Mr Holland, that industrious, useful, laborious, imitative actor, idolized his great instructor too much to be anything original; in Macbeth we deem him particularly unhappy; aiming to be great, he frequently lost all trace of character: untunably stiff in all his declamations; mechanical in action; ungracious in attitude; affected in feeling; unharmonious in tone; irregular in emphasis, and wild in passion...

Holland was popular, nevertheless, though he did not possess anything like the genius of Garrick. As Gentleman confesses, 'yet having an agreeable person, significant aspect and powerful voice', Holland as Macbeth 'often pleased his audience, and kept attention awake while judgement was obliged to slumber or seek safety in silence from popular prejudice'.[2]

The last performer of any real distinction to interpret Macbeth, before the advent of Kemble, was John Henderson, who played opposite both Mrs Hartley and Mrs Yates. Henderson belonged to the great tradition descending through Garrick from Betterton and Mrs Porter. 'Stick to Garrick' a friend wrote to Henderson from Bath on June 27, 1773, 'as close as you can for your life: you should follow his heels like his shadow in sunshine...for when he drops you'll have nothing but poor old nature's book to look in—you'll be left to grope it out alone, scratching your pate in the dark, or by a farthing candle.'[3]

Henderson was no mechanical disciple of Garrick: he had a strong individuality which showed itself in his interpretation of poetry and character: 'he was truly excellent', says Waldron, 'in some characters never exhibited by Garrick'. Yet as Macbeth 'he fell infinitely short of the admirable model on which he formed

[1] *Dramatic Censor*, I, 110.   [2] *Ibid.*
[3] See John Ireland, *Letters and Poems by the Late Mr John Henderson, with Anecdotes of his Life* (1786), p. 108.

1   Macbeth in the witches' cave. Reproduced from Rowe's edition, 1790

2 Garrick and Mrs Pritchard in *Macbeth* (II. ii). Reproduced from Green
mezzotint (1775) of a painting by Zoffany

Mr MACKLIN,
In the Character of MACBETH.
Act II.d Scene 3.d

3   Macklin as Macbeth (II. iii). Reproduced from *The London Magazine*,
November 1773

4   Sarah Siddons as Lady Macbeth (I. v. 37–8). Reproduced from a
painting by George Henry Harlow

5   Sarah Siddons as Lady Macbeth (v. i. 32). Reproduced from a
        painting by George Henry Harlow

6   Edmund Kean as Macbeth (ii. ii). Reproduced from
The Theatrical Inquisitor, November 1814

7 Macready as Macbeth (I. iii). Reproduced from *The Illustrated London News*, March 1, 1851, p. 177

8 Henry Irving as Macbeth (I. iii). Reproduced from a photograph
   of a drawing by Bernard Partridge, December 29, 1888

9 Ellen Terry as Lady Macbeth (v. i)

10   Sybil Thorndike as Lady Macbeth (v. i). Reproduced from
The Sketch, January 5, 1927

11   Laurence Olivier as Macbeth (i. iii)

himself'.[1] There were obviously some significant moments in Henderson's performance at Covent Garden. Romney painted the scene in which Macbeth encounters the witches. Henderson wears a tartan drawn across the shoulder, which suggests that, influenced by Macklin, he was experimenting with the new convention of historical realism. Particularly vivid and memorable, according to John Ireland, was Henderson's 'horror' and 'remorse' when he appeared after the murder of Duncan, with the daggers in his hand. Yet, on the whole, Henderson was not successful as Macbeth. Like other actors before him he was found wanting when judged by standards that Garrick had established. John Ireland thought that he lacked the expressive qualities of Mr Garrick's 'look and action', which could 'no more be described than they can be equalled'.[2]

[1] See 'Appendix to Downes's "Roscius Anglicanus"', in Smith, *Collection of Material*, II, 25.
[2] *Letters and Poems*, p. 248.

CHAPTER 6

SARAH SIDDONS AND KEMBLE

When one reads her essay, 'Remarks on the Character of Lady Macbeth', it is possible to imagine that had Mrs Siddons lived in the twentieth century she would have understood Stanislavsky. It is not surprising that Stanislavsky's translator, David Magarshack, thought the 'Remarks' contained 'all the essentials of Stanislavsky's system'.[1]

Mrs Siddons believed in the importance of concentration—in 'the circle of solitude'. William Robson, reflecting on Mrs Siddons's performance as Lady Macbeth, tells us that 'from the moment she assumed the dress she became the character: she never chatted or coquetted by the Green Room fire but placed herself where no word of the play could escape her, or the illusion for a moment be destroyed'.[2] This habitual discipline accounts for her distress when Sheridan knocked at her door and insisted on being let in on the night of February 2, 1785, just before she appeared as Lady Macbeth for the first time on the London stage.[3]

For her, acting was an intellectual discipline, the product of judgement and observation as much as of feeling. It was not the study of the dressing-glass alone 'wherein she schooled herself; she sought the cell of the maniac and the couch of the dying; and dared to carry away the shriek of frantic agony and the last flutter of the departing agonized spirit'.[4] There was something thoroughly objective about her method, and in 1785 the originality of her interpretation of the sleep-walking scene in *Macbeth* arose from the fact that she had observed a somnambulist in real life. Like Peter Brook who learned, by the simple and direct method of visiting asylums before he produced the *Marat/Sade* at the Aldwych in 1964, that conventional lunatics on the stage did not behave as real ones did, Mrs Siddons observed that conventional

---

[1] See *Stanislavsky on the Art of the Stage* (1950), p. 82.

[2] *The Old Playgoer* (1846), p. 19.

[3] See Thomas Campbell, *Life of Mrs Siddons* (2 vols. 1834), II, 37 (the whole of Mrs Siddons's essay is in this volume, 10–39).

[4] Robson, *Old Playgoer*, p. 19.

stage somnambulists had little connection with reality. In 1785, when she was 'compelled to admit' Sheridan into her room, he strongly advised her to play the scene conventionally, without the realism that she found necessary. Had she yielded to his suggestion, Mrs Siddons writes, 'It would have been against my own opinion, and my observation of the accuracy with which somnambulists perform all the acts of waking persons.'[1] In 1785 her interpretation of Lady Macbeth began at the conscious levels of judgement and observation. But by the time she had finished playing the character the interplay between the conscious idea and the subconscious impulse, which makes art seem like nature itself, had begun. Mrs Siddons went on living the part of Lady Macbeth after the play was over. Telling us that the new interpretation was well received, she writes:

Mr Sheridan himself came to me, after the play, and most ingenuously congratulated me on my obstinacy. When he was gone out of the room I began to undress; and, while standing up before my glass, and taking off my mantle, a diverting circumstance occurred, to chase away the feelings of this anxious night; for, while I was repeating, and endeavouring to call to mind the appropriate tone and action to the following words, 'Here's the smell of the blood still!' my dresser innocently exclaimed, 'Dear me, ma'am, how very hysterical you are tonight; I protest and vow, ma'am, it was not blood, but rose-pink and water; for I saw the property-man mix it up with my own eyes.'[2]

Six years earlier, on her first reading of the play, she had intuitively lived it. At this time, Mrs Siddons tells us, 'the necessity of discrimination' and the consciousness that a character may grow and develop in a play had scarcely entered her imagination. She began to read the play with the simple intention of getting the words of the part into her head:

I went on with tolerable composure, in the silence of the night, (a night I never can forget), till I came to the assassination scene, when the horrors of the scene rose to a degree that made it impossible for me to get farther. I snatched up my candle, and hurried out of the room, in a paroxysm of terror. My dress was of silk, and the rustling of it, as I ascended the stairs to go to bed, seemed to my panic-struck fancy like the movement of a spectre pursuing me. At last I reached my chamber, where I found my husband fast asleep. I clapt my candlestick down

[1] Campbell, *Mrs Siddons*, II, 38–9.   [2] *Ibid.* 39.

upon the table, without the power of putting the candle out; and I threw myself on my bed, without daring to stay even to take off my clothes.[1]

Mrs Siddons understood that Lady Macbeth deliberately chooses evil. She observed that Lady Macbeth could behave like a person in whom there was 'a deplorable depravation of all rational knowledge' as when, replacing the daggers by Duncan's body, she 'calmly and steadily' returns to Macbeth 'with the fiend-like boast,

My hands are of your colour;
But I would scorn to wear a heart so white.'[2]

In Mrs Siddons's time the word 'rational' was not in disrepute: it stood for positive, life-affirming values. Yet her interpretation of Lady Macbeth's character was built around no simple absolute— she recognised that Lady Macbeth had a certain kind of intellectual power and argued on logical grounds that she must have 'personal beauty' as well. It was only the association of these two qualities in Lady Macbeth, a 'subjugating intellectual power' and 'the graces of personal beauty' that could make Macbeth's capitulation to her believable.[3] The proposition that Lady Macbeth should be beautiful was not purely theoretical. We know, from Gainsborough's portrait of Mrs Siddons in the National Gallery, that she must have possessed an astonishing charm and grace. 'Her countenance', wrote Edward Mangin, 'might with strict justice be called beautiful. It was composed of the finest proportions imaginable; her mouth was wonderfully expressive of good sense, sweetness and scorn. Her eyes were brilliant and piercing.'[4] Lady Macbeth's beauty may have been a way of rationalising a fact which Mrs Siddons had no way of avoiding. Shakespeare's text provides no explicit support for the theory, but it is not implausible. Mrs Siddons made Lady Macbeth both 'fiend-like' and beautiful, a creature who fascinated not Macbeth only but the audiences at Drury Lane and Covent Garden as well.

The passion of ambition had 'almost' but not quite obliterated the characteristics of human nature within Lady Macbeth.[5] Mrs Siddons observed that, during the murder of Duncan, 'feeling' which Lady Macbeth so consistently denies, asserts its presence:

[1] Campbell, *Mrs Siddons*, II, 35–6.   [2] *Ibid.* 21.
[3] *Ibid.* 11.   [4] *Piozziana* (1833), p. 85.
[5] Campbell, *Mrs Siddons*, II, 10.

'Had he not resembled my father as he slept, I had done it.'[1]
When Flora Robson played Lady Macbeth in 1934, the line
became the 'clue' to her interpretation of the character.[2] While
the line was not a clue to Mrs Siddons's portrayal, her recognition
of its significance helps to account for the complexity of her
interpretation of Lady Macbeth's character.

She saw this not in terms of a static principle of evil—'possession' was not absolute—but in terms of growth and development.
In the 'Remarks' she sees the change take place in the third act,
and notes the disillusionment of Lady Macbeth in III. ii. 4–7:

> Nought's had, all's spent,
> Where our desire is got without content,
> 'Tis safer to be that which we destroy,
> Than by destruction dwell in doubtful joy.

She discovers 'striking indications of sensibility' and 'tenderness' in Lady Macbeth's attitude to Macbeth. She draws out
attention to:

> How now, my lord! Why do you keep alone,
> Of sorriest fancies your companions making,
> Using those thoughts which should indeed have died
> With them they think on? Things without all remedy
> Should be without regard. What's done is done   (III. ii. 8–12)

and compares it with her earlier reproaches and 'contemptuous
taunting' of Macbeth.[3]

Mrs Siddons saw Lady Macbeth in the fifth act as quite transformed, with 'wan and haggard countenance, her starry eyes
glazed' with the 'burning fever of remorse'. The 'smell of
innocent blood incessantly haunts her imagination':

Here's the smell of the blood still. All the perfumes of Arabia will
not sweeten this little hand.   (v. i. 48–9)

Demonstrating her responsiveness to Shakespeare's language,
Mrs Siddons contrasts these lines with 'the bolder image' used by
Macbeth when he expresses similar feelings:

> Will all great Neptune's ocean wash this blood
> Clean from My hand?[4]   (II. ii. 60–1)

---

[1] *Ibid.* 20.
[2] See Flora Robson, 'Notes on Playing the Role of Lady Macbeth', in *Macbeth*, ed.
Francis Fergusson (1959), p. 27.
[3] Campbell, *Mrs Siddons*, II, 22–3.   [4] *Ibid.* 31.

The two paintings by George Henry Harlow (see Plates 4 and 5) showing Mrs Siddons as Lady Macbeth dressed in austere browns 'invoking the spirits to take possession of her body (I. v.), and then radically transformed, in the sleep-walking scene, shrouded in white, corpse-like, as both Edward Mangin[1] and James Boaden[2] remembered her, suggest that she carried out her conception of the way in which Lady Macbeth's character grows and changes.

Mrs Siddons's essay is not always well written, and it is not a logically consistent document. The idea that Lady Macbeth's character alters in the third act, that she shows signs of disillusionment, seems to conflict with her speculation that in the third act Lady Macbeth instigates the murder of Banquo and Fleance. Mrs Siddons did not, however, interpret the line,

> But in them nature's copy's not eterne

on the stage as if she was suggesting that Banquo and Fleance should be murdered. She portrayed Lady Macbeth's disillusionment and melancholy instead, both at the commencement and the end of the third act.

It seems clear that Mrs Siddons's 'Remarks on the Character of Lady Macbeth', while being no substitute for her performance, was nevertheless related to it. Fanny Kemble's comment that Mrs Siddons's 'analysis of the part of Lady Macbeth was to be found *alone* in her representation of it—of the magnificence of which the "essay" which she has left upon the character gives not the faintest idea'[3] seems, in retrospect, to be not wholly just.

As Lady Macbeth, Mrs Siddons incarnated Talma's ideal of tragic acting—'the union of grandeur without pomp and nature without triviality'.[4] When she played Lady Macbeth in 1785 she was praised by the critic of the *Morning Post* for the naturalness with which she spoke Shakespeare's poetry, as Garrick had been praised before her for his unaffected naturalness by Aaron Hill, and Betterton by Cibber. The critic wrote: 'Mrs Siddons never exhibited such chaste, such accomplished acting. There being little or no declamation; our ears were not wounded with the

[1] *Piozziana*, p. 17.
[2] *Memoirs of Mrs Siddons* (2 vols. 1827), II, 146.
[3] See *Papers on Acting*, ed. Brander Matthews (1958), p. 207.
[4] *Ibid.* p. 70.

repetition of *the lark's shrill note*, or the blundering distribution of a vitiated emphasis.'[1] As Leigh Hunt expressed it in 1807, Mrs Siddons had 'the air of never being the actress'.[2] But natural though she was, she did not lack grandeur. James Sheridan Knowles wrote of her Lady Macbeth: 'An awe invested her... There was something absolutely subduing in her presence...'[3] Hazlitt saw her play the part and could conceive of 'nothing grander'.[4] Byron seemed to be referring to the extraordinary combination of grandeur and naturalness in Mrs Siddons when he wrote: 'Of actors Cooke was the most natural, Kemble the most supernatural, Kean the medium between the two. But Mrs Siddons was worth them all put together.'[5]

The union of the sublime with the natural, characteristic of Garrick's art at its best, was a feature of Mrs Siddons's art as well. When she worked at Drury Lane during Garrick's last days there, he paid special attention to her. 'He would even flatter me', wrote Mrs Siddons, 'by sending me into the Boxes when he acted any of his great Characters...'[6] Garrick communicated a concept of naturalness to her. He criticised the awkward, stiff movements of her arms,[7] and on one occasion, when she played Lady Anne to his Richard III, successfully terrified her.[8]

When Mrs Siddons made her first entrance as Lady Macbeth dressed, not in the elaborate, circumambient garments of Mrs Yates, but with neat elegance,[9] the effect she created was of easy naturalness. She entered reading Macbeth's letter in what appears to have been her familiar style and giving the impression that it was a continuation of something begun earlier:[10]

They met me in the day of success; and I have learn'd by the *perfect'st* report they have *more* in them than mortal knowledge...

(I. v. 1–3)

Professor John Bell, who saw Mrs Siddons play Lady Macbeth and described her performance in detail, reports that she stressed

[1] February 3, 1785.
[2] *Critical Essays on the Performers of the London Theatres* (1807), p. 18.
[3] *Lectures on Dramatic Literature: Macbeth* (1875), p. 19.
[4] *Works*, ed. A. R. Waller and A. Glover (13 vols. 1902), XIII, 312.
[5] *A Self-portrait: Letters and Diaries, 1798–1824*, ed. Peter Quennell (2 vols. 1950), II, 629.
[6] *The Reminiscences of Sarah Kemble Siddons*, ed. William Van Lennep (1942), p. 6.
[7] See Yvonne French, *Mrs Siddons* (1936), p. 33.
[8] *Ibid.*   [9] See *Morning Post*, February 3, 1785.
[10] See French, *Mrs Siddons*, pp. 111–12.

two words in the long opening sentence of the letter, 'perfect'st' and 'more'.[1] The rest of the sentence seems to have flowed smoothly on.

In stressing the word 'more', Mrs Siddons seems to have been concerned with bringing out the supernatural theme in *Macbeth*, the 'more than mortal knowledge' of the witches. The witches and their 'knowledge' are the subject of Macbeth's letter. She captured for her audience the surprise and wonder of Macbeth's first encounter with the witches, as she read on:

When I burn'd in desire to question them further, they made themselves air, into which they vanish'd.   (I. V. 3–4)

The effect she wanted was achieved with a slight pause before the word 'air'—'they made themselves—air'. Boaden, using Garrick's words, calls it a 'little suspension of the voice'.[2] Sheridan Knowles describes the effect she achieved: 'In the look and tone with which she delivered that word, you recognised ten times the wonder with which Macbeth and Banquo actually beheld the vanishing of the witches.'[3]

Mrs Siddons read the letter with easy naturalness, and paused to reflect when it was over. With the transition from prose to poetry

Glamis thou art, and Cawdor; *and shalt be*[4]
What thou art promis'd...   (I. V. 12–13)

John Bell remembered that the tone, for a moment became 'exalted, prophetic' and that she made the future seem a present reality.[5] But Mrs Siddons had too much good sense and was too responsive to the sense and texture of Shakespeare's language to keep the tone of exaltation going after the prophetic mood changed to one of doubt:

Yet do I fear thy nature;
It is too full o' th' milk of human kindness
To catch the nearest way. Thou wouldst be great;
Art not without ambition, but without
The *illness* should attend it.   (I. V. 13–17)

---

[1] The words Mrs Siddons chose to emphasise are italicised in Professor Bell's notes. See *Papers on Acting*, ed. Matthews, pp. 81–96.
[2] Boaden, *Mrs Siddons*, II, 133. Cf. chapter 4, pp. 43–4.
[3] *Dramatic Literature*, p. 20.
[4] Italicised in Bell. See *Papers on Acting*, p. 82.   [5] *Ibid.*

After 'and shalt be', 'illness'[1] was singled out for emphasis, though it could not have been stressed with the same energy. The verse seems to have flowed smoothly on, with a single emphatic stress on 'play' informed by 'a slight tincture of contempt throughout', while the voice dipped low at 'holily'.[2] Here and in the night scenes, writes Bell, Mrs Siddons as Lady Macbeth made it plain that she was fully aware of Macbeth's ambitious thoughts and wishes.[3]

As she went on, contempt appears to have given way to calculation:[4]

> Thou'dst have, great Glamis, that which cries
> 'Thus thou must do' if thou have it;
> And that which rather thou dost fear to do
> Than wishest should be undone...   (I. v. 19–22)

and at

> Hie thee hither,
> That I may pour my spirits in thine ear,
> And chastise with the valour of my tongue
> All that impedes thee from the golden round
> Which fate and metaphysical aid doth seem
> To have thee crown'd withal...   (I. v. 22–7)

contempt and calculation were replaced by impatience[5] and animation.[6] The variety of tone Mrs Siddons brought to her interpretation of Lady Macbeth's lines was not an imposition from outside, a device used to keep a drowsy audience awake. Her achievement consisted in responding intelligently to the varied and complex patterns of tone and feeling already there in Shakespeare's verse, and in communicating that response. Her interpretation of the text was like the best sort of 'practical criticism' functioning in the most practical way possible.

Mrs Siddons's sensitiveness to the changes of tone and feeling in Shakespeare's text was demonstrated in vivid fashion immediately after the first soliloquy, when the Messenger (Seyton in Kemble's production) arrived to announce the coming of the

---

[1] *Ibid.*
[2] *Ibid.*   What thou wouldst highly,
    That wouldst thou holily; wouldst not *play* false,
    And yet wouldst wrongly win. (I. v. 17–19)
[3] *Ibid.*   [4] See Boaden, *Mrs Siddons*, II, 133–4.
[5] *Ibid.*   [6] See *Papers on Acting*, p. 82.

king to Dunsinane. Boaden's analysis of Shakespeare's art at this point is at the same time a description of Mrs Siddons's acting:

Shakespeare alone, perhaps, would have written the daring compromise of all decorum, which bursts from the exulting savage upon this intelligence:

> 'Thou'rt MAD to say it.'

Aware of the inference to be drawn from an earnestness so marked, she immediately cloaks the passion with a *reason* why the intelligence could not seem true. The actress, fully understanding the process, after the violence of the exclamation, recovered herself with slight alarm, and in a *lowered* tone proposed a question suited to the new feeling:

> 'Is not thy master *with* him? who, were't so,
> Would have inform'd for preparation.'[1]

Silence followed the Messenger's departure. Bell[2] remembered the long pause that followed his going. The silence seems to have been dramatic—the kind of moment that Gordon Craig would have approved of. It ought to have helped Mrs Siddons to make the transition from the apparently matter-of-fact dismissal of the Messenger to the 'murmured mysteriousness' of the address to the spirits 'that tend on mortal thoughts'.[3] In the opening lines of the soliloquy Mrs Siddons picked out the word 'fatal' for emphasis:

> The raven himself is hoarse
> That croaks the *fatal* entrance of Duncan
> Under my battlements.[4]   (I. v. 35–7)

She pitched her voice low and in a 'whisper of horrid determination'[5] began her invocation to the spirits. Bell's description of the aural effect of her voice, and Boaden's visual impression of her, give us some idea of the way in which she attempted to realise her interpretation of the passage on the stage. Her interpretation, as we know from the 'Remarks on the Character of Lady Macbeth', was based on the idea of 'possession'. She seems to have literally called on the ministers of evil to take possession of her body. Bell reports that at

> Come to my woman's breasts,
> And take my milk for gall, you murd'ring ministers.

                                                (I. v. 44–5)

---

[1] *Mrs Siddons*, II, 134.   [2] *Papers on Acting*, p. 83.
[3] Boaden, *Mrs Siddons*, II, 135. [4] *Papers on Acting*, p. 83.
[5] *Ibid.*

which was spoken in a 'slow hollow whisper', her voice sounded 'quite supernatural, as in a horrible dream'. The slow rhythms of her speech, the whispering, made his blood run cold.[1] Boaden carried away with him a visual impression of eyes coming into play, of 'raised shoulders' and 'hollowed hands'.[2]

When Macbeth entered, however, there was one of those dramatic, but just and natural changes of tone which the text seems to call for.

> Great Glamis! Worthy Cawdor!   (I. v. 51)

was 'loud, triumphant, and wild in air'.[3] At the end of the brief, quick exchange that followed:

> *Macb.* My dearest love,
>   Duncan comes here to-night.
> *Lady M.* And when goes hence?
> *Macb.* To-morrow—as he purposes.
> *Lady M.* O, never
>   (never) Shall sun that morrow see!   (I. v. 55–8)

the voice dropped low again, the 'pronunciation became almost syllabic' though 'not unvaried'. Mrs Siddons introduced a second 'never' into the text. After the first 'never' there was a long pause as she turned away from Macbeth, her 'eye steadfast'. Bell observed a 'deep downward inflection' on the first 'never' and 'a strong, dwelling emphasis'. The 'full deep voice' dipped again at 'see':

> O, never
> (never) Shall sun that morrow see.[4]

Bell's observations show that Mrs Siddons had a voice of great range and depth and that she used it with fine technical skill, though he understandably confesses that her interpretation could not be fully recaptured in words. Though Bell points to the inadequacy of words, his close observations do give us an immediate, though not fully definable, experience of that interpretation.

Bell seems to have had a more acute ear than eye, but he was not insensitive to visual effects; he caught the movement of Mrs Siddons's face as she continued to speak, observing the effect of

> ...never
> Shall sun that morrow see

---

[1] *Papers on Acting*, p. 83.   [2] *Mrs Siddons*, II, 135.
[3] *Papers on Acting*, p. 83.   [4] *Ibid.*

upon Macbeth, and turning her eyes upon him:

> Your face, my thane, is as a book where men
> May read strange matters. (I. v. 59–60)

She spoke

> ...look like th' innocent flower,
> But be the serpent under't (I. v. 62–3)

very slowly, 'with a severe and cruel expression'.[1] In the closing couplet

> Which shall to all our nights and days to come
> Give solely sovereign sway and masterdom (I. v. 66–7)

the voice became reassuring again.[2] As Mrs Siddons made her exit, leading Macbeth out on the lines

> Only look up clear.
> To alter favour ever is to fear.
> Leave all the rest to me

Bell did not quite like her use of gesture, 'the hand on his shoulder —clapping him', because it seemed to reduce Macbeth in stature.[3] Boaden, however, seems to have had no objection, and saw Mrs Siddons's playing throughout the scene as 'the triumph of nature'.[4]

Mrs Siddons brought the idea of the murder of Duncan into sharp focus and made it appear a real and immediate possibility. When she appeared again, it was to receive Duncan graciously on his arrival at Dunsinane. There was nothing obvious about the deception. Mrs Siddons kept close to the text:

> All our service
> In every point twice done, and then done double,
> Were poor and single business to contend
> Against those honours deep and broad wherewith
> Your Majesty loads our house... (I. vi. 14–18)

She was 'dignified and simple'. The verse was 'beautifully spoken', writes Bell, her tones 'soothing and satisfying the ear'.[5] She bowed gracefully to the king, giving him the *pas* as he

---

[1] *Papers on Acting*, pp. 83–4.   [2] *Ibid.*
[3] *Ibid.*   [4] *Mrs Siddons*, II, 136.
[5] *Papers on Acting*, p. 84.

entered the castle, and then bowed 'graciously' and 'sweetly' to the nobles before she followed the king.[1]

When she reappears it is after Macbeth changes his mind in the soliloquy on judgement: alone with Macbeth there is no attempt to be courtly. When Macbeth enquires whether Duncan has asked for him, her 'Know you not he has?' was delivered in an eager whisper of anger and surprise.[2] Bell compares Kemble's playing in this scene with his sister's, and in doing so defines the naturalness of Mrs Siddons's approach to Shakespeare. Kemble appeared to speak the 'If it were done' soliloquy like a speech to be recited. There was 'none of that hesitation and working of the mind which in Mrs Siddons seems to inspire the words as the natural expression of the emotion'.[3]

Mrs Siddons contrived to change her expression solely from within. When Macbeth confesses that he has changed his mind:

> We will proceed no further in this business.
> He hath honour'd me of late; and I have bought
> Golden opinions from all sorts of people...   (I. vii. 31–3)

her expression appears to have altered in this way. Bell was of the opinion that the silent transition 'from animated hope and surprise to disappointment, depression, contempt, and rekindling resentment' was 'beyond any powers but hers'.[4]

When she began to speak:

> Was the hope drunk
> Wherein you dress'd yourself?   (I. vii. 35–6)

she was 'very cold, distant, and contemptuous'.[5] The 'cold, contemptuous reasoning' continued

> What beast was't then
> That made you break this enterprise to me?   (I. vii. 48–9)

until the rhythms of her speech became slow and her words sounded clear and distinct:[6]

> Nor time nor place
> Did then adhere, and yet you would make both;
> They have made themselves, and that their fitness now
> Does unmake you.   (I. vii. 51–4)

---

[1] *Ibid.* [2] *Ibid.* p. 85.
[3] *Ibid.* [4] *Ibid.*
[5] *Ibid.* [6] *Ibid.* p. 86.

At this point there occurred one of those dramatic changes of tone Mrs Siddons used with such controlled power. She had been up-stage. She now moved forward and close to Macbeth, down-stage, looking for some time into his face. Her manner changed entirely before she spoke again:[1]

> I have given suck, and know
> How tender 'tis to love the babe that milks me—
> I would, while it was smiling in my face,
> Have pluck'd my nipple from his boneless gums,
> And dash'd the brains out, had I so sworn
> As you have done to this.   (i. vii. 54–9)

Mrs Siddons appears to have been carrying out her own interpretation of the passage given in the 'Remarks': 'The very use of such a tender allusion...persuades one unequivocally that she has really felt the maternal yearnings of a mother towards her babe, and that she considered the action the most enormous that ever required the strength of human nerves for its perpetration.'[2] She spoke the passage, first 'softly and with tenderness' and then, as she went on, with 'appalling energy'.[3]

Mrs Siddons was a subtle and original player. The originality expressed itself in her interpretation of Lady Macbeth's response to Macbeth's

>   If we should fail?   (i. vii. 58)

Lady Macbeth's

>   We fail!   (i. vii. 59)

was spoken by Mrs Siddons in a new way. Oxberry tells us that her interpretation was against all the received ideas of contemporary actors. For, before Mrs Siddons, 'We fail!' had been spoken with surprise, 'as if scouting all possibility of failure'.[4] Instead, Mrs Siddons spoke the line with a 'strong downward inflection' on 'fail', in a quietly fatalistic tone, bowing, hands down, palms upward[5] giving the impression of 'a mind prepared for the worst', as if she had answered Macbeth's question with, 'why then, "We fail" and there an end'.[6] Mrs Siddons seems to

---

[1] *Papers on Acting*, p. 86.   [2] Campbell, *Mrs Siddons*, II, 18.
[3] See A. C. Sprague, *Shakespearian Players and Performances* (1954), p. 61.
[4] W. Oxberry, *Oxberry's Dramatic Biography* (3 vols. 1825), I, 138.
[5] *Papers on Acting*, p. 86.
[6] Oxberry, *Dramatic Biography*, I, 138.

have read into the line a primitive fatalism and stoic courage. Some considerable time before scholars perceived the connection between Shakespeare and the stoicism of Seneca, she seems to have responded to its presence in Lady Macbeth. With

> But screw your courage to the sticking place,
> And we'll not fail

the tone changed to one of 'strong assurance',[1] but it was the stoical 'We fail' that remained in the mind of her audiences and became the subject of some critical debate.[2]

The description of the plan for murdering the king

> When Duncan is asleep—
> Whereto the rather shall his day's hard journey
> Soundly invite him—   (I. vii. 61–3)

was spoken in a 'low whisper'.[3] Once again Mrs Siddons demonstrated the intelligence and flexibility of her approach to Shakespeare's verse. After outlining her plan to drug Duncan's guards with 'wine and wassail' Bell tells us that she paused, as if watching for its effect upon Macbeth. Then she renewed her plan 'more earnestly' and 'low still' but 'with increasing confidence'.[4]

Mrs Siddons's acting demanded a continuous and living relationship with her fellow actors on the stage. Throughout the scene, observes Bell, she appeared to feel her way, watching the wavering of Macbeth's mind, suiting her whole manner to it. 'With contempt, affection, reason, the conviction of her well-concerted plan...she turns him to her purpose with an art in which the player shares largely in the poet's praise.'[5]

Mrs Siddons interpreted Shakespeare's bare, terse line, 'He is about it', in 1816, bending towards the door, listening for the sounds of murder, during the great assassination scene in *Macbeth*, while J. H. Siddons stood back-stage, watching Kemble put the 'blood' upon his hands. He describes Mrs Siddons's interpretation of the murder scene:

The whispered words, 'he is about it', drew my attention to the half-opened door...Mrs Siddons was bending towards the door in the act

---

[1] *Papers on Acting*, p. 86.   [2] See *Monthly Mirror*, IV (1808), 189, 302.
[3] *Papers on Acting*, p. 86.   [4] *Ibid.*
[5] *Ibid.*

of listening—her ear so close that I could absolutely feel her breath. The words, I have said, were whispered—but what a whisper was hers! Distinctly audible in every part of the house, it served the purpose of the loudest tones...[1]

Bell confirms this description. He reports that Mrs Siddons seemed to breath with difficulty, and that her whisper sounded 'horrible'.[2] Her performance seems to have proved time and again the truth of Coquelin's statement that 'the power of a true inflexion of the voice is incalculable' and that 'all the picturesque exteriors in the world will not move an audience like one cry given with the right intonation'.[3]

Yet though she used her voice with memorable skill, J. H. Siddons's description indicates that Mrs Siddons, like Garrick, did not use her voice alone: she used all the resources of her body. In *Macbeth*, as in *King John*, 'her body thought'.[4] Bell writes that Mrs Siddons spoke her first line in the assassination scene, which tells of the drugged grooms—

> That which hath made them drunk hath made me bold
>
> (II. ii. 1)

—with 'a ghastly horrid smile'.[5] It was her acting alone that created the illusion of a murder taking place. This she did by the process, vivid and detailed, of becoming Lady Macbeth, living her terrible excitement and communicating it to the audience. Referring to the grooms again, when Lady Macbeth says

> Alack! I am afraid they have awak'd,
> And 'tis not done   (II. ii. 9–10)

Bell seems to have experienced with immediacy what he describes—the lines spoken with 'the finest agony', the 'tossing of the arms'.[6]

Mrs Siddons's interpretation of Lady Macbeth in the assassination scene was complex, subtle and varied, compounded not of one emotion only but of many. Lord Harcourt writes that in the

---

[1] *Memoirs of a Journalist* (1873), p. 17. Quoted in Sprague, *Shakespearian Players*, p. 62.
[2] *Papers on Acting*, p. 88.   [3] *Ibid.* p. 168.
[4] See Campbell, *Mrs Siddons*, I, 210; '...her very body seemed to think' as Constance in *King John*.
[5] *Papers on Acting*, p. 88.   [6] *Ibid.*

performance of 1785, referring to the sleeping king, she threw 'a degree of proud and filial tenderness'[1] into her delivery of

> Had he not resembled
> My father as he slept, I had done't.　　(II. ii. 12–13)

But as she speaks of her father, Macbeth enters, and her

> My husband!　　(II. ii. 13)

conveyed 'agonised suspense', as if she were 'speechless with uncertainty' at the thought of the murder being discovered.[2] After Macbeth has looked on his blood-stained hands, saying

> This is a sorry sight　　(II. ii. 20)

and Lady Macbeth has countered with:

> A foolish thought to say a sorry sight　　(II. ii. 21)

Bell observed that Mrs Siddons showed 'her wonderful power and knowledge of nature'. As if her inhuman strength of spirit was overcome by the contagion of Macbeth's despair, she put her arms 'about her neck and bosom, shuddering'.[3]

But when Macbeth refers to an imagined 'voice':

> Methought I heard a voice cry 'Sleep no more;
> Macbeth does murder sleep'—the innocent sleep...
> 　　　　　　　　　(II. ii. 35–6)

her horror changed 'to agony and alarm' at his derangement; uncertain what to do next, she seemed to be calling up 'the resources of her spirit'. With the question

> *Who* was it that thus cried?　　(II. ii. 44)

she attempted to bring Macbeth down to earth, moving up to him, emphasising 'who'. And

> Why, worthy Thane,
> You do unbend your noble strength to think
> So brainsickly of things.　　(II. ii. 44–6)

---

[1] See *Correspondence of Horace Walpole and William Mason*, ed. J. Mitford (2 vols. 1851), II, 404. Cf. Mrs Siddons's 'Remarks' in Campbell, *Mrs Siddons*, II, 20: '...one trait of tender feeling is expressed, "Had he not resembled my father..." Her humanity vanishes, however, in the same instant.'

[2] *Papers on Acting*, p. 88.　　　　[3] *Ibid.* p. 89.

was spoken in a tone of 'fine remonstrance'. At

> Why did you bring these daggers from the place?
> They must lie there...   (II. ii. 48–9)

Mrs Siddons seemed to notice the daggers for the first time, and
when Macbeth refuses to take them back to the dead king's room,
she seized them 'contemptuously'.[1] As she stole out to Duncan's
room, she turned, stooping, and pointing her finger at Macbeth,
said with 'malignant energy':

> *If he do bleed,*
> *I'll gild the faces* of the grooms withal,
> For it must seem their guilt.[2]   (II. ii. 55–7)

Sheridan Knowles remembered her calm self-possession when
she returned from the king's room. Mrs Siddons was calm,
though not placid, because there was 'contempt' in her voice
when she spoke:

> My *hands* are of your colour; but I shame
> To wear a *heart* so white...   (II. ii. 64–5)

'hands' and 'heart' being selected for emphasis.[3] When Kemble
played Macbeth, at this moment, says Bell, he stood rooted to the
spot, motionless, his eye fixed. Mrs Siddons at first spoke to him
with an 'assured and confident air':

> A little water clears us of this deed...   (II. ii. 67)

but as the knocking at the door became more insistent, she
became alarmed, 'agonized', says Bell, that Macbeth's reason
might 'be quite gone and discovery inevitable'. Their exit appears to have been remarkably effective. Bell, writing in the
present tense, recaptures the vividness of Mrs Siddons's 'action'
as she 'strikes him on the shoulder, pulls him from his fixed
posture, forces him away', Macbeth 'talking as he goes'.[4]

Mrs Siddons's interpretation of character on the stage, in the
assassination scene, provides a permanent object lesson to all
interpreters of Shakespeare, critics as well as actors, for its
detailed, accurate sensitiveness to Shakespeare's text. Her interpretation seems to demonstrate the validity of the approach

---

[1] *Papers on Acting*, pp. 89–90.   [2] *Ibid.*
[3] *Ibid.* p. 90.   [4] *Ibid.* pp. 90–1.

which considers that a grasp of the particular, local life of Shake-speare's verse is essential if the uniqueness and variety of the experience offered in his plays is to be grasped at all.

Like Mrs Pritchard, Mrs Siddons adhered to the old, unfortunate tradition that Lady Macbeth should not appear in the scene during which the murder of Duncan is discovered. When she appeared again, it was to open the second scene of the third act with a question to Macbeth:

Is Banquo gone from court?   (III. ii. 1)

The question is significant, argues Boaden. 'Their attention while apart has been directed to the same object...She is ready to suggest the murder of Banquo and his son: "In them nature's copy is not eterne."'[1] In 'Remarks on the Character of Lady Macbeth' Mrs Siddons expressed the same idea,[2] but she did not act the scene in this way. The idea possibly clashed with the conception also expressed in the 'Remarks' that Lady Macbeth's character grows and develops.[3]

In Mrs Siddons's enquiry there appears to have been no sinister implication. The question, 'Is Banquo gone from court?' was spoken, says Bell, with 'great dignity and solemnity of voice', with 'nothing of the joy of gratified ambition'. At

Nought's had, all's spent...   (III. ii. 4)

the voice was melancholy, and there was no trace of contempt in

How now, my lord! Why do you keep alone,
Of sorriest fancies your companions making...
(III. ii. 8–9)

The accents sounded 'plaintive' to Bell. The melancholy persisted in
Come on
Gentle my lord, sleek o'er your rugged looks;
Be *bright and iovial* among your guests to-night...
(III. ii. 26–7)

though once more the complexity of her approach to the character was finely demonstrated. Bell observed that with the words

[1] *Mrs Siddons*, II, 139–40.   [2] Campbell, *Mrs Siddons*, II, 30.
[3] *Ibid.* 22.

'Be bright and jovial', a forced cheerfulness seemed to break through Lady Macbeth's melancholy. There was no hidden irony in the line

> But in them nature's copy's not eterne. (III. ii. 38)

What Bell observed instead was a brief 'flash' of Lady Macbeth's 'former spirit and energy'.[1]

During the banquet, which according to the *Gazetteer* of February 3, 1785, was 'particularly magnificent', Mrs Siddons showed 'a growing uneasiness' from the point at which Macbeth moved apart and spoke to the murderer at the door. Mrs Siddons lived her role though she said nothing while the action progressed. When Ross speaks

> Pleas't your Highness
> To grace us with your royal company (III. iv. 44–5)

and Macbeth replies:

> The table's full (III. iv. 46)

her 'secret uneasiness', says Bell, 'was very fine'.[2] When Ross, surprised by Macbeth's unusual behaviour, decides to rise and Lady Macbeth intervenes, speaking for the first time since the commencement of the banquet,

> Sit, worthy friends. My lord is often thus, (III. iv. 53)

Mrs Siddons rose and moved among her guests.[3] To Edward Mangin her eyes which 'were brilliant and piercing could be seen to sparkle and glare at an incredible distance on the stage' as she descended from her throne.[4]

Just as Mrs Siddons does not seem to have carried out her theory that Lady Macbeth suggested the murder of Banquo and Fleance in the remark 'But in them nature's copy's not eterne', there is no conclusive evidence that she carried out the idea which flowed directly from this, that Lady Macbeth, being equally responsible for the second murder, sees the ghost of Banquo as well.[5] Her interpretation of the line,

> Why do you make such faces? When all's done,
> You look but on a stool (III. iv. 67–8)

---

[1] *Papers on Acting*, p. 92.
[2] *Ibid.*
[3] *Ibid.*
[4] *Piozziana*, p. 85.
[5] See Campbell, *Mrs Siddons*, II, 30.

as Bell describes it, offers no conclusive evidence that she carried out her theory at this point. She spoke the line softly in Macbeth's ear, writes Bell, 'as if to bring him back to objects of common life', though he adds that her anxiety made his flesh creep with apprehension.[1] When Macbeth sees the ghost for the second time and addresses it directly again

> Avaunt, and quit my sight. Let the earth hide thee.
> Thy bones are marrowless, thy blood is cold;   (III. iv. 93–4)

a 'secret agony seemed to agitate her',[2] though when Lady Macbeth says:

> Think of this, good peers,
> But as a thing of custom...   (III. iv. 96–7)

Mrs Siddons rose and spoke 'sweetly' to the company.[3]

As Macbeth goes on to speak of the ghost with no attention to his guests, Boaden remembered how Mrs Siddons rapidly cut into Ross's question

> What sights, my lord?   (III. iv. 116)

with

> I pray you speak not; he grows worse and worse;[4]
>   (III. iv. 117)

and dismissed her guests in 'haughty, hurried and apprehensive' tones.[5] The 'inimitable grace' of the 'congé to her guests' seems to have been immediately recognised.[6] But when the guests have gone, and Macbeth asks

> What is the night?   (III. iv. 126)

to which Lady Macbeth replies

> Almost at odds with morning, which is which   (III. iv. 127)

Mrs Siddons portrayed sadness and extreme exhaustion.[7] On the basis of what appear to be most elusive suggestions in Shakespeare's text, she prepared for the development of mood and feeling in the sleep-walking scene. At the end of the banquet scene, when Lady Macbeth says

> You lack the season of all natures, sleep   (III. iv. 141)

---

[1] *Papers on Acting*, p. 93.   [2] *Ibid.*
[3] *Ibid.*   [4] *Mrs Siddons*, II, 142.
[5] *Bell's Weekly Messenger* (July 5, 1812). Quoted in Sprague, *Shakespearian Players*. p. 65.
[6] See *Morning Post* (February 3, 1785).   [7] *Papers on Acting*, p. 94.

Mrs Siddons appeared to convey the impression of being 'quite as much in need of sleep' as Macbeth. Bell writes that at that moment she seemed 'feeble...as if preparing for her last sickness and final doom'.[1]

Mrs Siddons, like Garrick, had a sense of the dramatic possibilities in costumes rightly worn. Though she had no particular faith in historical realism,[2] she rejected the outlook which regarded costumes as primarily decorative, unrelated to character and possessing no other function than to look glamorous and expensive. Mrs Siddons reformed the voluminous skirts worn by Mrs Yates as Lady Macbeth, and appeared in the first act in austere browns. In later years the first costume worn by Mrs Siddons became more sombre. As queen (in 1803), black was the predominant colour in her costume. For the banquet scene she wore a silver tiara and silver coronet, from beneath which flowed a gauze veil. After 1805 she replaced the tiara and coronet with a heavy gold crown, 'lengthening her gauze veil and draping it somewhat intricately round her'.[3] In the sleep-walking scene she first wore white satin, which suggested madness,[4] but later changed to shroud-like white. Her costumes were on the whole dramatic and expressive rather than glamorous. And in the sleep-walking scene, particularly, the costume she wore lent support to her interpretation of the text.

She entered, carrying a 'taper', as Shakespeare's stage direction recommends. The significance of the candle is explained by the gentlewoman:

> She has light by her continually; 'tis her command. (v. i. 21–2)

As Mrs Siddons enacted the comments of the Doctor and the Gentlewoman—

> *Doct.* You see her eyes are open.
> *Gent.* Ay, but their sense is shut   (v. i. 23–4)

—Hazlitt felt that this was precisely what Mrs Siddons managed to convey. 'In coming on in the sleeping scene,' he wrote, 'her eyes were open but their sense was shut.'[5]

---

[1] *Papers on Acting*, p. 95.
[2] See J. R. Planché, *Recollections and Reflections* (revised edition, 1901), p. 39.
[3] See 'Macbeth on the Stage', *English Illustrated Magazine*, vi (December 1888), 248.
[4] See *Morning Post* (February 3, 1785).
[5] *Works*, ed. Waller and Glover, i, 189–90.

Leigh Hunt's description of her playing, however, suggests that she gave the lines a more than literal significance. He felt that 'the death-like stare of her countenance while her body was in motion was sublime'.[1] Mrs Siddons advanced swiftly, set down the candle and rubbed her hand, 'making the action of lifting up water in one hand, at intervals'.[2]

Bell thought that Mrs Siddons might have made her entrance less rapidly;[3] Sheridan, following convention, objected to the candle being set down at all,[4] and Leigh Hunt did not quite like 'the dribbling and domestic familiarity' with which she mimed the pouring of water over her hands and 'slid them over each other'.[5] But she based her interpretation partly on her observation of the real behaviour of somnambulists, partly on the logic of Shakespeare's text. When the Doctor remarks

Look how she rubs her hands (v. i. 26)

and the Gentlewoman replies

It is an accustomed action with her, to seem thus washing her hands; I have known her continue in this a quarter of an hour (v. i. 27–9)

they both use the plural 'hands'. When Sheridan burst into her room on the night of February 2, 1785, and protested against her decision to put the candle down, against all established convention, she referred him to the text:

…I urged the impracticability of washing out that '*damned spot*' with the vehemence that was certainly implied by both her own words, and by those of her gentlewoman…he insisted that if I did put the candle out of my hand, it would be thought a presumptuous innovation, as Mrs Pritchard had always retained it in hers. My mind, however, was made up…[6]

The great difference between Mrs Siddons's interpretation of the sleep-walking scene and previous interpretations lay in the unusual energy and vigour of her movements. As Professor Sprague justly observes: 'The hideous realities of the dream were more insisted upon rather than the fact of dreaming.'[7] That it was the hideous realities of the dream that concerned Mrs Siddons is

[1] *Dramatic Criticism, 1808–31*, ed. L. H. and C. W. Houtchens (1949), p. 72.
[2] *Papers on Acting*, p. 95.   [3] *Ibid.*
[4] Campbell, *Mrs Siddons*, II, 38.   [5] *Dramatic Criticism*, ed. Houtchens, p. 72.
[6] Campbell, *Mrs Siddons*, II, 38.   [7] *Shakespearian Players*, p. 66.

unwittingly confirmed by Leigh Hunt, who did not seem quite to understand the principle behind her interpretation. After she had washed her hands, and failed to get the blood off 'she made "a face" in passing them before her nose, as if she perceived a *foul smell*. We venture to think', comments Leigh Hunt, 'that she should have shuddered and looked in despair, as recognizing the *stain on her soul*.'[1] Boaden's description shows that Mrs Siddons was re-living the murder of Duncan: 'She ladled the water from the imaginary ewer over her hands—bent her body to listen to the sounds presented by her fancy, and hurried to resume the taper where she had left it, that she might with all speed drag her pallid husband to their chamber.'[2] Bell's notes confirm the impression given by Boaden that Mrs Siddons re-enacted the murder of the king in her dream. At

> One, two; why then 'tis time to do't   (v. i. 34)

she seemed to be 'listening eagerly' and 'why then 'tis time to do't' was spoken in a 'strange, unnatural whisper'. Towards the end of the scene, when Lady Macbeth remembers the old man who had 'so much blood in him', and finds the smell of blood overpowering:

Here's the smell of the blood still. All the perfumes of Arabia will not sweeten this little hand. Oh, oh, oh!   (v. i. 48–9)

Bell writes that what they heard was more than a sigh. It was a 'convulsive shudder—very horrible'.[3] The 'anxious whispering, with which she made her exit, as if beckoning her husband to bed, took the audience with her into the silent and dreaming horror of her retirement', wrote Leigh Hunt after seeing her last performance as Lady Macbeth.[4]

Sheridan Knowles tells us what it was like to be in the audience when Mrs Siddons played the sleep-walking scene. 'Though pit, gallery, and boxes were crowded to suffocation, the chill of the grave seemed about you while you looked on her;—there was the hush and damp of the charnel-house at midnight; you had a feeling as if you and the medical attendant, and lady-in-waiting, were alone with her; your flesh crept and your breathing became un-

---

[1] Leigh Hunt's *London Journal* (1834), I, 118. Quoted in Sprague, *Shakespearian Players*, p. 66.
[2] *Mrs Siddons*, II, 144.   [3] *Papers on Acting*, p. 96.
[4] *Dramatic Criticism*, p. 72.

easy.'[1] As Professor Sprague points out, Sheridan Knowles did better when he was talking to the American tragedian Edwin Forrest. Forrest asked Sheridan Knowles about Mrs Siddons's interpretation of the sleep-walking scene:

'I have read all the high flown descriptions of the critics, and they fall short. I want you to tell me in a plain blunt phrase just what impression she produced on you.' Knowles replied with a sort of shudder... 'Well, sir, I smelt blood! I swear that I smelt blood!'[2]

To actors and theatre people, it seemed, for many years after Mrs Siddons had left the stage, that the most complete statement possible about Lady Macbeth had been made, even though this realisation did not prevent players of genius like Rachel from imagining new possibilities. Coquelin tells us that Rachel, who once almost played Lady Macbeth in England, was haunted by the memory of Mrs Siddons. When Rachel was told that the English actress had exhausted every resource, especially in the sleep-walking scene, she replied—'Oh but I have an idea of my own, I should lick my hand'.[3]

Mrs Siddons had a judgement that Pope would have admired and an imagination that Blake and Coleridge would have understood. She first used Garrick's version of *Macbeth*, in 1785, and later Kemble's. In both stage texts Lady Macbeth's words were restored as they existed in the First Folio, with one or two minor alterations in metre, and with one major concession to contemporary taste—the omission of the fainting episode after Duncan's murder. Hazlitt was speaking as a representative of the critics of the nineteenth century when he wrote that to have seen Mrs Siddons as Lady Macbeth was 'an event in everyone's life, never to be forgotten'.[4] She seems to have established, beyond doubt, the capacity of the actor to interpret Shakespeare as no critic had done. Sheridan Knowles felt that her interpretation of Lady Macbeth's character on the stage went ultimately beyond a critic's powers of description and analysis; it was no more to be embodied in description than the speed and brightness of the lightning flash, which nothing can give you a conception of except the lightning.[5]

[1] *Dramatic Literature*, p. 22.
[2] W. R. Alger, *The Life of Edwin Forrest* (2 vols. 1877), II, 545. Quoted in Sprague, *Shakespearian Players*, p. 67. [3] *Papers on Acting*, p. 199.
[4] *Works*, XIII, 312. [5] *Dramatic Literature*, p. 21.

There was unanimity among the critics in the nineteenth century about the value of Mrs Siddons's interpretation of Lady Macbeth, with the exception of George Fletcher. Fletcher writes:

They who cite Mrs Siddons' Lady Macbeth as exhibiting the highest development of her histrionic powers are perfectly right; but when they speak of it as transcendentally proving her fitness for interpreting Shakespeare, they are decidedly wrong. It is not a statue-like simplicity that makes the essence of a Shakespearean character, but a *picturesque* complexity, to which Mrs Siddons' massive person and sculptured genius were essentially repugnant. Her genius, indeed, has been well described as rather epic than dramatic.[1]

Fletcher's judgement seems to rest on a surface knowledge of her performance. As I have tried to show, her interpretation of Lady Macbeth combined a classic grandeur with complexity, elements which are not irrevocably opposed, and which co-exist in Shakespeare's text. Fletcher had an axe to grind. His real concern was to establish the rightness of Helen Faucit's interpretation of Lady Macbeth.[2]

Fletcher's other implied criticism, that as a result of Mrs Siddons's interpretation Lady Macbeth displaced Macbeth as the central figure in the play, possibly deserves more attention.[3] In some of the productions of *Macbeth* in which Mrs Siddons took part, this undoubtedly happened. But it was not due to a faulty interpretation of the text. The displacement took place, as Professor Bell tells us, when Lady Macbeth was played by Mrs Siddons, and Macbeth was in the hands of an inferior actor. She then appeared to make him 'the mere instrument of her wild and uncontrollable ambition'.[4]

This must have happened in 1785, when Smith, who seems to have provided a caricature of Garrick's Macbeth, played the part. 'In its outline, I suppose him to have given what he remembered of Garrick', writes Boaden, adding that, though 'he *walked* the character...he never looked it...the multitudinous *passions*, in his expression of them, at the wafting of his hand, became *incarnadine*, or as Murphy would say—ONE RED'.[5]

The balance appears to have been redressed, to some extent,

---

[1] *Studies of Shakespeare* (1847), p. 194.
[2] *Ibid.* pp. 197–8.
[3] *Ibid.* pp. 190–1.
[4] *Papers on Acting*, p. 81.
[5] *Mrs Siddons*, II, 147.

when Kemble played the role. At his best, Kemble helped to make Mrs Siddons's interpretation of Lady Macbeth viable and true, within the pattern of meaning projected in *Macbeth*.

Those opinions of Leigh Hunt which have attracted attention suggest that John Kemble, as Macbeth, was a mannerist, a declaimer, a Quin unaccountably resurrected in the nineteenth century. In fact, Leigh Hunt's views are not at all consistent. A closer look at his criticism of Kemble's Macbeth, over the years, reveals puzzling contradictions.

On January 15, 1809, Hunt wrote: 'Kemble, who is excellent in all that there is of dignity in *Macbeth*, cannot forget, in the more impassioned scenes, those methodistical artifices of dropped eyes, patient shakes of the head, and whining preachments, which always do and ever will injure his attempts at heartfelt nature.'[1] On November 7, 1831, however, some years after Kemble had left the stage, Hunt began to praise him. On Monday, November 7, 1831, Leigh Hunt compared Mrs Siddons's Lady Macbeth to Clytemnestra, but added that 'more wonderful if not so complete, was Kemble's performance of the far more difficult part of Macbeth...The force of voice and gesture never approached nearer to an adequate expression of the most affecting and beautiful thoughts expressed by the force of terrible exigencies.' On November 7, Hunt expressed the view that Kemble's interpretation of Macbeth was far more satisfying than Kean's.[2] This almost unqualified praise of Kemble need not be puzzling, for Kemble matured through the years as an actor and Leigh Hunt as a critic; yet in the same year in which he praised Kemble's Macbeth, Hunt compared Kemble with Quin. On July 25, 1831, he wrote: 'Garrick's nature displaced Quin's formalism: and in precisely the same way did Kean displace Kemble.'[3]

These contradictions in Leigh Hunt's criticism are difficult to resolve. They could mean that he did not fully understand the principles of Kemble's art. Thomas Davies, who remembered the solemn monotony of Quin as Macbeth, and who had lived through the revolution accomplished by Garrick, appears to have seen no resemblance between Kemble and Quin. Davies, in the

---

[1] *Dramatic Criticism*, p. 22.
[2] *Dramatic Essays*, ed. W. Archer and R. W. Lowe (1894), pp. 231–3.
[3] *Ibid.* p. 222.

last years of his life, saw Kemble play Hamlet and wrote: 'There was nothing of...any man within our memory, in his delivery or deportment; he stood alone.'[1]

Kemble had not seen Garrick play, and therefore, Sir Walter Scott tells us, could not imitate him. Kemble carved out an original style, which the word 'formal', whether used in critical dispraise or as a term of approval, does not adequately describe. His originality seems to have consisted in a recognition and evasion of the formal. After weaving a formal pattern, Kemble would surprisingly hit the purely natural, and the effect, vivid and contrasting, seems to have been often cathartic.

Professor Sprague has drawn attention to an experiment conducted some years ago in a Russian production of *Romeo and Juliet*, which helps to describe the nature of Kemble's originality. When Romeo, encountering Juliet at the masked ball, begs a kiss, the language used during the exchange is stylised, the conversation conducted in the sonnet form. The Russian actors playing Romeo and Juliet kept close to the formal patterns of Shakespeare's poetry until Juliet said with sudden naturalness, 'you kiss by th' book'.[2] As Professor Sprague observes, 'Kemble's technique in his stateliest days lent itself to similar effects'.[3] Macready, writing of Kemble's interpretation of Macbeth, describes these effects as 'brilliant' and 'worked out with wonderful skill on a sombre ground, which only a great master of his art could have achieved'.[4]

When Kemble made his entrance as Macbeth, the first impression was one of grave formality, though his costume was more naturalisitic than Garrick's. Influenced by the new convention of historical realism, Kemble wore chain mail, and over it a plaid, in the manner of some of the clans of Scotland.[5] In the fashion of a chieftain of the clans, Kemble wore in his bonnet (after Sir Walter Scott had placed it there with his own hands), the single broad quill feather of an eagle, sloping across his brow.[6] The

---

1 *The European Magazine* (November 1783). Quoted in Sprague, *Shakespearian Players*, p. 44.
2 A. V. Morozov, *Shakespeare on the Soviet Stage* (1947), pp. 67–8. Quoted in Sprague, *Shakespearian Players*, p. 55.
3 *Ibid.*
4 William Charles Macready, *Reminiscences and Selections from his Diaries and Letters*, ed. Sir Frederick Pollock (2 vols. 1875), I, 148.
5 See William Winter, *Shakespeare on the Stage* (1911), First Series, p. 463.
6 See *The Quarterly Review*, XXXIV (1826), 226.

single feather, often worn by clan chieftains, probably gave Kemble the feel of reality, for he grew enthusiastic about it. In the same way as what he imagined to be a gull's feather brought the sea to Irving in *King Lear*,[1] it is quite possible that the single broad feather helped to bring the highlands to Kemble. Scott tells us: '...he was delighted when, with our own critical hands...we divested his bonnet of sundry huge bunches of black feathers... and replaced them with a single broad quill feather of an eagle sloping across his noble brow; he told us afterwards that the change was worth to him three distinct rounds of applause as he came forward in this improved and more genuine head-gear.'[2] Kemble was concerned to improve the 'accuracy of dresses' on the stage 'during his whole life'.[3] Scott, who knew the highlands well, tells us that Kemble wore 'the highland dress'[4] as Macbeth. While the costume was not historically accurate, in the sense that it was not that of the time of Edward the Confessor, it seems to have brought the atmosphere of the Scottish Highlands into the play.

At his entrance Kemble did not merely mirror reality, he transformed it. This certainly was the effect he had on Scott: 'Who crosses the blighted heath of Forres [wrote Scott] without beholding in imagination the stately step of Kemble as he descended on the stage at the head of his victorious army.'[5] The 'distant approach of the army was very well arranged'[6]. In his stage text of *Macbeth* Kemble retained Davenant's line 'Command they make a halt upon the heath',[7] as Garrick had done in his text, though Kemble did not, as has been mistakenly assumed, use Davenant's version. In at least three instances, Kemble, who had something of a scholar's eye, as I hope to show, approached closer to the First Folio than Garrick. After the interpolation from Davenant, the first act of Kemble's text unfolds as in the Folio.

In his response to the witches Kemble seems to have run daringly counter to what the audience had been used to.[8] Where

---

[1] Laurence Irving, *Henry Irving* (1930), pp. 548-9.   [2] *Quarterly Review*, p. 226.
[3] *Ibid.*   [4] *Ibid.*
[5] *Ibid.* p. 199.   [6] *Ibid.* p. 227.
[7] See *Macbeth written by Shakespeare as represented to their Majesties Servants on opening the Theatre Royal Drury Lane on Monday, April* 21, 1794 (1794), I. iii. p. 9.
[8] See Scott, *Quarterly Review*, p. 211. '...it was often objected to Kemble, that in playing Shakespeare's best-known characters he frequently sought to give them effect by a mode of delivery and action daringly opposed to what the audience had been used to.'

Garrick had shown astonishment, Kemble seems to have shown a studied indifference. A critic who could not accept Kemble's interpretation, who felt that Macbeth should run 'breathless with impatience, from one sorceress to another', tells us that

> Say from whence
> You owe this strange intelligence, or why
> Upon this blasted heath you stop our way
> With such prophetic greeting? Speak, I charge you
>
> (I. iii. 75–8)

was spoken by Kemble 'in a *stately* posture'. With a wave of the hand, with '*studied* dignity', and in 'measured accents', he said:

> Stay, you imperfect speakers, tell me more.[1]   (I. iii. 70)

It has been too easily assumed that Kemble always spoke in 'measured accents'. As Hotspur, Kemble assumed, says Scott, 'the rapidity and energy, and hurry and reckless indulgence of his humour, which are the chief ingredients of Henry Percy's character'.[2] And if Kemble assumed a '*studied* dignity' with the witches, it was almost certainly intentional. It seems likely that what the critic saw was precisely what Kemble intended to convey. For the air of studied indifference was observed again when Macbeth stood in Duncan's court and watched Malcolm named Prince of Cumberland. While Garrick let the audience see that his mind was in a tumult in the presence of the king, Kemble was '*easy* and *serene*',[3] though when he was alone with Lady Macbeth the ease and serenity were less in evidence. There was a hint of the disturbance within. J. H. Siddons writes that when Mrs Siddons, as Lady Macbeth, spoke the lines beginning

> Your face, my thane, is as a book where men
> May read strange matters...   (I. v. 59–60)

Kemble 'hung his head as if he could not withstand her penetrating gaze or the language which interpreted aright the ambitious whisperings of his own heart'.[4]

At the end of the first act, when Garrick spoke the soliloquy

---

[1] See *Critical Observations on Mr Kemble's Performance* (1811), p. 22.

[2] *Quarterly Review*, p. 219.

[3] See *Critical Observations*, p. 22.

[4] See 'Random Recollections of a Life', *Harper's New Monthly Magazine*, xxvi (December 1862).

'If it were done', Macbeth was 'agitated', his words seemed at times disjointed, his speech slightly incoherent.[1] In Kemble's interpretation of the lines, however, there was a marked absence of agitation. Bell thought that he 'recited' the soliloquy.[2] In 1811 another critic remarked that Kemble spoke the lines like a 'cool logician'.[3] Yet it is interesting to observe that Kemble's text of the soliloquy was closer in one important respect to that of the First Folio than Garrick's. The comma after 'well' in the first line of the Folio:

> If it were done, when 'tis done, then 'twere well,
> It were done quickly...[4]

indicates a pause both in the rhythm and sense of the line. Garrick dropped the comma, and the opening lines in his text seem to mean: 'If the murder is to be done, when I do it I had better do it quickly.' Kemble who had a scholar's eye, attempted to give back the lines their original depth of meaning by introducing a period after 'well':

> If it were done, when 'tis done, then 'twere well.
> It were done quickly, if the assassination
> Could trammel up the consequence, and catch,
> With his surcease, success.[5]

Kemble was accused of speaking the lines like 'a metaphysical speculator'. This is not altogether surprising because he appears to have given back the lines their original metaphysical significance. The repeated 'done' shows us what Macbeth's mind is circling round—when is a deed ever 'done'?

Writing in 1831, Leigh Hunt appears to have in the end set his seal of approval on Kemble's strategy:

With what an abstracted air he passed through the first act as his eye saw strange sights unseen of others! With what a trembling hand, confessing irresolution of purpose, did he grasp his contemptuous wife, and decline to proceed 'further in this business' while his eye yet seemed to gloat and glisten at the visionary crown which was leading him to Duncan's chamber.[6]

---

[1] See chapter 4, pp. 50–1.   [2] *Papers on Acting*, p. 85.
[3] *Critical Observations*, p. 24.   [4] Actus Primus, Scena Septima, p. 125.
[5] I. vii. pp. 18–19.
[6] *Dramatic Essays*, ed. Archer and Lowe, pp. 231–2.

Hunt seems to have felt that the 'abstracted air' of Kemble in the first act, with a hint of strong feelings submerged beneath, was right for Macbeth. In 1831 he clearly preferred Kemble's interpretation to Macready's. 'Mr Macready's Macbeth will scarcely bear to be thought of after Mr Kemble's...'[1]

During the first act, Kemble presented Macbeth's public image, as he had conceived it, with all its studied dignity. In the second act, when Macbeth murders Duncan, and when horror overwhelms him, Kemble tried to present the private figure, the hidden 'natural' man.

Unfortunately, it is difficult to decide what Kemble's interpretation of the dagger scene was, for there are five different versions of the way in which he played it. The dramatic critic of the *Theatrical Inquisitor* of August 1819, Professor Bell, and the *Times* reviewer of September 19, 1811, found Kemble's interpretation of the dagger scene unsatisfactory, for one reason or another. The dramatic critic of the *Theatrical Inquisitor* tells us:

Mr Kemble...always unsheathed his sabre, as Macbeth, when delivering the following lines:

> 'Or art thou but
> A *dagger* of the mind, a false creation,
> Proceeding from the heat-oppressed brain?
> I see thee yet, in form as palpable
> As *this* (i.e. Johnny Kemble's sword) which now I draw.'

'This' need not refer to a dagger but the critic of the *Theatrical Inquisitor* felt it ought to. Professor Bell thought that Kemble's acting was forced:

There is much stage trick and very cold in this scene of Kemble—walks across the stage, his eyes on the ground, starts at the sight of the servant whom he forgets for the purpose, renews his walk, throws up his face, sick, sighs, then a start theatric and then the dagger.[2]

Bell considered that Kemble's interpretation of the dagger scene was unnatural. At the point where Macbeth says 'There's no such thing:'

Kemble...hides his hand, then fearfully looks up, and peeping first over, then under his hand, as if for an insect whose buzzing had dis-

---

[1] *Dramatic Essays*, ed. Archer and Lowe, pp. 231–2.
[2] *Papers on Acting*, p. 87.

turbed him, he removes his hand, looks more abroad, and then recovers
—very poor—the recovery should be by an effort of the mind...A
change in the look, the clearing of a bewildered imagination, a more
steadfast and natural aspect, the hand drawn across the eyes or forehead, with something of a bitter smile.[1]

The *Times* reviewer thought that Kemble was not 'bewildered',
'terrified and brain-sick' enough.

Mr Kemble's conception was otherwise; he stretched his arms,
yawned and at once started at the dagger; all after this was *palpability*:
he made no doubt of its existence; he followed it with his eye steadily
through the air, and walked after it composedly to Duncan's door.

One doubts whether the *Times* reviewer would have agreed with
Bell that Macbeth should be 'steadfast'.

Bell made his observations around 1808, the *Times* reviewer in
1811. It is possible that by 1814 Kemble had improved. Henry
Crabb Robinson, writing on December 1, 1814, tells us that he
preferred Kemble's interpretation of the dagger scene to Edmund
Kean's, though Kean was well known for achieving brilliant
natural effects: 'His dagger scene pleased me less than Kemble's.
He saw the dagger too soon, and without any preparatory pause.
Kemble was admirable in the effect he gave to this very bold
conception. In his eye you could see when he lost sight of the
dagger.'[2] Lamb, in his essay on the 'Tragedies of Shakespeare
considered with reference to their fitness for stage presentation',
published in 1818, reports that he found Kemble's interpretation
of the dagger scene painfully immediate and convincing:

...when...we come to see a man in his bodily shape before our eyes
actually preparing to commit a murder, if the acting be true and impressive, as I have witnessed it in Mr K's performance of that part, the
painful anxiety of the act...the too close pressing semblance of reality,
give a pain and an uneasiness which totally destroy all the delight which
the words in the book convey.[3]

As the dagger soliloquy moved to its close, in Kemble's production of *Macbeth*, two strokes upon the bell[4] announced that the

---

[1] *Ibid.* pp. 87–8.
[2] *The Diary, Reminiscences and Correspondence of Henry Crabb Robinson*, ed. T. Sadler
(2 vols. 1872), I, 241.
[3] *The Works of Charles Lamb* (2 vols. 1818), II, 23–4.
[4] See *The Oracle* (April 22, 1794).

arrangements for the murder were complete. Kemble seems to have based this effect on a remark made by Lady Macbeth in the sleep-walking scene:

One, two; why then 'tis time to do't. (v. i. 34)

When Macbeth returned after murdering Duncan, the realism which had disturbed Charles Lamb was indisputably there. The playing of Kemble and Mrs Siddons had affinities with the playing of Garrick and Mrs Pritchard during the sharp brief exchange that followed Macbeth's entrance:

Macb. I have done the deed. Didst thou not hear a noise?
Lady M. I heard the owl scream and the crickets cry.
  Did not you speak?
Macb.   When?
Lady M.   Now.
Macb.   As I descended? (ii. ii. 14–17)

Kemble spoke his first brief lines extremely well, writes Bell, like 'some horrid secret—a whisper in the dark'.[1] Another critic, who did not agree with Kemble's interpretation of Macbeth in the first act, felt that his interpretation of the murder scene earned Kemble a title to greatness:

That scene particularly, 'I have done the deed', was beyond all possibility of description, fine, beautiful, sublime, and indeed it paid us with double usury, for our patience throughout the evening.—The face, the looks, the *every thing* of that moment in MACBETH, appalled us with hellish terror, and brought before us the corse of DUNCAN...[2]

In this crucial scene (ii. ii.), in Kemble's stage text, lines 36–41 were cut. It is the kind of 'editing' that one might associate with a film-director like Carol Reed: the pace increases while the poetry is sacrificed. One can imagine David Lean retaining the lines for exactly the opposite reason. Kemble telescoped Macbeth's comments on sleep, omitting Shakespeare's metaphor of the 'ravell'd sleave'.

Macb. Methought I heard a voice cry, Sleep no more!
  Glamis hath murder'd sleep, and therefore Cawdor
  Shall sleep no more, Macbeth shall sleep no more!

---

[1] *Papers on Acting*, p. 88.   [2] See *Critical Observations*, pp. 24–5.

Lady M. Who was it, thus cry'd? Why, worthy thane,
You do unbend your noble strength, to think
So brain-sickly of things—Go, get some water
And wash this filthy witness from your hand.[1]

At the end of the scene, when Lady Macbeth returned after plac-
ing the daggers by Duncan's body, Kemble played well, writes
Bell. He stood 'motionless; his bloody hands near his face; his
eye fixed, agony in his brow; quite rooted to the spot'. He was
pulled away by Lady Macbeth 'talking' as he went.[2]

In the murder scene the private figure emerged from behind
the proud and stately public image which Kemble had projected
in the first act. While Garrick played the sensitive murderer from
the commencement of the play, Kemble revealed Macbeth's sensitiveness to the evil in which he is caught, in the second act.
Kemble omitted the Porter from his text as Garrick had done, and
when he re-entered, to encounter Macduff and Lennox, he wore a
flowered satin night gown,[3] like that which Garrick had worn
before him. Scott's description of Kemble's interpretation of
Macbeth's encounter with Macduff suggests that it was supremely
natural and convincing. Scott's account demonstrates how
Kemble's face could alter from within and express a whole world
of meaning:

We can never forget the rueful horror of his look, which by strong
exertion he endeavours to conceal, when on the morning succeeding
the murder he receives Lennox and Macduff in the ante-chamber of
Duncan. His efforts to appear composed, his endeavours to assume the
attitude and appearance of one listening to Lennox's account of the
external terrors of the night, while in fact he is expecting the alarm to
rise within the royal apartment, formed a most astonishing piece of
playing. Kemble's countenance seemed altered by the sense of internal
horror, and had a cast of that of Count Ugolino in the dungeon, as
painted by Reynolds. When Macbeth felt himself obliged to turn
towards Lennox and reply to what he had been saying, you saw him,
like a man awakening from a fit of absence, endeavour to recollect at
least the general tenor of what had been said, and it was some time ere
he could bring out the general reply, 'Twas a rough night'.[4]

[1] Kemble, *Macbeth*, ii. ii. p. 25.   [2] *Papers on Acting*, pp. 90–1.
[3] See Mangin, *The Parlour Window* (1841), p. 123.
[4] *Quarterly Review*, p. 219.

Other observers besides Sir Walter Scott were struck by the way in which Kemble interpreted character with his face. In the second scene of the third act, J. R. Planché remembered the 'wonderful expression' on Kemble's face when he vividly rendered the tragic moral condition of Macbeth:

I can see him now standing in the doorway in the centre of the scene. The kingly crown appeared a burthen and a torture to him. How terribly clear it was, before he uttered a word, that his mind was 'full of scorpions'—that he acutely felt—

> —'Better be with the dead,
> Whom we, to gain our place have sent to peace,
> Than on the torture of the mind to lie
> In restless ecstasy.'[1]

The reference to a 'kingly crown' suggests that Kemble changed his costume for the third act. A remark by Leigh Hunt appears to confirm this. Hunt writes that in the banquet scene Kemble's Macbeth was 'kingly' and 'superbly attired'.[2] What the attire was can be guessed at. The changes of costume in a production of *Macbeth* described by Charles Lamb possibly reflected Kemble's practice—indeed it could well have been a performance by Kemble himself that Lamb was describing: 'The coronation robe of the Scottish monarch was fairly a counterpart to that which our king wears when he goes to the Parliament house,—just so full and cumbersome, and set out with ermine and pearls.'[3] Charles Lamb was writing of 'the last time'—unfortunately he is not more specific—that he had seen the play: he did not like Macbeth's changes of costume which he compared with 'the shiftings and re-shiftings of a Romish priest at Mass...'[4]

During the banquet scene, Kemble appears to have been, on the whole, formal in his manner—Leigh Hunt describes him as 'tame and kingly'.[5] In his approach to the poetry of the banquet scene Kemble seems to have emphasised the formal elements in Shakespeare's language, bringing in 'brief touches of feeling' when he detected their presence in the poetry. This, at any rate, is the impression given by Boaden. Talking of Shakespeare's use of language, Boaden writes:

[1] *Recollections and Reflections*, p. 15.
[2] *Dramatic Essays*, ed. Archer and Lowe, p. 232.   [3] *Works*, II, 34.
[4] *Ibid.* 33.   [5] *Dramatic Esssay*, p. 232.

...He, at intervals, throws in brief touches of feeling in the language of daily life; and the simpler the expressions are, the more brilliant are the effects they produce. Write the whole play in such a diction, and it would be a creeping, prosaic, vulgar performance. One of these familiar touches (the reader will supply hundreds) occurs to me in Macbeth; after the spirit of Banquo has vanished, the trembling usurper falters out to his approaching queen—

'If I stand here, I saw him.'

The reader, who remembers the tone and gesture which from Mr Kemble conveyed this assertion to the audience, will know how truly he could hit the merely natural, when no other consideration called upon him for a more elevated style of utterance.[1]

To some critics a second natural touch was Kemble's refusal to let Banquo's ghost appear on the stage. On April 21, 1794, Kemble dispensed with the physical presence of the ghost, following up a suggestion by Robert Lloyd in the *Actor*:

The king alone should form the phantom there
And talk and tremble at the vacant chair.[2]

Macbeth now bent 'his eye on vacancy'. The critic of the *Morning Chronicle* approved,[3] but Campbell felt that the innovation was 'an out-rage on the rights' of stage ghosts: 'If we judge by sheer reason, no doubt we must banish ghosts from the stage altogether; but if we regulate our fancy by the laws of superstition, we shall find that spectres are privileged to be visible to whom they will.'[4] Kemble was, in fact, no thoroughgoing rationalist, for he made a curious distinction 'between a ghost and an apparition'. Banquo was a ghost and to be 'pictured only in words as an idea, while Hamlet's father was 'an apparition' with a part to perform.[5]

Banquo's ghost, as a physical presence, was banished from Drury Lane and then from Covent Garden, when Kemble moved there in the autumn of 1803, until, London audiences clamouring for the restoration of a visible ghost, Kemble was forced to resurrect him, as he told Joseph Farrington, against his better judgement.[6]

---

[1] *Memoirs of the Life of John Philip Kemble* (2 vols. 1825), I, 177.
[2] (1760), p. 15.
[3] April 22, 1794. Quoted in Sprague, *Shakespeare and the Actors*, p. 256.
[4] *Mrs Siddons*, II, 186, 187.
[5] See Herschel Baker, *John Philip Kemble* (1942), p. 186.
[6] See Joseph Farrington, *Diary*, November 8, 1811.

Kemble's conviction that the actor should make the audience imagine the ghost, not see him,[1] may help to explain the violence of his Garrick-like approach to the business with the cup. Garrick would fling his drinking-glass away with some violence at the sight of Banquo, 'as if he saw a spider in the wine'. Kemble followed Garrick's practice, though he was criticised for it. A critic who had seen Kemble play wrote:

I ask my readers, those particularly who may have had opportunities of witnessing the effects of strong fear, would MACBETH, thus surprised, dash the cup from him with a violence requiring wilful strength, and put up a frown, and take a threatening posture?...Or rather would not the cup drop unconsciously from the powerless hand, and, after a few staggering paces, would not the distressed wretch recoil in himself, and exclude the horrible sight from his eyes with both spread hands?[2]

When Kemble threatened the vision, however, in 'the bold language of *sound* courage', he was less like Garrick: 'Now Mr K ...seemed not to fear while yet he said he *trembled*.'[3] During those years in which Kemble addressed a vacant chair, this approach was possibly necessary. The fear and trembling shown by Garrick might have looked excessive when the audience saw no ghost. In later years, when the ghost was restored, Kemble's interpretation would have been consonant with the idea expressed in his essay on the character, that none of Macbeth's actions is based on fear. In 'Macbeth Reconsidered' (1786), Kemble contested the argument that Macbeth plunges into fresh crimes in order 'to get rid of personal fear'.[4] As Kemble saw it: ...'Ambition is the predominant vice of Macbeth's nature but he gratifies it by hypocrisy, that reveres virtue too highly to be perfectly itself...'[5]

At the end of the banquet scene Kemble restored the 'correct' pronunciation of maggot-pies, when Macbeth remarks to his wife, after the guests have left:

> It will have blood; they say blood will have blood.
> Stones have been known to move, and trees to speak;
> Augurs and understood relations have
> By maggot-pies and choughs and rooks brought forth
> The secret'st man of blood.[6]

[1] See Joseph Farrington, *Diary*, November 8, 1811.
[2] *Critical Observations*, p. 25.   [3] *Ibid.* p. 26.   [4] See p. 19.
[5] 'Macbeth Reconsidered', p. 35.   [6] Kemble, *Macbeth*, III. iv. p. 42.

Scott describes the reaction of a provincial audience to Kemble's Elizabethan pronunciation of maggot-pies with some amusement:

Performers had been in the habit of pronouncing the word *mag-pies* though the blank verse halted for it. But Kemble resumed the proper pronunciation of *magot-pies*, with an emphasis which made the audience look round them in astonishment, scarcely trusting their eyes, and marvelling how any species of augury could be derived from what they apprehended to be a stale pastry.[1]

Kemble's pronunciation of maggot-pies, like his stress on dignity in tragedy, may be regarded as an instance of his scholarly, classical bent.

It may be argued that the introduction of several 'imps', one of whom was Edmund Kean, for 'the black spirits and white', in the fourth act was hardly classical. But after Edmund Kean tripped his fellow spirits so that they trembled and fell like 'a pack of cards', Kemble abandoned the experiment.[2]

In 1794, though he retained the traditional music, dances, songs and aerial exits and entrances in the fourth act, Kemble's approach as director was 'classical' in its total rejection of the traditional comic interpretation of the witches. His purpose was to 'strike the eye with supernatural power...and likewise to avoid all buffoonery in those parts that *Macbeth* might no longer be termed a *Tragi-comedy*'.[3]

Kemble's interpretation of his own role in the first four acts could be compared to his interpretation of the witches. He possibly tended to avoid disparate elements in Macbeth's personality, yet he created a character which, though formal and aristocratic in conception, profoundly satisfied the romantic imagination. Part of his success was due to the fact that the portrait he created was not entirely formal. Moments purely natural would break through to cause a ripple across the formal surface. And in the fifth act, the formal pattern so carefully established seemed to disrupt and explode.

Leigh Hunt thought the fifth act was a 'great intellectual triumph'.[4] And Macready writes that Kemble's really memorable *coup de théâtre* came in the fifth act:

[1] *Quarterly Review*, p. 217.   [2] See *ibid.* p. 228.
[3] W. C. Oulton, *History of the Theatres of London* (2 vols. 1796), II, 140.
[4] *Dramatic Essays*, ed. Archer and Lowe, p. 232.

...when the news was brought, 'The queen, my lord, is dead', he seemed struck to the heart; gradually collecting himself he sighed out, 'She should have died hereafter'. Then, as if with the inspiration of despair he hurried out distinctly and pathetically the lines

> 'To-morrow, and to-morrow, and to-morrow,
> Creeps in this petty pace from day to day
> To the last syllable of recorded time,
> And all our yesterdays have lighted fools
> The way to dusty death. Out, out, brief candle!
> Life's but a walking shadow, a poor player,
> That struts and frets his hour upon the stage,
> And then is heard no more; it is a tale
> Told by an idiot, full of sound and fury,
> Signifying nothing.'

rising to a climax of desperation that brought down the enthusiastic cheers of the closely packed theatre. All at once he seemed carried away by the genius of the scene.[1]

Kemble did not, as Garrick had once done, assault the Messenger who brought the news that Birnam Wood was moving. In the second version of his essay, 'Macbeth and Richard III', published in 1817, Kemble argued that the stage direction, 'Striking him', after 'Liar and slave!' (v. v. 35), is not to be found in any of the Folios, being first introduced by Rowe. 'Such outrageous violence does not belong to the feelings of a person overwhelmed with surprise, half doubting, half believing an event,—at once, in nature most strange, and to himself of the most fatal importance. It is a direction irreconcilable to Macbeth's emotions at the moment for which it is given...'[2] 'At the tidings of "the wood of Birnam moving" he staggered', says Macready, describing Kemble's interpretation of Macbeth's response to the news brought by the Messenger, 'as if the shock had struck the very seat of his life'. In a 'bewilderment of fear and rage' he could barely 'ejaculate the words "Liar and slave!"'[3] Once again Kemble hit the purely natural. And the critic of *The Drama: or Theatrical Pocket Magazine*, notes with enthusiasm: '...let his enemies assert that his "Liar and slave!" was not natural if they can; and the tears and thrilling hearts of thousands shall answer them! Mr K was regarded by cavillers as a mere mannerist, only

---

[1] *Reminiscences*, ed. Pollock, I, 148.   [2] P. 110.
[3] *Reminiscences*, I, 148.

because his manner was the finest in the world.'[1] The violence of despair came after 'Liar and slave'. Lashing himself into a 'frantic rage', Kemble ended the scene in a 'perfect triumph',[2] says Macready. The creation of a formal pattern in the first four acts seems to have been a preparation for the fifth act, when the pattern was shattered and broken by the force of disillusionment and despair.

Kemble's essay on the character of Macbeth is less subtle than his actual performance seems to have been. One has to remember that in both versions of his essay he was more concerned with contesting other views than with his own interpretation of the character on the stage. In both versions Kemble stressed Macbeth's courage. He took the description of Macbeth as 'Bellona's bridegroom' seriously:

Could Shakespeare call a man brave, and insist upon his well deserving that appellation; could he grace a man with the title of valours minion, and deem him, as he does in a subsequent passage, worthy to be matched even with the goddess of war;—could he do this, and not design to impress a full idea of the dignity of his courage?

In his performances Kemble modified this view of Macbeth's character. As Macready writes: 'His shrinking from Macduff when the charm on which his life hung was broken by the declaration that his antagonist was "not of woman born" was a masterly stroke of art...' Kemble was no anti-hero, however. Macready adds that 'his subsequent defiance' of Macduff was 'most heroic'.[3] Like Garrick, Kemble believed in the ideal dignity of the tragic role, though not in that alone. His success lay partly in his ability to play off the real against the ideal. This was clearly one reason why Kemble's interpretation of Macbeth appealed to the contemporary imagination.

It might be argued, of course, that Kemble's Macbeth was not 'real' enough; that there was little of the 'dead butcher' in his portrait; that while Garrick inspired both pity for and horror of the character, Kemble inspired more of pity. One might go further and suggest that Kemble stamped his image of Macbeth 'touching in crime and noble in infamy' on a whole generation of critics, that his Macbeth was really one of the great 'Romantics', and that he smuggled in more sympathy for the character than

---

[1] iv (1823), 373.　　　[2] *Reminiscences*, i, 148.　　　[3] *Ibid.*

Shakespeare would have allowed. The tone of Leigh Hunt's account of Kemble's Macbeth might point to this, as he writes in 1831 of the way in which Kemble's '...voice trembled and fluttered among the fond images of decay and clung with melancholy grace to the blessings "which should accompany old age" and touched on the emptiness of human hope...'[1] The word 'fond' qualifying 'images of decay' contains more than a hint of romantic indulgence.

With these qualifications in mind it is yet necessary to remember that Macready compared Kemble's interpretation of Macbeth on the stage to a portrait by Rembrandt, consisting of brilliant effects created against a sombre background,[2] and that Scott believed Kemble's interpretation of Macbeth to be more satisfying than Garrick's:

...In Macbeth, Kemble has been as yet unapproachable; nor can we conceive that the bold and effective manner of Garrick, touching on the broad points of the character with a hand however vigorous, could at all compare with Kemble's exquisitely and minutely elaborate delineation of guilty ambition, drawn on from crime to crime, while the avenging furies at once scourge him for former guilt, and urge him to further enormities.[3]

While Scott's description of Garrick's Macbeth is far from just— (he did not see Garrick play)—it does show that Kemble's performance was the first after many years that could stand sustained comparison with Garrick's. Kemble's performance had the merit, unlike Macklin's, of being both original and successful.

As Garrick had done, Kemble established a standard by which actors who came after him were judged. Leigh Hunt preferred Kemble's portrait of Macbeth to either Edmund Kean's or Macready's,[4] both of which were brilliantly effective in some ways. And Hazlitt, commenting on Macready's interpretation of Macbeth, felt that 'the *ideal*, and preternatural' had eluded him. There was 'not a weight of superstitious terror loading the atmosphere and hanging over the stage'. Macready, wrote Hazlitt, had '*struck short* of the higher and imaginative part of the character... John Kemble was the best *Macbeth* (upon the whole) that we have

[1] *Dramatic Essays*, p. 232.   [2] *Reminiscences*, I, 150.
[3] *Quarterly Review*, pp. 218–19.
[4] *Dramatic Essays*, pp. 232–3.

seen'.[1] It seems evident enough that Kemble, at his best, did not allow Mrs Siddons, powerful and compelling though she was, to displace Macbeth as the central character in the play.

In 1805, Thomas Holcroft wrote in *The Theatrical Recorder*:

...Mrs Siddons is a noble actress! In her impassioned scenes, the man who can listen without frequent surprise and ecstasy must have no discrimination, no feeling, nor any sense of the true dignity of excellence. Mr J. P. Kemble is too often cold and declamatory; but he has his inspired moments, which give, perhaps, the greatest delight by bursting upon the audience when they are least expected. Both brother and sister, however, are the practical patrons of this hateful recitative, and are therefore theoretically its defenders. Mr Kemble contends that blank verse demands a recitation peculiar to itself...As a tragedian, Mr Cooke has a proud honour of being nearly free from this sing-song defect...[2]

Holcroft's view that Mrs Siddons believed in the declamatory approach to Shakespeare's verse seems to conflict sharply with the view expressed by the critic of the *Morning Post* twenty years earlier, in 1785, that 'there was little or no declamation' in Mrs Siddons's speech when she played Lady Macbeth: '...our ears were not wounded by the repetition of the *lark's shrill note*'.[3]

An explanation for this conflict of views may lie in the fact that Holcroft was himself a thoroughgoing 'naturalist'—his standard was set by Cooke, who seemed to Byron the 'most natural actor' he had seen. Mrs Siddons incorporated natural elements in her art—this explains why Holcroft could not avoid listening to her without 'frequent surprise and ecstasy', but she was not anti-formal when Shakespeare's verse showed a formal organisation with a special function and purpose. Kemble's approach to Shakespeare's poetry, like his sister's, appears to have been based upon the principles on which the verses he spoke were constructed.[4] Hazlitt thought that Kemble's 'formality[5] did not displease, because there was always sense and meaning in what he did'. Mrs Siddons seems to have been better equipped than her brother to deal with the principles on which Shakespeare's verse were constructed, because her voice was richer and more flexible

---

[1] *Works*, ed. Waller and Glover, XI, 315–16.
[2] (2 vols.), I, 274.
[3] February 3.
[4] See Boaden, *Mrs Siddons*, II, 49.
[5] *Works*, VIII, 378.

than Kemble's; but neither of them would have thought it helpful to impose a thoroughgoing naturalism on Shakespeare's verse at all points, in the fashion of realistic actors.

At the same time one notes that the stage speech of both Kemble and Mrs Siddons seemed to become slower as the years went by. When Mrs Siddons returned to play Lady Macbeth on June 16, 1816, after her retirement, Hazlitt thought that 'the machinery of the voice' seemed 'too ponderous' for the power that wielded it. There was 'too long a pause between each sentence, and between each word in each sentence'.[1] How much this slowing-down was due to advancing years, and how much it was due to the altered structures of the Covent Garden and Drury Lane theatres and their changing audiences, it is difficult to guess.

Both Drury Lane and Covent Garden were rebuilt on the principle that the bigger the theatre the better it is. Drury Lane, where *Macbeth* was staged by Kemble in 1794, was rebuilt in the same year, with a stage 'upon a much larger scale than...any other theatre in Europe'.[2] The 'opening for the scenery' was '43 feet wide, and 38 high'. The aquatint by Rowlandson and Pugin of the interior of Drury Lane Theatre, reproduced in Odell, shows the actors looking diminutive and rather lost on a vast stage, at an incredible distance from the audience in a huge auditorium.[3] The engraving by J. Fittler of Covent Garden Theatre in 1804, given in Odell,[4] has much the same distancing effect. The actors again look diminutive. Drury Lane could seat an audience of 3,611 people in 1794,[5] and Covent Garden 3,000 at the end of 1809, when Kemble presented *Macbeth* during the winter season of the same year.[6] As the years went by, spectators began to complain that they could hear only the 'ranted speeches' at Drury Lane and Covent Garden.[7] Moreover, the new audiences at Drury Lane and Covent Garden were scarcely likely to follow the complexities of Shakespeare with any degree of ease, whether the theatres were large or not. As H. Barton Baker points out:

...poetry and wit had no charms for these new patrons of the drama, because they were too ignorant to comprehend them; they required

[1] *Works*, VIII, 313.   [2] Oulton, *Theatres of London*, II, 136.
[3] Odell, *Shakespeare from Betterton to Irving*, II, facing 6.
[4] *Ibid.* II, facing 98.
[5] See R. Mander and J. Mitchenson, *The Theatres of London* (1961), p. 64.
[6] *Ibid.* p. 52.
[7] See F. G. Tomkins, *A Brief View of the English Drama* (1840), p. 73.

something more highly spiced, something that would produce in a milder form the excitement of seeing a dog gored to death by a bull, or a couple of bantams spurring each other to shreds.[1]

Drury Lane and Covent Garden found that 'such pieces as *A Tale of Mystery*, *Raymond and Agnes*, *The Castle Spectre*, *The Miller and his Men*, were more attractive than Shakespeare or Sheridan'.[2] It seems possible that when Kemble and Mrs Siddons spoke Shakespeare's verse more slowly than they had earlier done, it was partly the result of an instinctive effort to be heard—and understood.

Richard Cumberland, who knew Garrick and remembered the state of the theatre in his time, points out that Kemble had to present Shakespeare on stages used for lavish spectacle, and so large that Garrick would have looked lost in them:

...He [Garrick] was the great promoter of...that legitimate taste for the early dramatists, particularly Shakespeare, which Mr Kemble to his honour be it spoken, struggles to uphold, but struggles against a torrent of mummery and machinery and song and spectacle, which the circumstances of the time he lives in, and of the stage he treads, renders it impossible for him to do more than struggle with; it is a turbid torrent which he cannot stem. If he cannot trust himself to the character even of Macbeth on the little stage in the Haymarket without Mother Goose to cackle in his after-piece, neither could Garrick have filled the *Colliseum*, which is now in ruin, unless Johnson had drawn out his elephants to allure the gapers in the galleries: All the intelligence of his eye, the archness of his smile, the movement of his brow, the touching pathos of his undertones, spent in their passage through the musty void, would have failed to reach the outskirts of the greedy theatre; and he would have found himself only understood in the neighbourhood of the orchestra, while the rest of the spectators would have discovered little else in the finest actor that ever lived, but the diminutiveness of his figure.[3]

Though Garrick, in his time, had to battle with the spirit of the 'commercials' of John Rich, the forces arrayed against him were not quite as formidable as those arrayed against John Kemble.

[1] *The London Stage* (2 vols. 1889), II, 3-4.
[2] *Ibid.*
[3] See 'Theatrical Retrospections', *The Theatrical Inquisitor*, II (February 1813), 100.

CHAPTER 7

FROM KEMBLE TO MACREADY

Kemble's approach to Macbeth might be usefully described as 'intellectual'.[1] He would seize an idea and pursue it with intensity.[2] Kemble's most successful portraits were remembered for their unity of conception, their total impact. Scott appreciated the total effect of Kemble's interpretation of Macbeth—'the exquisitely and minutely elaborate delineation of guilty ambition, drawn on from crime to crime...'[3] Kemble, like Garrick, created standards by which actors who attempted the role of Macbeth after him were judged.

When Cooke attempted Macbeth in December 1800, at Covent Garden,[4] his interpretation seemed inadequate compared with Kemble's. As Dunlap, Cooke's biographer, writes: 'Mr Kemble's dignified person, noble face, graceful attitudes, deliberate manner, in short, all his peculiarities were congenial to Macbeth; and all the peculiarities of Mr Cooke adverse.'[5] Dunlap's reactions are revealing. They confirm the impression created by Hazlitt and Leigh Hunt, that Kemble had succeeded in stamping his own image of Macbeth on the imagination of a whole generation of critics.

Byron thought that Cooke was the most natural actor he had seen. But Cooke's naturalism in Macbeth was not always apt. Cooke had faith in a doctrine of naturalism which revealed itself in details of movement and gesture; yet he does not always seem to have discriminated between one character and another. In *Richard III*, when Stanley refuses his support to the king and the king says,

> Off with his son George's head,

Norfolk interposes saying,

> My Lord, the foe's already past the marsh:
> After the battle let young Stanley die

---

[1] The word used by Leigh Hunt in 1831, to describe the effect of Kemble's playing as Macbeth in the fifth act. See *Dramatic Essays*, ed. Archer and Lowe, p. 232.
[2] See Hazlitt, *Works*, ed. Waller and Glover, VIII, 379.
[3] *Quarterly Review*, XXXIV (1826), 218.
[4] See William Dunlap, *Memoirs of George Frederick Cooke* (2 vols. 1813), I, 136.
[5] *Ibid.*

FROM KEMBLE TO MACREADY

and Richard agrees
                          Why, after be it then. . .

Cooke, as Boaden tells us, 'fastened upon this precise point. . .to
affect deliberation, and stood. . .swaying his body backwards and
forwards, till he settled the fate of young George, and relieved the
almost agonized spectators, by "*after be it then*".'[1] Cooke repeated
the realistic touch, the swaying movement, when he played
Kitely in Ben Jonson's *Every Man in his Humour*, where it was apt
and successful. It ceased to be effective, however, when Cooke
tried it again as Macbeth. As Boaden writes, Cooke's 'hasty
striding of the stage backwards and forwards, the circular position
of his arms, and the see-saw of the body during his meditation,
were in Kitely appropriate, but in Macbeth vulgar and insufferable'.[2] The evidence provided by Boaden suggests that Cooke did
not discriminate enough in his mind between the characters of
Richard III, Kitely and Macbeth. Naturalistic 'action', initially
fresh and surprising, became a cliché, a convenient formula,
which no longer served the purposes of the actor's imagination.

   Cooke, in this matter of gesture and movement, suffered for a
principle imprecisely enforced. But when it came to speaking
Shakespeare's verse, his failure to enforce consistently his own
naturalistic principle yielded novel and effective results. Cooke,
we know, believed in turning verse into prose. Quite early in his
career, when acting in a verse play, he wrote out his part in prose,
to avoid the lilt of poetry, carefully working out each inflexion of
the voice.[3] But when he came to speak the poetry of disillusionment in *Macbeth*, he abandoned any attempt at consistent naturalism. When the news of Lady Macbeth's death was brought to him,
Cooke, as Macbeth, said with 'suppressed agitation':

                     She should have died—

but after a pause, 'with a tone lowered almost to a whisper',
added
                          —hereafter.

He used a similar change of tone and feeling in the lines describing life in terms of a guttering candle, a tale told by an idiot—

                  . . .full of sound and fury,
            Signifying nothing

[1] See *Life of Kemble*, ii, 281; the text, as quoted in Boaden, is probably a stage-text.
[2] *Ibid.* 288–9.   [3] See Dunlap, *Cooke*, ii, 357–8.

when a pause followed 'signifying' and the voice sank to a whisper, saying

—nothing.

with 'suppressed feeling and heart-breaking disappointment'.[1] Sir John Gielgud brought out the disillusionment in this line, in much the same fashion, when he played Macbeth more than a hundred years after Frederick Cooke.[2]

Cooke seems to have achieved his best effects in the closing scenes of *Macbeth*; his dying became him, being neither 'vulgar nor insufferable'. As Hazlitt wrote: 'We recollect that Mr Cooke discovered the great actor in the death-scene in *Macbeth*, and in that of *Richard*. He fell like the ruin of state, like a king with his regalia about him.'[3] Cooke did not, however, succeed in presenting a unified conception of Macbeth. His performance was remembered rather for its brilliant, isolated moments.

If one is to do justice to Edmund Kean, it must be said that though his portrait of Macbeth was, like Cooke's, remembered not for its coherence, but for its brilliant or surprising isolated moments, he seems to have started out with a logical and naturalistic conception of the role, the result primarily of a reaction to the theory and practice of John Kemble. Giles Playfair, in his life of Kean, quotes a revealing extract from the *Champion*: 'Let me here remark a most important difference between the acting of Mr Kemble and Mr Kean', a critic wrote. 'To Lady Macbeth's question, "When does Duncan go hence?", Mr Kemble replies indifferently, "Tomorrow as he purposes". With Mr Kean it assumes a very different aspect. In an emphatic tone, and with a hesitating look...he half divulges the secret of his breast— "To-morrow as he...purposes!"'[4] Using a pause and a stress Kean 'gave the impression that the idea of murdering Duncan at Dunsinane had already occurred to him. From then on he appeared not the pawn of his wife's ambition but the master of his own destiny'.[5] Kean's decision to stress the dominant role of Macbeth was doubtless partly a reaction to the way in which Kemble and Mrs Siddons had approached the play, but it was

[1] See Dunlap, *Cooke*, II, 356.
[2] This effect was described to me by one member of the audience, who had no knowledge of Cooke, after he saw Sir John Gielgud play Macbeth.
[3] *Works*, VIII, 207.   [4] *Kean* (1950), p. 126.
[5] *Ibid.*

quite possibly a matter of necessity as well. Mrs Bartley, who played opposite Kean, seems to have been ineffectual and 'very ordinary',[1] though the text makes the decisive importance of Lady Macbeth's role quite clear, a fact appreciated by Garrick and Mrs Pritchard, as well as by Kemble and Mrs Siddons. Mrs Bartley appears to have used a 'high declamatory tone' without success, according to the *Theatrical Inquisitor*. She lacked Mrs Siddons's 'flexibility of expression' as much as she lacked her dignity.[2] Partly as a matter of choice, partly as a matter of necessity, Kean does not seem to have allowed for the centrality of Lady Macbeth's role in Macbeth's tragedy. To Kean, Macbeth seems to have been responsible in isolation for his own tragedy. Kean is said to have remarked to Dame Madge Kendal's father that Macbeth, though initially 'Bellona's bridegroom' and the quintessence of bravery, having sinned, became a moral coward after the murder of Duncan, Banquo and Macduff's wife and children.[3]

When Kean and Mrs Bartley played Macbeth and Lady Macbeth on November 5, 1814, they were inevitably judged by standards which Kemble and Mrs Siddons had established together. Kean's initial conception of Macbeth as a dominating, brave, ruthless character, quite unlike Kemble's tortured stately thane, caused Hazlitt to say on November 13, 1814, that Kean, who had played Richard III with brilliant effectiveness, did not distinguish between the characters of Richard and Macbeth 'as completely as he might'. Hazlitt thought that Kean's Richard came 'nearer to the original than his Macbeth: Richard is not a character of imagination, but of pure will or passion. There is no conflict of opposite feelings in his breast. The apparitions which he sees are in his sleep, nor does he live like Macbeth, in a waking dream.'

Yet it was not merely Kean's initial conception of the character that failed to satisfy Hazlitt. Macbeth's poetic insights, and therefore Shakespeare's poetry, seem to have eluded Kean. 'He was deficient in the poetry of the character', wrote Hazlitt. 'In the delivery of the beautiful soliloquy "My way of life is fallen into the sear, the yellow leaf", Mr Kean was unsuccessful. That fine thoughtful melancholy did not seem to come over his mind,

[1] See H. N. Hillebrand, *Edmund Kean* (1933), p. 140.
[2] November 1814, p. 335.
[3] *Dame Madge Kendal by Herself* (1933), p. 7.

which characterises Mr Kemble's recitation of these lines. The very tone of Mr Kemble's voice has something retrospective in it —it is an echo of the past.'[1] A review in *The Times* of November 7, 1814, provides further evidence of Kean's failure to respond accurately to Shakespeare's poetry. During the soliloquy on judgement he 'wandered over those potent words as if they formed the mere preface to the lines that followed'. When he came to 'We still have judgement here', Kean, by pressing his hand on his heart at the closing 'here' gave the idea that he had 'mistaken for the warnings of conscience, the murderer's terror of the world's outcry'.

In *The Drama: or Theatrical Pocket Magazine*, one of Kean's most favourable critics found him 'generally inferior' to Young and Macready in his interpretation of the poetry of the soliloquies, even though during the first soliloquy his audience could read in Kean's eye 'the contrived murder his mind contemplates'. The critic thought that Kean did not, on the whole, deliver the soliloquies as inward 'cogitations of the mind': on the contrary he seemed to 'address them to the audience as speeches'.[2] As G. H. Lewes recognised, though Kean was an actor of 'genius' his range was 'very limited',[3] and watching him act was, in Coleridge's justly celebrated description, like reading Shakespeare by flashes of lightning. There were sudden illuminations and patches of darkness in Kean's acting.

A 'flash of lightning' occurred after the murder of Duncan. 'The hesitation, the bewildered look, the coming to himself when he sees his hands bloody; the manner in which his voice clung to his throat, and choked his utterance, his agony and tears, the force of nature overcome by passion—beggared description', wrote Hazlitt. 'It was a scene which no one who saw it can ever efface from his recollection'.[4]

The reviewer in *The Times* describes the reactions in the auditorium at Drury Lane, 'the unbreathing suspense' of the 'vast audience', the 'vehement applause that followed the actor's departure'. The dramatic critic of *The Times* thought that the 'voice broken by terror, inward torment and hopeless despair' was extraordinarily convincing.

[1] *Works*, VIII, 207.   [2] VI (1824), 6.
[3] *On Actors and the Art of Acting* (1875; paperback ed. 1957), p. 13.
[4] *Works*, VIII, 207.

Kean's interpretation of the scene was strikingly original. As the critic of the *Theatrical Inquisitor* observed:

Instead of beating violently on the door, and rushing on with gigantic strides, he crept on with the stealthy pace of fear, as if every faculty were for the time un-strung. When his timid eye first rested on Lady Macbeth, his frame was convulsed and wound up to the highest pitch of terror; even upon recognising her, he is but half-assured; in broken half-smothered tones, forced upon him by violent exertion and evident pain, he slowly stammers—'I have done the deed'. It was so terribly true to nature, that every heart and mind was electrified by the shock.[1]

Kean's interpretation of the scene after Duncan's murder was both naturalistic and illuminating. It throws light on his conception of Macbeth as 'Bellona's bridegroom' turned timorous.

When Kean re-entered in the third act the 'huge cloak in which he dressed the character of "King Macbeth" was from its magnitude entirely disproportionate to the slenderness of his figure . . .'[2] Kean may have wanted to enforce in visual terms the point made by Angus:

> Now does he feel his title
> Hang loose about him, like a giant's robe
> Upon a dwarfish thief. (v. ii. 20–2)

Dr Caroline Spurgeon was to draw the attention of critics in the twentieth century to the significance of this remark, in her analysis of the clothes imagery in *Macbeth*. Dr Spurgeon writes that the imaginative picture drawn by Angus of a 'small ignoble man encumbered and degraded by garments unsuited to him should be put against the view emphasised by some critics (notably Coleridge and Bradley) of the likeness between Macbeth and Milton's Satan in grandeur and sublimity'.[3] Shakespeare had a double vision of Macbeth, showing him both as Bellona's bridegroom, a heroic figure, and as a dwarfish thief, limited and treacherous. Kean seems to have wanted to draw the attention of his audience to the dark and limited side of Macbeth's character, in reaction possibly to Kemble. In the battle scenes he stressed the idea of the dwarfish thief again. John Finlay writes that the great

---

[1] November 1814, p. 336.
[2] John Finlay, *Miscellanies* (1835), p. 248.
[3] 'Leading Motives in the Imagery of Shakespeare's Tragedies', in *Shakespeare Criticism*, ed. Bradby, p. 35.

helmet which Kean wore for the battle in the fifth act, 'must by "its weight have galled his leaden brow" and by its height it appeared almost as tall as himself'.[1]

When Kean played Macbeth at a theatre in Lincoln, Dame Madge Kendal's father remembered another brilliant and startling interpretation, a good example of one of Kean's 'rapid descents from the hyper-tragic to the infra-colloquial'.[2] At Lincoln, Kean's voice 'rang like a clarion until the very rafters reverberated':

When Macbeth rushed on to the stage and spoke, 'Hang out our banners on the outward walls' he shouted the command in a voice like thunder. Suddenly he paused, dropped his double-handed sword to the ground and leaning on it whispered 'The cry is still they come, they come', at the same time seeming to become ashy grey with fear.[3]

Dame Madge Kendal's father thought Kean's interpretation of the lines 'startling in its revelation of his conception of the part'.

Kean's final touch of originality was in the last scene of the fifth act. Kean appears to have used a text no different from Garrick's or Kemble's, and he retained Garrick's dying speech for Macbeth. But his critics agreed that his interpretation of Macbeth's death was original and illuminating. 'His death was admirable', wrote the *Times* reviewer, 'full of that fine contrast of fierceness and feebleness, the spirit fighting while the body was perishing under mortal faintness...'[4] Hazlitt tells us that he 'fell at last finely, with his face downwards, as if to cover the shame of his defeat'.[5] Crabb Robinson describes Kean's interpretation in more detail: 'After falling he crawls on the floor to reach again his sword and dies as he touches it. This is no less excellent than his dying in Richard, but varied from it.'[6]

When Mrs Siddons was asked whether Kean reminded her at all of Garrick, she said: 'In some respect he does; he is forever energetic and often natural, which Garrick was *always*: and then he is short and sprightly; and like Garrick's his little frame seems constantly full of fire.'[7] Scott wrote that Kean revived the school of Garrick.[8] In fact, Kean lacked Garrick's range and his fine

[1] *Miscellanies*, p. 248.
[2] Samuel Taylor Coleridge, *Table Talk*, ed. T. Ashe (1888), p. 25.
[3] *Dame Madge Kendal by Herself*, p. 7.   [4] November 7, 1814.
[5] *Works*, VIII, 207.   [6] *Diary*, ed. Sadler, I, 241.
[7] See Mangin, *Piozziana*, p. 66.   [8] *Quarterly Review*, XXXIV (1826), 240.

decorum. Though Kean at his best managed, like Garrick, to make the heroic seem natural, there were moments when he seemed to be making 'points' rather than living his role, appealing to the sensational appetite. When Mrs Siddons remarked that Garrick was always natural, what she is likely to have meant was that Garrick was always apt. It was said of Mrs Siddons that on the stage she had 'the air of never being the actress'.[1] It could not be said of Kean that on the stage he had the air of never being the actor. Mrs Siddons 'did the greatest things with childlike ease', whereas Kean gave the impression of being 'all effort, all violence, all extreme passion'.[2] Kean appears to have been a child of a new age, an actor whom the new audiences could appreciate. As Hazlitt pointed out in February 1820, Kean's acting was not of 'the patrician order'. He was 'one of the people' and what might be termed 'a *radical* performer'.[3] Kean's 'radical' approach, however, was not adequate for Macbeth. To Leigh Hunt, who believed in Kean, and to Hazlitt, who once said that Kean's acting made him an apostate from the Kemble religion,[4] Kemble's interpretation of Macbeth seemed more satisfying.

Kean's costumes in Macbeth seem to have been patterned on John Kemble's: the Highland costume in the first two acts (see Plate 6) and the royal robes in the third, were of striking costliness and taste.[5] But he offered an interpretation of Macbeth's character that was radically opposed to Kemble's. For Kemble Macbeth, though touched in the end by fear, remained 'Bellona's bridegroom'. Kean saw the character much more in terms of disintegration.

After the first act of murder, Kean began his transformation of Macbeth into a moral coward, timorous, cowering at the touch of Lady Macbeth's hand. After the murder of Banquo, during the second appearance of Banquo's ghost, where Kemble had shown courage, Kean retreated from the ghost 'with head averted and in fear'.[6] As Malcolm advanced toward Dunsinane, Kean grew 'grey with fear', and he fell in the end 'with his face downward, as if to cover the shame of his defeat'.

Despite the novelty and force of Kean's conception, it was Kemble's interpretation of Macbeth that Leigh Hunt and Hazlitt

---

[1] See Leigh Hunt, *Critical Essays on the Performers of the London Theatres*, p. 18.
[2] Hazlitt, *Works*, VIII, 389.   [3] *Ibid*. 402.
[4] *Ibid*. 345.   [5] See *The Times*, November 7, 1814.
[6] See Finlay, *Miscellanies*, p. 282.

preferred. It was not that Kemble's patrician air in *Macbeth* was more contemporary than Kean's. Rather, Kemble in *Macbeth*, though not dissociated from the contemporary romantic climate, could still express a depth and range of poetic suggestion where Kean seemed to be merely hurried or unresponsive. It is possible that Kemble's idea of Macbeth as Bellona's tragic bridegroom could include more of the poetry of the play than Kean's more 'radical' conception of Macbeth, as a figure of courage turned into a moral coward.

Though Kemble appreciated propriety and decorum as much as Chesterfield or Pitt, his patrician air became less representative as England became more industrial and, with the increasing accumulation of men in cities, probably less secure and gracious. As the years passed, Cooke and Kean as actors seemed more 'contemporary' than Kemble. By 1814 Kean seemed more in tune with his time, though Kean at his best, like Kemble at his best, could bring the timeless and the temporal together. Kean brought new values into the theatre, and it seemed to Hunt and Hazlitt that he accomplished a revolution.

It would be a mistake to assume, however, that all traces of the 'Kemble religion' were wiped out. As late as March 17, 1838, the *Athenaeum* could report that 'Mr Young and Mr Vandenhoff are the only two whom we can, at this moment, call to mind as followers of the Kemble school; the former at a respectful—the latter at an immeasurable—distance'.[1] There was Charles Kemble as well, who helped to keep the old tradition alive.

Young had dignity and restraint and a voice 'full bodied, rich and powerful and capable of every variety of modulation'.[2] He was no mere elocutionist, however, and he could act. As Iago he won a remarkable tribute from Edmund Kean:

Everyone about me told me he could not hold a farthing rushlight to me; but he can! He *is* an actor; and though I flatter myself that he could not act Othello as I do, yet what chance should I have in Iago, after him, with his personal advantages and his d—— musical voice?[3]

Like Kemble, Young believed in achieving a unity of conception; but as Macbeth he did not succeed in projecting a fully realised

---

[1] P. 204.
[2] See Julian Charles Young, *A Memoir of Charles Mayne Young* (1871), p. 55.
[3] See William Clark Russell, *Representative Actors* (n.d.), p. 326.

character. Like Kean he failed in *Macbeth*, though unlike Kean he was remembered not for 'flashes of lightning' but for one exquisitely restrained moment. At one point in *Macbeth* Young achieved what critics at the end of the eighteenth century would have called 'chaste' acting. As Leigh Hunt wrote:

The awful description of night,

> 'Now o'er the one half world
> Nature seems dead, &c.'

[particularly when] it raises the figure of murder moving towards his design like a ghost, was perhaps the best delivered passage in the whole performance. It was full of the solemnity for which the lower tones of Mr Young are so excellently qualified, and he managed to give a personal character to the idea of the ghost, by just rising slowly and shrinkingly as if preparing to glide, without precisely acting the description which would have been unseasonable and unnatural.[1]

Hunt, interestingly enough, objected to Young's naturalistic pronunciation of 'oppresséd' in the dagger scene:

Mr Young also in that passage,

> 'a false creation
> Proceeding from the heat-oppressed brain'.

should not have shortened the word in *oppress'd*. The language has suffered enough already from these contractions, and we should at least preserve all the metre we can in our great poet. The wonderful difference of effect between the proper and the familiar pronunciation of this single word in a line so full of harsh syllables will be evident to everybody who reads it.[2]

Hunt preferred the 'proper' to the more 'familiar' naturalistic pronunciation because he believed that the virtue of propriety could yield dramatic and vivid results. The irony, of course, lies in the fact that Young, an actor of the Kemble school, which believed in propriety and decorum, should have at this point mistakenly sacrificed propriety to a naturalistic principle. The evidence provided by Hunt suggests that the dividing line between the school of Kemble and the school of Kean was sometimes blurred. In 1822, Young's preparation for the scene with the imaginary dagger, the prelude to Duncan's murder, was

---

[1] *Dramatic Criticism*, ed. Houtchens, p. 23.
[2] *Ibid.* pp. 22–3.

naturalistic, but here naturalism was probably more apt. He turned his eyes to 'the several parts of the hall in an inquisitive yet perturbed manner'. He then fixed them on the door that led to Duncan's chamber but turned from it 'as if it were the way to perdition: ...deeply agitated...his eyes wander unconsciously around, till suddenly, he fixes them on the air and starts'.[1] The paradox of the history of Macbeth interpretation in this period is that actors of the 'classical' school are largely remembered for their naturalistic effects in *Macbeth*.

Charles Kemble, known for his natural dignity and grace, his unstudied courtesy, the perfect modulation of his tones within the limits of a formal speech—Marston had not imagined, until he heard Kemble speak, that there could be so much charm in words as mere sounds[2]—introduced a new and naturalistic piece of business into the play before the murder of Duncan. Oxberry tells us that Charles Kemble's 'look and attitude' while listening at Duncan's chamber before the murder was a 'point' as 'excellent' as it was 'novel'. Oxberry thought that Kemble's Macbeth though 'unequal' was a 'talented' performance.[3]

It was Charles Kemble who, as Macbeth in 1809, 'threw the cup from him in the Banquet scene with such violence that it broke the arm of a glass chandelier, which stood on the table, and sent it very near to Mrs Siddons's face'. Mrs Siddons seems to have narrowly escaped injury though she 'sat as if she had been made of marble'.[4]

Both Charles Kemble and the elder Vandenhoff went on playing well into the age of Macready. In roles such as Macbeth and Othello, comments Westland Marston in 1838, Vandenhoff had no great intensity of passion 'but it was his power of facial expression, his excellent elocution, largeness of style and fine bearing that carried him through'.[5] If Kemble and Vandenhoff helped to control the excesses of the new romantic and naturalistic school, they did not themselves totally avoid naturalistic strategies, as Vandenhoff's interpretation of the dagger scene indicates. Here Vandenhoff created a naturalistic effect which was to be developed (very much as if he had known of it) by Phelps,

[1] *Theatrical Observer* (October 31, 1822). Quoted in Sprague, *Shakespeare and the Actors*, pp. 237–8.
[2] John Westland Marston, *Our Recent Actors* (2 vols. 1888), I, 113.
[3] *Dramatic Biography*, III, 10.   [4] See Genest, *Some Account*, VI, 338.
[5] *Our Recent Actors*, I, 22.

and brilliantly taken further by Henry Irving. On March 9, 1824, in the dagger scene, Vandenhoff

...seemed first to view the 'fantasy of his brain' slowly and reluctantly; he fixed his eye upon it until the image seemingly acquired a reality of existence in his bewildered and troubled mind; he shrunk from the belief of this reality, but still returned to it with a struggling conviction of its existence.[1]

Twenty years later, writes Sprague, a London newspaper printed a 'strikingly similar' description of Phelps, who, instead of staring at once when he saw the dagger 'kept his eyes fixed on the "painting of his fear"' until he came at length to accept its reality.[2] Irving's acting in this scene at first seemed disappointing

...but therein lay one of its chief excellencies. So much the apparition accorded with Macbeth's thought that he scarcely seemed to notice it ...It was not until the direction it took gave a practical hint of its terrible meaning, that the man became appalled and the true power of the actor became apparent.[3]

The history of the interpretation of Macbeth after Kemble and Kean suggests that the two traditions nurtured by them were not always kept rigidly apart.

[1] *Edinburgh Theatrical Observer*, quoted in Sprague, *Shakespeare and the Actors*, p. 238.
[2] *Lloyds Weekly London News*, September 27, 1947. Quoted in Sprague, *Shakespeare and the Actors*, p. 238. Cf. W. May Phelps and J. Forbes-Robertson, *The Life and Life-work of Samuel Phelps* (1886), p. 101.
[3] *Dramatic Review*, January 5, 1889. Quoted in Sprague, *Shakespeare and the Actors*, p. 238.

CHAPTER 8

MACREADY

From one point of view it would appear that Macready kept old traditions alive. Writing on October 13, 1849, the dramatic critic of the *Illustrated London News* felt that Macready was to be looked on rather 'as the last survivor of the old school of acting than as the head of the new'. By other observers he was thought to be a modernist. When Macready staged *The Patrician's Daughter*, by Westland Marston, he appeared to be anxious to invest the action with every detail of the most 'modern realism'. He wanted the players to carry and use parasols as they would in ordinary life. When Mrs Warner objected that 'blank verse and parasols' were 'quite a new combination', she was informed that the 'present time has its poetical aspect'.[1] When Macready played Macbeth, his approach seemed anti-heroic to Hazlitt and Lewes. 'Macbeth comes out a mere modern,' wrote Hazlitt, 'agitated by common sense and intelligible motives.'[2] George Henry Lewes felt that 'nothing could have been less heroic than Macready's presentation of the great criminal...he stole into the sleeping-chamber of Duncan like a man going to purloin a purse, not like a warrior going to snatch a crown.'[3]

John Forster took a different view of Macready's interpretation of Macbeth. On October 4, 1835, Forster wrote in the *Theatrical Examiner* that when Macready made his entrance as Macbeth, he was welcomed like 'the last of the tragic kings of our time returned to his proper dominion'. As Forster saw it, Macbeth's death, when Macready enacted it, had a heroic grandeur:

...Mr Macready's attitude in falling, when he thrusts his sword into the ground, and by its help for one moment raises himself to stare into the face of his opponent with a gaze that seemed to concentrate all Majesty, Hate and Knowledge, had an air of the preternatural, fit to close such a career.

[1] See Marston, *Our Recent Actors*, I, 285–6.
[2] *Works*, ed. Waller and Glover, XI, 315.
[3] *On Actors and the Art of Acting*, p. 41.

Macbeth's death had a non-human and preternatural quality, when Macready played the role. John Coleman wrote that the 'desperation of his final defiance of fate was appalling to witness. So might the fallen star of morning have confronted the archangel in the last dread conflict.'[1] Macready seems to have successfully brought out the theme of doomed evil in the play and expressed a suggestion contained in Malcolm's allusion to Macbeth:

> Angels are bright still, though the brightest fell.   (IV. iii. 22)

Clearly there were heroic elements in Macready's interpretation of Macbeth, but just as clearly there were moments when it seemed to contain anti-heroic realistic elements. It seemed to Leigh Hunt that at times Macready's modern and realistic approach made him lose sight of the troubled depths, the mysterious, strange life of Shakespeare's verse. In March 1831, Leigh Hunt felt that after his first entrance as Macbeth, Macready spoke the line

> So foul and fair a day I have not seen   (I. iii. 38)

—which significantly recalls the words of the witches: 'Fair is foul, and foul is fair' (I. i. 10)—'like a good-humoured conquering general looking cheerily up at the sky, and playing, as it were, with the harmless struggle of the elements'. Hunt could not agree that the words should be delivered 'like a mere commonplace'. He observed again that Macready spoke the richly expressive lines

> Light thickens, and the crow
> Makes wing to th' rooky wood   (III. ii. 50–1)

as merely intimating a fact—a note of time—pointing with his hand as he did it, as he might have pointed to a clock, to convince his witness of the truth of what he was saying. If Hunt is right, Macready spoke Macbeth's disturbing invocation to evil

> Good things of day begin to droop and drowse,
> Whiles night's black agents to their preys do rouse
>   (III. ii. 52–3)

with 'rapidity and indifference'.[2]

The evidence suggests that Macready's interpretation of Macbeth was both traditional and realistic, homely and heroic.

---

[1] 'Facts and Fancies about Macbeth', *Gentleman's Magazine* (March 1889), p. 223.
[2] *Dramatic Essays*, ed. Archer and Lowe, pp. 210–11.

Macready did not want anything like a clean break with the past. When he played Macbeth for the first time in London, at Covent Garden on June 9, 1820, the influence of the Kembles and Kean was still strong. It was but three years after Kemble's retirement and his interpretations lingered in the theatrical air, while Kean was unmistakably there, radical, sensational at times, yet at his best capable of supreme dignity. Kemble, and Kean in his most successful roles,[1] kept the heroic tradition alive. Macready absorbed what he could of the traditions established by them.[2] We know that when he played with Mrs Siddons in *The Gamester* at Newcastle, during the season of 1811–12, she applauded him from the wings, and told him he was 'in the right way'. Macready took note of the quality that distinguished all Mrs Siddons's portraits: their unity of design, the just relation of parts to the whole, which made her audiences forget the actress in the character she assumed. 'Her acting', wrote Macready, 'was a revelation to me, which ever afterwards had its influence on me in the study of my art.'[3]

Macready was not, then, as Hunt's account might suggest, totally insensitive to the virtues of the old tradition, but he was at the same time responsive to changes in contemporary life, to new currents of feeling, new attitudes. It has been said that the test of a first-rate intelligence is the ability to hold two opposed ideas in the mind, and still retain the capacity to function. Macready attempted to reconcile the heroic tradition with the new realism, and seems to have succeeded finally in achieving something coherent and unified, even though in the process the heroic tradition suffered some diminution.

This wholeness and unity of creation was the result of thirty years of endeavour. To Macready, the interpretation of character was an inductive process; it was like becoming acquainted with a person. This ceaselessly active and imaginative process of knowing a character went on over the years. After playing Hamlet, Macready could write on July 17, 1844:

It seems to me, as if only now, at fifty-one years of age, I thoroughly see and appreciate the artistic powers of Shakespeare in this great

[1] Richard III, Shylock, Othello.
[2] See *Illustrated London News* (October 13, 1849). 'The traditions of the stage cling to him, and his style is a compromise between the Kean and Kemble schools with some traces of Talma super-induced.'
[3] See *Reminiscences and Selections from his Diaries and Letters*, ed. Pollock, I, 55–8.

human phenomenon; nor do any of the critics, Goethe, Schlegel, Coleridge, present to me in their elaborate remarks, the exquisite artistical effects which I see in this work, as long meditation, like long straining after sight, gives the minutest portion of its excellence to my view.[1]

The entries in Macready's *Diaries* suggest that his encounter with Macbeth was of a similar kind. It was a long acquaintance, growing in intimacy and knowledge over the years. From the beginning one finds Macready groping for sincerity, for a real knowledge of the character. An entry made on January 2, 1833, twelve years after he had first played Macbeth, suggests that Macready is still unconvinced about the 'truth' of his interpretation:

I acted with much energy, but could not (as I sometimes can when holding the audience in wrapt attention) listen to my own voice and feel the truth of its tones. I was crude and uncertain, though spirited and earnest; but much thought is yet required to give an even energy and finished style to all the great scenes of the play, except perhaps, the last, which is among the best things I am capable of.[2]

In January 1834, Macready was still grappling with the character in an effort to achieve a genuine identification that could be felt on the pulse and along the heart. He was sharply self-critical:

...acted Macbeth in a very inferior manner; there was scarcely even reality, and very often positive affectation. A total absence of that directness of look, voice, and attitude, that tells to the actor far more truly than the thunders of an audience that he is possessed with his part...[3]

To the end of his life, Macready seems to have kept Mrs Siddons's injunction in mind—'You are in the right way, but remember what I say: study, study, study...'[4] and on September 2, 1835, after reading 'the sixth book of Milton' he went over the third act of *Macbeth* again:

My object is to increase the power and vigour of my performance, and to subdue all tendency to exaggeration of gesture, expression and deportment, to make more simple, more chaste, and yet more forcible and real, the passions and character I have to portray.[5]

[1] *Reminiscences*, II, 249.   [2] *Ibid.* II, 348–9.
[3] *Ibid.* I, 406.   [4] *Ibid.* I, 57.
[5] *Ibid.* I, 467.

It was not until 1840 that Macready seems to have been able to satisfy himself about the validity and coherence of his own interpretation of Macbeth. The entry, 'J'ai été le personnage', on April 26, 1840,[1] is reassuring. But it was not until February 26, 1850, the date chosen for his farewell performance, that Macready seems to have achieved an unalloyed enjoyment of the role, a full and rich realisation:

> ...acted Macbeth as I never, never before acted it, with a reality, a vigour, a truth, a dignity that I never before threw into my delineation of this favourite character. I felt everything, everything I did, and of course the audience felt with me. I rose with the play and the last scene was a real climax.[2]

The entry of February 26, 1850, contains no self-delusive fancy. Macready had satisfied himself as well as his audience. Bulwer Lytton, speaking at a farewell dinner to the actor, asserted that Macready's last interpretation of Macbeth conveyed 'a more exact notion of what Shakespeare had designed than he could recollect to have read in the most profound of the German critics'. Speaking about Macready's method, Bulwer Lytton pointed out, '...we do not much say "How well this was spoken, or how finely that was acted", but we feel within ourselves how true was the personation of the whole...'[3] How 'exact' Macready's notion of Shakespeare's design in *Macbeth* was, and how true his personation of the whole character, can be arrived at by reconstructing the details of his interpretation.

In Macready's production, before Macbeth's entrance the curtain rose on foggy darkness. With the entry of the witches the light increased gradually. As the witches spoke, an off-stage march began softly, on the right. The Weird Sisters danced, the lights continued to rise, and the mist dissolved slowly, revealing a barren heath.[4] The highland landscape revealed, as the mist lifted, was a barren rocky heath, with two gaunt trees in the background and a mountain range in the distance, a perspective effect

---

[1] *Reminiscences*. II, 177.   [2] *Ibid*. II, 368.
[3] See *ibid*. II, 376.
[4] See Alan S. Downer, 'Macready's Production of Macbeth', *Quarterly Journal of Speech* (April 1947), pp. 172–3. Professor Downer bases his reconstruction on Macready's prompt book, dated 1821, at Princeton University Library, and on contemporary descriptions.

possible on the deep stage at Covent Garden. In the foreground, at the same time, a primitive bridge was revealed.[1]

Macbeth's army came first into sight and Macbeth's voice was heard before the audience saw him:[2]

> Command they make a halt upon the heath.

Macready retained Davenant's line in his stage text, as Garrick and Kemble had done before him. The sky was dappled with pale white and ominous black clouds,[3] as Macbeth entered, crossed the rustic bridge at stage centre, and moved towards the footlights.[4] The rustic bridge, the highland landscape, Macready's costume and make-up helped to give him a primitive air. A black wig, a clipped beard and moustache outlined his face. He wore a tam-o-shanter with a single feather, a plaid scarf over his shoulder, a knee-length kilt-like garment, open sandals, a dagger, sword, round shield, and carried a baton in his right hand.[5]

'He looked like one who had communed with himself among his native mountains',[6] wrote Lady Pollock, giving the impression that Macready created a character Wordsworth would have understood. Coleman, with Kemble probably in mind, thought that there was 'little of "Bellona's bridegroom"' about Macready's Macbeth 'when he made his first appearance upon the blasted heath'. As Coleman saw him he was 'simply a rugged, semi-barbaric chief, a being of another age; a man physically brave, but eerie and superstitious; a believer...in all the mysteries of second sight'.[7]

Macready gave the impression of subdued power in the first act.[8] And though Leigh Hunt observed that he looked 'cheerily' up at the sky when he spoke the words,

> So foul and fair a day I have not seen   (1. iii. 38)

when Coleman saw him, Macready appears to have glanced at the sky and spoken the line with 'a guttural growl'.[9] Though there

---

[1] See George Scharf jr, *Recollections of the Scenic Effects of Covent Garden Theatre* (n.d.), '*Macbeth*, Act 1, Scene i'.
[2] Downer, p. 173.   [3] See Plate 7.
[4] Downer, p. 173. See Scharf, '*Macbeth*, Act 1, Scene i'.
[5] See engraving after a painting by Tracey (Enthoven Collection).
[6] *Macready as I Knew Him* (1885), pp. 117–18.
[7] 'Facts...about Macbeth', *Gentleman's Magazine*, p. 221.
[8] *Literary Gazette* (June 17, 1820), p. 397.
[9] 'Facts...about Macbeth', p. 222.

was the elation of a soldier 'flushed with victory'[1] about him
when he first entered, 'martial and erect',[2] this mood swiftly
changed as the witches hailed him, each pointing with a crooked
finger.[3] Macready turned towards them in surprise, his left hand
clutching at his plaid scarf, his mouth slightly open, his eyes wide
(see Plate 7). As the dramatic critic of the *Theatrical Journal* saw it
in 1842: 'The Witches stop him, a rejoicing conqueror on the
blasted heath. Immediately he becomes an altered man; the shadow of destiny has fallen on and darkened him, and from that
moment he is dragged, inexorably dragged towards Duncan's
chamber.'[4] To Coleman, 'from that moment onwards, Fate and
metaphysical aid seemed to surround him with death and doom'.[5]
When the witches began to withdraw, Macready crossed over to
them[6] saying, 'Stay, you imperfect speakers', curt and yet disturbed.[7]

Macready was left alone for his first soliloquy after Ross and
Angus arrived with the news that Macbeth had been made Thane
of Cawdor. Banquo moved apart to confer with them,[8] a piece of
business conceived originally by Garrick.[9] Macready began with
an air of 'brooding revery',[10] his mind haunted by the prediction
of the witches.[11] At

> This supernatural soliciting
> Cannot be ill; (I. iii. 130–1)

he 'seemed to be endeavouring to deceive himself'. He continued
the line in 'a startled and hurried fashion' as if 'a thought of
indefinable evil shot through his mind'—

> —cannot be good.—[12] (I. iii. 131)

He was shaken by dark emotions. One 'could instinctively
realise', wrote Coleman, 'that the horrid image that unfixed his
hair and made his seated heart knock at his ribs...was the gory
image of the gracious Duncan, his white hair dabbled in blood'.[13]

[1] *Theatrical Journal*, I (1840), 277–9.
[2] Marston, *Our Recent Actors*, I, 76.
[3] Downer, *Quarterly Journal of Speech*, p. 173.   [4] III, 106.
[5] 'Facts...about Macbeth', *Gentleman's Magazine*, p. 222.
[6] Downer, p. 173.   [7] *Ibid.*
[8] *Ibid.*   [9] See above, p. 41.
[10] Marston, I, 75.   [11] *Theatrical Journal*, I, 277.
[12] *New York Mirror*, IV (October 14, 1826), 95.
[13] 'Facts...about Macbeth', p. 222.

Recalled to his senses, Macready spoke to his friends with 'over-done warmth'.[1] The martial music resumed as he ordered them towards the king, and the curtain fell on a general exit.

Before the curtain rose again the music shifted to a royal march. The royal procession entered from stage right. Duncan, with two chamberlains, moved towards the centre of the stage, Malcolm and Donalbain crossed to the left, Ross and the physician moved down right, and three officers grouped themselves behind the king. After Malcolm delivered his report on the death of Cawdor, a second procession entered on the left: Macduff and Lennox, who crossed to the right, Macbeth and Banquo and six lords, one of whom, carrying two banners, knelt down and placed them at the king's feet. This was Macready's statement, as director, of the theme of royal power: and when the king created Malcolm Prince of Cumberland (heir to the throne) Macready showed agitation and bewilderment. When the king moved up-stage with his courtiers, Macbeth was isolated for his comment on the scene:[2]

> Stars, hide your fires... (I. iv. 50)

The next scene shifted to Dunsinane. Lady Macbeth entered reading a letter and Macbeth entering, embraced her[3] (an interesting survival from Garrick's production). While Lady Macbeth continued to speak, Macready showed restlessness, his lips moved involuntarily, and the words

> My dearest love,
> Duncan comes here to-night (I. v. 55–6)

burst from him.[4] The dramatic critic of the *New York Mirror* described the way in which Macready answered Lady Macbeth's question, 'And when goes hence?' (I. v. 57). His answer came at once—'To-morrow', spoken quickly, 'as if stating a fact.' Then came 'the pause, the look, the sinking of the voice. The slow and conscious manner of adding "as he purposes", spoke volumes.'[5] The dramatic critic of the *Theatrical Journal* thought that the pause after 'To-morrow', and the sequel, seemed to indicate Macbeth's awareness of the fact that 'his wife *guessed at his thought* but saw his want of resolution to do the deed'.[6]

---

[1] Marston, *Our Recent Actors*, I, 75. [2] Downer, p. 174.
[3] *Ibid.* [4] *New York Mirror*, IV, 95.
[5] *Ibid.* [6] I, 278.

After Duncan's arrival at Dunsinane, the scene for the banquet in his honour was set at night. A lamp burned in a room in the castle, and at the back of the stage was an entrance beyond which servants passed from right to left, carrying torches and dishes of food. It was through the rear door that Macbeth entered, thinking about the murder of Duncan[1] with a 'tremulous expression of horror of himself':[2]

> If it were done, when 'tis done, 'twere well.
> It were done quickly...[3]

Macready, like Kemble, made 'It were done quickly...' a separate sentence and not joined to the previous line. When the images of pity crowded into Macbeth's brain:

> And pity, like a naked new-born babe,
> Striding the blast, or heaven's cherubin hors'd
> Upon the sightless couriers of the air,
> Shall blow the horrid deed in every eye,
> That tears shall drown the wind   (I. vii. 21–5)

Macready gave them utterance in what seemed like an 'irrepressible wail of agony'.[4] At the end of the soliloquy there came one of his celebrated contrasts of tone. After 'rising to heaven' on the words

> Vaulting ambition, which o'er-leaps itself,
> And falls on th' other   (I. vii. 27–8)

'he dropped to the earth with a growl':[5]

> How now! What news?   (I. vii. 28)

To us in the 1960s, Macready's interpretation of the soliloquy on judgement might seem mannered, but in his own day the dramatic critic of the *New Monthly Magazine* thought that Macready spoke the soliloquy with 'uncommon vigor and freshness', with 'naturalness and spontaneity...as if thought were suggesting thought'.[6]

After Lady Macbeth entered, Macready spoke the lines

> We will proceed no further in this business.
> He hath honour'd me of late   (I. vii. 32–3)

---

[1] Downer, p. 175.   [2] *New York Mirror*, IV, 95.
[3] *Theatrical Journal*, I, 278.
[4] Coleman, 'Facts...about Macbeth', p. 222.
[5] *Ibid.* p. 223.   [6] December 1, 1827.

in 'an expostulatory manner'.[1] When Lady Macbeth poured scorn on what seemed to her mere weakness, Macready, pre-occupied, taut—'I dare do all that may become a man' (I. vii. 46) —crossed abruptly to the left, saying 'Who dares do more is none' (I. vii. 47). At the end of the scene, music, beginning quietly, rose to a crescendo as Macbeth left the stage.[2]

The opening scenes of the second act were played in a courtyard at Dunsinane. The set was a walled square, with a main arched entrance under a heavy tower up-stage centre, and two smaller doors down-stage, on the left leading to Duncan's apartment, on the right to Macbeth's. When the curtain rose the lights were dimmed.[3]

After Banquo and Fleance entered and left the courtyard, Macbeth, 'having sent Seyton off right with a touch of almost paternal consideration',[4] remained alone and silent 'like a man on the verge of fate'.[5]

It was at this point that Macready saw the dagger 'wavering in the air'.[6] He did not 'start according to prescribed rule' at the sight of the dagger when Charles Durang saw him play, but kept his eye fixed constantly on the imagined object, at length drawing his own dagger.[7] The early part of the soliloquy, wrote Forster, was 'majestic' and created awe, but the lines immediately before the murder were spoken with an expression of imaginative terror.[8] As he came to the end of the soliloquy the bell struck twice. In an almost imploring voice Macready cried

> Hear hear it not Duncan, for it is a knell,
> That summons thee to heaven or to hell.[9]

Macready's exit into Duncan's room excited a great deal of comment in his day. Coleman wrote:

Had not one been entirely carried away by the cunning of the scene, his exit into Duncan's chamber must have excited derision. Up to that moment he had reached the highest pitch of tragic horror, but his

[1] *New York Mirror*, IV, 95.   [2] Downer, p. 175.
[3] *Ibid.*   [4] *Ibid.*
[5] *Theatrical Examiner* (October 4, 1835).
[6] Sprague, *Shakespeare and the Actors*, p. 239.
[7] *The Philadelphia Stage*, chapter 32 (scrapbook, Harvard College Library Theatre Collection). Quoted in Downer, p. 175. Cf. *John Bull* (May 26, 1839).
[8] *Theatrical Examiner* (October 4, 1835).
[9] *Spectator* (November 11, 1837). See Downer, p. 175. (The text here is Macready's.)

desire to over-elaborate made him pause, and when his body was actually off the stage, his left foot and leg remained trembling in sight, it seemed, fully half a minute.[1]

Lewes thought that Macready looked like a common thief going to purloin a purse, but Westland Marston wrote that Macready's 'crouching form and stealthy felon-like step' as he entered Duncan's room made 'a picture not to be forgotten'. Marston felt that Macready was making a point and making it well, when he made Macbeth look like a common thief. 'In contrast with the erect, martial figure that entered in the first act, this change was the moral of the play made visible.'[2] The dramatic critic of the *New York Mirror*, who had obviously not read Lewes, observed that Macready's 'stealthy manner of stealing into Duncan's chamber was universally admired'.[3]

After the murder of Duncan, Macready rushed on to the stage clasping the blood-stained daggers, his face pale with fear, his limbs trembling, his tongue whispering the question

> ...Didst thou not hear a noise?　　　　(II. ii. 14)

Macready's interpretation appears to have convinced his audiences that it was 'a dread reality they beheld and not a mimic scene'.[4] Like Kemble before him he appears to have created a Macbeth 'touching in crime', though more primitive in his responses. When the knocking at the door began he buried his face in his hands, and

> Wake Duncan with thy knocking! I would thou couldst!　(II. ii. 74)

was a 'savage howl'.[5] Westland Marston remembered him 'as with his face averted from his wife, and his arms outstretched as it were to the irrecoverable past, she dragged him from the stage'.[6]

The Porter scene was omitted in Macready's production, as it had been omitted by Kemble and Garrick. There was no relaxation of tension. Macready re-entered in a flowered dressing-gown to face Macduff and Lennox, continuing the tradition begun by Garrick. Pückler Muskau saw Macbeth's steel armour glitter beneath the gown when he witnessed a performance by Macready which otherwise impressed him. He disliked the gown because it

---

[1] 'Facts...about Macbeth', p. 223.　　[2] *Our Recent Actors*, I, 76–7.
[3] IV, 95.　　[4] *Theatrical Journal*, I, 278.
[5] *Political and Literary Journal* (October 13, 1849). Quoted in Downer, p. 176.
[6] *Our Recent Actors*, I, 78.

seemed too fashionable and contemporary and did not effectively conceal Macbeth's armour.[1] More significantly perhaps, the fashionable dressing-gown clashed with Macready's own conception of Macbeth's character as primitive rather than sophisticated.

After the murder of Duncan was discovered, the alarm bell tolled through twenty lines, and ceased as Macduff explained to Malcolm and Donalbain that their father was dead. Macbeth repented of the murder of the guards, speaking the lines

> O, yet I do repent me of my fury
> That I did kill them   (II. iii. 105–6)

'very quick'.[2]

In the brief scene with Lady Macbeth (III. ii.), after he succeeds Duncan to the throne, Macready brought out Macbeth's sense of loss—the tragedy of his success. Coleman tells us that Macready re-created the 'dull, leaden despair'[3] of Macbeth when he spoke of the dead king:

> Duncan is in his grave;
> After life's fitful fever he sleeps well...   (III. ii. 22–3)

Marston describes the way in which Macready brought out the increasing moral isolation of Macbeth, turning away from Lady Macbeth with a 'furtive' glance and a 'sinister ill-suppressed laugh'[4] on:

> Be innocent of the knowledge, dearest chuck,
> Till thou applaud the deed.   (III. ii. 45–6)

The 'dull' despair, the 'furtive' look suggest again that Macready was portraying a primitive hero, sensitive, yet unsophisticated in his responses. One is reminded again of Hazlitt's comment on Macready's interpretation of Macbeth. Natural expression, human feeling seemed 'to woo him like a bride', but the ideal beckoned him only at a distance.[5]

The banquet scene was grand and spectacular: the tables piled high with fruit, gorgeous dish-covers glittering in endless perspective. Music added to the 'high festivity'. The music stopped

---

[1] *Briefe eines Verstorbenen* (4 vols. 1831), IV, 263: *Tour in England*, trans. Sarah Austin (4 vols. 1832), IV, 248.
[2] Downer, p. 176.   [3] 'Facts...about Macbeth', p. 222.
[4] *Our Recent Actors*, I, 79.   [5] *Works*, ed. Waller and Glover, XI, 315.

as Macbeth came down to the centre table among his guests, and the gaiety must have been shadowed for a moment as Macbeth moved forward towards the footlights to talk to the murderer.[1]

The ghost entered through a trap, hidden by the gathering servants. When the servants moved away, Lennox pointed to the chair in which the ghost sat, requesting Macbeth to sit down. Banquo, 'pale as chalk', with a gash across his throat, turned slowly to face Macbeth. When Macbeth cried out

Which of you have done this?　　　(III. iv. 48)

all noise and festivity ceased.[2] Where Garrick had shown fear and then a wild courage, Macready showed fear and then courage, followed by a lapse into fear again. At first he shuddered and trembled, shielding his eyes from a sight that seemed to burn them.[3] But when Lady Macbeth crossed down to him from her throne saying,

Are you a man?

and tried to restore his courage—

You look but on a *chair*,[4]

Macbeth seemed to regain control over himself, his voice hardened, his body tensed, and he looked boldly at the ghost as it rose, moving slowly backward and off the stage.[5] Macready's interpretation of Macbeth's response to the second appearance of the ghost was much written about in his day. When it made its second appearance, the ghost entered stage left and not through the trap. Macready looked at the ghost with petrified horror 'as if the sight had frozen every faculty'.[6] The dramatic critic of the *New York Mirror* thought that Macready's manner of shrinking from the ghost was an innovation[7]—though it was probably inspired by Edmund Kean.[8] Macready seems to have elaborated effectively on Kean's strategy, however, falling into his chair and 'convulsively burying his head in his mantle, as if to shut out sight, sense and recollection'.[9] After the ghost and the guests had gone, Macready, as Macbeth, regaining something of his old spirit, laid

---

[1] See Downer, p. 177.　　　[2] *Ibid.*
[3] *Literary Gazette* (June 17, 1820).　　　[4] Macready's text.
[5] *New Mirror* (December 9, 1843). Quoted in Downer, p. 178.
[6] *New York Mirror*, IV, 95.　　　[7] IV, 95.
[8] See above, chapter 7, p. 149.
[9] *New York Mirror*, IV, 95. Cf. *Papers on Acting*, ed. Matthews, p. 93.

plans for the defence of his shaky position in 'a new and hardened manner'. To one critic this was a turning point in the play, the point at which Macbeth seemed to swing round from 'soft to stern'.[1] Once again in the third act Macready portrayed a man swayed by emotions primitive in their force and variety.

The cauldron scene in the fourth act and the entrance and exit of Hecate were excellently directed by Macready, who showed in this, as in other scenes, a fine sense of timing and a brilliant, pure theatricality.[2] When he entered as Macbeth after the sleep-walking scene in the fifth act he played the primitive hero again, showing haughty self-confidence and contempt for his opponent, drawing back his head, with a curl of his lip at

What's the boy Malcolm?[3] (v. iii. 3)

When Macbeth was told a moment later that the English were moving towards Dunsinane, Macready portrayed a change of emotion that was swift and sudden, though predictable and consistent with the character that he had created, detail by detail. At

I have liv'd long enough... (v. iii. 22)

he made Macbeth look suddenly 'cheerless'. There was 'a deep melancholy pathos in his voice, and his whole frame seemed to become as relaxed and nerveless as his mind'.[4] Later on, as Macbeth called for his armour and addressed the Doctor at the same time, Macready employed a change of tone which was implicit in Shakespeare's lines, even though Marston could not quite accept 'the much celebrated transition from the impetuous command to Seyton, "Give me mine armour", to the ultra-colloquial, "How does your patient, doctor?"'[5]

In the next scene, when Macbeth entered, with Seyton and some of his soldiers, his courage wound up to the highest pitch, he was first shaken by the crying of women and then by the news of Lady Macbeth's death. The baton fell from Macready's hand, a piece of business suggesting the sudden onset of grief, the muscles of his face seemed to slacken[6] as he began to speak,

There would have been a time for such a word... (v. v. 18)

[1] *New Mirror*. Quoted in Downer, p. 178.
[2] See Downer, pp. 178–9. [3] *New York Mirror*, IV, 95.
[4] *Ibid.* [5] *Our Recent Actors*, I, 79.
[6] *Examiner* (May 2, 1846). Quoted in Sprague, *Shakespeare and the Actors*, p. 274.

Macready paused after 'word', and there was a slight break in his voice after the first syllable in 'To-morrow', when, as if suddenly struck with the thought that followed, he went rapidly through the whole passage. The dramatic critic of the *New York Mirror* remembered that this was not the 'slow and moralizing delivery' they had been used to.[1] Macbeth steeped from head to heel in blood, to obtain the glories of the earth, descanted on their nothingness in a voice of chill despair and a look of blank desolation. To the dramatic critic of the *Theatrical Journal* Macready's interpretation of the lines brought out their moral significance, 'wholly unforced and unobtrusive', but there.[2]

When the Messenger brought the news that Birnam Wood was moving, however, there was a sudden change of mood, startling but predictable. Macready roared, 'Liar and slave!' half-drawing his sword over the trembling form of the Messenger, who fell on his knees in fright.[3] As the news sank in, for a second time Macbeth seemed to waver in irresolution, but recovered sufficiently to end the scene with a ringing defiance of his foes.[4]

After the English army marched on to the stage, each man screened by an immense bough—a scene effectively directed by Macready, as Downer shows[5]—the stage was set for the climactic encounter between Macbeth and Macduff. The duel took place on the ramparts of the castle with a great iron gate in the background.

The iron gate had a definite function for it was burst open with a tremendous shout as Macduff rushed on, crying

Turn, hell-hound, turn.[6]   (v. viii. 3)

Driving Macduff back, Macready stood holding up his sword with careless ease, secure in the illusion that he was invulnerable. When the illusion was shattered by Macduff, Macready stood in breathless horror like 'one who looks on a wild beast about to devour him', every muscle suddenly relaxed.[7] At 'I'll not fight with thee', Macready retreated 'cowardly towards his castle' and then stood at bay[8] looking himself like a cornered and dangerous

---

[1] IV, 95.   [2] III, 106.

[3] *Tallis's Dramatic Magazine* (November 1850). Quoted in *Shakespeare and the Actors*, p. 277.

[4] Downer, p. 180.   [5] *Ibid.* Cf. *Shakespeare and the Actors*, pp. 273–4.

[6] See Downer, p. 180.   [7] *New Monthly Magazine* (December 1, 1827).

[8] *Theatrical Journal*, I, 279; Marston, *Our Recent Actors*, I, 79.

animal; he crouched like a tiger for his last deadly spring on Macduff.[1] Nobility seemed to return to Macbeth, as Macready played him, after he received his death-wound. 'Nothing can possibly be grander', wrote Forster, 'than his manner of returning, with that regal stride, after he has received his mortal thrust, to fall again on Macduff's sword in yielding weakness.' After he had fallen, wounded, Macready thrust his sword into the ground and raised himself by its help to his knees, staring 'into the face of his opponent with a gaze that seemed to concentrate all Majesty, Hate and Knowledge'[2] falling down again in death, as Malcolm and his thanes entered. Hunt declared that any actor of ability could portray individual passions but that only an actor of genius could show their gradations—'It is not in simple passions but in their gradations and changes that the actor is most admirable.'[3] And Macready, as Lady Pollock writes, was 'a master in the gradations of passion. He knew well how to raise an emotion by degrees to its full height, and had the skill to fill the cup of anguish drop by drop till it overflowed.'[4] Macready had demonstrated this ability in the last scene without the assistance of Garrick's dying speech, which both Kemble and Kean had retained.

Forster thought that Macready's greatest achievement was in the fifth act, in which he played magnificently from its commencement to its close.[5] The main elements of Macready's interpretation were concentrated in the fifth act—the animal ferocity and the sensitiveness, the courage and cowardice, the assurance and the insecurity, the primitive impulsiveness and dignity of his Macbeth. Decorous and conventional though he was off the stage, while on it Macready seems to have discovered his primitive, hidden self. Macready's conception of Macbeth's character, which seems to have been that of 'the noble savage', helped him to bring these opposed elements together in a convincing way. While Kemble's Macbeth was more noble than savage, Macready's was more savage than noble. Macready created a character which the new audiences in the London theatres[6] could believe in.

[1] *Theatrical Journal*, III, 106. [2] *Examiner* (October 4, 1835).
[3] *Dramatic Criticism*, ed. Houtchens, p. 220.
[4] *Macready as I Knew Him*, pp. 104. [5] *Examiner* (October 4, 1835).
[6] Audiences not at all sophisticated according to Pückler Muskau. See description of Macready's production of *Macbeth* in *Briefe eines Verstorbenen*, IV, 263; *Tour in England*, IV, 248.

As Leigh Hunt demonstrated, Macready certainly neglected the poetry of some of Shakespeare's finest passages in an effort to create a character that his contemporaries could understand, but the neglect was not, like Charles Kean's, total. Macready's interpretation of the poetry of the murder scene and the fifth act shows that he could express character through Shakespeare's poetry, not by battling against it. Though Fanny Kemble accused Macready of chopping Shakespeare's verse into prose,[1] Bulwer Lytton held rather a different view. Speaking during the dinner to Macready after his last performance as Macbeth, he remarked that Macready had done more than accomplish the essential graces of the actor— the look, the gesture, the intonation, the stage play; he had placed his study far deeper. He had sought, said Bulwer Lytton, to penetrate the subtle intentions of the poet and make poetry the key to the secrets of the human heart.[2] It must be supposed that Macready succeeded at times in doing just this. Shakespeare's intention in *Macbeth* was to penetrate beneath the surface of things and reveal their inner nature. Clearly there were moments in Macready's performance when he understood this intention and carried it out.

Macready played with many Lady Macbeths throughout his career. All of them, with the possible exception of Helen Faucit, dwindled in the shadow of Mrs Siddons's Lady Macbeth. Those who tried to realise her conception afresh could not match her complexity, or achieve the same union of grandeur without pomp, and nature without triviality. George Fletcher, who could not agree with her interpretation, wrote in 1847 that the most respectable efforts since her time 'had never amounted to anything beyond a vastly inferior expression of Mrs Siddons's conception of the character, to which the stage, as well as the audience, were accustomed to bow with a sort of religious faith and awe'.[3] When Fletcher wrote, however, that Mrs Siddons's Lady Macbeth was really 'an impassive heroine of antique tragedy',[4] though it was not a good description of Mrs Siddons's interpretation, it described what her imitators were doing.

Helen Faucit attempted a fresh interpretation as Fletcher had

---

[1] *Records of Later Life* (3 vols. 1882), III, 376.
[2] *Reminiscences*, ed. Pollock, II, 376.
[3] *Studies of Shakespeare*, p. 196.　　　　[4] *Ibid*. p. 193.

hoped she would, and Fanny Kemble had some interesting new ideas about the character, though she wrote of them more effectively than she re-created them on the stage; but Macready himself seems to have preferred imitations of Mrs Siddons rather than the more novel approaches, which did not suit his own interpretation. Macready seems to have preferred the probably grand, though not always natural Lady Macbeth of Mrs Warner to the affectionate, natural and civilised Lady Macbeth of Helen Faucit. Both Macready and Phelps assured Coleman that Mrs Warner was '*the* Lady Macbeth, the only possible one since Siddons'.[1]

Mrs Warner played opposite Macready at the beginning of his career and at the end of it, when he gave his last interpretation of Macbeth. Macready obviously did think Mrs Warner's interpretation harmonised best with his own conception, even though her Lady Macbeth was a creation of the will rather than of the imagination. 'There was all the difference between it and a genuine conception arrived at and expressed by the understanding', wrote Marston, making a distinction Stanislavsky would have appreciated. Mrs Warner's Lady Macbeth was 'a character seized by the will and inspired with its energy'.[2]

Mrs Warner's traditionalism was willed rather than felt, and while she remembered Mrs Siddons's grandeur, she had little of her variety of tone. As Marston tells us, Mrs Warner made a declamatory attempt in the first scene to realise the supernatural, but there was no real awe. In the later scenes she was dignified and remorseful, and the solemnities of the sleep-walking scene were punctiliously rendered with all the time-honoured traditions, but she lacked depth, incisiveness, the interchange of the shifting moods of emotion, and the ability to communicate different shades of the same emotion. Mrs Warner lacked the infinite variety of Mrs Siddons and yet, says Marston, there was such 'a constant *physique* of Lady Macbeth' in her delineation, and 'such a propriety in her somewhat surface exhibition of the character that she was held for years to be its most satisfactory representative'.[3]

If Mrs Warner made no conscious attempt to depart from the main lines of interpretation laid down by Mrs Siddons, neither did Miss Cushman. And, like Mrs Warner, Miss Cushman seems to have pleased Macready. When he first played opposite her, in

---

[1] 'Facts...about Macbeth', p. 224.
[2] *Our Recent Actors*, I, 276.   [3] *Ibid.* 277.

New York in October 1843, he found her aware and responsive to his strategy: '...Miss Cushman who acted Lady Macbeth interested me much. She has to learn her art, but she showed mind and sympathy with me; a novelty so refreshing to me on the stage.'[1] Miss Cushman concentrated on those elements in Mrs Siddons's interpretation which she found congenial, bringing out the dark grandeur of Lady Macbeth, but not her variety of feeling. Marston found that Miss Cushman's 'unrelieved, level earnestness of manner' gave her Lady Macbeth 'a sameness of gloom which fatigued admiration'. Marston writes that she lacked the 'quick careless strokes' of Mrs Betterton which Cibber had spoken of with so much delight. Miss Cushman's acting in *Macbeth* 'had the effect of one of those scenes in which land and water lie beneath a dense sky. You hear the hoarse breaking of the tide, but are not roused from the pervading gloom by the sudden flash and peal of the storm.'[2]

Charlotte Cushman's acting had power, of a direct and unavoidable kind, though it lacked variety. The power of Helen Faucit's art was less direct, more subtle, more original. Yet Macready probably preferred working with Charlotte Cushman and Mrs Warner. Helen Faucit's originality could have endangered the logic of his own interpretation of Macbeth, as remarks made by Fletcher show. When Fletcher asked for a new conception of Lady Macbeth—which he thought Helen Faucit was suited for—and a totally new conception of Macbeth to harmonise with it, one of his principal targets must clearly have been Macready.

To Fletcher, writing in 1847, it seemed that Macbeth, 'the most poetical of selfishly ambitious assassins', had been mistakenly transformed into a 'sentimental butcher' on the contemporary stage. Fletcher argued that to make Macbeth a victim of destiny, driven by supernatural forces and by a commanding woman, was a moral evasion, a distortion of Shakespeare's intention: 'The mighty artist wasted not his moralizing on persuading inherent villainy to be honest; he expended it more profitably, in teaching the honest man to see through the fairest visor of the incurable knave.' Fletcher saw Lady Macbeth, not as Mrs Siddons saw her, a woman driven by the pride of ambition, but as a tragic victim, torn by the 'continual *struggle*, between her compunction for the

---

[1] *Reminiscences*, II, 219.
[2] Sprague, *Shakespeare and the Actors*, p. 232.

criminal act, and her devotion to her husband's ambitious purpose'. This 'conscious struggle', wrote Fletcher, 'should give to the opening invocation

> "Come, come you spirits
> That tend on mortal thoughts," &c.—

a *tremulous* anxiety as well as earnestness of expression'.

Fletcher was sharply critical of what he must have believed to be the moral evasion involved in Macready's conception of Macbeth, as a creature trapped by destiny. Fletcher wanted a quite unsympathetic Macbeth, attracted to the pursuit of a selfishly and criminally ambitious object, whose career was 'destructive to the nearest domestic ties as to political and social security'. Fletcher's tragic victim was not Macbeth but Lady Macbeth. He appears to have been looking for a tragic heroine rather than a tragic hero, and he found her in Helen Faucit.

When Helen Faucit played Lady Macbeth, Fletcher wrote that at last Mrs Siddons's grand but mistaken vision of Lady Macbeth had been overthrown. He was referring exclusively to Mrs Siddons's stage portrait, and not to her essay on the character. Mrs Siddons's essay, it will be recalled, contained the stray suggestion that Shakespeare may have intended Lady Macbeth to be beautiful, even fragile. Helen Faucit seems to have developed this idea in a logical and imaginative way. As Fletcher wrote, after her performance of Lady Macbeth, Helen Faucit's

> ...possession of that *essentially feminine person* which we have seen Mrs Siddons herself contending for as Shakespeare's own idea of Lady Macbeth—together with that energy of intellect and of will, which this personation equally demands—have enabled her to interpret the character with a convincing truth of nature and of feeling, more awfully thrilling than the imposing but less natural, and therefore less impressive grandeur of Mrs Siddons' representation. Her performance, in short, would seem to have exhibited to her audience—not the 'fiend' that Mrs Siddons presented to her most ardent admirers—but the far more interesting picture of a naturally generous woman, depraved by her very self-devotion to the ambitious purpose of a merely selfish man.[1]

Fletcher's view of Helen Faucit's interpretation of Lady Macbeth was confirmed by other voices. When Helen Faucit replaced

[1] See *Studies of Shakespeare*, pp. 192–8.

Mrs Warner as Lady Macbeth for one night at Drury Lane, R. R. M'Ian wrote to her: '...you hold that Lady Macbeth is the most difficult of Shakespeare's female characters, and yet you made quite a new thing of it. It was different in feeling and effect from any one else's I ever saw...'[1]

The critic of the *Morning Post* wrote on August 5, 1851, that Helen Faucit's Lady Macbeth was not the conventional stage portrait. In her interpretation 'the ambition of the heroine o'erswayed but did not extinguish the sentiments of the woman'. There was throughout 'a strong and passionate love for her husband, expressed in many tender and graceful passages' which she delivered 'with exquisite pathos'. A striking example occurred after the banqueting scene. When Helen Faucit spoke the line—

You lack the season of all natures, sleep   (III. iv. 141)

'the mingled love and pity conveyed in the words revealed the real character of Lady Macbeth'. Her speech was 'charmingly musical'.[2] During the banquet scene, wrote W. Carleton, where other Lady Macbeths had shown a cold ferocity combined with the desire to conceal Macbeth's crime, Helen Faucit showed the same desire for concealment, combined with 'ill-suppressed anguish'.[3] As Carleton wrote to Dr Stokes, after he had seen Helen Faucit play,

The first thing that began gradually to creep upon me last night was an unaccountable yet irresistible sense of propriety in Miss Faucit's management of the character (of Lady Macbeth)...I said to myself: This woman, it seems to me, is simply urging her husband forward through her love for him, which prompts her to wish for the gratification of his ambition, to commit a murder. This, it would appear, is her sole object, and in working it out she is naturally pursuing a terrible course, and one of singular difficulty.[4]

Helen Faucit's interpretation of Lady Macbeth gave a new and gentle quality to every scene she appeared in. The moment at which Lady Macbeth faints after the discovery of Duncan's murder had hitherto been avoided because it was felt to be a piece of Machiavellian duplicity that audiences would not stomach. But

---

[1] Quoted in Theodore Martin, *Helena Faucit* (1900), p. 109.
[2] *Morning Post* (August 5, 1851).
[3] Martin, *Helena Faucit*, p. 178.   [4] Quoted *ibid.* pp. 177–8.

when Helen Faucit did faint, later in her career, after Lady Macbeth's part in the scene had been restored, audiences had no doubt of the genuineness of it. Professor Morley was persuaded that she collapsed at this point because of the recurrence of the image which recalled her father when he slept:

> Here lay Duncan,
> His silver skin lac'd with his golden blood...[1]   (II. iii. 111)

What had previously been deliberate and Machiavellian, Helen Faucit seems to have made suddenly human. It had become traditional for Fleance to appear with Banquo during the brief meeting with Macbeth at the beginning of the third act. Macready had made a point of his presence, fondling Fleance with a 'cat-like propensity' as if playing with his victim.[2] In December 1864, Helen Faucit, playing opposite Phelps, took over the business herself and made it immensely sentimental. As Professor Morley saw it: 'The fingers of the woman who has been a mother, and has murder on her soul, wander sadly and tenderly over the type of her lost innocence.'[3] This was logical and believable, as Helen Faucit made it clear that Lady Macbeth had no idea of Macbeth's intention to murder Banquo and Fleance.[4]

Helen Faucit's great moment, however, came in the sleep-walking scene when her own domestic vision of Lady Macbeth was most fully revealed. With a wandering and uncertain step she advanced towards the audience, and in a low moan of great mental agony, gave expression to the remorse which was 'weighing her down to the grave'.[5] Macready praised her when she first played Lady Macbeth in 1842, for emphasizing the nature of sleep disturbed by fearful dreams.[6] And though her walk was 'heavy and inelastic'[7] when she entered, 'her final flight to bed was weird and startling, wholly unlike the usual stilted exit.'[8] Carleton remembered the corpse-like hands, the terrible remorse.[9] After seeing her play, Professor Wilson ('Christopher North'), a

---

[1] Henry Morley, *Journal of a London Playgoer* (1866), p. 354. Cf. Helen Faucit's own account of the character in Martin, p. 175.
[2] *John Bull* (May 26, 1839). Quoted in Sprague, *Shakespeare and the Actors*, p. 248.
[3] See *ibid*.   [4] *Ibid*.
[5] *Morning Post* (August 5, 1851).
[6] Helen Faucit, *Some of Shakespeare's Female Characters* (1891), p. 288.
[7] *Ibid*.
[8] *Liverpool Post*, quoted in Martin, *Helena Faucit*, p. 314.
[9] Martin, p. 178.

devotee of Mrs Siddons, is reported to have said: 'We have all been wrong...This is the true Lady Macbeth! Mrs Siddons has misled us.'[1]

Macready however was not fully satisfied with Helen Faucit's interpretation. While he thought her first scene was promising, and her playing in the fourth and fifth acts particularly effective, he found her interpretation of the second act unhelpful. She failed altogether, he told her, to chastise him with the valour of her tongue.[2] Though Fletcher found her interpretation of these scenes effective, Helen Faucit herself admitted being unhappy with them.[3] 'I had no misgivings after reaching the third act,' she wrote, 'but the first two always filled me with shrinking horror.' While Helen Faucit could 'recognize the stern grandeur of the indomitable will of Lady Macbeth'[4] she herself played not a grand but a sensitive Lady Macbeth.

It would have been surprising if Fanny Kemble had not reacted sharply to Helen Faucit's interpretation of Lady Macbeth. Fanny Kemble was in her own way original. Partly because of an innate conservatism, and partly one feels in reaction to Helen Faucit's interpretation, Fanny Kemble's approach to Lady Macbeth's character, which is presented in her *Notes upon some of Shakespeare's Plays*, was uncompromising in its moral rigour. Where Mrs Siddons had seen an underlying sensitiveness in Lady Macbeth's character, though she did not make it the basis of her interpretation, Fanny Kemble saw only coldness and unimaginative evil. Fanny Kemble looked at Shakespeare's creation in exclusively moral terms. Of Lady Macbeth she wrote: 'The *unrecognized* pressure of her great guilt killed her. I think her life was destroyed by sin as by a disease of which she was unconscious.' To Fanny Kemble the tragedy of Lady Macbeth was the tragedy of spiritual self-extinction through sin.

While Helen Faucit saw Lady Macbeth as essentially feminine, Fanny Kemble saw her as possessing characteristics 'which generally characterize men not women—energy, decision, daring, unscrupulousness, a deficiency of imagination, a great preponderance of the positive and practical elements'. If Lady Macbeth possessed a high degree of courage, Fanny Kemble thought that

---

[1] Martin, p. 159. [2] *Shakespeare's Female Characters*, p. 289.
[3] See *Literary Gazette*, quoted in Martin, p. 228.
[4] Martin, p. 175.

it was due to a deficiency of imagination and 'a certain obtuseness of the nervous system which goes with that rare quality'.[1]

The difference between Helen Faucit's approach to Lady Macbeth and Fanny Kemble's can best be illustrated by their differing interpretations of a single line. While Helen Faucit read a mingled love and pity into the line

> You lack the season of all natures, sleep

Fanny Kemble saw in it Lady Macbeth's 'habitual tone', a sort of 'contemptuous compassion' for her husband.[2]

It is not surprising, given Fanny Kemble's interpretation of Lady Macbeth, that when she came to play opposite Macready in 1848 she delivered the invocation to the forces of evil successfully: 'The terrible great invocation to the powers of evil, with which Lady Macbeth's part opens, was the only thing of mine that was good in the whole performance.'[3] For the rest of the performance Fanny Kemble could not successfully realise her interpretation. Macready's primitive upsurges of feeling put her off. She was much 'astonished and dismayed when at the exclamation, "Bring forth men-children only", he seized me ferociously by the wrist, and compelled me to make a demi-volte or pirouette, such as I think that lady surely did never perform before under the influence of her husband's admiration'.[4]

Macready, as Fanny Kemble's remarks show, was something of what is currently described as a 'method' actor, and directly experienced the feelings he portrayed. 'I really believe', she wrote, that 'Macready cannot help being as odious as he is on the stage. He very nearly made me faint last night in "Macbeth", with crushing my broken finger, and by way of apology, merely coolly observed that he really could not answer for himself in such a scene, and that I ought to wear a splint.'[5] On another occasion in *Macbeth*, Fanny Kemble claims that Macready pinched her black and blue, and almost tore the point lace from her head.[6]

Clearly Fanny Kemble was not, as Charlotte Cushman was, in sympathy with Macready's mind and feelings. She found his emotional violence disquieting and his stage arrangements for the banquet scene profoundly unsatisfactory. Fanny Kemble's

---

[1] See *Notes upon some of Shakespeare's Plays* (1882), pp. 50–7.
[2] *Notes*, p. 69.
[3] *Records of Later Life*, III, 389.   [4] *Ibid.* 375.
[5] *Ibid.* 394.   [6] *Ibid.* 386.

account of the way in which Macready changed the traditional position of the tables in the banquet scene is worth quoting in full because it shows how traditional she could be, and how, in the banquet scene, her interpretation of Lady Macbeth depended upon where a table stood:

From time immemorial the banquet scene in 'Macbeth' has been arranged after one invariable fashion: the royal dais and throne, with the steps leading up to it, holds the middle of the stage, sufficiently far back to allow of two long tables, at which the guests are seated on each side, in front of it, leaving between them ample space for Macbeth's scene with Banquo's ghost, and Lady Macbeth's repeated rapid descents from the dais and returns to it, in her vehement expostulations with him, and her courteous invitations to the occupants of both the tables to 'feed and regard him not'. Accustomed to this arrangement of the stage, which I never saw different anywhere in all my life for this scene, I was much astonished and annoyed to find, at my first rehearsal, a long banqueting table set immediately at the foot of the steps in front of the dais, which rendered all but impossible my rapid rushing down to the front of the stage, in my terrified and indignant appeals to Macbeth, and my sweeping back to my place, addressing on my way compliments to the tables on either side. It was as much as I could do to pass between the bottom of the throne steps and the end of the transverse table in front of them; my train was in danger of catching its legs and my legs, and throwing it down and me down, and the whole thing was absolutely ruinous to the proper performance of my share of the scene. If such a table had been in any such place in Glamis Castle on that occasion, when Macbeth was seized with his remorseful frenzies, his wife would have jumped over or overturned it to get to him.

All my remonstrances were, however, in vain. Mr Macready persisted in his determination to have the stage arranged solely with reference to himself, and I was obliged to satisfy myself with a woman's vengeance, a snappish speech, by at last saying that, since it was evident Mr Macready's Macbeth depended upon where a table stood, I must contrive that my Lady Macbeth should not do so. But in that scene it undoubtedly did.[1]

Clearly, Fanny Kemble's interpretation of Lady Macbeth must have suffered from her disagreements with Macready. At the same time she did well as Desdemona when Macready played Othello. It is quite possible, therefore, that if she failed as Lady

---

[1] *Records of Later Life*, III, 379–80.

Macbeth, her failure was due as well to limitations in her conception of the role.

Macready's desire for a third table could not have been arbitrary. We know how much he valued the total effect of a scene—he had a painter's eye, as Fanny Kemble herself tells us, a fine sense of the possibilities of colour and design, and impeccable taste. He built up an impression of festive magnificence to achieve a dramatic contrast between the rich royal setting and the scenes of madness played against it.[1] A third table could have been a necessary part of his total vision of the scene. Macready attempted, as a director, to marry poetry in the theatre with the poetry of the theatre. As he told Lady Pollock, he had attempted to enrich Shakespeare's poetry with scenes worthy of its interpretation, to give his tragedies their due magnificence, and to his comedies their entire brilliancy.[2] Fanny Kemble in all probability fell victim to this principle.

[1] See Downer, *Quarterly Journal of Speech*, p. 178.
[2] *Macready as I Knew Him*, p. 83.

CHAPTER 9

THE YEARS BETWEEN MACREADY
AND IRVING

'The public is willing to have the magnificence without the tragedy', commented Macready to Lady Pollock, during his retirement, after reading a review in which every detail of the décor, costume and grouping of a production of *The Winter's Tale* had been described, while the acting was barely mentioned. 'The accessories swallow up the poetry and the actors', said Macready, and added:

...I feel myself in some measure responsible...in my endeavour to give Shakespeare all his attributes, to enrich his poetry with scenes worthy of its interpretation, to give his tragedies their due magnificence, and to his comedies their entire brilliancy, I have set an example which is accompanied with great peril...[1]

Macready himself escaped the 'peril'. Though Fanny Kemble's experience might suggest otherwise,[2] he had maintained the importance of the actor's role in *Macbeth*, without sacrificing him to the *mise-en-scène*.

Macready maintained a just balance between the needs of the actor and the needs of the production as a whole, but in Charles Kean's *Macbeth*, despite some brilliantly successful effects, the accessories threatened to swallow up the poetry. Kean himself was, on the whole, more interested in problems of grouping, costume and décor, than in the interpretation of Shakespeare's lines. It is useful to compare Coleman's account of Macready's *Macbeth* at Covent Garden with Charles Kean's at the Prince's Theatre, which began on February 14, 1853. When he describes Macready's production, Coleman's attention is drawn to the actor's interpretation of character; when he talks of Kean's *Macbeth*, his attention shifts to effects achieved by careful grouping and solid, realistic sets.

Kean was called 'the great Shakespearean upholsterer' in his day; but in fairness to him it must be said that some of his best

---

[1] *Macready as I Knew Him*, p. 83.   [2] See above, pp. 177–8.

effects were functional. Coleman's description of Duncan's camp at Forres shows Kean's skill in achieving satisfying visual effects:

The scene was discovered in night and silence, a couple of semi-savage armed kerns were on guard prowling to and fro with stealthy steps. A distant trumpet call was heard, another in reply, another and yet another; a roll of the drum—an alarum. In an instant the whole camp was alive with kerns and gallowglasses, who circled round the old king and the princes of the blood. The Bleeding Sergeant was carried in upon a litter, and the scene was illuminated with the ruddy glare of burning pine-knots.[1]

It had been the practice for the wounded soldier to enter gasping as if he had run a long distance. Lewes thought that Kean did well in altering the old business, and in having the wounded soldier brought in instead on a litter.[2]

At their best, Kean's scenic effects were functional. They helped to focus attention on the central character in the scene. The grouping after the discovery of the murder of Duncan was, however, a trifle sensational:

When the alarm bell rang out, crowds of half-dressed men, demented women and children, soldiers with unsheathed weapons, and retainers with torches, streamed on and filled the stage in the twinkling of an eyelid. Wild tumult and commotion were everywhere, while in the centre of the seething crowd, with pale face and flashing eyes, the murderer held aloft his blood-stained sword.[3]

And in the banquet scene the elaborate realistic set seems to have displaced the hero of the play. Lewes thought that the banquet afforded a real glimpse into feudal times.[4] White-bearded bards occupied a gallery up-stage and aloft, where they played on harps[5] under a sloping timber roof supported by Saxon pillars.[6] On tables placed, one at the back of the stage facing the audience, the other two right and left and extending down-stage, food smoked as if it were real. Observers remembered the colour and animation of the movement of the feudal lords, ladies, soldiers,

---

[1] 'Facts...about Macbeth', *Gentleman's Magazine*, p. 225.
[2] *Dramatic Essays*, ed. W. Archer and R. W. Lowe (1896), p. 239.
[3] Coleman, 'Facts...about Macbeth', p. 226.
[4] *Dramatic Essays*, p. 239.
[5] Coleman, p. 226. Cf. Cuthbert Bede, 'Macbeth on the Stage', *N & Q*, VIII, seventh series (July 13, 1889), 22.
[6] Bede, p. 22.

and retainers behind two pillars left and right, which gave the impression of solidity and supported a semi-circular arch down-stage. It was between the pillars and the footlights that the Keans enacted the main business of the scene. Banquo's ghost appeared for the first time in an eerie blue light on a seat of state beside Lady Macbeth. When Macbeth turned round to pledge his guests, the pillar down-stage opposite him became transparent, and Banquo's ghost was seen within it.[1] Kean seems to have wanted to create the impression that the ghost of the 'blood-boltered Banquo' was a projection of the feverish imagination of Macbeth.

Kean was criticised in his day for not making the banquet grand enough. In his farewell speech on August 29, 1859, he remembered the charge and defended himself against it:

Fault was also found with my removal of the gorgeous banquet and its gold and silver vessels, together with the massive candelabra (such as no Highlander of the eleventh century ever gazed upon), and with the substitution of the more appropriate feast of coarse fare, served on rude tables, and lighted by simple pine torches. I was admonished that such diminution of regal pomp impaired the strength of *Macbeth*'s motive for the crime of murder, the object being less dazzling and attractive. Until that hour I had never believed that the Scottish Thane had an eye to King *Duncan*'s plate. I had imagined that lofty ambition, the thirst of power, and the desire of supreme command, developed themselves with equal intensity in the human heart, whether the scene of action might be the palace of a European monarch or the wigwam of an American Indian.[2]

One suspects, however, that it was not merely the removal of the gold and silver and the massive candelabra that robbed the scene of its grandeur, but Kean's own acting as Macbeth, and his limiting approach to the poetry of the play. Cuthbert Bede tells us that after the ghost appeared, at 'Prythee see there' Kean clung in terror to his wife.[3] Whatever the plate was, whether gold and silver or not, this kind of business was hardly likely to have created an illusion of dignity and grandeur.

Westland Marston, who was a warm friend of Kean's, speaks of the 'painstaking inadequacy' of his *Macbeth*.[4] Kean took immense pains with externals, with the grouping, the décor, the costumes,

[1] Coleman, p. 226; Bede, p. 22.
[2] See J. W. Cole, *The Life and Theatrical Times of Charles Kean* (2 vols. 1859), II, 381.
[3] 'Macbeth', *N & Q*, VIII, 22.   [4] *Our Recent Actors*, I, 176.

but his grasp of the poetry in the play was inadequate. His programme note dated June 8, 1853, shows the scientific pains he took to discover the right period costumes for the play. Kean wrote that there was no certain information to be had about the dress worn by the people of Scotland in the eleventh century. He had to work not on established facts but on reasonable assumptions:

I have introduced the tunic, mantle, cross gartering and ringed byrnie of the Danes and Anglo-Saxons, between whom it does not appear that any very material difference existed; retaining, however, the peculiarity of 'the striped and chequered garb', which seems to be generally admitted as belonging to the Scotch long anterior to the history of this play; together with the eagle feather in the helmet, which, according to Gaelic tradition, was the distinguishing mark of a chieftain. Party-coloured woollens and cloths appear to have been commonly worn among the Celtic tribes from a very early period.

Charles Kean was a historical realist but he was not without a sense of the possibilities of colour and design. He adds to his programme note:

Strabo, Pliny and Xiphilin, record the dress of Boadicia, Queen of Iceni as being woven, chequer-wise, of many colours, comprising purple, light and dark red, violet and blue.
    There is every reason to believe that the armour and weapons of the date of *Macbeth* were of rich workmanship.
    Harold Hardrada, King of Norway, is described by Snorre as wearing in the battle with Harold II, King of England, A.D. 1066, a blue tunic and a splendid helmet.

Yet in spite of his aesthetic realism, Kean's approach to costumes was obviously external: his conception of the costume for Macbeth grew not out of an inward conception of the character, but out of a conception of a particular historical period.
    When Lewes reviewed the production of *Macbeth* at the Prince's Theatre his complaint was that Kean had no real conception of the character of Macbeth: 'We cannot be said to take any view of the *character* at all; he tries to embody the various feelings of each situation; taking, however, the literal and un-intelligent interpretation, so that almost every phase of the character is falsified.' At times Kean's acting seemed wooden, When the witches addressed him, Kean gave expression to Mac-

beth's fluctuating emotions by standing still and open-mouthed, with a fixed stare. Kean spoke the verse, when he was not being vehement, in a conversational tone. When he did become impassioned, it seemed to Lewes that there were times when he did so in the wrong place. In the dagger soliloquy Kean did not rise to 'a crescendo of horrible amazement on the words

> Thou marshall'st me the way that I was going;

but at

> ...such an instrument I was to use.'

He flew into a 'paroxysm of horror' again when he saw on its 'blade and dudgeon gouts of blood'. While it is possible to make a case for the second crescendo, it is difficult to justify the first, either on grounds of economy or relevance. Lewes thought that both paroxysms of horror were irrelevant, and that Kean's transitions from 'explosive rant' to 'calmness' were artificial and unconvincing. At one moment he was ranting till his voice was hoarse and at the next he was as quiet as a melancholy recluse.

'In Charles Kean's Macbeth', wrote Lewes, 'all the tragedy has vanished; sympathy is impossible because the mind of the criminal is hidden from us. He makes Macbeth ignoble—one whose crime is that of a common murderer, with perhaps a tendency towards Methodism.' Kean's interpretation was not, of course, entirely artificial and wooden; there were moments when it came to life. The weariness of Macbeth's guilt was imaginatively portrayed; the terror after the murder *was* terror, even though it looked more like a house-breaker's fear of the police than the expression of a tortured conscience; Macbeth's desperation at the close of the play *was* desperation;[1] but even though there were moments in Kean's performance which were emotionally convincing, his Macbeth lacked tragic dignity. Like Lewes, Marston, who had no reason to be hostile to Kean, wrote that watching Kean play Macbeth 'You had less the thought of a combat with Fate than of a bull fight and of the brave and frantic efforts of the tortured animal in the arena.'[2]

Mrs Charles Kean, when she played Lady Macbeth in 1853, had more dignity and grandeur than her husband, though her conception of the role had not always been in the Warner-Cushman tradition. As Ellen Tree she had played Lady Macbeth

---

[1] *Dramatic Essays*, pp. 235-7.   [2] *Our Recent Actors*, I, 175.

opposite Macready on October 4, 1835, and was described by Forster as being the most civilised and sensitive actress the stage had seen for years, though he felt that her 'irresistible artillery of tenderness' was inadequate for the role: '...her acting is pure elegance, nature and pathos, and is utterly deficient in the grander as well as in the more physical requisites for Lady Macbeth'.[1]

In 1835 Mrs Kean approached the role as Helen Faucit had. In 1853 she radically changed her strategy. Lewes, who was 'very much of Mrs Siddons' opinion, that Lady Macbeth was a fair, delicate *womanly* woman, capable of great "valour of the tongue", capable of nerving herself for any one great object but showing by her subsequent remorse and broken heart that she had been *playing* a part', and who argued that Mrs Kean's interpretation of Lady Macbeth in 1835 was probably better than her audiences, accustomed to the 'received notion' of Lady Macbeth's character, would allow, thought nevertheless that Mrs Kean was more successful in 1853 than in 1835. 'I do not accept her view of the part', wrote Lewes 'but at any rate she *has* a view, and realises it with vulture-like ferocity. In no scene was she weak; in the sleep-walking scene she was terrific.'[2]

This account by Lewes of Mrs Kean's performance in 1853 is confirmed by the dramatic critic of the *Athenaeum*, who observed on February 15, 1853, that she 'was not at all deficient, as might have been expected, in the requisite physical force', and by the critic of *The Times*, who wrote on February 15, 1853, that Mrs Kean had created a new character essentially different, more terrible and more tragic than the character created by her in 1835. Her new interpretation combined savage ferocity with grandeur. If her luring on of Macbeth had an appalling intensity, her sleep-walking was calm and dignified, the 'incarnation of agony'. It would appear from all accounts that Mrs Kean's interpretation of Lady Macbeth in 1853 was more successful than Kean's interpretation of Macbeth.

With Macready, the director's imagination and the actor's were part of a single vision. With Charles Kean this unity of vision no longer seemed to exist—the pursuit of the *mise-en-scène* so excited his attention that he forgot the purpose and meaning of his text. This was particularly evident in his treatment of the witches;

---

[1] *Theatrical Examiner* (October 4, 1835).   [2] *Dramatic Essays*, pp. 237–8.

though it was quite charming—a myriad white arms gleamed in the moonlight during the dance of the witches, and the ascent of Hecate revealed a distant view of 'steeples, towers and turrets' in a city miles away—[1] it seems to have done little to advance Shakespeare's theme of evil. Lewes thought, quite justifiably, that it was a violation of the poet's meaning to multiply Shakespeare's three Weird Sisters into fifty witches called 'in managerial English...the vocal strength' engaged for the occasion.[2] In this case, clearly, the accessories swallowed up the poet's meaning. Charles Kean established a new tradition of spectacle which reached its peak with Beerbohm Tree.

Meanwhile other directors like Samuel Phelps were resisting the 'peril' that Macready had feared would sweep away Shakespeare's poetry from the theatre. Phelps, who had worked with Macready and shared his attitudes, was considered his logical heir.[3] Phelps's treatment of the witches, unlike Charles Kean's, was functional rather than spectacular, and more chaste and severe than Macready's. As the *Athenaeum* tells us, in Phelps's production of *Macbeth* 'the interpolated choruses, Locke's music —with its own prescriptive charm, the accustomed multitude of ragged and illegitimate witches were all swept away'.[4] But if Phelps swept away the accessories, he kept the substance. In the first scene the Weird Sisters grew, as it were, out of the mist, and their intangible, spiritual nature was suggested again when they met Macbeth on the blasted heath and melted from him in the shadowy distance 'like "breath in the wind"'[5]...The poetry of their presence was never, to our feeling, so brought out before', wrote the critic of the *Athenaeum*.[6] Phelps's theatricality was exceptional for its purity.

He perceived the theatrical possibilities of scenes omitted in productions of *Macbeth* since Betterton's day. The scene with the drunken Porter was restored in its original form, and so was the conversation between Ross, Lady Macduff and her son. The murder of Macduff's son was enacted on the stage. The dramatic critic of the *Athenaeum* could not stomach the realism of the scene, and thought it inflicted a needless pang; his reactions suggest that Phelps succeeded in communicating the full horror

[1] Coleman, 'Facts...about Macbeth', p. 226.
[2] *Dramatic Essays*, pp. 239–40.
[3] See Coleman, p. 224.
[4] (October 2, 1847), p. 1037.
[5] *Ibid.*
[6] *Ibid.*

of Macbeth's third murder. Phelps came closer to the First Folio than any of his predecessors, from Betterton to Macready. At the end of the play Macbeth was killed off-stage and his head was brought in on a pole[1] as a stage direction in the Folio recommends. The dramatic critic of *The Times* thought that Phelps had preserved the integrity of his text and liked the 'freshness' of his approach.[2]

Though Phelps approached the text of *Macbeth* with a fresh outlook, his interpretation of the character of Macbeth did not differ radically from Macready's. There were some changes in detail, but Phelps did not alter the conception of Macbeth's character established by Macready. He abandoned the tartan and wore instead a primitive-looking mantle with heavy bars and ponderous folds.[3] His interpretation of the dagger scene was probably more successful than Macready's though, like Macready, he did not start at once, as if he was immediately convinced of the existence of the dagger, but kept his eye fixed on the 'painting of his fear', till the brain-sick bewildered imagination made it real. Phelps seemed to shrink away from belief in the dagger, returning to it with a struggling conviction until it obtained full possession of him.[4] Phelps did not radically alter Macready's interpretation of the dagger scene, but developed it with more subtlety. The alteration in Macbeth's position on the stage during the banquet scene was a more clear-cut and obvious change. Phelps placed Banquo's chair up-stage and addressed the ghost with his back to the audience. The dramatic critic of the *Athenaeum* (October 2, 1847), thought the new position of Macbeth was a great mistake, because as a result one 'of the grandest, psychological expressions of the play' was lost to the house—probably a fair criticism. We know from the new text he used that Phelps did not die on-stage in heroic fashion, like Macready, but off, where the noise of battle roared. The battle scenes in Phelps's production of *Macbeth* were excellently managed, giving the impression of a real conflict between opposing armies.[5]

Phelps made no radical changes in Macready's conception of the character. He was, like Macready, 'a half-barbarous warrior-

[1] *Ibid.*   [2] September 27, 1847.
[3] See Phelps and Forbes-Robertson, *Life-work of Phelps*, pp. 100–1.
[4] *Ibid.* p. 101.
[5] *Athenaeum* (1847), p. 1037. Cf. *The Times* (September 27, 1847).

chieftain'[1] but his performance was no mechanical imitation of Macready's. In 1845 his interpretation was considered both chaste and awe-inspiring.[2] According to the *Athenaeum*, Phelps's interpretation of Macbeth in 1847 was marked by 'taste, discrimination and pathos', and was 'often indisputably great'.[3] On March 23, 1850, the dramatic critic of the *Illustrated London News* observed that Phelps's Macbeth was 'occasionally animated with wild fire, skilfully indicating the supernal influence under which he acted; but throughout, the vehemence of the style was regulated with most excellent judgement'.

In 1850, Phelps had Isabella Glyn playing opposite him at Sadler's Wells—the most original and successful Lady Macbeth he had the good fortune to play to. Isabella Glyn was Charles Kemble's pupil,[4] and her performance in 1850 was said to possess a finely developed vigour, an overwhelming energy, 'chastened by a presiding taste, worthy of the Siddonian school'. Brought up in the Siddonian tradition, Isabella Glyn was not external in her approach to the character. Though Mrs Siddons's interpretation must undoubtedly have influenced her—her reading of Lady Macbeth's first soliloquy, like Mrs Siddons's, was 'electric' in its 'power'[5]—there were points at which her interpretation of the character clearly diverged from that of Mrs Siddons.

Unlike Mrs Siddons, Isabella Glyn was sceptical of the 'murdering ministers'. The lines

> *Wherever* in your *sightless* substances
> You wait on nature's mischief   (I. v. 46–7)

in Lady Macbeth's second soliloquy, were spoken with an emphasis on 'Wherever' and 'sightless', that implied at once a doubt of the existence of the 'murdering ministers'. Isabella Glyn treated them as fictions of a superstitious fancy, the sort of fancy by which Macbeth was hag-ridden. Her voice, calm, staid and subdued, seemed to be devoid of all moral feeling.[6] The dramatic critic of the *Illustrated London News* observed that she gave a severe intellectual outline to a definite conception of a 'cold, calculating, materialistic woman'.[7]

---

[1] Morley, *Journal of a London Playgoer*, p. 349.
[2] *Athenaeum* (August 23, 1845), p. 845.   [3] P. 1037.
[4] C. E. Pascoe, *The Dramatic List* (1880), p. 158.
[5] *Illustrated London News*, XVI (March 23, 1850), 194.
[6] *Ibid.* XX (January 3, 1852), 10.   [7] *Ibid.*

There were two ways, wrote a critic in the *Birmingham Journal*, of dealing with Lady Macbeth's successful attempt to influence her husband in the first two acts. The first was to overcome the reluctance of Macbeth by 'dint of sheer dragooning'—this was probably Mrs Kean's way of doing it. The energy of Lady Macbeth, her physical vehemence, her declamation, overcame Macbeth's softer and more pliant nature. The second way was Mrs Glyn's, and it was colder and more calculating. It was intellectual, and the reverse of declamatory. In her interpretation, Lady Macbeth seemed to possess a more subtle intelligence, detecting the weak points in Macbeth's character and offering the stimulant of ambition, or administering the anodyne of selfish fear, according to the action to which she desired to mould his mind. Isabella Glyn's voice was capable of a wide range of modulation and, like the play of her features, obeyed every phase of passion and emotion.[1]

In the murder scene and during the banquet, Isabella Glyn was 'self-possessed, appalling, sustained, triumphant...the guardian demon of the crowned assassin'.[2] Before the banquet, and after the guests dispersed, however, melancholy seemed to overcome her. The old murderous spirit revived for a moment with

> But in them nature's copy's not eterne   (III. ii. 38)

but after the line was uttered her 'moodiness' returned.[3] The sleep-walking scene seems to have been exceptionally effective. As Isabella Glyn interpreted the scene, conscience seemed to assert its being with all the force of remorse—she appears to have succeeded in communicating the idea that Lady Macbeth took her own life.[4] The idea of suicide finds support in the text. At the end of the play, Malcolm refers to the 'dead butcher'

> and his fiend-like queen,
> Who, as 'tis thought, by self and violent hands
> Took off her life...   (v. viii. 69–70)

Trained in the Siddonian school, Isabella Glyn seems to have had a clear conception of the character of Lady Macbeth, and saw it in terms of a single line of development. She seems to have portrayed the disillusionment that follows the pursuit of the temporal

[1] Quoted *ibid.* XXIX (November 1, 1856), 448.
[2] *Ibid.* XVI (March 23, 1850), 194.
[3] *Ibid.* XXIV (August 23, 1851), 234.   [4] *Ibid.* XVI (March 23, 1850), 194.

as an end in itself. For all its scepticism of the supernatural, her performance was a genuine exploration of evil.

Isabella Glyn did not reduce Macbeth to a nonentity. When the Italian actress Ristori played Lady Macbeth in an Italian translation of *Macbeth* at the Lyceum in 1857, Macbeth, played by Signor Vitaliani, was clearly not the hero of the play. Both Professor Morley and Coleman testify to Macbeth's reduction in stature. Professor Morley tells us that it was Macbeth's business at the Lyceum to serve 'as foil and contrast to his lady'.[1] And Coleman, who grew enthusiastic about Ristori's interpretation, writes that Macbeth 'was but the veriest slave of her will and pleasure. In the murder scene she was everything, he was nothing—in fact, all throughout she overshadowed and extinguished the wretched creature.'[2]

There was no scepticism in Madame Ristori's attitude to the supernatural. When she read the letter, the line 'they made themselves air' (I. v. 4) was spoken with deep awe.[3] When she finished reading the letter and began the invocation to the spirits of evil, 'she crooned forth the opening words until the voice changed to the hiss of a serpent'. As her voice rose like 'the diapason of an organ', her eyes seemed particularly expressive to Coleman; 'her white hands clutched her ample bosom': it required but little imagination to conceive that '"the dunnest smoke of hell" would burst forth' and surround her.[4] Ristori seems to have wanted to make 'the murdering ministers' as real as her body. Metaphysical aid seemed to be, within the terms of her interpretation, quite immediate and real.

Ristori saw the character of Lady Macbeth in terms of contrast and development. She played a strong woman, who does not talk about her inner fears and tensions 'until her heart gives way under the weight it is forced...to bear'. She brought into sharp contrast 'the innate force of the wife's character, with the weakness of the man who cannot keep his troubles to himself, who gives all his emotions tongue'. Signor Vitaliani, as Macbeth, in an 'excess of zeal, wriggled, leaped and pirouetted', serving as a foil to Lady Macbeth who, when Macbeth was at his most emotional, commonly stood by his side. The interpretation of

[1] *Journal of a London Playgoer*, p. 186.   [2] 'Facts...about Macbeth', p. 232.
[3] Morley, *Journal of a London Playgoer*, p. 187.
[4] 'Facts...about Macbeth', p. 232.

Macbeth by Signor Vitaliani was probably more explicable in Italian terms than in English. At 'We will speak further' (I. v. 68), Madame Ristori laid her hands upon him and, with a persuasive yet compelling force, urged him on, smiling with firm-set lips and nodding satisfaction at her work. The business suggested that Macbeth was in her power and moved at her urging.[1]

In comparison with Isabella Glyn's approach to Lady Macbeth, Ristori's interpretation was less sophisticated, more primitive and unsubtle; it had a popular folk quality, all the directness and obviousness of an archetypal creation. She displayed the spirit of a fox when she invited Duncan into her castle, and the false tone in her voice was immediately evident.[2] During the murder scene, when she came to the line

> Had he not resembled
> My father as he slept, I had done't   (II. ii. 12–13)

she hurried over the thought as one not to be dwelt upon. When the association was unconsciously revived by Macbeth after the discovery of the murder:

> Here lay Duncan,
> His silver skin lac'd with his golden blood   (II. iii. 110–11)

Madame Ristori fainted, and in the banquet scene, when Macbeth resurrected the memory again—

> When now I think you can behold such sights
> And keep the natural ruby of your cheeks,   (III. iv. 114–15)

a turning point appears to have been reached in her interpretation of the character. Madame Ristori flinched, her strength seemed to fail her and she hurried away the guests at the banquet in a voice which betrayed intense nervous emotion. At

> You lack the season of all natures, sleep   (III. iv. 141)

there was a great weariness in her voice and manner, and with a tired step she made her exit with Macbeth. In the sleep-walking scene, her look was haggard, she moved slowly, her voice was pitched low and was full of the weariness that follows acute and exhausting pain. When she made her exit with a ghostly repetition of the old gesture of urging Macbeth on before her, Madame

---

[1] Morley, *Journal of a London Playgoer*, pp. 186–7.
[2] *Ibid.* p. 187.

Ristori seemed to be reliving the night of Duncan's murder.[1] After Lady Macbeth's final exit, the rest of the play was condensed, says Professor Morley, 'into a single page of libretto'.[2]

Madame Ristori was undoubtedly an artist of genius. Henry James thought that she was a supreme exponent of the grand style of acting. 'No one whom we have seen, or are likely to see in this country, can interpret tragedy in the superbly large way of Madame Ristori—can distribute effects into such powerful masses', wrote Henry James, after seeing her perform at the Lyceum in New York. James observed that Madame Ristori had the good fortune to come of a great artistic race 'in whom the feeling of the picturesque is a common instinct, and the gift of personal expression so ample that, even when quite uncultivated, it begins where our laborious attempts in the same line terminate'.[3] Madame Ristori had the simplicity, the 'naiveté' which James regarded as essential to great tragic art. While it must be acknowledged that Madame Ristori's interpretation of Lady Macbeth had elements of tragic grandeur, it must be remembered as well that the Italian production of *Macbetto* in which she played at the Lyceum, altered Shakespeare's own design and deprived the play of a tragic hero.

Charles Kean had no instinctive sympathy with Shakespeare's tragic vision,[4] as Madame Ristori undoubtedly had. Isabella Glyn and Phelps attempted, like Macready, to fuse an 'ancient' and a 'modern' mentality. Other players like Wallack and Mrs Wallack, Creswick and Sullivan attempted, with varying degrees of success, to join the traditional with the new. They formed an important though, as the years went by, increasingly tenuous link with the past, at a time when Charles Kean's spirit, with its passion for spectacle, and its preference for realistic detail and conversational rhythms, seemed to meet the needs of the Victorian imagination.

Wallack's style was a not always successful blend of modern elements found in the art of Macready, with traditional elements associated with the art of John Kemble.[5] As Macbeth, he appears to have tried to follow the main lines of interpretation laid down by Macready. When Wallack played Macbeth on March 17, 1851, at the Haymarket, the critic of the *Athenaeum* observed that in the

[1] Morley, pp. 188–90.　　　　　　　[2] *Ibid.* p. 190.
[3] *The Scenic Art*, ed. Allan Wade (1948), p. 29.
[4] See Lewes, *On Actors*, pp. 24–5.
[5] *Athenaeum* (March 22, 1851), p. 332.

early scenes of the play much of Macbeth's 'primitive nobleness was preserved'.[1] The style of the Wallacks, wrote the dramatic critic of the *Athenaeum* in 1853, was distinguished by an 'elaborate' concern for passionate and poetic speech. Descriptions of Wallack's acting suggest, however, that the element of calculation in his art was not always concealed, and that his dignity was the result of effort, something he took care to preserve. Looking back, Marston recognised 'a touch of theatricality' in Wallack's manner, a tendency to 'attitudinize', which in the 1880s, 'when even tameness was preferred to exaggeration', would have gone ill with him.[2]

The dignity of Barry Sullivan seems to have been more instinctive than the dignity of Wallack. Shaw remembered the lightning swiftness of his action, and his stage walk, which was the perfection of grace and dignity.[3] At his best, Sullivan appears to have spoken Shakespeare's verse with elegance and delicacy.[4] Yet though his Falconbridge in *King John*, reminiscent of Charles Kemble's, was a memorable and sensitive interpretation of Shakespeare, his interpretation of Macbeth a month later, in October 1866, suggests that Sullivan did not respond to some aspects of the poetry of the play, even though his attitudes, noble and graceful, resembled a painting by Flaxman.[5] Immediately after the encounter with the witches, Macbeth seemed fully resolved to murder Duncan. Sullivan's Lady Macbeth was like Edmund Kean's, weak rather than commanding. As the dramatic critic of the *Daily Telegraph* wrote on October 3, 1866:

It may be fairly objected to Mr Barry Sullivan's notion of the rapidity with which the thought of the murder entered the mind of *Macbeth*, that his wife who considers him 'too full o' the milk of human kindness', could have had but little knowledge of the darker moods of his disposition, or else we must be enforced to believe that his nature entirely changed on being accosted by the witches. Whatever opinion may be entertained it is in favour of the *Macbeth* of Tuesday night that he was unconsciously assisted by Miss Amy Sedgwick, who, venturing for the first time in London on the personation of Lady Macbeth, gave a suggestive rather than a powerful rendering of the character. Her

[1] *Ibid.*   [2] *Our Recent Actors*, II, 229.
[3] See *Ellen Terry and Bernard Shaw: a correspondence*, ed. Christopher St John (1931), p. xxii.
[4] R. M. Sillard, *Barry Sullivan and his Contemporaries* (2 vols. 1901), II, 3.
[5] *Ibid.* II, 189–90.

performance is not lacking in intelligence, but it is deficient in force, and much less decided in form and colour than could be desired.

Sullivan did justice to his own conception, and it seemed at the time novel, though open to logical objections.

New conceptions of realism, however, had captured the Victorian imagination in the 1870s. As he grew older and less resilient, as the years advanced and ideas of what was both tragic and natural changed, Sullivan's acting, which had appeared to be natural as well as grand, seemed, after 1890, to represent 'the grandiose and the violent on its last legs'.[1]

By 1887, Samuel Phelps himself seemed the representative tragedian of a school 'the merits of which are these days not very readily allowed'.[2] The change in taste, however, was already evident by the end of 1860. When Charles Dillon and Phelps played Macbeth on alternate nights in March 1869, Phelps seemed by contrast monotonous in style, though he made each of his characters a distinct individual, not a mere variation of the same type. In general Phelps's perception of poetry and recital of blank verse was considered excellent.[3] As Shaw pointed out, after seeing a performance by Wilson Barrett in *Othello*, the more reasonably you speak 'Farewell the tranquil mind', the more absurd it seems. 'It must affect us', instead, wrote Shaw, 'as "Ora per sempre addio, sante memorie", affects us when sung by Tamagno.'[4] One suspects that there were traces of what Shaw would have called 'the orchestral quality' in Phelps's art. As Dr Bertram Joseph points out,

Whatever his faults, Phelps knew how to speak verse: he was specially fine as the Duke in *Measure for Measure*, in which 'his voice rang out with an earnestness rare even with the best declaimers...He closed the third act with a splendid delivery of the rhymed verses'. He was also splendid in the beginning of Prospero's 'Ye elves', and in his action as well as his elocution in Coriolanus: the harangue, 'I banish you', had a fierce sarcasm, 'mounting syllable by syllable to a taunt which, even for the most ignoble order of humanity would have a bitter sting', and which suited his 'passionate declamation' better than anything else in the part, except for the last scene in which Coriolanus lashes himself 'into the mood of taunting invective'. Turner admired the action with

---

[1] George Bernard Shaw, *Our Theatres in the Nineties* (3 vols. 1931), I, 191–3; 297.
[2] *Athenaeum* (1887), I, 73.
[3] *I.L. News*, LIV (1869), 251.　　　　　[4] *Our Theatres in the Nineties*, III, 156.

which Phelps 'accompanied his utterance of the word "fluttered", which came after a seemingly enforced pause, and with that lifted emphasis and natural break in his voice, remembered, I dare say, by all who heard him in his prime. Lifting his arm to its full height above his head, he shook his hand to and fro, as in the act of startling a flock of doves.'[1]

In 1869, however, when contrasted with Phelps, Dillon as Macbeth appeared to be very different. It seemed to the critic of the *Illustrated London News* that 'the actor appeared instead of the elocutionist' only in Phelps's last act, whereas, he observed, 'From the first scene to the closing one Mr Dillon *acts* Macbeth'.[2] Dillon brought out the sense of Shakespeare's verse, but to Marston, who saw his Macbeth, 'there was a sense in the spectator that the agitation of the passions, however real, wanted the charm of dignity for its completeness'. When Dillon played Othello on December 1, 1856, 'he was natural, not at all declamatory, sometimes familiar, always domestic, and rather intensely passionate, than vehemently demonstrative. The great scenes between the Moor and his tempter were for the most part gone through in a sitting position...'[3] Dillon was a forerunner of players like Fechter and Henry Irving.

[1] *The Tragic Actor*, pp. 326–7.
[2] *I.L. News*, LIV (1869), 251.
[3] *Athenaeum* (February 15, 1856), p. 1504.

CHAPTER 10

INTERPRETATIONS FROM
1875 TO 1911

In a lecture delivered at Oxford, Henry Irving pointed out that every revolution in acting was apt to announce itself as a return to nature.[1] His examples were Burbage, Betterton, Garrick and Edmund Kean. Irving saw himself in the same role, as a technical innovator who had resuscitated an old art by making it seem natural again. Yet Irving's conception of the natural was not that of Burbage, and it was not Betterton's, Garrick's or Kean's. It was an Augustan view that the beauty of nature was order. In the nineteenth century, nature seemed much less orderly, and at times even melodramatically cruel, 'red in tooth and claw'. Irving's view of the natural was realistic in late nineteenth-century terms, rather than ideal. The story told by Ellen Terry of Irving's encounter, as a boy, with a lamb which looked like the traditional symbol of innocence but in fact bit him when he tried, after clambering up a steep bank, to kiss it,[2] was not intended to be flippant and is not without significance.

Irving seems to have had a gift for attracting this kind of sharply disillusioning experience. But frequently disillusioned though he was by the real,[3] this did not make him any the less fascinated by it. Gordon Craig's description of Irving's first entrance as Mathias in *The Bells*—of Mathias getting rid of his coat as he stood by the door and brushing the snow off it, taking off his boots, and wearing his buckled shoes, shows how much realistic business counted in his performance. Craig remembered the long hands stretched down over the buckles, and the fingers suddenly stopping their work when the murdered Jew was mentioned.[4]

Irving's realism seemed most vivid and original when it was touched by scepticism and disillusionment. When Shaw saw him play, he felt instinctively that a new drama inhered in the man.[5]

---

[1] *English Actors* (1886), p. 5.
[2] *Memoirs*, ed. Edith Craig and C. St John (1933), p. 130.
[3] See L. Irving, *Henry Irving*, pp. 548–9.   [4] *Ibid.* pp. 58–61.
[5] See *Our Theatres in the Nineties*, I, 287; III, 152.

Irving's interpretation of Macbeth attracted so much comment because it was marked by this special quality, a sense of disillusioned realism. His special brand of realism suited Irving's peculiar gifts and limitations. As Ellen Terry wrote: 'Irving at first had everything against him as an actor. He could not speak, he could not walk, he could not *look*...His amazing power was imprisoned, and only after long and weary years did he succeed in setting it free.'[1] At all times Irving worked hard to achieve a realistic veracity, both as an actor and a director. When he was preparing for his second production of *Macbeth* in 1888, he visited Scotland 'to get ideas for the scenes'. Ellen Terry made an entry in her diary describing an incident in the quest of reality: 'Visited the "Blasted Heath". Behold a flourishing potato-field. A smooth softness everywhere. We must blast our own heath when we do *Macbeth*.'[2]

Irving staged *Macbeth* in 1875 and again in 1888. His idea of the character did not change in essentials between 1875 and 1888, but in 1888 he was a much better craftsman and possessed the ability to realise his conception. When Henry James saw Irving play Macbeth in 1875 he thought his acting was that of 'a very superior amateur'. His personal gifts were rather meagre, his voice was without charm, his utterance without subtlety, and he failed to give their great imaginative value to many of the superb passages he had to speak. James had no quarrel with Irving's conception of the part—he felt there was fair warrant in the text for it—but with his execution of it.[3] Had James seen Irving play in 1888, however, he might have qualified his view. When Bernard Shaw saw Irving's interpretation of Macbeth in that year, he thought that it possessed a 'refined beauty' and that it was 'fine and genuine' within its limits.[4]

In 1875 both Clement Scott of the *Daily Telegraph* and E. R. Russell of the *Daily Post* agreed with Irving's interpretation. Even though Scott felt that Irving did not carry out his conception of the character effectively—'Point upon point is lost and idea upon idea squandered by the actor's extraordinary delivery'—he took the view that Irving's conception of Macbeth was implicit in the

---

[1] *Memoirs*, ed. Craig and St John, p. 61.   [2] *Ibid.* p. 231.
[3] *The Scenic Art*, ed. Wade, pp. 36–7.
[4] See *Ellen Terry...a Correspondence*, ed. St John, p. xxxi.

text: 'The world thinks Macbeth must be a good fellow because he is a brave soldier; but Shakespeare who mirrors the conscience of Macbeth, tells us what a moral coward a brave soldier can be.'[1]

Irving's conception was also accepted by E. R. Russell. 'As Macbeth stands there in clear outline against the lurid sky', he wrote, on September 17, 1875, 'no one could fancy him an ordinary successful general on his way home from victory to honour. There is more in him, and the overplus is high-reaching, gloomy, and mischievous...let us hope, though the notion still seems to flourish that Macbeth was a noble character, that we have heard the last of the theory that he was an amiable tool in the hands of a fiendish woman.' Irving told Ellen Terry in 1888 that he had arrived at the right idea of the character of Macbeth in 1875 by intuition, and that he knew after fresh study in 1888 that it was right. He was not shaken, Ellen Terry writes, by criticisms of his realistic, sceptical conception of the character and always maintained that in *Macbeth* he did his finest work.[2] Irving's conviction that it was Shakespeare's intention to show how a brave soldier could be a moral coward, was found acceptable by Henry James, Clement Scott and E. R. Russell in 1875 and by Bernard Shaw and William Archer in 1888.[3]

Irving's part-book[4] of *Macbeth* for his 1875 production reinforces the description of his conception given by the critics. The passage in I. ii. describing Macbeth's courage and loyalty is omitted. Irving seems to have felt at first that it would not be in harmony with his interpretation. The critic of the *Illustrated London News* (October 2, 1875) noted the omission and pointed out that it was Shakespeare's design to obtain respect for Macbeth before he entered. What Cawdor had lost 'noble Macbeth' had won. To the critic of the *Illustrated London News*, who accepted the truth of the wounded soldier's description, Macbeth's fall from integrity made his character doubly interesting, and his remorse understandable. In 1888 Irving seems no longer to have felt that the passage describing Macbeth's physical courage was inconsist-

---

[1] *Daily Telegraph* (September 27, 1875).

[2] *Memoirs*, p. 232.

[3] 'For my part I have no quarrel whatever with Mr Irving's conception of Macbeth. I do not think he has misunderstood the part in any vital point'—W. Archer. Quoted in A. Brereton, *The Life of Henry Irving* (2 vols. 1908), II, 142.

[4] See analysis of Irving's part-book in Bertram Shuttleworth, 'Irving's Macbeth', *TN*, v (Jan.–March 1951), 28–34.

ent with his view of the character, for he restored it. Except for the omission of this passage there was little difference between Irving's entrance in 1875 and in 1888. As Clement Scott tells us in the *Daily Telegraph* of September 27, 1875, the witches created awe, not laughter or amusement, as they were seen in the air revealed by an occasional lightning flash and heard above the rumbling of the storm. Macbeth came hurriedly upon the scene. Standing in front of 'a wild picture' and 'in the lurid glare of a setting sun' wearing a winged helmet and carrying a great double-handed sword (see Plate 8), Irving seems to have looked 'wonderfully picturesque'. In 1888, when the curtain went up it disclosed nothing. The stage was pitch dark and out of the black-ness came the hollow crooning of the witches. Again they were glimpsed in flashes of lightning. After the restored scene with the wounded soldier, Macbeth made his entrance against a 'blood-red sky': '...a strange, gaunt figure, with thin moustache floating in the wind, clad in chain-mail and winged head-piece, long dagger on hips and huge broad-sword'.[1]

The part copy of 1875 suggests that Irving swiftly unfolded his conception of the character as the scene developed. Against Macbeth's exhortation to the witches 'Stay, you imperfect speak-ers...' (I. iii. 70 ff.), Irving wrote, 'Burning in desire', and against Banquo's exchange with the witches 'Macbeth notes this', as if to indicate that he was considering how far Banquo would stand in the way. The aside 'Two truths are told...' (I. iii. 128 ff.), was marked 'Whisper'. When Malcolm is created Prince of Cumberland in I. iv. Irving's interpretation of Macbeth's response was contained in the direction, 'Very intent'. Duncan's speech at the end in praise of Macbeth, which was cut in 1888, was left untouched in 1875.[2] Irving's cuts at all times suggest that he was trying to pull everything into line with his conception of the character of Macbeth. Even the critic of *St. James's Gazette*, who was clearly not happy with Irving's idea of the character in 1888, recognised the consistent logic of the portrait.[3]

Both Miss Bateman in 1875 and Ellen Terry adapted their own interpretations to suit Irving's. If Macbeth was entirely the creator of his own fate, driven not by the forces of destiny nor by his wife, but by an ambitious impulse within him, then Lady

[1] *Star* (December 31, 1888).   [2] Shuttleworth, 'Irving's Macbeth', p. 29.
[3] December 31, 1888.

Macbeth clearly had to play a subordinate role. Miss Bateman did not read Macbeth's letter 'with the grand sweep of a tragedy queen' but seemed 'too genuine to give herself nonsensical tragedy airs in private'. Miss Bateman's appeal to the infernal powers was 'gloriously interrupted by a warm and natural embrace at Macbeth's entrance'.[1]

What was only hinted at in Miss Bateman's interpretation of Lady Macbeth was developed more fully and consistently when Ellen Terry came to play the role in 1888. Irving had been influenced by G. Fletcher, who described Macbeth in 1847 as 'the most poetical of selfishly ambitious assassins'. Fletcher, it will be recalled, had entirely approved of Helen Faucit's conception of Lady Macbeth. When Ellen Terry was cast as Lady Macbeth, Irving gave her Fletcher's essay with its strong plea for Helen Faucit. Yet, though Ellen Terry's interpretation of Lady Macbeth was influenced by Helen Faucit's conception of the character, she was much too original an actress merely to repeat an old idea. After reading Fletcher she decided to play to the best of her powers and to adapt the part to her own personality with the knowledge that 'nature *does* sometimes freak and put an honest eye into a villain's heart'.[2]

Helen Faucit's Lady Macbeth was domestic and gentle, while Ellen Terry's Lady Macbeth was domestic and practical. She was familiar, realistic and her conversation before the murder had a 'tetchy briskness'.[3]

She fell into a chair by the fireside as she read Macbeth's letter, and while describing his character she gazed at his miniature and kissed it.[4] Her make-up and costume made her look like 'a woman such as Rossetti might have painted'. Throughout the play, she wore 'a series of most wonderful and admirable dresses'.[5] A reviewer in the *Lady's Pictorial* of January 5, 1889, mentions 'the original gown of curious green with its decoration of beetle's wings', a 'wonderful arrangement of mignonette', and a 'glittering gold embroidered skirt and coif'. Ellen Terry began a tradition of dressing Lady Macbeth in exotic costumes which went on into the twentieth century.

[1] *Daily Post* (September 27, 1875).
[2] The copy of Fletcher's essay, with Ellen Terry's comments pencilled in blue, facing p. 72, is on view at the British Theatre Museum. Cf. above, pp. 172–3.
[3] *Liverpool Daily Post* (December 31, 1888).
[4] *Star* (December 31, 1888).   [5] *Liverpool Daily Post* (December 31, 1888).

For her first entrance she wore the gown of peacock green and over it a mantle of dull claret.[1] The critic of the *Star* felt that when she spoke the lines 'Come, you spirits/ That tend on mortal thoughts, unsex me here' (I. v. 37–8), nothing of the kind happened. Ellen Terry's Lady Macbeth was 'redolent, pungent with the *odeur de femme*...She rushed into her husband's arms, clinging, kissing, coaxing, flattering' and even her taunts when his resolution began to fail were 'sugared with a loving smile'.[2] She was full of 'bright, prompt, fascinating impulse with an audacity of realism' that had not been seen before in high tragedy.[3] Her interpretation was adapted to Irving's, and must have pleased him well, for he liked to pull everything into line with his conceptions.

The consistency of his portrait emerges clearly in his treatment of the 'If it were done' soliloquy. In his part copy of 1875 'Besides, this Duncan', (I. vii. 16) was altered to 'Besides this, Duncan'.[4] Shakespeare's punctuation clearly puts the stress on 'Duncan'; in Irving's alteration, 'this' receives emphasis, and the attitude to Duncan seems colder. On the stage in 1875, Irving's interpretation was strikingly evident in his 'calm, cold, over-logical style' of uttering the soliloquy. At the Lyceum in 1875, Macbeth seemed to be swayed solely by the fear of failure, afraid of consequences only in this life. It is just possible that Irving qualified this reading in 1888, when he restored Shakespeare's punctuation, going back to 'Besides, this Duncan',[5] but there is little evidence that he radically altered his interpretation of the rest of the soliloquy and the encounter with Lady Macbeth that followed it. In the part copy of 1875, Lady Macbeth's plan 'When Duncan is asleep' (I. vii. 61–72) was marked, 'Macbeth jumps at this' and Irving's comment against Macbeth's next speech

> ...Will it not be receiv'd,
> When we have mark'd with blood those sleepy two
> Of his own chamber, and us'd their very daggers,
> That they have done't? (I. vii. 74–7)

was 'eagerly'.[6] By the end of the scene Macbeth had completely recovered from the hesitation of 'If we should fail',[7] (I. vii. 59).

---

[1] *Sunday Times* (December 30, 1888).   [2] *Star* (December 31, 1888).
[3] *Liverpool Daily Post* (December 31, 1888).
[4] Shuttleworth, 'Irving's Macbeth', p. 29.
[5] *Ibid.* p. 30.   [6] *Ibid.*   [7] *Ibid.*

There is no clear evidence of any essential change in this approach in 1888.

In his part copy, before the dagger soliloquy, Irving had written emphatically 'Ambition'. Irving evidently regarded the dagger as the embodiment of Macbeth's ambition. A 'sigh' was marked before 'Now o'er the one half-world...' (II. i. 49) and the rest of the soliloquy was to be spoken 'dreamily' with Macbeth coming out of the dream—'he awakes'—at the sound of the bell.[1] What he actually did on the stage must have been more subtle than his notes suggest, though they help to account for the vivid realism of Irving's playing.

On September 21, 1875, the dramatic critic of the *Daily News* wrote:

We believe it has always been customary in the dagger scene to confront the audience looking upwards, as if the imaginary dagger was hovering in the air somewhere between the performer and the audience. Mr Irving on the contrary sees the dagger at a much lower point as he follows it across the stage, drawn as it were by its fascination towards the arched entrance to the chamber of the king—a fine point being his averted hands as if the man 'infirm of purpose', and conscious of the spell that is around and about him, could not trust himself to clutch the airy weapon save in words.

To the critic of the *Dramatic Review* (January 5, 1889), the dagger scene at first seemed disappointing but 'therein lay one of its chief excellencies. So much the apparition accorded with Macbeth's thought that he scarcely seemed to notice it...It was not until the direction it took gave a practical hint of its terrible meaning that the man became appalled and the true power of the actor became apparent...'[2]

E. R. Russell thought in 1888 that of all the scenes this was the most effective. The courtyard in which Irving saw the air-drawn dagger was of irregular construction in the style of Norman architecture when it was just becoming decorative. The entrance hall faced the spectators. Above the passage leading to it were murky, arched galleries. On the right was a staircase, on the left a round tower-like structure suggestive of a spiral stairway. Against this Lady Macbeth leaned back restlessly while the murder was in progress. The place was comparatively dark.[3]

[1] Shuttleworth, p. 30.   [2] Quoted in Sprague, *Shakespeare and the Actors*, p. 238.
[3] *Liverpool Daily Post* (December 31, 1888).

The part-book of 1875 provides slight though significant evidence of the way in which Irving and Miss Bateman interpreted the scene between Macbeth and Lady Macbeth after the murder of Duncan. On the re-entry after the murder, Irving's note says 'don't look at each other', and 'I'll go no more' (II. ii. 50) is marked 'cow', presumably for 'cowardly', while Lady Macbeth's return with the daggers has 'He lost—she firm'.[1] Irving was being consistent, but this enactment of Macbeth's cowardliness and terror seems to have been achieved at the expense of the poetry of the murder scene, even if one agrees with Henry James that his representation of 'a nature trembling and quaking to its innermost spiritual recesses' excited the imagination.[2] In 1875 Irving seems to have been so preoccupied with portraying the terror of Macbeth, that he made 'a ranting screaming exit',[3] at the end of the scene. In 1888, Ellen Terry's portrait of Lady Macbeth presented a sharp contrast to Irving's terrified murderer. There was a commonplace practical tone in her voice when she asked the question 'Who was it that thus cried?' and when she declared the sleeping and the dead were but as pictures, she gave the impression of 'cool and perfect sincerity'. When she returned after replacing the daggers by Duncan's body, there was 'a curious curdling touch of detail' as she lifted a robe (probably her own) that had fallen on the ground, by the tips of her fingers,[4] evidently to avoid staining it with blood. Ellen Terry wore a series of mantles and robes of varying colours for nearly every change of scene.[5] The robe could have fallen before she made her exit with the daggers. The gesture of picking up her own robe would have brought out Lady Macbeth's cool detachment.

The part copy of 1875 provides only one clue to the way in which Irving approached the scene after the discovery of the murder of Duncan. The dialogue with Macduff and Lennox is twice marked 'vacant'.[6] Yet it would not be accurate to assume that Irving played the entire scene vacantly. During Macbeth's speech in his own defence, we know that Irving was very eloquent and powerful, taking the only opportunity afforded by his reading of the character to show how Macbeth obtained his power

[1] Shuttleworth, 'Irving's Macbeth', p. 30.
[2] *The Scenic Art*, p. 37.   [3] *The Figaro* (October 2, 1875).
[4] See *Liverpool Daily Post* (December 31, 1888).
[5] *Ibid.* Cf. *Daily Telegraph* (December 31, 1888); *Lady's Pictorial* (January 5, 1889); *The Political World* (January 5, 1889).   [6] Shuttleworth, p. 30.

over the thanes in council.[1] In 1888, as Irving spoke to the assembled thanes, Ellen Terry stood behind Banquo, nervously assenting with unconscious nods and inarticulate lip-movements until her strength failed her. She was carried out with her head thrown back over a thane's shoulder, and her red hair hanging down.[2]

Irving appears to have played a Machiavellian Richard III-like Macbeth in III. i. When Macbeth enquired about Banquo's movements he was 'smiling'. And the scene with the murderers in the part-book of 1875 was marked heavily with such comments as 'sneeringly' and 'very black all this'. In III. ii., however, the mood changed. A 'sigh' was marked before Lady Macbeth's 'Nought's had, all's spent' (III. ii. 4), and after Macbeth's '... these terrible dreams / That shake us nightly' (III. ii. 18–19), Irving wrote 'hand to head and sigh'.[3] The reviews confirm those notes in the part-book. In 1875, 'Nought's had, all's spent...' brought out the 'sad plight' of the Macbeths. Irving entered 'lost in gloom'.[4] Most of the markings in the part-book seem to show a growing rift between Macbeth and Lady Macbeth. On Macbeth's entrance 'abstractedly', Lady Macbeth 'appearing happy...puts her arms around him', he 'removes her arms quickly' and speaks 'impatiently'. Irving wanted to make it clear that Lady Macbeth had no knowledge of Macbeth's scheme. After 'Thou marvell'st at my words' (III. ii. 54) Irving commented, 'and she *does—no knowledge of his scheme*. She doesn't understand and goes off abruptly.'[5]

The comments on the banquet scene in the part-book were surprisingly few and general. The comment after 'If thou canst nod, speak, too' (III. iv. 70), was 'very bold and excited' and at the end of the scene Irving felt that Macbeth was 'wandering and desperate'.[6] For details one has to go to the reviewers. The hall for the banquet in 1875 was neither 'too barbaric nor too glossy', and the spectral illusion was considered novel. The figure of Banquo was painted on gauze and on this a pale blue light was thrown. Irving raged at the phantom on its second appearance, and moved towards it as if he 'would trample it'. But his horror got the better of him. He clutched furtively at his red mantle, flung it before his face, burying his head in it and 'grovelling in

[1] *Daily Post* (September 27, 1875).
[2] *Liverpool Daily Post* (December 31, 1888).
[3] Shuttleworth, p. 30.   [4] *Daily Post* (September 27, 1875).
[5] Shuttleworth, p. 30.   [6] *Ibid.*

impotent terror at the foot of the throne'.[1] Clement Scott, writing in the *Daily Telegraph* on September 27, 1875, thought that Irving's idea of covering his face with his cloak as he fell shrieking to the foot of the throne would have been thoroughly effective 'had his strength been as powerful as his welcome imagination'. This seems to have been a fair criticism. Irving appears to have lacked the resources to carry out fully this exhibition of terror and despair even in 1888. In 1888, Bernard Shaw thought that Irving's performance as a whole was a thing of 'refined beauty' with the exception of the scene with Banquo's ghost which was 'rather ludicrously beyond his powers'.[2] Irving's distracting lighting effects in 1888 would not have helped. The dramatic critic of the *Star* (December 31, 1888) tells us that on each appearance of the ghost the stage was plunged in darkness and concludes that this was Irving's way of indicating that the ghost was visible only to Macbeth. After the guests had gone Ellen Terry spoke

You lack the season of all natures, sleep   (III. iv. 141)

'mechanically', quite unlike Helen Faucit, in tones not of comfort, but as if she was relinquishing her grip on 'practical wifehood'. As he passed her, Macbeth took a torch from behind a pillar and hurled it blazing to the ground. He shrouded his face in his robe as he leaned against a pillar and Ellen Terry knelt behind him, clinging to his robe with an upturned tragic face.[3]

Irving made very few notes on the scenes that followed the banquet. The idea of seizing Macduff's castle and murdering his children seems to have been interpreted by him, in the cauldron scene, as 'a sudden thought'. According to E. R. Russell, in 1888, as the play moved to its conclusion Irving showed Macbeth sinking deeper and deeper into wretchedness; as he indulged in 'nervous boasting of bravery' his tones sounded hollow. It was an intensely thought-out portrayal, writes E. R. Russell, of the degeneracy of an able and powerful general.[4] In 1875, Irving introduced two new readings[5] in the final scenes which, one suspects, were consistent with the portrait he was drawing—

She *would* have died hereafter

---

[1] *Daily Post* (September 27, 1875).
[2] See *Ellen Terry...a correspondence*, p. xxxi.
[3] *Liverpool Daily Post* (December 31, 1888).
[4] *Ibid.*   [5] Shuttleworth, p. 31.

and
> Hang out our banners. On the outer walls
> The cry is still they come...

Bertram Shuttleworth's assertion that Irving abandoned the new readings in 1888 does not seem true, however, because 'An Old Playgoer', after seeing Irving play, objected to them in a letter published in *St. James's Gazette* on December 31, 1888. The 'Old Playgoer' protested against 'She *would* have died hereafter', as a platitude unworthy of Shakespeare and Mr Irving, and he could not see why the cry 'they come' should have been confined to the outer walls. It is possible, however, that the alterations helped Irving to suggest the hollow assurance, the nervous boasting, E. R. Russell writes about. It is not surprising that Irving thought the lines '...full of sound and fury, / Signifying nothing' (v. v. 27–8) should sound 'very determined'.[1] Where Garrick, Kemble, Cooke and Macready had aroused pity, Irving seems to have suggested not self-knowledge here but self-assertion.

If Irving interpreted Macbeth more in the spirit of realism, the sleep-walking scene when Miss Bateman played it in 1875, 'not as a gaunt spirit of evil but as a wife', was domestic and melancholy. She re-enacted the murder scene in her sleep 'in a manner closely resembling the original occurrence', supported by a 'simple domestic arrangement for her entrance and exit down and up a stair-case'. Ellen Terry, on the other hand, was charming rather than realistic. The dramatic critic of the *Stage* wrote on January 4, 1889: 'The sleep-walking scene is full of charm by reason of Miss Terry's personality. She looks like a beautiful picture, the conception of a poetic mind. But her pure white clinging garments and pain-strained face call for admiration rather than pity and awe.' The pre-Raphaelite charm achieved by Ellen Terry (see Plate 9), was not adequate for the harsh, tragic intensity of the sleep-walking scene. Irving himself seems to have been conscious of deficiencies in her approach. Characteristically, his objections were made on realistic grounds—in an undated letter written to Ellen Terry, possibly after the dress rehearsal. 'The sleep-walking scene will be beautiful too', Irving wrote, 'the moment you are in it—*but* Lady Macbeth should certainly have the appearance of having got out of bed, to which she is

[1] Shuttleworth, p. 31.

returning when she goes off. The hair to my mind should be wild and disturbed, and the whole appearance as distraught as possible, and disordered...'[1] As Ellen Terry herself pointed out, however —'the cause of my being all wrong in the scene lay deeper than my appearance...'[2] She seems to have been right when she observed that Sargent's pre-Raphaelite picture of her—now in the Tate Gallery—embodied all that she had meant to do: 'The picture of me is newly finished and I think it magnificent. The green and blue of the dress is splendid, and the expression as Lady Macbeth holds the crown over her head, quite wonderful.'[3]

If Ellen Terry in the sleep-walking scene seemed to radiate a charm that was irrelevant, Irving in his last scene succeeded in achieving an arresting power which, if not fully tragic in its force, had an animal intensity. He looked 'like a great famished wolf' after the battle, wrote Ellen Terry.[4] Conscious of doom but resolved to meet it, his hair dishevelled, his face drawn and tense,[5] Irving met his death in a conflict short, sharp and savage while 'many mysterious thrilling sounds of war' were heard in the distance and a war-song kept rising and falling away.[6] After receiving his death-wound Irving, like Edmund Kean, fell with his face downward.[7]

For all its power and beauty, however, Irving's interpretation of Macbeth was not tragic in the fullest sense. While it had a positive originality and provided a refreshing contrast to merely conventional Macbeths 'with their posturing...and unbroken accents',[8] it made the tragic experience of *Macbeth* more and not less elusive. As Henry James pointed out, when reviewing a realistic interpretation of Macbeth by George Rignold, in New York: 'Realism is a very good thing, but in a Shakespearean production it is like baking a pudding in a porcelain dish; your pudding may be excellent but your dish gets cracked.'[9] One is inclined to believe that though the pudding was excellent when Henry Irving and Ellen Terry played in *Macbeth*, the dish did get cracked. At the end of the nineteenth century Henry James

---

[1] See *Memoirs*, ed. Craig and St John, p. 233.
[2] *Ibid.*   [3] *Ibid.*   [4] *Ibid.* p. 232.
[5] See H. A. Saintsbury and Cecil Palmer, *We Saw Him Act* (1959), p. 91.
[6] *Liverpool Daily Post* (December 31, 1888).
[7] *Daily Post* (September 27, 1875).
[8] *Liverpool Daily Post* (December 31, 1888).
[9] *The Scenic Art*, p. 34.

thought that 'the simplicity, the naiveté' essential to tragic art was rapidly passing out of human life:

> To produce very good acting there should be a class of performers and a public in whom subtlety has not attained its maximum. If evidence in favour of this assertion were needed, I should venture to point to two striking cases of essentially modern acting which I have lately witnessed as samples of the harm that can be done by the absence of what I have called naiveté. One is the Macbeth of Mr Henry Irving, which I lately saw in London; the other is the Macbeth of Signor Ernesto Rossi, which I saw the other night here. I do not know how Garrick or Charles Kemble or Edmund Kean played the part, or how Talma would have played it if he had been allowed; but as I watched the English and the Italian tragedian I murmured with myself, 'Oh, for one touch of Kemble or of Talma!' one touch of good faith, of the ideal, the simple.[1]

James recognised, however, that Irving and Rossi were very clever actors, and that his remarks at the time had 'perhaps an air of aberration'.[2]

Realism was in the air when Henry Irving and Ellen Terry staged *Macbeth*. The audacity of Ellen Terry's realism in the first act of *Macbeth* was in fact anticipated by Sarah Bernhardt, and some of Rossi's strategies in *Macbeth* had an Irvingesque quality. Like Irving, Rossi invented business of a startling kind in the banquet scene.

When Sarah Bernhardt played Lady Macbeth at the Gaiety Theatre on July 4, 1884, she was attuned to the spirit of the age, anticipating the realism of Ellen Terry by four years. While pouring into Macbeth's ear the thought of Duncan's murder, she wrapped him in a clinging embrace, as if she would play upon his senses rather than his reason.[3] Sarah Bernhardt was less decorous and more realistic than Ellen Terry in the sleep-walking scene. She startled her audience by making her entrance 'with naked feet'.[4] Bare-footed and in 'a clinging night-dress', the *Times* reviewer reports, she had 'aroused an extraordinary degree of enthusiasm in Paris'. Sarah Bernhardt's interpretation of the sleep-walking scene was violent and hysterical. After apostrophising the 'damned spot' she fell back shrieking hysterically and

[1] *The Scenic Art*, p. 45. [2] *Ibid.*
[3] *The Times* (July 4, 1884). [4] *Ibid.*

finally rushed off to the wings, calling out lustily, 'To bed, to bed!' (*Au lit, au lit!*).[1] Her portrayal of Lady Macbeth was sensational rather than serious, though it must be remembered that both she and Marais, who played Macbeth, used Richepin's melodramatic translation. Richepin's version of *Macbeth* was 'a literal translation of the poetry with the poetry left out'.[2]

Rossi played Macbeth at Drury Lane on May 10, 1876, with Signora Glech-Pareti as Lady Macbeth. Like Irving, Rossi was a clever, realistic actor, fascinated by the possibilities of stage business. Moy Thomas, writing in the *Academy*,[3] thought that the most imaginative portion of his portrayal of Macbeth was 'perhaps' during the dagger scene, a very fine point being made of a 'long pause' before the famous soliloquy, while the eyes were 'fixed on air or wandering, as if following the movements of the shadowy weapon'. It is noteworthy that Rossi's most imaginative effect seems to have been achieved outside the words.

The desire to achieve effects outside and almost independent of Shakespeare's poetry led Rossi in the banquet scene to create business reminiscent of Henry Irving's, though more sensational. It seemed to Henry James that Rossi over-stepped the modesty of nature in the banquet scene, when he saw him play in Paris:

As Macbeth leaves the apartment with his wife, after the departure of the guests, he stumbles upon his long mantle, trips, falls, and rolls over his heels in the air. His mind is so full of supernatural horrors that he thinks the ghost of Banquo is still playing him tricks and he lies crouching and quaking to see what is coming next. It is a handsome somersault, certainly, but I do not think it can be called acting Shakespeare.[4]

The experiments of Rossi and Sarah Bernhardt illustrate the presence of an old tendency (though in the late nineteenth century it looked like a new tendency) to sacrifice Shakespeare rather than sacrifice to him.

Neither Salvini nor Forbes-Robertson altered the taste for realistic interpretations of Macbeth established by players like Irving. Salvini, who was both a grand and a natural Othello, seems to have taken a rather limited view of the character. Salvini's Macbeth was the reverse of Garrick's sensitive murderer

---

[1] *Ibid.* [2] See *The Saturday Review* (June 14, 1884).
[3] May 13, 1876. [4] *The Scenic Art*, p. 47.

when he played the role in April 1876, at Edinburgh, and in London at Covent Garden in March 1884.

He saw 'nothing great in Macbeth' beyond 'the royalty of muscle' and the courage 'which comes from strong and copious circulation', wrote R. L. Stevenson, when he saw Salvini play at Edinburgh.[1] Stevenson had no quarrel with Salvini's conception of the character and held that it was a thoroughly convincing creation, though he reports that Salvini, shuddering with uncontrollable jealousy when he observed Duncan embracing Banquo, insisted on the moral smallness of Macbeth from the beginning. His caresses were singularly hard and unloving—and, as Stevenson points out, Salvini could give a great deal of meaning to a caress. At times he would lay his hand on Lady Macbeth, as he might take hold of anyone who happened to be nearest to him in a moment of excitement. Love had fallen out of the marriage by the way and left a curious friendship. Stevenson writes:

Only once—at the very moment when she is showing herself so little a woman and so much a high-spirited man—only once is he very deeply stirred towards her; and that finds expression in the strange and horrible transport of admiration, doubly strange and horrible on Salvini's lips.—'Bring forth men-children only!'[2]

In the banquet scene Salvini seemed at first to show 'a purely physical dislike for Banquo's spirit and the "twenty trenched gashes".' He was both abject and blustering and so far forgot himself, his terror and the nature of what was before him, that he rushed upon the ghost as if it were a man. When Lady Macbeth told him that he needed repose, there was something really childish in the way Salvini looked about the room; seeing nothing, with an 'expression of almost sensual relief', he plucked up heart enough to go to bed.[3]

In the fifth act, the moral and physical transformation effected in the character by Salvini seems to have been totally convincing. R. L. Stevenson described the transformation from the physical well-being of the first act to the moral degradation of the fifth:

From the first moment he steps upon the stage you can see this character is a creation in the fullest meaning of the phrase; for the man before you is a type you know well already. He arrives with Banquo on

[1] *Academy* (April 15, 1876). [2] *Ibid.* [3] *Ibid.*

the heath, fair and red-bearded, sparing of gesture, full of pride and the sense of animal well-being, and satisfied after the battle like a beast who has eaten his fill. But in the fifth act there is a change. This is still the big, burly, fleshy handsome-looking Thane; here is still the same face which in the earlier acts could be superficially good-humoured and sometimes royally courteous. But now the atmosphere of blood, which pervades the whole tragedy, has entered into the man and subdued him to its own nature; and an indescribable degradation, a slackness and puffiness, has overtaken his features.

In the last scenes of Salvini's Macbeth, there was nothing human left in the character; there was only 'the fiend of Scotland' and Macduff's 'hell-hound', whom 'with a stern glee' the Scottish audience saw baited 'like a bear' and 'hunted down like a wolf!'[1] It seems clear from Stevenson's enthusiastic and approving account of Salvini's Macbeth, that behind Salvini's portrait, as behind Irving's, there was a realistic principle at work and a feeling of profound disillusion which, though impressive, fell short of the truly tragic.

To R. L. Stevenson, Salvini, 'fair and red-bearded, full of pride and the sense of animal well-being' when he made his first entrance, 'looked Macbeth to the full as perfectly as ever he looked Othello'.[2] To the dramatic critic of The Times, Forbes-Robertson, 'ruddy, robust, unkempt, strong in physical courage', looked the 'living picture of the rude, northern soldier'.[3] But here all resemblance between the portraits drawn by Forbes-Robertson and Salvini ends.

Salvini adopted a consistent realism. But at the Lyceum, on September 17, 1898, Forbes-Robertson's well-bred tones clashed with his looks. The tones, natural and poetic, civilised and yet alive which had suited Hamlet so well, seemed unrelated to his new costume and make-up. The Times reviewer was obviously sympathetic. He liked the visual impression of 'rugged strength' but found Forbes-Robertson's Macbeth disappointing in comparison with his Hamlet. Though the character was visually there —'a type which might have been placed on canvas by a great painter who remembered that the uncouth Scottish thane of the eleventh century was as likely as not to be half-Norwegian in blood and ruddy with the ruddiness of the Scandinavian stock'— Forbes-Robertson's speech did not accord with his visual con-

---

[1] Ibid.   [2] Ibid.   [3] September 19, 1898.

ception: 'The very scholarliness, the preachiness, that accord with the character of the philosophic Dane are drawbacks to the shaggy warrior.'[1] Clearly realism, if it was to work at all, could not stop with costume and make-up.

But the same clash between costume and character appears to have occurred in the case of Mrs Patrick Campbell, who played Lady Macbeth opposite Forbes-Robertson. Her first dress was magnificently barbaric, the bodice like a coat of mail, being covered with blue, green and gold sequins almost suggesting serpent's scales; and at the banquet she wore 'a gorgeous robe of golden tissue, glittering with multi-coloured jewelled embroideries, and with various strange birds wrought upon the golden background'.[2] Her manner, however, was 'essentially modern': the dramatic critic of *The Times* thought it 'decadent' as well. Mrs Campbell approached the scenes, in which Lady Macbeth plays the role of temptress, like Ellen Terry and Sarah Bernhardt. She attempted to coax and charm, to lull and cling, and was a modern 'temptress à la Baudelaire'.[3] The truth of this description is confirmed by the critic of *The Times*, who wrote that within her limits Mrs Patrick Campbell possessed 'a very special quality which has been aptly described as the suggestion of "dangerous love".'[4]

Mrs Campbell, who had played the second Mrs Tanqueray successfully, was in 1898 clearly unhappy with Shakespeare's verse. She told Graham Robertson one night after a performance '...I can't do it. I feel all the time that the woman would not speak like that—she couldn't say such things—I shouldn't say such things.' To this reasoning, relevant to the realistic play, Robertson ventured to point out that Lady Macbeth's thoughts were being turned into words by a great poet. Mrs Campbell interrupted with a remark which showed that realism of this kind eluded her: 'But you can't say such words *naturally*. Ellen Terry tried, and what did *she* do? She chopped the line into little bits, and pumped them out in staccato jerks.'[5] Clearly, Forbes-Robertson could not have had much help from Mrs Patrick Campbell.

The production was a disappointment though Forbes-Robert-

[1] *The Times* (September 19, 1898).
[2] *Pall Mall Gazette*. Quoted in Alan Dent, *Mrs Patrick Campbell* (1961), p. 161.
[3] *The Speaker*. Quoted in Dent, *Mrs Campbell*, pp. 160–1.
[4] September 19, 1898.   [5] See Dent, *Mrs Campbell*, p. 162.

son achieved one brilliantly chaste effect in the banquet scene; without the employment of spectacular business he achieved a result that was pure, unembellished and yet theatrical. He made the ghost of Banquo stalk in by the open door like an ordinary guest, except that he was arrayed in a bluish and spectral costume, in contrast with which the bloody gash upon his face showed up vividly. It was customary, says the dramatic critic of *The Times*, for actors playing Macbeth to become aghast at the apparition and apostrophise it loudly, 'Thou canst not say I did it...' (III. iv. 50). But Forbes-Robertson delivered the line very quietly, almost in a whisper.[1]

Yet, despite the intelligence and tact of Forbes-Robertson's interpretation of this scene, the total effect of his performance was less satisfying. Both Forbes-Robertson and Mrs Patrick Campbell seemed contemporary in a limiting sense. To the critic of the *Athenaeum* Forbes-Robertson's Macbeth seemed to be a courteous rather than a tragic figure: 'Our actors in tragedy...are most courteous and well-bred, and loth, apparently to do anything that might not decently be done in a drawing-room...To our pursuit of the beautiful we are sacrificing the terrible and the grotesque. We watch with pleasure...But we are not moved.'[2] When Arthur Bourchier and Violet Vanbrugh played Macbeth and Lady Macbeth at Stratford on November 13, 1906, and when Beerbohm Tree staged *Macbeth* at His Majesty's on September 5, 1911, this description of tragic acting in 1898 still seemed relevant.

When Bourchier played Macbeth at Stratford the dramatic critic of the *Birmingham Post* thought he had 'thrown tradition to the winds and presented a new conception of Macbeth'.[3] In fact, Bourchier's 'fair and portly Thane, with a mellow voice and genial manner'[4] resembled Forbes-Robertson's Macbeth in one important respect—there was a suggestion of the Victorian drawing-room in his voice. Like Forbes-Robertson, Bourchier approached the banquet scene with restraint. As the critic of the *Birmingham Post* pointed out, there was much of the milk of human kindness in him and he did not rave or make a grimace even when he saw the ghost of Banquo.

If Bourchier played Macbeth as a Victorian gentleman, Violet Vanbrugh's Lady Macbeth was 'not a fiend-like queen': 'Even

[1] September 19, 1898.   [2] September 24, 1898.
[3] November 14, 1906.   [4] *Ibid.*

when inciting her more scrupulous husband to murder she was every inch a woman and a very charming woman too. In the sleep-walking scene she looked exceedingly beautiful and was the personification of pathos. His performance was pleasing rather than powerful.'[1] Like Ellen Terry and Mrs Patrick Campbell, Violet Vanbrugh wore costumes interesting in themselves. As hostess to Duncan, she wore a simple gown of flowing red with narrow green embroidery. As queen she wore a startling and gorgeous robe that seemed to contain all the colours of the rainbow, 'suffused and modified'.[2] Her Lady Macbeth was not radically different from Mrs Patrick Campbell's, but was probably, at times, a more dramatic creation. Her colourful robe in the banquet scene hung loose on the shoulders of a stricken and miserable woman, with watchful red eyes and sunken cheeks.[3]

Violet Vanbrugh attracted the attention of Herbert Beerbohm Tree, for he chose her to play Lady Macbeth in his production of the play at His Majesty's Theatre in 1911. In Tree's *Macbeth*, the pre-Raphaelite cult of beauty, first glimpsed in Irving's production of 1888, now seemed to assert itself without restraint.

For her first scene as Lady Macbeth, Violet Vanbrugh wore a dress which showed 'a beautiful harmony in exquisite shades of blue and purple', the 'soft fabrics' draped one over the other, falling in graceful folds which seemed 'to take upon them fresh beauties at every movement of the wearer'.[4] She sat at a low window which revealed a sunlit landscape, brilliant against the sombre frame of the castle walls, reading Macbeth's letter. Tree's property plot for *Macbeth* lists a 'box seat in the window',[5] and his prompt copy contains the direction—'distant Trumpet off-stage. Lady Macbeth looks through window, sees nothing and goes on reading.'[6] The low window, the sunlit landscape, the trumpet heard in the distance, create a picture of medieval England that one associates with the pre-Raphaelite imagination.

Beauty seemed to be the truth pursued in Tree's production. When Lady Macbeth came out of the grey castle gate to welcome King Duncan as her husband's guest, she wrapped round her head and shoulders 'a long scarf of dull crimson silk, which gave

---

[1] November 14, 1906. [2] *Herald* (November 18, 1906).
[3] *Ibid.* [4] *Lady's Pictorial* (September 16, 1911).
[5] Gabrielle Enthoven Collection—see H. B. Tree Gift.
[6] *Ibid.* See also *The Times* (September 6, 1911).

her the air of some old-world Madonna'.[1] In the banqueting
scene Lady Macbeth wore a black veil upon which rested a
jewelled crown, and a magnificent court-train of crimson velvet,
elaborately embroidered.[2] Lady Macbeth's 'kind good night to
all' was beautifully said. And 'You lack the season of all natures,
sleep' (III. iv. 141), was 'accompanied by a beautiful action'; she
'gently removed the crown from Macbeth's head as from the
tired head of a child'.[3] In the sleep-walking scene she wore a long,
straight robe of some soft, clinging fabric of a sober shade of
russet brown.[4] Beauty was insisted upon in flat defiance of the
text. Lady Macbeth descended and ascended a long flight of stone
steps;[5] to the *Times* reviewer she seemed to 'go up and up';[6] and
at the end of the scene, as the Doctor and Gentlewoman talked to
each other, Lady Macbeth was 'still walking'.[7]

In his programme note Beerbohm Tree wrote: 'Among the
many instructive works written upon the subject none is more
inspiring than that of Dr Bradley.'[8] Bradley had published
Shakespearean Tragedy in 1904, and seven years later Tree attempted
to translate his comments on the imagery in *Macbeth* into literal
terms. Bradley reminds us that darkness broods over this tragedy:
'...almost all the scenes which at once recur to memory take
place either at night or in some dark spot.'[9] Tree accordingly set
most of his scenes 'in the solemn splendour of the night'.[10] Bradley
draws our attention to the torches that glow in the darkness, the
torch carried by Macbeth's servant when they meet Banquo in II.
i., the torch carried by Fleance, the torches that flared in the hall on
the face of the ghost,[11] and Tree's property plot lists torches to be
used in his production[12]—Tree added to Bradley's list, and made
his entrance carrying a torch. Bradley wrote that the witches are
associated with tempests that blow down 'trees and churches,
castles, palaces and pyramids',[13] and before Macbeth made his first
entrance carrying a torch, the wind howled, lightning flashed, and

---

[1] *Lady's Pictorial* (September 16, 1911).   [2] *Ibid.*
[3] *The Times* (September 6, 1911).
[4] *Lady's Pictorial* (September 16, 1911).
[5] See prompt copy, G. Enthoven Collection—H. B. Tree Gift.
[6] September 6, 1911.
[7] See prompt copy. Cf. *Morning Post* (September 6, 1911).
[8] September 5, 1911. On view at the London Museum.
[9] A. C. Bradley, *Shakespearean Tragedy* (reptd 1964), p. 279.
[10] See programme note.   [11] *Shakespearean Tragedy*, p. 280.
[12] H. B. Tree Gift.   [13] *Shakespearean Tragedy*, p. 281.

a tree was heard crashing down.[1] Tree introduced Davenant's 'Halt, halt', which was shouted off-stage in the storm, before Macbeth's entrance.[2]

Tree was inspired by those elements in Bradley's essay which excited his imagination. Bradley saw Macbeth's haunted poet's imagination as one aspect of his character: 'This bold ambitious man of action, has, within certain limits, the imagination of a poet...His imagination is thus the best of him, something usually deeper and higher than his conscious thoughts; and if he had obeyed it he would have been safe.'[3] The idea seems to have excited Tree because the dramatic critic of *The Times* tells us that he 'brought out the poet' in Macbeth: 'In the lyrical passages on sleep he became almost the virtuoso, pausing to enjoy the poetry, to turn it over on his tongue—it was Macbeth as the exponent of *l'art pour l'art?*'[4] Yet one suspects that Bradley would not have approved of Beerbohm Tree's interpretation of his idea. For Bradley saw the poetic imagination of Macbeth as part of an inescapable moral vision, 'something usually deeper and higher than his conscious thoughts', whereas Tree's impression of Macbeth's poetic imagination seems to have been aesthetic rather than moral. 'Terror, remorse, blood-thirst, all the other tragic elements had to give way wherever there was a chance for sheer beauty',[5] in Tree's production.

The murder of Duncan was presented as *'un beau crime'*.[6] The set was beautiful and possessed a pre-Raphaelite symmetry, with opposite flights of steps leading to the door of Duncan's room in the centre of the scene. To the critics of *The Times* and the *Daily Chronicle*[7] the closed door became, in one sense, the protagonist. 'Victor Hugo and Maeterlinck knew the fascination of the closed door but Shakespeare knew it before them.'[8]

In the pursuit of beauty, Tree made extensive cuts in the text. It appeared to one critic that the omission of the scene after the murder of Duncan, and the omission of Banquo's murder made everything too sudden.[9] Tree seems to have concentrated all his attention on the banquet scene, which seems to have had its ballet-like moments as he staged it. There was a 'fierce dance of

[1] See prompt copy.
[2] *Ibid.*
[3] *Shakespearean Tragedy*, p. 295.
[4] September 6, 1911.
[5] *The Times* (September 6, 1911).
[6] *Ibid.*
[7] September 6, 1911.
[8] *The Times* (September 6, 1911).
[9] *Evening Standard* (September 6, 1911).

retainers' and even the ghost of Banquo appears to have been a beautiful ghost. It had 'rhythmic movement'—gracefully 'eluding', almost 'dodging' Macbeth all round the walls.[1] In his programme note Beerbohm Tree writes that he had intended to establish an 'awe-inspiring atmosphere'[2]—but the response he got was not one of awe. 'We were never shaken with terror', wrote the dramatic critic of *The Times*, 'Sir Herbert certainly is without a trace of it; he gives you what he can—sweetness, perfect taste, romantic melancholy, a sense of beauty. He interests and charms you but never dominates or thrills.'[3]

It could be said of Beerbohm Tree, when he cut scenes from *Macbeth*, that at least he had an aesthetic end in view. When Matheson Lang played Macbeth with Hutin Britten as Lady Macbeth on April 27, 1911, at one in the afternoon in Stratford, the encounter with the 'bleeding Sergeant' and the murder of Lady Macduff and her children were not given, while the closing scenes of war were severely cut, because 'the stars had to catch their London train'.[4]

Matheson Lang had been, rather like Tree, a 'romantic' actor, but when he returned from a tour abroad 'the occasional, somewhat lackadaisical movements' had disappeared, and his voice was no longer liable to huskiness when overtaxed. Lang's interpretation of the verse in *Macbeth* appears to have been 'thoughtful and free from affectation'. Yet his performance seems to have lacked 'colour', and his characterisation appears to have been vague.[5] While Tree, six months later, seems to have been less comfortable with Shakespeare's verse, he was able to communicate a more distinct, though limited idea of Macbeth's character. All that could be said in favour of the Stratford production in April 1911 was that some value seems to have been placed on restraint. From the time of Duncan's murder Miss Hutin Britten watched Macbeth 'with anxious intensity' and her sleep-walking scene was 'quietly poignant'.[6]

The most satisfying interpretation of Macbeth given during the early years of this century seems to have been F. R. Benson's when he was playing at his best. Gordon Crosse preferred Ben-

---

[1] *The Times* (September 6, 1911).   [2] September 5, 1911.
[3] September 6, 1911.   [4] *Morning Post* (April 28, 1911).
[5] *Ibid.*   [6] *Ibid.*

son's interpretation of Macbeth to Beerbohm Tree's. Crosse writes that there was an improvement in Benson's tragic acting after 1900: 'His Macbeth became one of the best I have seen, thoughtful, restrained, with hardly a trace of his earlier manner-isms.'[1] This impression of Benson's Macbeth appears to have been shared by James Agate. When Agate saw a performance by Donald Wolfit as Macbeth, which he regarded as unsatisfactory because Wolfit was not in the maximum degree simultaneously extrovert and introvert, it was Benson's Macbeth which he seems to have had in mind. To James Agate, among all the actors he had seen, Benson alone before 1945 appeared to make some attempt to understand the mighty opposites in Macbeth's character, as Shakespeare had perceived them. After seeing Wolfit play in February 1945, Agate wrote: 'I have seen one first-class Macbeth and one only—Benson. Benson was a superb Henry V and an exquisite Richard II, and his Thane was the result of adding the two together.'[2] Mrs Benson, who played Lady Macbeth, seems to have worn the kind of brilliant, exotic costume that had been fashionable since the days of Ellen Terry. In the banquet scene she wore an elaborate dress of red silk (on view at the London Museum), with green embroidery and strips of orange-patterned brocade. Her red velvet train was a gift from Henry Irving. The dramatic critic of the *Herald* wrote on April 27, 1906, that as Lady Macbeth, she was 'fiend-like in the savage obduracy of her nature' but 'a faithful and affectionate wife'.

In 1906 Benson had worked out the main lines of his interpreta-tion of Macbeth, though he had not realised his full powers. He showed Macbeth's development from a brave soldier to a tyrant, timorous, cunning and bloodthirsty,[3] but seemed to lack sus-tained physical power and to fall short of ideal excellence.[4] In May 1908 there was no essential change in Benson's approach. In the earlier scenes Macbeth seemed brave and just, and it was in the scenes after the murder of Duncan that 'cunning' and 'blood-thirstiness' seemed to dominate his actions. 'Was it not yesterday we spoke together?' (III. i. 72)—Macbeth's casual remark to the first murderer—was spoken 'with perfect indifference to the in-tended destruction of his old associate'.[5] But in July 1910

---

[1] *Shakespearean Playgoing*, 1890–1952 (1953), p. 31.
[2] *Sunday Times* (February 18, 1945).   [3] *Herald* (April 27, 1906).
[4] *Stratford-upon-Avon Herald* (April 27, 1906).   [5] *Ibid.* (May 8, 1908).

Benson's interpretation of Macbeth seems to have been both 'powerful and subtle'.[1]

A prompt copy of *Macbeth* at the Shakespeare Centre in Stratford, provides some indications of the way in which the Bensons interpreted their roles. At 'screw your courage to the sticking place, / And we'll not fail' (I. vii. 60–1), Lady Macbeth seized Macbeth's hand and knelt down before him. The business indicates the tone in which the lines must have been spoken. Mrs Benson seems to have been 'feminine' at this point, pleading with Macbeth rather than commanding him. Lady Macbeth's fainting in the scene after the murder was represented as genuine, and Benson crossed the stage and carried her 'up left'—a natural gesture that could have suggested Macbeth's capacity for affection, his sensitiveness, and the fact that at this stage in the action he seemed to be in control. After the guests left the banquet and the stage was empty, the tensions within her seemed to overpower Lady Macbeth again. The Benson prompt copy tells us how the moments after the departure of the guests were dealt with. At 'A kind good night to all' (III. iv. 121) 'Lady M. falls by the throne'. At the end of the banquet scene, the prompt copy seems to contrast the sudden weakness of Lady Macbeth with Macbeth's new, cold decisiveness. At 'We are yet but young in deed' (III. iv. 144), Macbeth 'Sticks his dagger into a stool and drinks'. In v. v., Benson beat the unfortunate Messenger with his dagger and made him kiss it—Garrick, it will be remembered, in his earlier performances beat the Messenger with his truncheon.

Benson could be surprisingly, at times refreshingly, unprofessional. He could invent business that now seems over-elaborate, as when he wrote the letter to Lady Macbeth on the stage. His improvisations gave his Shakespearean productions, at their worst, a rather ragged quality; at their best a lively spontaneity. At Stratford, Benson had the advantage of working in an atmosphere which seemed to W. B. Yeats refreshing and alive. Yeats tells us how his own imagination was liberated and describes the shared intellectual excitement when Benson staged Shakespeare's plays there. 'There is no one', wrote Years in 1901, 'who has come merely because one must go somewhere after dinner...It is certainly one's fault if one opens a newspaper, for Benson gives one a play every night, and one need talk of nothing

[1] *Herald* (August 6, 1910).

but the play in the inn-parlour, under oak beams blackened by time and showing the mark of the adze that shaped them.'[1]

But the revolution which was to make even Benson seem archaic[2] had begun unobtrusively at the end of the nineteenth century, with William Poel as its prophet. The student of the history of acting gets accustomed to the thought of revolutions. Garrick, Kean and Irving had looked like prophets of revolution in their day, and each of them had helped to accomplish a return to the natural. Yet Poel, who was much less of an actor than Garrick, Kean or Irving, began changes on many fronts, possibly more radical on the whole than any that had occurred in the history of Shakespearean theatre since the days of Betterton.

Poel had some points in common with earlier innovators. He believed that Shakespeare's poetry was created out of the staple of common speech and should be spoken 'trippingly on the tongue', easily and naturally: 'In the delivery of verse, therefore, on the stage, the audience should never be made to feel that the tones are unusual. They should still follow the laws of speaking, and not those of singing.[3] This does not mean that Poel was insensitive to the variety of tone, the musical qualities expressive of both feeling and sense in Shakespeare's verse. As Robert Speaight tells us, while Poel was never satisfied with a merely mellifluous voice, he wanted the 'tuned tongue'. Speaight writes that Poel wanted more vocal splendour and variety than is generally found on the stage today.[4]

Poel went back to the original Folio text of *Macbeth* though he was not the first to do this. It was Garrick who abandoned Davenant's version after it had been in use for eighty years, and Phelps who played the full text for the first time, including the scene in which Lady Macduff and her child confront the killers sent by Macbeth. When Phelps staged *Macbeth* on March 20, 1850, at Sadlers Wells, Miss Edwards played Lady Macduff and Miss Bullen the 'Son of Macduff'.[5] Poel was wrong when he made the claim in *The Times* on January 3, 1927, that '...Lady Macduff

[1] *Ideas of Good and Evil* (1903), pp. 142 ff.
[2] See Audrey Williamson, *Theatre of Two Decades* (1951), p. 14.
[3] *Shakespeare in the Theatre* (1913), p. 7.
[4] *William Poel and the Elizabethan Revival* (1954), p. 273.
[5] See letter by Arden Foster in *The Times* (January 6, 1927). See also, review of Phelps's 1847 production in *Athenaeum* (October 2, 1847), p. 1037.

made her appearance on the stage after more than two hundred years absence on January 22, 1909, when the Elizabethan Stage Society...revived the tragedy in the Elizabethan manner at the Grand Theatre, Fulham...' More important than Poel's claim that Lady Macduff was included in his production of Macbeth for the first time after two hundred years was his analysis of her role. Lady Macduff was the only other woman besides Lady Macbeth in the play. Poel showed how the two characters were contrasted,[1] and Bernard Shaw commented, after seeing the performance at Fulham: 'I never before realised with absolute certainty that Macbeth was a doomed man if he ever let Macduff catch him.'[2] Poel helped to establish a veneration for Shakespeare's text and a respect of his powers as a dramatist, even though he failed to appreciate that the first steps in the restoration of the Folio text were taken by Garrick, and that Phelps had used the original uncut text in 1850.

Poel's third revolutionary idea was more radical than his first two principles, and it was not anticipated by any of the great innovators before him. Poel realised that when Shakespeare wrote *Macbeth* the play was staged in Elizabethan costume, not in Scottish kilts or Anglo-Saxon dress. To him the tragedy was Elizabethan in feeling, and the blood-guiltiness of Holyrood and Fotheringay seemed to darken the corridors of Dunsinane.[3] Poel's discovery that Shakespeare's plays were contemporary in feeling and that they were staged in what was 'modern dress' in his time, was to have far-reaching consequences.

Poel's fourth great principle was that Shakespeare's plays could be best produced on the kind of stage for which he wrote. Shakespeare had no naturalistic sets, but Poel did not think this a deprivation. 'One of the chief fallacies', he wrote, 'in connection with the modern notion of the Elizabethan stage is that of its poverty of colour.'[4]

The stage projected into the yard surrounded by spectators. The action was brought into prominent relief and placed close before the eye. Deprived of perspective, it acquired a special kind of realism which the vast distances of Victorian theatres rendered unattainable—the realism of an actual event at which the audience assisted, not the realism of a scene in which the actor

---

[1] See Speaight, *William Poel*, p. 187. [2] *Ibid.* Cf. *The Times* (January 3, 1927).
[3] See Speaight, *William Poel*, p. 184. [4] *Shakespeare in the Theatre*, p. 5.

seemed to play a subordinate role.[1] Poel's ideas about the apron-stage were not understood in his day, though they seem to have a better chance of being understood now.

The struggle for the preservation of the apron-stage had been a long, losing battle. In the days of Betterton, Cibber noted with regret that when Drury Lane was rebuilt by 1700 the apron-stage was smaller by ten feet, and it seemed to him that some of the old intimacy between actor and audience was lost.[2] Yet a sizable though smaller apron was still in use at Drury Lane during the eighteenth century, in the days of Garrick and Mrs Siddons. It was at the end of the nineteenth century, when spectacle and elaborate sets became completely dominant, that the apron went quite out of use. Poel's demand for an uncluttered open stage, with the audience surrounding it, and not shut out by a curtain, may prove to be the most fruitful idea he had.

Poel was an exciting theorist. As a practitioner he was less successful. In May 1895, Poel directed Lillah McCarthy as Lady Macbeth in a production by the Shakespeare Reading Society at St George's Hall. Bernard Shaw wrote of her interpretation on that occasion: 'The banquet scene and the sleep-walking scene were quite successful; and if the earlier scenes were immature, unskilful and entirely artificial and rhetorical in their conception, still they were very nearly thrilling.'[3] Shaw's remarks reveal that Poel only achieved a partial success in his direction on this occasion.

Poel seems to have been more interested in Lady Macbeth than in Macbeth. Robert Speaight writes that Poel challenged tradition most deliberately in his conception of Lady Macbeth, taking Mrs Siddons's suggestion that she was 'fair, feminine, nay perhaps fragile' as his text.[4] Poel's conception was very much in the tradition established by Helen Faucit, and, like Helen Faucit's, has some justification in Shakespeare's text. Both

> O *gentle* lady,
> 'Tis not for *you* to hear what I can speak!   (II. iii. 81–2)

and

> All the perfumes of Arabia will not sweeten this *little* hand
>   (V. i. 50)

---

[1] *Shakespeare in the Theatre*, p. 6.   [2] See above, p. 24.
[3] *Our Theatres in the Nineties*, I, 139–40.   [4] *William Poel*, p. 185.

could be indications that Shakespeare saw Lady Macbeth as feminine and fragile. Where Poel differed from Helen Faucit was in his translation of the idea into concrete terms. He saw Lady Macbeth's hair as bright red and her complexion as flushed pink. Her eyelids were painted light green and there were flecks of gold under her eyes. Her mouth was very clear and carmined. Her neck and hands were white, tinted with pale blue. She carried her head high, with straightened back and squared shoulders, and moved with a slight swing. She was a woman of thirty-five.[1]

Poel felt that Lady Macbeth lacked imagination and was at heart a materialist, not from conviction but from shallowness. Her invocation to the murdering ministers, as Poel saw it, was sceptical in tone; 'Even the "spirits", to which her husband has alluded; those which she mockingly invokes to her feminine aid, have no reality for her...'[2] With Poel every problem of interpretation was referred to the kind of woman he thought Lady Macbeth was. In the line 'Give me the daggers', he thought there were two possible emphases, on 'Give' or on 'me'. But he chose 'Give' because he believed that a woman of Lady Macbeth's practical disposition would put the emphasis on 'give'. Besides, he argued, an emphasis on 'me' could not be meaningful because there was nobody else to whom Macbeth could give the daggers.[3]

All the evidence suggests that Poel believed in much more than good platform recitals, and his innovations did not stop with changes in Lady Macbeth's costume, make-up and character. He introduced new business of a realistic, though not sensational, kind into the sleep-walking scene. He showed Lady Macbeth at her dressing-table, playing mechanically with her brushes and comb and going through the motions of doing her hair. Poel believed the scene would be more convincing if the audience could see Lady Macbeth moving gradually into the rhythm of her sleep-walking, instead of being fixed in it at the moment of her first appearance. The business at the dressing-table seems to have gone on in an inner chamber while the Doctor and the Gentlewoman watched and commented from outside.[4] The whole idea of Lady Macbeth 'doing her hair' strikes one as modern and realistic. It is difficult to see the business outside a picture-frame stage—on Shakespeare's open platform stage it might not have

---

[1] Speaight, *William Poel*, p. 188.   [2] *Shakespeare in the Theatre*, p. 64.
[3] *Ibid.* pp. 58-9.   [4] Speaight, *William Poel*, p. 188.

worked at all; there is certainly no provision for it in his text. It makes one wonder whether Poel had fully worked out the consequences of his most revolutionary principle. He was a great innovator, a courageous experimentalist, but some of the implications of his ideas have still to be fully worked out.

It is possibly because Poel's revolution has far from reached completion that critics involved in the theatre like Professor Wilson Knight look back with some nostalgia to the days of Beerbohm Tree. To Wilson Knight, Tree was an artist and a good one and in 1935 it seemed that 'the richness and dignity which the Shakespearean play demands died with him':

For at his Majesty's you attended always something beyond entertainment, of ceremonial grandeur and noble if extravagant artistry. I well remember Tree's marvellous make-up as Othello; and the Weird Sisters floating through smoky clouds at the opening of Macbeth; and how appropriate this a symbol of his whole approach—the incense filling the theatre from the Forum scene in *Julius Caesar*.[1]

Tree carried on a tradition of grand realism in production established by Charles Kean and Henry Irving. But his interpretation of Macbeth's character was melancholy and romantic, while Irving's was sceptical and realistic. It is with reservations of this sort that one must accept Wilson Knight's remark that, even if we differ from Tree's principles, 'we have nevertheless scrapped one great tradition without properly creating another'.[2] The revolution begun by Poel, one feels, has yet to complete itself.

[1] See *Shakespearean Production* (1964), p. 21.
[2] *Ibid.*

CHAPTER 11

TRADITION AND INNOVATION
(1912–55)

When Granville-Barker, who had worked with William Poel, staged *The Winter's Tale* at the Savoy in September 1912, he was carrying the revolution begun by Poel into the commercial theatre. Footlights were abolished, pauses between scenes eliminated, symbolic décor substituted for the realistic sets that had become traditional since the days of Charles Kean, and Henry Ainley delivered Leontes's speeches with swift intensity. When Granville-Barker staged *A Midsummer Night's Dream* in New York in 1914, Professor G. C. D. Odell, who preferred the old tradition represented by Tree in the Edwardian age, wrote: 'It would require a brave man to predict the future manner of presenting Shakespeare on the stage. I suspect it will not be Tree's way. I hope it will not be Mr Granville-Barker's.'[1] Brought up in the realistic tradition, Odell could not understand how Granville-Barker's silk curtains lighted in changing tones of green, blue, purple or violet, and his light gauze canopy where fireflies and glow-worms flickered,[2] could be substituted for forest trees. Yet, though critics like Odell and Wilson Knight believed that with the end of the tradition begun by Tree, something that was accustomed and ceremonious went out, with Granville-Barker new ceremonies were substituted for old.

To later critics who had no experience of the old tradition at first hand, the lavish displays of Irving and Tree seemed a natural expression of the later Victorian age, the Indian summer of the European bourgeoisie.[3] Tree's approach to Shakespeare seemed 'capitalistic', his audiences elegant. In contrast the 'simplicity' of Granville-Barker and Poel appeared to have social as well as formal implications. Certainly, productions were less expensive at the Old Vic and they were aimed at a less wealthy public. Eric Bentley has claimed that Miss Lilian Baylis[4] of the Old Vic was

[1] See *Shakespeare from Betterton to Irving*, II, 469.
[2] See J. C. Trewin, *Shakespeare on the English Stage 1900–1964* (1964), p. 58.
[3] See Eric Bentley, *In Search of Theatre* (1954), p. 114.   [4] *Ibid.*

more important to the revolution in the staging of Shakespeare than Granville-Barker.

While the war stopped Granville-Barker's invasion of the commercial theatre between 1915 and 1918, Sybil Thorndike, who was very much an exponent of the new tradition, played Lady Macbeth at the Old Vic. It seems relevant from more than one point of view that Dame Sybil should see Macbeth and Lady Macbeth as rather like 'big capitalists' in a tragic partnership.[1] This sort of judgement could restrict the universality of the characters, could indeed become a limiting formula, except that in Dame Sybil's case the phrase defines an emotional attitude to the characters. It is a view of the characters that would be understood today more easily than in the eighteenth and nineteenth centuries. We live at a time when the phrase and its connotations are widely known. Yet in some ways Dame Sybil's attitude to the characters resembles William Poel's. Poel regarded Macbeth and Lady Macbeth as Renaissance individualists—a view of the characters that evidence unearthed by L. C. Knights might support. L. C. Knights has shown in *Drama and Society in the Age of Jonson* (1937), how playwrights like Shakespeare and Jonson evaluated the individualist spirit that was altering old patterns of living at the end of the sixteenth century.

Though she had what one might describe as a contemporary view of Lady Macbeth, it seems ironic that in the 1920s Sybil Thorndike should have played the role of Lady Macbeth in a production which was closer in some ways to Tree than to Granville-Barker. Sir Lewis Casson, who had directed a *Julius Caesar* indebted to Poel and Granville-Barker at Manchester in October 1913, with a full text, a modified apron and a permanent set,[2] and received a hostile reception from the Press, staged, on December 24, 1926, a production of *Macbeth* in which there were realistic sets reminiscent of Tree's. This shows that the changes initiated by Poel and Granville-Barker had yet to be accepted in the commercial theatre.

Lewis Casson embarked on the production of *Macbeth* in 1926 with some reluctance, attempting to reconcile the elaborate aesthetic realism of Tree with fidelity to the text.[3] There were

---

[1] An opinion expressed in conversation with the writer.
[2] Trewin, *Shakespeare on the English Stage*, pp. 56–7.
[3] See *The Times* (December 24, 1926).

twenty-two changes of scene. The dramatic critic of *The Times* reported that eager imagination sat in half-darkness, thwarted by the recurrent curtain, wondering when Mr Rickett's next picture would be ready. The repeated fall of the curtain seemed to break up the dramatic form of the tragedy into brilliant fragments, and to rob individual performances of some of their concentration and power. Though there was a consensus of agreement among the critics about the 'high accomplishment' of Sybil Thorndike's interpretation of Lady Macbeth, the critic of *The Times* felt that if she failed nevertheless to stir the blood or to freeze it, if the tendency of her acting was to encourage appreciative criticism rather than to quell the impulse to criticise while emotion lasted, the reason lay in the fact that her own part, like the play itself, was broken up and robbed of its evocative force.

In spite of this loss of concentration, Sybil Thorndike's Lady Macbeth was still a consistent and natural creation. Lewis Casson has pointed out that Lady Macbeth's terrible prayer to the forces of evil, beginning

Come, you spirits...   (I. v. 37 ff.)

was rightly whispered by Mrs Siddons, and that the full horror of the invocation is lost by declamation.[1] Dame Sybil whispered Lady Macbeth's commitment to evil, showed common sense during the intrigue, majesty at the banquet, and evoked pity for the queen at the end.[2] Her Lady Macbeth was both natural and majestic. Gordon Crosse remembered the unforgettable picture she made in her red dress as she stood framed in the doorway awaiting Duncan's approach, how she listened crouched against the wall as the murder was committed, and made a bold, almost jaunty exit with the daggers.[3] During the sleep-walking scene the terror of Lady Macbeth's subconscious awakening was controlled by regal restraint. It was, said the critic of the *Sketch*, as if she would have conveyed remorse, but could not forget that she was a queen even in her slumbers (see Plate 10).[4] Yet the majestic dignity of the sleep-walking scene was not monotonous or unvaried. For the traditional sigh at the end of the scene Sybil Thorndike substituted a shrill agonised whisper.[5]

[1] See Introduction to *The Tragedy of Macbeth*, Folio Society edition (1951), p. 7.
[2] See James Agate, *Brief Chronicles* (1943), p. 217.
[3] *Shakespearean Playgoing*, p. 53.
[4] January 5, 1927.   [5] *The Times* (December 24, 1926).

Given her understanding of the role it seems a pity that the demand for elaborate scenery should have reduced the effectiveness of Sybil Thorndike's playing, and that Henry Ainley as Macbeth should have been acting below his capacity—'there was more terror in the little finger of his Gauguin', wrote James Agate, 'than in the whole of his Macbeth'. To James Agate, Ainley's auburn wig, his fullness of countenance and his short beard gave him a distinct likeness to a Van Dyke Charles the First 'well in flesh'. He was never 'daemonic' and did not 'quite touch pathos'. In his interpretation of Macbeth Ainley ignored the variety of feeling and tone in Shakespeare's verse. Agate observed that Ainley passed from 'My way of life / Is fall'n into the sear, the yellow leaf' (v. iii. 22–3) to 'I'll fight till from my bones my flesh be hack'd' (v. iii. 32) without a change of intonation.[1]

There appears to have been a gap between intention and performance in Ainley's Macbeth. He differed from previous interpreters like Irving, rejecting the idea that Macbeth had the thought of murdering Duncan in his mind from the outset. Ainley made it clear that when he spoke the line 'My thought, whose murder yet is but fantastical' (I, iii. 139) the crime did not at this point present itself. His interpretation of the line caused Agate to suggest that Gould's reading of 'matter for murder' should be adopted.[2] Unfortunately, Ainley seems to have lacked the capacity to realise his conception of Macbeth's character in any consistent way in 1926.

When Lewis Casson played Macbeth with Sybil Thorndike in Wales in 1941, he adopted Gould's reading and the view of Macbeth's character that it implies. In his introduction to *The Tragedy of Macbeth* brought out by the Folio Society in 1951, Lewis Casson has left on record his view that Macbeth does not yield at once to the temptation of murder, and that

> My thought, whose matter yet is but fantastical

is more in harmony with Macbeth's actual state of mind. Lewis Casson sees 'murder' as a 'scrivener's error'. Macbeth succumbs to the temptation of murder only in the crucial scene during which Duncan appoints Malcolm Prince of Cumberland.[3]

[1] *Brief Chronicles*, pp. 216–17.
[2] *Ibid.* p. 216. Cf. G. Gould, *Corrigenda and Explanations* (1884), p. 37.
[3] See pp. 5–6.

Lewis Casson's conception of Macbeth has both traditional and modern elements, and he has given a contemporary significance to Macbeth's lines

> To-morrow, and to-morrow, and to-morrow,
> Creeps in this petty pace... (v. v. 19 ff.)

He sees the lines as the expression of a doctrine of atheistic nihilism, as the logical result of Macbeth's commitment to evil, and when I discussed the passage with him, he was not too happy about eighteenth- and nineteenth-century interpretations of the lines. Garrick drew pity when he spoke the lines, evidently seeing them as an expression of a state of mind rather than the assertion of a doctrine; so did Kemble and Macready, who saw the passage as an expression of tragic despair and disillusionment. Looking on earlier interpretations as 'sentimental', Lewis Casson would perhaps have equated Shakespeare's lines with the line given to the Four Tempters in T. S. Eliot's *Murder in the Cathedral*:

> Man's life is a cheat and a disappointment;
> All things are unreal...[1]

What he has given us is a modern reading which pays little attention to the pathos of the image of the 'poor player' who 'struts and frets his hour upon the stage' and is 'heard no more'—though surely Macbeth sees himself here. In my own view any interpretation which regards the passage as the expression of a doctrine rather than a particular experience threatens to divorce the conceptual content of the lines from their connotations. Shakespeare thought in images, and one cannot ignore the metaphors of the guttering candle and the poor player in arriving at the total experience conveyed by the lines. T. S. Eliot has pointed out that Shakespeare's imagery has tentacular roots reaching down to the deepest terrors and desires. What we seem to have in the 'To-morrow' soliloquy is the end of desire, an experience which has its own kind of terror.

Lewis Casson was a traditionalist in some ways, an innovator in others. When he staged *Macbeth* in Wales, he and Dame Sybil wore the costumes of the Forty-Five. His production of *Macbeth* in 1926 showed tradition and innovation commingling uneasily. The 1920s did not immediately accept the changes initiated by

[1] (1935), p. 41.

Poel and Granville-Barker. The commercial theatre in London was still conservative, though at Stratford and Birmingham the spirit of innovation was strong.

When James Hackett, the American, with 'his splendid Salvini-like Voice' and 'no perceptible American accent'[1] played Macbeth to Mrs Patrick Campbell's Lady Macbeth at the Aldwych on November 2, 1920, Bernard Shaw described the production as an 'ancient Victorian absurdity'. Shaw thought that 'the intervals with the *entr'acte* music played sixteen times over, killed the play'.[2] Mrs Patrick Campbell found Hackett a curiously unresponsive actor. 'It seemed to me', she wrote, 'he realised my presence only at his cues, and more than once seized the opportunity during a strong speech of mine to turn his back to the audience and clear a troublesome catarrh.'[3] Hackett seems to have believed in a purely elocutionary and non-dramatic approach to Shakespeare's verse. Mrs Campbell herself found Forbes-Robertson much easier to act with.

Her own interpretation had not changed since the days in which she had played Lady Macbeth with Johnston Forbes-Robertson. Shaw's comments on her performance, in his letters to her, indicate this. 'You should not have played the dagger scene in that best evening dress of Lady Macbeth's', he wrote on December 22, 1920, 'but in a black wrap like a thundercloud, with a white face...If you are determined to be a Paffick Lady all the time (Mrs P.C.'s dresses by HS & Co.) you cannot be Lady Macbeth or Mrs Siddons.'[4] As Lady Macbeth, Mrs Campbell evidently attempted to coax James Hackett as she had coaxed Forbes-Robertson in the scene in which Lady Macbeth persuades Macbeth to murder Duncan. Shaw wrote again on January 13, 1920, criticising her approach to this particular scene: 'It is not by tootling to him *con sordino* that Lady Macbeth makes Macbeth say "Bring forth men children". She lashes him into murder.'[5]

In his letter to her of December 22, 1920, Shaw suggested that if they had the good sense to invite Bridges-Adams to produce *Macbeth* for them and followed his direction, she and Hackett

---

[1] See Mrs Patrick Campbell, *My Life and Some Letters* (1922), p. 142.
[2] *Bernard Shaw and Mrs Patrick Campbell: Their Correspondence*, ed. Alan Dent (1952), p. 216.
[3] See *My Life and Some Letters*, p. 142.
[4] *Bernard Shaw and Mrs Campbell: ...Correspondence*, p. 216.
[5] *Ibid.* p. 219.

could go round the world with the play.[1] When *Macbeth* was produced by Bridges-Adams at Stratford with other players, it was undoubtedly interesting, though perhaps less successful than Shaw's letter might have led one to expect. When he directed *Macbeth* in the spring of 1923 with Frank Cellier and Dorothy Green in the leading roles, Bridges-Adams appears to have seen the play initially as a statement of evil. Macbeth and Lady Macbeth were 'two splendid figures' caught in 'a fog rolling up from dismal hell'. It was when 'the great doors opened on the dawn' that the voice of Baliol Holloway as Macduff brought 'daylight, fresh air, and the challenge of the good earth'.[2] Bridges-Adams, who had worked with Poel and Granville-Barker and was no believer in elaborate Victorian realism, seems to have translated Shakespeare's themes into symbolic visual terms.

Bridges-Adams was not as successful, however, in his direction of Frank Cellier and Dorothy Green as he was with visual and symbolic effects. Cellier presented Macbeth as prepossessed with the ridiculousness of extreme action, as a murderer who finds subterfuge embarrassing. When Lady Macbeth told him that he had been a fool to bring the daggers from Duncan's room, he gave 'a dismal and embarrassed shake of the head'.[3] Cellier's interpretation, clearly contemporary though it was, appears to have been 'interesting, subtle, but extraordinarily unsatisfying'. While his Macbeth seemed 'immensely underacted',[4] Dorothy Green appears to have played Lady Macbeth in 'the tradition of an earlier day'. Her iron will, her cunning and terror suggested the struggles of an evil animal, but at times she seemed to be striving after over-sensational effects.[5] At Stratford, during the regime of Bridges-Adams, it would appear that old traditions were not entirely obliterated.

It was at the end of the 1920s that an attempt was made to sweep away traditional elements altogether. When Sir Barry Jackson of the Birmingham Repertory Theatre staged the play he intended to make Macbeth and Lady Macbeth his contemporaries in a deliberate and conscious way.

The photographs at the Victoria and Albert Museum of Barry

[1] *Ibid.* p. 217.
[2] See Ruth Ellis, *The Shakespeare Memorial Theatre* (1948), p. 48.
[3] *The Times* (May 17, 1923).
[4] *Ibid.* (May 24, 1923).   [5] *Ibid.* (May 17, 1923).

Jackson's production of *Macbeth* suggest that we are looking at a play about the 1914–18 war. Eric Maturin, as Macbeth, is a general in khaki with red tabs, and he wears a silk dressing-gown for the scene of the discovery of Duncan's murder. It is possibly true that the English imagination in the 1920s was haunted by the memory of the 'Great War', but if there was a connection established between the 1914–18 war and Shakespeare's tragedy, it was superficial. The connection emerged when Macbeth turned 'blasted heath' into an expletive; when Duncan, in Field Marshal's uniform, stressed the epithet in 'What bloody man is that?'; when Lady Macbeth took a stiff whisky before 'That which hath made them drunk hath made me bold'.[1] Eric Maturin, in an effort to be consistent, spoke with 'a machine gun rattle that annihilated the verse'.[2]

The result of all these innovations was a displacement of Shakespeare's themes and interests. To James Agate, Eric Maturin's Macbeth did not grow 'either in perception, terror or sadness of heart'.[3] Barry Jackson appears to have succeeded in blurring the struggle between essential good and evil in the play, and Eric Maturin between the good and evil within Macbeth. Agate seems to have been right when he observed that the 'shadow not of tragedy but of the furniture dealers' plain van hung over the lounge-hall with its tasteful little table, standard lamp and pot of primulas accurately recalling windows in Kensington High Street and Tottenham Court Road'. Mary Merrall spoke the passage beginning

> What beast was't then
> That made you break this enterprise to me?

'reclining in abandonment and luxury in the arms of her Sheik on an art coloured divan with a distant gramophone playing the opening to the first act of Carmen'. It is not surprising, therefore, that Agate should have left the Court Theatre where Barry Jackson's production of *Macbeth* was staged in the spring of 1928 with 'no feeling of having attended *Macbeth* or even a tragedy by anybody'.[4]

[1] Trewin, *Shakespeare on the English Stage*, p. 111.
[2] J. C. Trewin, *The Birmingham Repertory Theatre 1913–1963* (1963), p. 94.
[3] *Brief Chronicles*, p. 223.
[4] *Ibid.* pp. 223–4.

The poetry of *Macbeth* was sacrificed in Sir Barry Jackson's production of *Macbeth*, and with it the tragic vision implicit in the poetry. In 1930 at the Old Vic, John Gielgud attempted to bring the poetry of *Macbeth* to life again, and with it the play's tragic significance. José Ferrer has left on record his first impression of hearing John Gielgud liberate Shakespeare's poetry from dead conventions and unintelligent rhythms:

I remember vividly having to control myself, literally control myself, to keep from standing up in my seat and asking him from the audience to say a certain speech over again so that I might never, so long as I lived, forget how he had read it. Gielgud revealed to me the fact that you could understand Shakespeare, that it was not a foreign tongue, that you could weep with him, and that there was a way to play the bard that did not just drive people out of the theatre mentally humiliated.[1]

Ferrer's account suggests that Gielgud was making Shakespeare contemporary in the best way possible by attempting to communicate the experience both ancient and modern which his poetry embodies. Though Gielgud did not capture the full tragic complexity of Macbeth either in 1930 or in 1942, he made a serious attempt to do it through the poetry and not outside it.

Gielgud showed that Macbeth was a prisoner of his own fantasy. This was Robert Speaight's impression,[2] and the idea of evil as unreal, as partaking of the nature of fantasy, is unfolded in the poetry of the play. Macbeth's first soliloquy closes with the words

> function is smother'd in surmise,
> And nothing is but what is not.   (i. iii. 141–2)

The word 'nothing' occurs again in Macbeth's last soliloquy, in the metaphor of life as an idiot's tale

> full of sound and fury,
> Signifying nothing.   (v. v. 27–8)

It was consonant with this conception of the role that Gielgud should pause after the word 'signifying' and whisper 'nothing'. To Robert Speaight, Gielgud succeeded in communicating the moral isolation (implicit in the text), which Macbeth brings down upon himself.

---

[1] See *The Listener* (April 23, 1964).
[2] Stated in conversation with the writer.

Gielgud seemed to explore Macbeth's nightmares with compelling sincerity. James Agate described the authentic, disturbing quality of his playing after the murder of Duncan:

Every good performance of any Shakespeare play is recognizable by the fact that it arouses fresh shock at something one knows so well that one takes it for granted...My own occurred when Macbeth came away from the murder carrying with incredible clumsiness both daggers as witnesses. To experience this shock is to believe in the murder, and this again is to believe in the actor.[1]

Gielgud's interpretation seemed most successful after the murder of the king. He was able to communicate a sense of the nightmare world which Macbeth begins to inhabit. To the dramatic critic of *The Times* he painted 'imaginary horror' in words that seemed 'dipped in the witches' cauldron'.[2] To Agate, Gielgud 'did not begin as so many Macbeths do' in the fifth act, but came on the stage as though he had lived the interval—occupied by IV. ii. and iii., and V. i. and ii., scenes which deal with the murder of Lady Macduff and her children, with the encounter between Malcolm and Macduff and the news of the murder brought by Ross, the sleep-walking of Lady Macbeth, and the meeting between Menteith, Caithness, Angus and Lennox. Macbeth says,

> I have supp'd full with horrors (V. v. 13)

and Gielgud made the audience realise that this is precisely what Macbeth had been doing while he was absent from the stage.[3] Gordon Crosse remembers the weariness of Gielgud's Macbeth in the last act, suggestive touches of wildness, 'not actual insanity, but something on the way towards it'.[4]

It was, in 1930 and in 1942, an individual interpretation, though there were some traditional touches. Irving's double-handed sword had excited Gielgud, and he decided to use one himself, though unlike Irving he got rid of it during the encounter with the witches. When the witches hail Macbeth:

> All hail, Macbeth, that shalt be King hereafter! (I. iii. 50)

Gielgud revealed Macbeth's shocked surprise by dropping the great sword.[5] In the last act an effort seems to have been made to

---

[1] *Brief Chronicles*, p. 228.   [2] July 9, 1942.
[3] Agate, *Brief Chronicles*, p. 227.   [4] *Shakespearean Playgoing*, p. 142.
[5] See Sprague, *Shakespeare and the Actors*, p. 230.

resurrect another memory of Irving. Gielgud's make-up, his 'hair whitened and eyes bloodshot' seems to have been designed to restore the 'gaunt famished wolf'[1] of Irving. The total effect however, was different. To Ivor Brown, Gielgud's make-up and acting suggested 'a fine kaleidoscope of ruin'.[2]

It was said of Gielgud's Macbeth that there was little of 'Bellona's bridegroom' about it. Certainly the business of the dropped sword may have worked against such an interpretation. Agate, it is true, expressed relief in 1942 that Gielgud did not enter like 'Kitchener at Omdurman' or bark Shakespeare's lines as 'if they were words of command in an Aldershot review'. At his first entry he had a martial bearing, but having discharged his formal reply to Duncan, after 'Stars, hide your fires...' (I. iv. 50–3) Gielgud dropped the warrior, Agate writes, and set out to interpret 'the most poetic of all murderers'.[3] However, Macbeth is not Richard II, or Hamlet, and Gielgud does not appear to have been able to command the mighty opposites in Macbeth's character—the fear and the courage, the sensitiveness and the reserves of violence—as Garrick had been able to command them. It seemed to the critic of *The Times* in 1930 that in the dagger speech, 'delivered rather too much in the platform manner', Gielgud failed to convey 'the full sense of the bloody business'[4] he intended to perform.

The dramatic critic of *The Times* wrote that in creating a Hamlet-like Macbeth, in letting 'conscience make a coward of him', Gielgud was assisted by Miss Martita Hunt, who after reading Macbeth's letter spoke the lines beginning 'Glamis thou art...' (I. v. 12 ff.) as though the plans had been talked over for years.[5] While assisting Gielgud to realise his conception of Macbeth's character, Martita Hunt does not seem to have been completely successful in her own portrayal of Lady Macbeth. Agate felt that the fault with her Lady Macbeth was that 'it was always too likeable'.[6] In 1942, when Gwen Ffrangcon-Davies played Lady Macbeth opposite John Gielgud, she seems to have had similar faults. The quality of her interpretation was defined as Tennysonian rather than Shakespearean.[7] Like Martita Hunt she

[1] See Trewin, *Shakespeare on the English Stage*, p. 117.
[2] *Observer* (March 31, 1930).   [3] *Brief Chronicles*, p. 244.
[4] March 18.   [5] See *The Times* (March 18, 1930).
[6] *Brief Chronicles*, p. 227.   [7] *Observer* (July 12, 1942).

seems to have been charming and succeeded in arousing pity but not terror.[1] Miss Ffrangcon-Davies appears to have been 'merely querulous' when she should have been terrible.[2] 'Scorn is the deepest note in this actress's register', wrote Agate, 'scorn accompanied by an expression of faint disgust.'[3]

When Gielgud first played Macbeth at the Old Vic the sets were simple, the action swift. While his interpretation of Macbeth seems to have been less satisfying than his interpretation of Hamlet in the period after 1930, he did represent a spirit of change in the theatre. During the 1930s the tendency first observed by Macready—'The public is willing to have the magnificence without the tragedy'[4]—was being combated at the Old Vic. There was an attempt to satisfy the ear as well as the eye.

Today, in the 1960s, Gielgud seems mannered, and it is easy to forget that he represented the forces of change thirty years ago. Poel, Granville-Barker and Gielgud attempted to restore the dominion of the human voice in the theatre, to reassert its value against what seemed to be excessive devotion to the needs of the *mise-en-scène*. Inevitably the new emphasis had its dangers. It would seem today that Gielgud's speech changes little with each Shakespearean character he plays and that his power of impersonation is limited, that in reasserting the dominion of the human voice he has not always evaded the real danger of acting with the voice only. In more recent years, some of Sir John Gielgud's pronouncements have tended to support what seems to be an illusory belief in the power of the pure sound of Shakespeare's verse, a belief possibly linked to Gielgud's cultivation of the physical resources of his voice. Of Cleopatra's lamentation over Antony, Gielgud has written: '...you have to know that a great speech like Cleopatra's speech on the death of Antony is written for the sound and not for the sense'.[5] This is indeed difficult to accept unless Gielgud is giving a special meaning to 'sound'. While it is true that some of Shakespeare's speeches are like arias, this could not mean that they possess no sense. In fact, Cleopatra's speech on the death of Antony contains rich and elusive feelings which she is trying to express. The sound of the verse is intimately related to real feelings and sensations (which make up

[1] *The Times* (July 9, 1942). [2] *Brief Chronicles*, p. 245.
[3] *Ibid.* [4] See above, p. 180.
[5] *Actors Talk About Acting*, ed. Lewis Funke and John E. Booth (1962), p. 32.

the meaning of it), feelings and sensations which the actress playing the part must understand and experience if she is to capture the true sound of Shakespeare's verse at all.

Today, if John Gielgud seems mannered, this may be partly due to a faulty principle; though it could be due as well to the fact that what was natural in 1930 seems mannered in 1966. In 1930, Gielgud was clearly one of the innovators of his time, during the interesting experimental years at the Old Vic.

In the 1930s at the Old Vic, Harcourt Williams and Gielgud were believers in the methods of Granville-Barker. In 1932, however, Edward Carrick, the son of Gordon Craig, was invited to produce *Macbeth*, and for a brief space the Old Vic experienced an approach to Shakespeare different from Granville-Barker's. The dramatic critic of *The Times* reports that Edward Carrick made use of a drum in the most dramatic scenes in *Macbeth* as if it were 'an Indian tom-tom'.[1] The critic found the drum overpowering: 'He builds up the atmosphere of impending doom with a sure hand and keeps the action taut enough for the intrusion of the drum beats to be overpowering.'[2] Descriptions of Edward Carrick's production suggest that *Macbeth* was approached as a melodrama rather than a tragedy.

Malcolm Keen, who played Macbeth, seems to have captured the soldier, the 'tyrant driven by remorse and his own daemon' but not the Macbeth who has an affinity with Hamlet.[3] Margaret Webster, who played Lady Macbeth in Edward Carrick's production, seems to have kept the idea of possession before her— she was 'terrible' in her invocation to the spirits. In her own description of the soliloquy, however, there is more than a hint of melodrama. Her comment on the opening lines of the invocation

> The raven himself is hoarse
> That croaks the fatal entrance of Duncan
> Under my battlements   (I. v. 35–7)

—that 'we can almost hear the soft beat of wings'[4]—has a slightly melodramatic flavour—in fact, it is the hoarse croak of the raven that we hear—and her analysis seems to lead to a simplified view of the character:

[1] November 22, 1932.   [2] *Ibid.*
[3] *Ibid.*   [4] See *Shakespeare Today*, pp. 227–8.

And they come, those sightless substances; there should be no smallest doubt about that. They use her, possess her, just exactly as she had prayed them to do; they make of her a creature as relentless as she had desired, they shroud the stars and charge the blackened night with terror.[1]

If Edward Carrick had made the supernatural theme in *Macbeth* seem melodramatic, when Tyrone Guthrie produced *Macbeth* at the Old Vic in 1934, with Charles Laughton as Macbeth and Flora Robson as Lady Macbeth, the influence of Granville-Barker re-asserted itself. As if in sharp reaction to Edward Carrick's inter-pretation, Tyrone Guthrie's view of the play seemed to be severe-ly rationalist. Granville-Barker regarded the opening scene with the witches as 'almost certainly' not Shakespeare's. He was con-vinced that the words spoken by the witches in the first act had 'all the tang of the Hecate lines' and that 'we do not meet Shakespeare's true text till Macbeth's own entrance'. He argued that the producer of *Macbeth* ought to omit the opening scenes altogether 'in line with the forthrightness of the play's action'. Granville-Barker regarded the whole text of *Macbeth* as 'exten-sively corrupted'.[2]

Obviously influenced by Granville-Barker, Tyrone Guthrie dropped the opening scene with the witches in his production at the Old Vic, carrying his argument to its logical conclusion in his programme note:

By making the three Weird Sisters open the play, one cannot avoid the implication that they are a governing influence of the tragedy, that throughout its turgid and tempestuous action these three hover through the fog and filthy air inspiring its motives and bringing about its catastrophe. But surely the grandeur of the tragedy lies in the fact that Macbeth and Lady Macbeth are ruined by precisely those qualities which make them great; he by the imagination and intellectual honesty which enable him to perceive his own loss of integrity and to realise the fullest implications of the loss; she by the relentless driving-force and iron self-control that would in different circumstances have made her so great a queen; both by their genuine love for one another. All this is undermined by any suggestion that the Weird Sisters are in control of events. On this account only those of their scenes will be played which are essential to the plot. But I wish to make it clear that

[1] See *Shakespeare Today*, pp. 227–8.
[2] See C. B. Purdom, *Harley Granville-Barker* (1955), p. 217.

the cuts are not solely due to an arbitrary decision of taste but are supported by arguments in textual criticism.[1]

Guthrie advised his cast to read Bradley, and one can detect traces of Bradley's view of *Macbeth* in Tyrone Guthrie's note. Bradley saw Macbeth as imaginative, but here all resemblance between Guthrie's view of the character and Bradley's ends. To Guthrie, it is Macbeth's imagination that ruins him. Ruin has obviously very practical connotations here. Bradley believed that if Macbeth had obeyed his imagination, 'something usually deeper and higher than his conscious thoughts', he 'would have been safe'. It is when Macbeth ceases to be imaginative, argues Bradley, that he becomes 'domineering, even brutal,' a 'cool pitiless hypocrite'.[2]

Tyrone Guthrie's view that Macbeth is ruined by precisely those qualities which make him great, appears to have led to some loss of the element of conflict in Macbeth's character, the conflict between essential good (imaginatively apprehended) and essential evil (unimaginatively grasped). As Guthrie saw it, it was the essential good in Macbeth which ruins him. There is a curiously limiting, perhaps unconscious cynicism in this view of the character and it was not in practice likely to create the impression of 'marred nobility' that Tyrone Guthrie elsewhere in his programme note claims for Macbeth.[3]

When James Agate saw the play he wrote, 'nobility must come out of your stage player, and when Macbeth falls he must fall like Lucifer. Mr Laughton was never within measurable distance of any kind of grandeur.'[4] It is possible that the cynicism of Tyrone Guthrie's view of the character infected Charles Laughton's interpretation. Shakespeare's poetry was reduced to the status of vivid prose; the line

I dare do all that may become a man   (I. vii. 46)

was spoken 'in accents of elvish expostulation', and at 'Avaunt, and quit my sight' Laughton bounced away from the ghost and landed 'half-way up the stairs like an indiarubber-cat'.[5] There were moments in Laughton's performance that seemed both genuine and relevant. Macbeth's love for Lady Macbeth at the

---

[1] Quoted by Trewin in *Shakespeare on the English Stage*, p. 161.
[2] *Shakespearean Tragedy*, pp. 295, 298.
[3] See Agate, *Brief Chronicles*, pp. 232–3.
[4] *Ibid.*   [5] *Ibid.* p. 231.

outset seems to have been strongly emphasised and 'Come, we'll
to sleep' at the end of the banquet scene was conceived 'as a
lullaby, the sad pair rocking breast to breast'.[1] At the end of the
play this relationship no longer existed. Charles Laughton spoke
the line 'She should have died hereafter' with a kind of hatred of
Lady Macbeth, as if to suggest that she ought to have died at a
time when he was less occupied.[2] Yet the total effect of Laughton's
interpretation of Macbeth's character was to simplify it. He
presented a character who was 'the slave not of evil destiny but
his own passions'.[3] Macbeth is not of course the 'slave' of his
passions in any conventional sense: his sharp awareness of their
consequences both before and after he gives way to them suggests
that to look on him as 'a slave of his own passions' is to see him
in terms of an inadequate metaphor and to place the stress
wrongly.

Tyrone Guthrie attempted to fit Lady Macbeth, played by
Flora Robson, into his conception of the play as he had attempted
to fit Macbeth into it. At rehearsals, when Flora Robson attempted to read the line in Macbeth's letter

they made themselves air. . .   (I. v. 4)

with a pause before 'air' so as to bring out the strangeness and the
wonder of Macbeth's encounter with the witches, Tyrone Guthrie
objected to the reading because he did not wish too much to be
made of the witches.[4] Her interpretation, reminiscent of a very
similar approach to the line by Mrs Siddons, was dropped. As
Guthrie wanted to indicate as clearly as possible that the Macbeths were solely responsible for their own tragedy, the supernatural theme was not taken too seriously. The letter was read
swiftly and the invocation to the 'murd'ring ministers' was taken
as a rather fanciful melodramatic statement. Flora Robson played
it accordingly, like a figure out of Disney's *Fantasia*, not with her
hands raised up, but stooping, with a curved, downward movement of the hands, raising the spirits up from below.[5]

Flora Robson saw Lady Macbeth as essentially an unimaginative woman. Here she was following Bradley. She has herself
written that while Macbeth has an excess of imagination, Lady

[1] *Brief Chronicles*, p. 231.
[2] Stated in a letter to the writer by Dame Flora Robson.
[3] *The Times* (April 3, 1934).
[4] Stated in conversation with the writer.   [5] *Ibid.*

Macbeth has no imagination at all: 'What could be more mundane than her lines (Act II, Scene 2):

> "The sleeping and the dead
> Are but as pictures"

Or when Macbeth's eyes see the bloody ghost of Banquo (Act III, Scene 4):

> "When all's done,
> You look but on a stool."'[1]

Flora Robson did not herself think that she was ideally suited to bring out a coldly unimaginative Lady Macbeth; her own voice had possibly too many tones in it for unimaginative coldness to be successfully rendered, though she made a serious attempt to do so. She spoke the line

> *Give* me the daggers...

with a stress on 'give', in matter-of-fact tones.[2]

Unlike Macbeth, Lady Macbeth as Flora Robson saw her, could not imagine either the reality or the consequences of murder. This is why Lady Macbeth seems unaffected, Flora Robson argues, when she returns from the dead king's chamber—'A little water clears us of this deed. / How easy is it then.' As she saw it, Lady Macbeth suffered a 'delayed shock'.[3] The shock experienced by Lady Macbeth first reveals itself during the scene after Macbeth has murdered the grooms, when all eyes turn on him and he flounders deeper and deeper in explanation.[4] As Laughton looked more and more like a cornered creature, Lady Macbeth fell down a flight of steps on stage right, and was caught as she fell by the lords below. With this piece of business, Tyrone Guthrie made it clear that there could be no doubt about the genuineness of Lady Macbeth's collapse.[5]

As Flora Robson played the role, after the murder of Duncan Lady Macbeth wanted no more killing. The line

> But in them nature's copy's not eterne   (III. ii. 38)

---

[1] See Flora Robson, 'Notes on Playing the Role of Lady Macbeth', in *Macbeth*, ed. Francis Fergusson, p. 27.
[2] Stated in conversation with the writer.
[3] See 'Notes on Playing...Lady Macbeth', *Macbeth*, ed. Fergusson, p. 29.
[4] *Ibid.* p. 30.
[5] Stated in conversation with the writer.

was spoken by her, not as if to incite Macbeth to murder Banquo and Fleance (Mrs Siddons had suggested such an interpretation, though she did not, in fact, carry it out), but with 'a horrified question mark'.[1]

In the sleep-walking scene Flora Robson fully revealed the shock that Lady Macbeth had experienced during Duncan's murder. She has written in her 'Notes on Playing...Lady Macbeth'[2] that the key to Lady Macbeth's character lies in the lines:

> Had he not resembled
> My father as he slept, I had done't.   (II. ii. 12–13)

After the murder of Duncan, Flora Robson had attempted to grasp Charles Laughton's hand, taking the suggestion from an implicit Shakespearean stage direction placed at a much later point in the play, during the sleep-walking scene:

> Come, come, come, come, give me your hand.   (v. i. 65)

Developing further Shakespeare's own suggestion for the playing of the murder scene, as she felt the blood on Macbeth's hand, Flora Robson had withdrawn her own blood-stained hand, shuddering. In the sleep-walking scene, she re-created every detail of Duncan's murder and repeated the gesture, stretching out her hand to Macbeth and withdrawing it, shuddering, as she relived the experience.[3]

Clearly Flora Robson's interpretation of Lady Macbeth was original and impressive within its limits. What the limits were is hinted at in a letter to her from Bernard Shaw, on November 15, 1958. Shaw wrote:

Most Lady Macbeths imagine that the sleep-walking scene is the great scene. It isn't. Anybody can play it. It plays itself. The scene that takes out of you all that you have in you is the one in the first act (I suspect Mrs Siddons primed herself for it with a pint of porter): for all star Macbeths try to steal it by swaggering instead of cowering in a chair and crying piteously 'I prithee peace. I dare' etc....while she [Lady Macbeth] towers over him storming and raging and dominant. But if he will not play down you must play up and let yourself go for all you are worth; for you must get on top at all costs...[4]

---

[1] See *Macbeth*, ed. Fergusson, pp. 30–1.   [2] *Ibid.* p. 27.
[3] Stated in conversation with the writer.
[4] Quoted in Janet Dunbar, *Flora Robson* (1960), p. 249.

Agate, we know, had not approved of Flora Robson's 'wifely solicitude and mothering'[1] of Macbeth in the first act. Yet within its limits, her interpretation of Lady Macbeth was a consistent whole. When she played Lady Macbeth opposite Michael Redgrave in New York, Professor Garrett Mattingly wrote: 'I have never seen—and indeed never hoped to see—a performance as perfect and illuminating as yours, intelligently analysed, deeply felt, completely integrated, and therefore profoundly moving. To watch it developing was a major artistic experience—and like any such experience, a revelation.'[2] Flora Robson's success was due to a consistent conception of the role and her easy command of Shakespeare's verse. Unlike Charles Laughton she did not turn it into prose, but yet made it seem perfectly spontaneous and natural. W. A. Darlington tells us that 'she took Shakespeare's utterances on her lips with a natural dignity and beauty'.[3]

Interpretations of Macbeth and Lady Macbeth during the 1930s were at times satisfying; at times they merely repeated old errors. When Komisarjevsky produced *Macbeth* in modern dress at Stratford, he was merely repeating an unsuccessful experiment of Barry Jackson's, though he was more sceptical in his treatment of the witches. The scenery was of aluminium, and howitzers fingered the sky. Macbeth met the witches near a chateau ruined by artillery. George Hayes as Macbeth looked like a dapper German officer of the Great War[4] in field grey uniform.[5] Fabia Drake as Lady Macbeth appeared to one critic to possess an 'attractive touch of the gypsy'.[6] Komisarjevsky had induced George Hayes and Fabia Drake to speak in a series of spasmodic rushes, with long pauses in between. The passages on sleep, and phrases like 'the shard-borne beetle with his drowsy hums' (III. ii. 42), were jerked out as casual observations.[7] The supernatural element (considerably toned down by Tyrone Guthrie) was in Komisarjevsky's production entirely eliminated. The witches were old hags, who were discovered plundering the slain after the battle, and told the fortunes of Macbeth and Banquo by palmistry.[8] Banquo's ghost in the banquet scene was Macbeth's own shadow.[9]

[1] *Brief Chronicles*, p. 232.
[2] Quoted in Dunbar, *Flora Robson*, p. 243.
[3] *Daily Telegraph* (April 3, 1934).   [4] See *Birmingham Gazette* (April 19, 1933).
[5] See *Birmingham Mail* (April 19, 1933).
[6] *Ibid.*   [7] *Morning Post* (April 19, 1933).
[8] Crosse, *Shakespearean Playgoing*, p. 97.   [9] *Morning Post* (April 19, 1933).

After the banquet, Macbeth went to bed on the stage, and his second encounter with the witches was played as in a dream, with the speeches of the witches spoken 'off'. Gordon Crosse writes, that Komisarjevsky's design was 'to remove all colour and poetry from the play leaving everything stark and drab'.[1] In an effort to make Shakespeare contemporary, and Macbeth acceptable on the literal and realistic plane, Komisarjevsky robbed the tragedy of a dimension that was archetypal and symbolic, eroding much of its meaning.

Komisarjevsky's *Macbeth* was a repetition of a modern heresy. When Ion Swinley played Macbeth at the Old Vic in December 1935, he propagated a much older error. His Macbeth resembled Richard III, and Agate advised him to set about discovering the humanity in the character.[2] Vivienne Bennett, who played Lady Macbeth, seemed ill-suited to the role. Agate spoke of her 'round and dimpling countenance' and her idiosyncratic interpretation of individual lines. In the passage about the milking babe, she put so much emphasis on the word 'brains' that she seemed to suggest a choice of injuries to the child. She had 'no tragic bearing', wrote Agate, and gave the impression of 'striving to play the part'.[3] In the passage beginning 'Come, thick night,' and ending 'To cry "Hold, hold"' (I. v. 47–51), 'Lady Macbeth tells Heaven not to interfere, but Miss Bennett, by shouting the last two words at the top of her voice, transferred the horror from Heaven to herself, as though she, Lady Macbeth, would prevent the murder'.[4] Ion Swinley and Vivienne Bennett seem to have changed *Macbeth* from a tragedy into a melodrama without consciously intending to do so.

The 1930s were experimental years. The last serious experiment with *Macbeth* during this period at the Old Vic was conducted in 1937 by Michel St Denis. The lighting was obtrusive and Shakespeare's tragic themes were not completely realised at all points, yet there was a serious attempt to approach *Macbeth* as a tragedy. From the moment the curtains went up there was a sense of impending evil in the air.[5] The evil was not so much in the man Macbeth—Laurence Olivier made the most of his courage and charm and the poetry that 'sings through his brain'—'as in the

---

[1] *Shakespearean Playgoing*, p. 97. [2] *Brief Chronicles*, p. 235.
[3] *Ibid.* [4] *Ibid.*
[5] See *The Times* (December 28, 1937).

circumstances in which his own weakness, his wife's overriding ambition, and the promptings of the supernatural have placed him'.[1] A more just balance between the forces within Macbeth and the forces outside him which determine his tragic fate was achieved when Olivier played Macbeth again in 1955 at Stratford-upon-Avon. In 1937 there was still evidence of a romantic naïveté which marred Olivier's portrait: the dagger speech seems to have been treated as 'the last despairing cry of a human being written in the stars'[2] and there were excesses which suggest a basic lack of control. The dramatic critic of the *Manchester Guardian* observed that Olivier had three voices: 'a head voice for passion, a middle or workaday voice of fine sonority, and a lower voice as melancholy as the wind in pine-woods', but suggested that he would do well to economise in the first of these attributes. This critic thought that Olivier used his 'head voice for passion' far too often, and at times when it was 'not at all indicated—as in the instructions to Banquo's murderers and in the "sleep no more" speech when he made more than enough noise to wake the castle up and discover his guilt'.[3] Judith Anderson played 'a fiend-like little queen'[4] and though evidently not convincing in the first act—it was 'difficult to believe that she could have the influence over him she did'—once the murder was committed, her performance gathered depth and persuasion.[5] Like Olivier's, however, her performance seemed at times overstrained and forced.[6]

This production of *Macbeth* by Michel St Denis coincided with the death of Lilian Baylis, and seemed to confirm the suspicion among theatre people that productions of the play were doomed to attract disaster, a suspicion entertained by Lilian Baylis herself. A curiously widespread superstition, and half-believed in, the idea does not seem to have occurred to Irving, Macready, Kemble or Garrick, in centuries that one might have thought were less knowledgeable about such matters.

Certainly the history of productions of *Macbeth* after 1937 might seem to lend some weight to a cherished superstition, if one did not suspect that there were more natural causes behind

[1] *Ibid.* [2] *Ibid.*
[3] November 27, 1937. [4] *Ibid.*
[5] *The Times* (December 28, 1937).
[6] See *The Times* (November 27, 1937). Cf. *Daily Telegraph* (November 27, 1937).

the disasters. Not all productions of *Macbeth*, of course, attracted disaster. When George Rylands produced the play at the Arts Theatre, Cambridge, in 1939, the production seems to have had a smooth enough passage. Rylands set out with conscious intent to stage *Macbeth* as 'a romantic melodrama' of 'lost glamour'. His programme note makes this intention clear.[1] The actors wore 'resplendent costumes of the '45'. The witches clustering round the gallows and, later, a splendid pantomime fire, were given an importance appropriate to romantic melodrama. The apparitions were rendered with luminous masks and the show of eight kings was considered 'a superb effect'.[2]

'Yet', as the dramatic critic of *The Times* wrote, 'the anonymous actors, fortunately, discovered in some of the characters a vitality, a searching into conscience, and a not inhuman terror that plainly disposed of the romantic idea.'[3] The actress playing Lady Macbeth alone seemed to be influenced by her court dress and powdered curls. Rage and determination were reduced to shrewishness, and the producer seems to have 'gravely hampered her' by turning the sleep-walking scene into a promenade backwards and forwards on the stage.[4] The actor playing Macbeth seems to have been influenced 'both in manner and diction by Sir John Gielgud'.[5]

If Cambridge seems to have survived the widespread notion that *Macbeth* was doomed to be accompanied by physical disaster of some sort, in 1939 the Sheffield Repertory Theatre evidently did not. When Alec Guinness played Macbeth at the theatre he took over 'at too short notice' from the previous interpreter, 'who collapsed and was unable to open'. Sir Alec Guinness writes that he 'learned and rehearsed the part in three or four days with a cold wet towel' round his head, and 'wore the costume Laurence Olivier had worn in Michel St Denis' production at the Old Vic ...Any question of interpretation', writes Sir Alec, 'was entirely governed by remembering the lines and moves.'[6] The critic of the *Sheffield Telegraph* reports, however, that Guinness had a 'rare clearness and force of utterance...he never whined as Macbeths are wont to do, and he never lost control of the part', though he was perhaps 'too heavily clothed'. Miss Joan Knowles played

[1] Quoted in *The Times* (February 22, 1939).   [2] *Ibid.*
[3] *Ibid.*   [4] *Ibid.*
[5] *Ibid.*   [6] Stated in a letter to the writer.

Lady Macbeth—'her reading of the part was one of perverted wifely devotion, a kind of terrible, unselfish ambition on her husband's behalf'.[1]

Through the 1940s the superstitious awe around the tragedy seemed to be felt still more strongly as actors of established reputation found themselves defeated by the complexities of the play. After Gielgud failed in 1942 to capture the 'mighty opposites' in Macbeth's character, Ernest Milton failed to project a dramatically realised character at all. Milton's playing of Macbeth (it was hardly an interpretation) demonstrated the fallacy of the theory that to play Shakespeare satisfactorily all one needs to do is to speak the lines clearly. Mr Milton appears to have been 'the most audible Macbeth of our time'. He appeared to have promised himself that 'every word, indeed every syllable shall be heard'.[2] The result of the elocutionary approach, and the avoidance of any serious attempt to interpret character, was that the words in the end lost their complexity. The dramatic critic of *The Times* observed that, under the measured tread of the syllables, every part of the verse seemed to have much the same value as any other. Macbeth instructing the murderers was 'every bit as sonorous' as Macbeth 'saying things about sleep, life, the passage of time...' The elocutionist too often absorbed the actor, 'who was satisfied to put forth an occasional expressive gesture'.[3] Miss Vivienne Bennett, who had played Lady Macbeth earlier opposite Ion Swinley, was described as being 'beautifully audible'[4] when she played the role again at the Lyric, Hammersmith, opposite Ernest Milton.

When Donald Wolfit played Macbeth at The Winter Garden in 1945, he did not substitute elocution for characterisation, even though the character he created seemed to be a caricature of Shakespeare's Macbeth. James Agate, who thought Donald Wolfit's portrait of Lear a grand and convincing creation, wrote that Wolfit had turned *Macbeth* into 'a ranting, roaring Saturday night melodrama, full of sound and fury but signifying nothing of the play's pity and melancholy'.[5]

Agate concluded that Donald Wolfit's Macbeth failed because

[1] See *Sheffield Telegraph* (May 9, 1939).   [2] See *The Times* (August 1, 1944).
[3] *Ibid.*   [4] *Ibid.*
[5] *Sunday Times* (February 18, 1945).

the character did not lie in the actor's personality. Macbeth is advised to be 'bloody, bold, and resolute' (IV. i. 79), but Wolfit was already 'bloody, bold, and resolute' from the beginning, having, as Agate saw it, deprived Macbeth of his 'poetry, introspection, vacillation and remorse'.[1] During the exchange

> *Macb.*　　　My dearest love,
> 　　Duncan comes here to-night.
> *Lady M.*　　　And when goes hence?
> *Macb.*　To-morrow—as he purposes.
> *Lady M.*　　　O, never
> 　　Shall sun that morrow see!　　　　(I. v. 55–8)

Agate thought that there should be no more than a glimmer of the possibility of murder in the lines 'To-morrow—*as he purposes*' whereas Wolfit gave to 'as he purposes' a wealth of innuendo. Agate gives us a detailed description of his interpretation of the line: 'At his wife's question, he disengages himself, steps back a pace, goes through prodigies of winking and nodding which would stagger the blindest horse and incidentally ruins Lady Macbeth's "O never shall sun that morrow see!"'[2] When Donald Wolfit played Macbeth at the King's, Hammersmith, eight years later, his performance had altered in details though not in essentials. In armour that glinted in a ruby light he looked 'like the image of one of Kean's heroic figures', but the portrait was still based on a conception of Macbeth as 'a heroic villain' rather than a 'tragic hero'.[3]

The review in the *Manchester Guardian* lends support to this description of Wolfit's interpretation of Macbeth: 'Mr Wolfit allowed no let or hindrance to the mounting obsession of his subject save in the last scene where the demoniac turned for a moment contemplative, was allowed to linger over his "to-morrows" with every syllable weighing a ton and taking an eternity.'[4] In 1953, Rosalind Iden's interpretation of Lady Macbeth, with its 'stately purpose' and 'sinister glamour' was in harmony with Wolfit's portrait of Macbeth.[5]

During the period under review, before Olivier proved it was possible, English players seem to have interpreted Macbeth as

[1] *The Sunday Times* (February 18, 1945).　　[2] *Ibid.*
[3] *The Times* (March 20, 1953).　　[4] March 21, 1953.
[5] *News Chronicle* (March 21, 1953).

either 'bloody, bold, and resolute', or as haunted and imaginative, never as both. When Robert Harris played Macbeth in Jacobean dress at Stratford-upon-Avon in 1946, he made Macbeth an honest man feeling the full horror of his own evil.[1] He was a civilised Jacobean nobleman, and during the murder scene suggested that Macbeth was in a nightmare from which he would eventually awake.[2] Rosemary Taylor, on the other hand, seemed to have the 'intensity' that Shakespeare wrote into the part of Lady Macbeth. Yet Michael MacOwan's production as a whole, despite the interesting Jacobean décor (an idea that Poel might have approved of), seems to have failed to come to terms with the complexity of *Macbeth*.

When Michael Redgrave played Macbeth at the Aldwych in 1947, according to Ivor Brown he left 'Macbeth the poet almost unnoticed'. Speeches of 'incomparable beauty' were 'hurled out' 'in martial rage'. The approach was realistic even though *Macbeth* is not by any means a consistently naturalistic play. As Ivor Brown observes: 'Soldiers don't naturally stop in the midst of deadly battle to make observations on the sereness of the leaf.' It seemed to Brown that Redgrave caught 'the *farouche*, defiant Macbeth' of the latter half of the play, though the crumbling conscience of the 'noble Macbeth' was less well established.[3] This description of Redgrave's interpretation is re-echoed by the dramatic critic of *The Times*: 'But the plainest reason for Mr Redgrave's failure to move us 'is the monotonous hoarseness of his speech. There is no music in his voice and the psychological consistency which he achieves is gained at the expense of the poetry and tragic emotion.'[4] While Michael Redgrave played a rough soldier, Miss Ena Burrill created an almost exclusively charming Lady Macbeth. To the critic of *The Times*, she seemed immensely decorative, 'flower-like, rather than the serpent beneath the flower'.[5]

In 1949, at Stratford, Godfrey Tearle seemed at first 'the powerful soldier, wild and shaggy, embarrassed by compliments'.[6] But, as the tragedy unfolded, the imaginative side of Macbeth seemed to exclude the more calculating aspects of his character. This is probably why the critic of the *Daily Telegraph* wrote that

[1] *The Stage* (June 27, 1946).   [2] *Stratford-upon-Avon Herald* (June 8, 1946).
[3] *Observer* (December 21, 1947).   [4] December 19, 1947.
[5] *Ibid.*   [6] *Sunday Times* (April 17, 1949).

while Tearle's 'performance had moments of great beauty' it failed to suggest a necessary 'ferocity'.[1] Tearle was a 'great general', wrote the dramatic critic of the *Liverpool Post*, 'a sensitive poet, a loving husband, but never an ambitious, scheming, lying despicable murderer'.[2] And the reviewer for the *Birmingham Mail* observed that at times Godfrey Tearle looked 'apostolic and even Christ-like'.[3] Tearle's costume, created by Edmund Carrick, was realistic—the costume of a Caledonian chieftain of the eleventh century. The costumes, decorated with shaggy fur,[4] suggested a wild primitive culture, but do not seem to have been related in any consistent way to Godfrey Tearle's conception of Macbeth's character.

Diana Wynyard, who played Lady Macbeth opposite Godfrey Tearle, was given similarly primitive clothes which W. A. Darlington described as 'barbarically hideous'. Her make-up was 'baleful'.[5] Diana Wynyard seems to have related her conception of Lady Macbeth's character to her make-up and clothes. Critics observed that she was 'forceful and malignant'. At

> Go get some water
> And wash this filthy witness from your hand   (II. ii. 46–7)

she slapped Macbeth to bring him to her purposes, and during the banquet scene she seemed to 'browbeat husband and guests' becoming 'hysterically shrill'.[6] Both the conception and the costumes seem to have had their roots in melodrama rather than tragedy.

Godfrey Tearle was not 'bloody, bold, and resolute' enough, though he communicated the poetry of anguish and despair in his portrayal of Macbeth. When Ralph Richardson succeeded him in the role at Stratford in 1952, using a soft Scottish brogue, he created the illusion of 'a desperate unmelodic mania'.[7] His Macbeth, like Ion Swinley's in 1935, achieved the stature of Richard III.[8] Richardson emphasised the Machiavellian elements in Macbeth's character. Margaret Leighton, who played Lady Macbeth, saw her role in the same harsh terms. She appears to have made Lady Macbeth a creature taut of nerve, jerky in action,

---

[1] April 18, 1949.
[2] April 18, 1949.
[3] April 18, 1949.
[4] See *Liverpool Post* (April 18, 1949).
[5] *Daily Telegraph* (April 18, 1949).
[6] *Birmingham Post* (April 18, 1949).
[7] *Birmingham Gazette* (June 11, 1952). Cf. *Daily Telegraph* (June 12, 1952).
[8] *Coventry Evening Telegraph* (June 11, 1952).

unbalanced in mind and strident in voice from the start, and declined into doddering insanity in the sleep-walking scene.[1]

The most eminent actors of the modern period (before Laurence Olivier essayed the role again in 1955) either failed, or did not try, to capture the mighty opposites in Macbeth's character. The actresses on the whole fared better with Lady Macbeth (as the performances of Sybil Thorndike and Flora Robson bear witness), but as the years went by they tended to blur the Shakespearean complexity of the character.

During the years between 1940 and 1955, interpretations of Macbeth and Lady Macbeth were not, of course, confined to the better known theatres. Other players attempted these roles at theatres like the Bristol Old Vic in 1946, the Arts Theatre in 1950 and the Mermaid in 1951 and 1952. While there is no evidence to show that *Macbeth* was explored in all its complexity, for their originality and inventiveness these productions command a certain attention.

At the Bristol Old Vic in 1946, Hugh Hunt's production of *Macbeth* was 'three-dimensional'. Hunt used not only the length and breadth, but the height of the stage as well. This added considerable excitement to the final fight between Macbeth and Macduff. William Devlin, who played Macbeth, leapt from the top of the middle rostrum, only to be 'impaled' on Macduff's sword, and fell to his 'death' on the stage beneath.[2] During the whispered terror of the murder scene, Pamela Brown used the gesture of slapping Macbeth's face to still his hysterical outburst. It was a gesture later to be adopted by Diana Wynyard at Stratford.[3] Hugh Hunt's production was full of new invention—as when Macbeth shut the castle gates 'excluding the forces which would have saved Duncan', or when Lady Macbeth rolled up her sleeves before she entered the room of the dead king to replace the daggers, evidently to avoid smearing them with blood.[4] It was said of Devlin that he was more 'kingly than the kings' and of Pamela Brown that she was cobra-like and evil.[5] There is no indication in these descriptions, however, that they portrayed the

[1] See *Birmingham Gazette* (June 11, 1952).
[2] See Audrey Williamson and Charles Landstone, *The Bristol Old Vic* (1957), pp. 34–5.
[3] See above, p. 250.
[4] See Williamson and Landstone, *The Bristol Old Vic*, p. 35.
[5] *Ibid.*

characters of Macbeth and Lady Macbeth in all their human complexity.

At the Arts Theatre in 1950 when Alec Clunes played Macbeth, he stood at a great open window, the shutters of which had been flung open by Lady Macbeth, when he spoke of the crow making wing to the rooky wood. He spoke several of the long 'asides' which in the play amount to soliloquies, on a darkened stage, his face lit only by a spotlight.[1] Margaret Rawlings held out shaking hands to the hall fire, showing frayed nerves under her forced resolution in the murder scene. After the discovery of Duncan's murder, she held up her hands to her face 'hiding all but her great frightened eyes' vividly showing Lady Macbeth's disquiet as Macbeth overplayed the scene after killing the grooms. Her swoon was patently contrived to distract attention from Macbeth.[2] The production by Alec Clunes was certainly inventive, though his own interpretation lacked the haunted awareness implicit in the poetry that Macbeth speaks.[3] His Macbeth seems to have been a reasonable rather than an imaginative man, and his dagger soliloquy appears to have sounded 'prosaic'.[4]

The spirit of inventiveness was perhaps most strongly shown in this period at the Mermaid Theatre, where rhetorical gestures were used to explore and interpret character. In 1952 and 1953 Bernard Miles, who played Macbeth at the Mermaid, entered in the second scene of Act III 'with the crossed or wreathed arms which were for the Elizabethans a typical sign of brooding and melancholy'. Dr Bertram Joseph describes the way in which the gesture was used to reveal the character of Macbeth:

...when Lady Macbeth...asked him why he brooded alone and admonished him to forget what he had done, or not to brood on it, he replied at first with his arms still folded. But when he came to the words 'let the frame of things disjoint, both the worlds suffer', he attained his inner reality and externalized it in a breaking apart of the knot of his arms, while his two clenched fists, falling slowly and as though with effort (yet still gracefully) to his sides, completed the full imaging of the selfish determination to triumph at no matter what cost to others.

Dr Joseph points out that part of this movement, the breaking apart of the wreathed arms and the two clenched fists, was not

---

[1] See Williamson, *Theatre of Two Decades*, pp. 272–4.
[2] *Ibid.* pp. 273–4.   [3] *Ibid.*   [4] *Ibid.*

derived from the Elizabethan rhetorical tradition, though 'the passion was released and realized by the typical gesture of crossed arms, the "token" of melancholy'.[1]

At the Mermaid Theatre in 1952 and 1953, both Bernard Miles and Josephine Wilson, who played Lady Macbeth, seem to have felt an obvious delight in resurrecting the old rhetorical gestures described in John Bulwer's *Chironomia* and *Chirologia*, and in making use of them to express real feelings and sensations. 'To wring the hands', writes Bulwer, 'is a natural expression of excessive grief, used by those who condole, bewail and lament.'[2] Lady Macbeth wrung her hands in this way in the second scene of Act III, as she considered 'the dangers into which she and her husband had run', when she spoke the lines:

> Naught's had, all's spent,
> Where our desire is got without content.
> 'Tis safer to be that which we destroy,
> Than by destruction dwell in doubtful joy.[3]   (III. ii. 4–7)

The productions of *Macbeth* at the Mermaid Theatre in 1952 and 1953 were experimental and, as Dr Joseph admits, in many ways imperfect. They were not 'artistic successes',[4] but they do seem to have held out the possibility that rhetorical gesture, if employed intelligently, could be genuinely dramatic. Gesture is a necessary part of the interpretation of character on the stage, and whatever its origins, if used with skill and tact, could help to correct a tendency sometimes observable on the stage today, which has led the Shakespearean actor to rest too much on the resources of the human voice. The power of a true inflection of the voice is incalculable, but so indeed is the power of the true gesture.

[1] *Acting Shakespeare*, p. 108.   [2] *Chirologia* (1644), p. 28.
[3] See Joseph, *Acting Shakespeare*, p. 100.   [4] *Ibid.* p. 99.

CHAPTER 12

STRATFORD (1955)—THE MERMAID (1964)

It seems appropriate that the most successful interpretation of *Macbeth* in this century should have taken place at Stratford-upon-Avon. Though the apron-stage at Stratford is by no means as large as we know the platform at the Globe to have been,[1] a whisper is heard, and the actor's face with its modulations of expression can be clearly seen. It is not surprising, therefore, that critics noted fine modulations of tone, changes of expression, gestures, movements, which revealed much of the subtle complexity of Macbeth's character, when Sir Laurence Olivier played the role in 1955 at Stratford.

The existence of the apron-stage, of course, lies outside the actor's control. If it is there he takes advantage of it. Other problems which lie outside the control of the principal actor can seriously affect his interpretation of character in the theatre. Fortunately, Glen Byam Shaw, who directed *Macbeth* at Stratford when Olivier played the principal role, was aware of them. As rehearsals got under way, he wrote:

Macbeth and Lady Macbeth can only achieve their right significance in the story if everyone round them reacts to them in the right way.

The discovery of the King's murder can only have its true impact on the audience if *every* individual on the stage is imagining the terrible situation to the full...

The difference between such characters as Angus, Caithness, Menteith, etc. is negligible but it is through the reactions of these men that we see the reflections of the fire that burns at the centre of the play.[2]

If the scene of the discovery of Duncan's murder was one of the most successful scenes in the play, this was partly because Byam Shaw seems to have achieved his intention of making every individual on the stage imagine the terrible situation to the full. As a result Olivier and Vivien Leigh, who played Lady Macbeth,

---

[1] See above, p. 4.
[2] From part 1 of MS notebooks in two parts by G. Byam Shaw, who was good enough to let me read his notes dated April 11, 1955.

were able to make their interpretation of the scene after the discovery of Duncan's murder completely effective. Both Olivier and Byam Shaw decided that the creation of atmosphere in *Macbeth* was primarily the actors' responsibility, not that of the stage designer.[1] The sets were to be bare and functional, the costumes expressive but severe. Olivier was conscious of the scope and magnificence of the role of Macbeth, and wanted to command the full range of meaning in it.

Byam Shaw fixed the dramatic time for Macbeth's first entrance at six in the evening, and outlined what he thought Olivier should convey when Macbeth is seen by the audience for the first time: 'From the way he behaves we see at once that the possibility of becoming King, and the idea of murdering Duncan is already in Macbeth's mind, however vaguely.'[2] At the sound of Macbeth's drum, the witches in rags of silvery grey shrank into the prompt corner, their greyness blending with the colour of wings and proscenium.[3] Macbeth, in cloak and kirtle, entered up-stage right, black-bearded, stepping on to a rock at stage centre (see Plate 11) in the light of the setting sun. Attention was concentrated on his face as he stiffened at the sight of the witches.[4] With arms folded, motionless and expectant, he seemed to radiate a brooding sinister energy while the commonsensical Banquo, rather doubting his senses, moved forward to question the witches.[5] Olivier seems to have been completely successful in communicating his director's idea that the thought of murdering Duncan is already in Macbeth's mind, for during this first entrance, the dramatic critic of *Tribune* glimpsed 'the black abysses in the general's mind, the pre-history of life at Dunsinane'.[6] And Kenneth Tynan of the *Observer* thought that Macbeth gave the impression of 'having already killed Duncan time and time again in his mind'.[7] 'Good sir, why do you start...' (I. iii. 51) says Banquo. But Macbeth showed no surprise. From his first sight of the witches he was 'rapt withal'.[8] It is only after Banquo has finished speaking and

[1] Reported by G. Byam Shaw during a conversation with the writer.
[2] MS notebook, part 1. [3] *The Theatre* (June 17, 1955).
[4] See Richard David, 'The Tragic Curve', *Shakespeare Survey* 9 (1956), p. 127. G. Byam Shaw's director's copy, dated March 17, 1955, which he has allowed me to read, indicates the movement described.
[5] See *Tribune* (June 8, 1955). [6] June 8, 1955.
[7] June 12, 1955. [8] *Tribune* (June 8, 1955).

the witches have answered him, that Macbeth, who has hitherto given the impression of motionless expectancy, moves forward to interrogate the witches:[1]

> Stay, you imperfect speakers, tell me more.   (I. iii. 70 ff.)

'By Sinel's death I know I am Thane of Glamis' was spoken to the first witch, 'But how of Cawdor...' to the second, and at 'to be King / Stands not within the prospect of belief', Olivier moved further down-stage towards the third witch.[2] The 'bland daylight remained undisturbed over all', writes Richard David. 'As Macbeth fixed on the second witch the first slid like a lizard from the scene; when attention shifted to the third the second was gone; and as Macbeth and Banquo turned on each other in eager surmise the third too vanished.' Richard David justly observes this was indeed 'genuine producer's sleight of hand, worth all the flying-ballet apparatus in the theatre workshop'.[3]

Darkness had begun to fall when Ross and Angus arrived to confirm the first prophecy of the witches. As they turned to go up-stage left and Banquo stopped them with 'Cousins, a word, I pray you' (I. iii. 127), crossing in front of Macbeth towards them, Olivier moved down-stage right and on to the apron to speak his first soliloquy;[4] showing 'no more than a head-shaking puzzlement' till a sudden tremor on 'unfix my hair and make my seated heart knock at my ribs' (I. iii. 135–6), betrayed the hidden disturbance.[5]

The scene at Forres when Duncan makes Malcolm Prince of Cumberland was set at nine in the evening of the same day.[6] Servants brought in candelabra, and to the blowing of trumpets Duncan, having made his entrance, stood at stage centre surrounded by his courtiers. Malcolm stood down-stage left on the apron. Macbeth entered down-stage right and, kneeling down before[7] the king, rose when Duncan touched him on the shoulder.[8] After Duncan placed the crown on Malcolm's head, Olivier moved down-stage left on to the apron to speak the 'aside' which is Macbeth's comment on Duncan's appointment of Malcolm as

---

[1] Director's copy, p. 8.   [2] *Ibid.*
[3] See 'The Tragic Curve', *Shakespeare Survey* 9, p. 128.
[4] Director's copy, p. 11.   [5] 'The Tragic Curve', p. 128.
[6] G. Byam Shaw, notebooks, part 1.   [7] Director's copy, p. 12.
[8] See prompt copy of *Macbeth* directed by G. Byam Shaw, at the Shakespeare Memorial Library, Stratford.

his successor. Olivier seems to have been on the whole successful in his treatment of the asides and soliloquies in *Macbeth*. A critic observed that when Olivier whispered in soliloquy so quietly (yet with every word perfectly intelligible) it was almost as if one were trespassing in Macbeth's mind.[1] And T. C. Worsley wrote in the *New Statesman* of June 18, 1955, that half the time Olivier took a stance that might have been borrowed from an old print of Kean...'and holding it on the bare stage, worked on the audience with his speech...He made every syllable, every consonant and vowel do its maximum of work, and had appreciated every nuance of the weight and feel of the words.' While Olivier understood Shakespeare's verse and communicated his understanding, he did not, as this account may suggest, act with his voice only. The body of the actor expressed character. Looking at his performance from this point of view, the dramatic critic of the *Financial Times*, on June 9, 1955, also compared Olivier with Kean and Booth: 'This sinuous tigerish Macbeth puts one continually in mind of old prints of Edmund Kean; the deep black-socketed brooding eyes achieve a like chilling effect to what we know of Edwin Booth...' Acting with his body and his voice, Olivier seems to have approached the character of Macbeth through the poetry and not outside it, which was precisely what a player like Kean achieved, at his best.

Vivien Leigh was less comfortable with the arias composed for Lady Macbeth. Effective in the short passages and brief exchanges with Macbeth, she appears to have lacked the gift of phrasing necessary to carry her through a long speech. When she made her first entrance opening Macbeth's letter,[2] she seemed to have 'superb attack'. Richard David thought that the opening was rendered with vivid power. But the power was not sustained. This disability was evident in her first scene; but for the rest Vivien Leigh's force and drive whipped up the play and saved it from the courted risk of dragging. 'Infirm of purpose—', 'Are you a man?'—such explosions gave to their scenes the propulsion that the spell-stopped Macbeth could not provide.[3]

When Vivien Leigh played Lady Macbeth she followed the main lines of interpretation laid down by Glen Byam Shaw. She

[1] *Western Daily Press* (Bristol, June 9, 1955).
[2] Director's copy, p. 16.
[3] 'The Tragic Curve', pp. 126–7.

presented a Lady Macbeth who was passionate, and had an extra-ordinary intensity of purpose, but who was incapable of under-standing 'the strange imaginative Celtic side of Macbeth's nature'. Byam Shaw saw Lady Macbeth as attractive, and argued as well that her will power and passionate ambition were out of all proportion to her physical strength: '...It is this which makes her faint after the discovery of the murder, and which makes her walk in her sleep and finally commit suicide'.[1] The critics were not all in agreement. A reviewer in the *Evening Standard* thought that Vivien Leigh was too beautiful and fragile for anyone to take seriously her cry to be unsexed and filled with direst cruelty.[2] Kenneth Tynan of the *Observer* thought on the other hand that Vivien Leigh's interpretation of Lady Macbeth was quite genuine, though limited, and described her as 'more viper than anaconda'.[3] And T. C. Worsley wrote: 'We do not expect a Mrs Siddons exhibition from Vivien Leigh. What we expect from her is the vixen, sharp and hard as nails, and that she was, and it is perfectly acceptable.'[4] Mrs Siddons was entirely charming and gracious when Duncan arrived at Dunsinane, but Vivien Leigh played the scene a little differently. When Duncan arrived, she curtseyed to him. As she rose, the king held out his hand to her. The prompt copy of *Macbeth* (1955) at Stratford-upon-Avon indicates that she hesitated at this point and then slowly put her hand in his.

Vivien Leigh seems to have been particularly successful during Lady Macbeth's second meeting with Macbeth. Olivier seemed merely 'petulant' in the 'If it were done' soliloquy. The succeed-ing interchange with Lady Macbeth during which Duncan's fate is sealed, was, however, 'a perfectly modulated "movement"'.[5] At

We will proceed no further in this business (I. vii. 31)

Vivien Leigh ran towards Olivier who, turning away,[6] remained obstinately impervious to her first taunts.[7] She then 'drew closer, and launched into the horrible boast of her own callous-ness that is to shock him into compliance'.[8] At this Olivier swung round to her, his back now to the audience, and laid his hand on

---

[1] Notebooks, part II.   [2] June 8, 1955.
[3] June 12, 1955.   [4] *New Statesman* (June 18, 1955).
[5] 'The Tragic Curve', p. 128.   [6] See prompt copy.
[7] 'The Tragic Curve', p. 128.   [8] *Ibid.*

her elbow 'in a gesture at once deeply affectionate and protest-
ing'.[1] Olivier's capitulation was not sudden but gradual. Richard
David describes the fine modulations leading up to it:

As she persisted in her self-torture, he tore himself away and moved
across the stage, but his rejoinder, over his shoulder, the last weak
objection of 'If we should fail', showed that his defences were shaken.
Lady Macbeth again moved to him and seizing him by the shoulders
from behind murmured in his ear the final temptation—how easy is it
then. He turned to her with 'Bring forth men-children only', but it was
said wryly, in almost mocking praise of her lack of scruple, and he still
did not take her hand. There needed a further pause for reflection, the
growing confidence of 'Will it not be received...?', before with 'I
am settled' he was her own again.[2]

As the scene ended with 'False face must hide what the false heart
doth know' (i. vii. 82), a harp cadenza took over.[3]

Olivier's interpretation of the dagger soliloquy which follows
immediately after seems to have been remarkably successful. Far
from recoiling in melodramatic fashion, he greeted the air-drawn
dagger with 'sad familiarity' as if it was 'a fixture in the crooked
furniture of his brain'.[4] The opening lines of the soliloquy were
spoken with a 'sort of broken quiet,' while only the sudden
shrillness of 'Mine eyes are made the fools o' th' other senses'
(ii. i. 44) and 'There's no such thing' (ii. i. 47) revealed the
intolerable tension within Macbeth. The second part of the
soliloquy was delivered in 'a drugged whisper', while Macbeth
moved 'as in a dream' towards the king's room but with his face
turned away from it. Tarquin's strides were only dimly reflected
in the dragging pace, and Macbeth implored trodden stones
behind him to silence with a deprecating hand.[5] Olivier seems to
have caught unerringly the sensitiveness intermingled with the
evil in Macbeth.

After the murder, however, Olivier's Macbeth seemed almost
indifferent to it, as if the murder itself was unreal. 'I have done
the deed...' (ii. ii. 14) was spoken in a flat tone of voice.[6] The
whole scene after the murder seems to have been conducted at a
deliberately slow pace. The prompt copy of *Macbeth* at the Shakespeare Memorial Library in Stratford provides evidence of this

[1] *Ibid.*   [2] *Ibid.*
[3] See prompt copy.   [4] *Observer* (June 12, 1955).
[5] 'The Tragic Curve', pp. 128–9.   [6] *Evening Standard* (June 8, 1955).

intention. The opening dialogue between Macbeth and Lady Macbeth is accompanied by the following prompter's note: 'They move slowly to each other and meet right of centre.' Most reviewers felt that, as a result, much of the suspense of the murder scene was dissipated, though there were other gains. Richard David remembered 'the despairing, fumbling abhorrence with which Olivier sought to ward off the multitudinous seas of blood that seemed to be swirling about his very knees.'[1] When the knocking was heard Vivien Leigh rushed away, but turned back again to push Macbeth towards the stairs. As the knocking continued, a prompter's note indicates that they moved 'slowly' up the stairs and out.

By contrast with the slow pace of this scene, the scene of the discovery of Duncan's murder was full of swift movement. Olivier reappeared in a black monkish gown tied with a rope. To Harold Hobson, writing in the *Sunday Times* on June 12, 1955, he looked a 'Judas who, in his dark brooding silence, has begun to already think of the potter's field and the gallows'. Olivier paced the stage uneasily during the conversation with Lennox, his arms folded and his hands concealed in his long sleeves. In a sudden movement 'at once furtive and half-automatic, he withdrew them for a moment and hurriedly inspected them front and back'. As the stage filled 'confusedly and yet without confusion', Vivien Leigh's 'What, in our house?' (II. iii. 86) was but faintly off-key. Aware of the mistake, however, she felt her way to the proscenium arch. When Macbeth re-entered, playing his role of a contrite and loyal subject, he was separated from his wife by the whole diagonal of the stage. He glanced uneasily at her for support. She seemed to step forward instinctively to assist him. As Macbeth spun his tangled web of deception, the two seemed 'drawn together by the compulsion of their common guilt to the centre of the stage'.[2] And as Lady Macbeth reached her husband she fainted. To critics viewing the performance, the whole movement appeared natural and right.

Throughout the play Olivier seems to have been able to suggest a latent nobility in Macbeth's character, and this was true even in his encounter with the murderers. After the meeting with Banquo, in which there were no obviously sinister overtones,

[1] 'The Tragic Curve', p. 129.
[2] *Ibid.*

Olivier played the scene with an 'enchantingly easy banter'[1]—
the colloquy with the murderers, commonly considered dull,
became one of the most revealing and dramatic moments in the
play. On the fore-stage[2] the murderers 'half-scared, half-fasci-
nated by the now evil magnetism of the King, shrank back each
time he approached them in a swirl of robes, while he, pacing the
stage between and around them, continuously spun a web of
bewildering words about their understandings, about his own
conscience, about the crime that between them they were about to
commit'.[3] Despite the evil magnetism, however, that made the
murderers shrink away from Macbeth, the dramatic critic of *The
Times* observed that Macbeth's contempt for the murderers was
shot through by overtones of self-contempt.[4] When Macbeth bade
his wife take comfort from the fact that Banquo and his son were
doomed, a note of resentment against crime's terrible necessities
crept into his ironic: 'Then be thou jocund' (III. ii. 40).[5] Olivier
was particularly effective in the closing passages of this scene.
Unlike Macready he did not speak

> Light thickens, and the crow
> Makes wing to th' rooky wood   (III. ii. 50–1)

as if making a note of the time. Instead, without breaking the
thread of the play he seems to have been able to 'step for a
moment outside it and project an authentic spell over the auditorium. What a chill was in his rooky wood!'[6] comments Richard
David.

In the banquet scene which followed, Olivier put forth his full
powers. The private anguish of Macbeth became public, 'flaming
across the darkness with terrifying power'.[7] It was in the banquet
scene that Laurence Olivier brought out most vividly the idea of
a soul in torment.[8] When the banquet began, Lady Macbeth was
seated on her throne up-stage, facing the audience, and slightly
left of centre. Macbeth stood before his throne slightly right of
centre. The thrones stood on a raised platform with steps leading
down towards the middle of the stage. The guests filed in and
took their seats facing the king and queen at a semi-circular table.

[1] *Ibid.* p. 130.
[2] Director's copy, p. 46.
[3] 'The Tragic Curve', p. 130.
[4] June 8, 1955.
[5] *Ibid.*
[6] 'The Tragic Curve', p. 125.
[7] *The Times* (June 8, 1955).
[8] *Ibid.*

From stage right to left sat the third Lord, Caithness, Menteith, Angus, Lennox, the first Lord, the second Lord and Ross. The fifth seat in a central position at the table, reserved for Macbeth, was empty. It was this seat that Banquo's ghost occupied.[1] The positioning of the guests, servants and retainers gave the audience a clear view of Macbeth. If, as Richard David says, the attention of the audience was focused on the face of Macbeth,[2] this was due to the grouping and movements of the characters on the stage.

At 'The table's full', Macbeth came down the steps of the platform. As Lennox says 'Here is a place reserv'd, sir' (III. iv. 46) and Macbeth answers 'Where?' (III. iv. 47), Olivier saw the ghost seated in his place. At 'Which of you have done this?' (III. iv. 49), he began backing up the steps of the platform. After 'Thou canst not say I did it' (III. iv. 50), Lady Macbeth rose from her throne. Ross and the nobles began to rise until Lady Macbeth's 'Sit, worthy friends...' (III. iv. 53) made the lords sit down again, though Ross remained standing. As Lady Macbeth made an attempt to reassure her guests—'My lord is often thus' (III. iv. 53)—at 'If much you note him, / You shall offend him' Macbeth suddenly rushed round the opposite prompt end of the table and on to the fore-stage. The ghost, turning on his stool, followed Macbeth round with his eyes. Lady Macbeth, who had come down from the platform, moved round the prompt side end of the table at

Feed, and regard him not.   (III. iv. 58)

She crossed over to the prompt side of Macbeth, now standing on the fore-stage isolated from his guests, saying

Are you a man?   (III. iv. 58)

The rest of the exchange between Macbeth and Lady Macbeth was continued on-stage, right of the apron.[3] When Macbeth said 'Prithee see there' the ghost rose and moving towards Macbeth, walked between them and out. Macbeth's

If I stand here, I saw him   (III. iv. 74)

[1] Director's copy, pp. 54–7.
[2] 'The Tragic Curve', p. 130.
[3] See diagram and notes reproduced from pp. 56–7 of director's copy—below, appendix II, pp. 280–1.

was whispered with all the agony of a scream.[1] The phrase about the dead rising again to 'push us from our stools' was accompanied by 'a convulsive shoving gesture'.[2]

After the departure of the ghost, Macbeth, recovering control over himself, moved back to his place at the centre of the table at

> Then I'll sit down. (III. iv. 88)

Saying 'Give me some wine, fill full' (III. iv. 88) he turned with his cup towards a servant on his prompt side, who poured out the wine for him. The lords rose from their seats and moved a little down-stage left and to stage right. Macbeth faced the audience with the lords on either side of him. After

> I drink to the general joy of o' th' whole table,
> And to our dear friend Banquo, whom we miss.
> Would he were here! (III. iv. 89–91)

the ghost appeared for the second time between the thrones on the platform.[3] When Macbeth turned to sit he saw the ghost, and dropped the cup in his hand,[4] retreating backwards down-stage left towards the platform. Lady Macbeth saying

> Think of this, good peers,
> But as a thing of custom (III. iv. 96–7)

crossed in front of the lords on stage right to the centre of the stage and moved towards Macbeth. At

> What man dare, I dare (III. iv. 99)

Macbeth pushed her aside, while the ghost began to move down the throne steps towards the centre of the table. With

> Or be alive again,
> And dare me to the desert with thy sword;
> If trembling I inhabit, then protest me
> The baby of a girl (III. iv. 103–6)

Macbeth walking up-stage jumped on the table at stage left and moved towards the ghost, confronting him directly. After 'Un-

---

[1] *Daily Mail* (June 8, 1955).   [2] *Observer* (June 12, 1955).
[3] See diagram and notes from pp. 58–9 of director's copy—below, appendix II, pp. 282–3.
[4] See prompt copy.

real mock'ry, hence!' (III. iv. 107) the ghost disappeared through a concealed trap.[1] The reviewers liked the 'wonderful histrionic jump on the table', and appear to have thought it convincing. The dramatic critic of the *Nottingham Guardian Journal*, writing on June 8, 1955, retained a vivid memory of Macbeth striding along the banquet table and banishing the ghost of Banquo with a flourish of his crimson cloak. As the scene moved to its close, it seemed to the same critic that Vivien Leigh's Lady Macbeth had the quality of ice melted in her for the first time when she said in sorrow:

You lack the season of all natures, sleep.   (III. iv. 141)

The cavern scene which followed in the fourth act appears to have been handled again with originality. The cauldron was small and the witches plucked their horrible emblems from it—a severed head transfixed on a pike, a bloody foetus, a waxen crowned child. The severed head was a replica of Macbeth's and, having entered from up-stage, Olivier stood behind it, 'echoing with his own head its agonized pose, and the message came as in a trance from his living lips'.[2]

The sleep-walking scene in the fifth act, in which Lady Macbeth's tragedy is revealed, was also given with an original clarity and power. Vivien Leigh had changed her wig from auburn to a lank mousy colour. Her playing was powerful yet restrained. The appearance of the sleep-walker's taper at the narrow end of a long cloister-like corridor was particularly effective. Vivien Leigh revealed the inward panic of Lady Macbeth not in large gestures but 'in her secret, vicious wringing of the hands that would "ne-er be clean", not in the expected phrases ("Hell is murky" was firmly objective) but in the sudden high-pitched quaver of "The Thane of Fife had a wife; where is she now?"'[3] Vivien Leigh's interpretation of the sleep-walking scene was thought to be 'true and exact and thoroughly upsetting'.[4]

Richard David says that in Glen Byam Shaw's production of *Macbeth* the scene of the murder of Macduff's family was given in all its brutality. 'The murderers entered to a startled hush; they paused, and then the boy made his ungainly run across the stage,

---

[1] See diagram and notes from pp. 58–9 of director's copy—below, appendix II, pp. 282–3.
[2] 'The Tragic Curve', p. 130.   [3] *Ibid.* p. 127.
[4] T. C. Worsley, *New Statesman* (June 18, 1955).

a puny, unplanned, forlorn attempt at defence. A blow with the hilts, a thrust. The murderer hung back, as if himself aghast at what he had done, leaving the boy standing isolated in mid-stage, with both hands huddled over his wound. For a long moment he hung, wavering, then crumpled slowly to the ground. There was still silence, a long, shocked silence, before the first animal scream broke from his mother.' It was not until this moment that the full horror of Macbeth's actions bursts upon the audience.[1] Yet, in spite of this, Olivier seems to have contrived to obtain sympathy for Macbeth's character in the closing scenes of the play, so that the audience could feel pity for the latent nobility of the man and at the same time recognize with horror the evil that flowed from him. The 'mighty opposites' in Macbeth's character seem to have been fully grasped by Olivier and communicated to his audience. Looking at one of the numerous photographs of himself after the performance, he remarked to Byam Shaw that in it one eye was good and the other evil.[2]

In the speech to the Doctor, drawing the necessary distinction between 'Cans't thou not minister to a mind diseas'd...' and 'Throw physic to the dogs' Olivier with 'a tender flexibility of phrasing, not only showed...the bond of affection between husband and wife but also (the hands gesturing dumbly and half-unconsciously towards his own breast) included himself in the plea for mercy'.[3]

Following Shakespeare's suggestion, Olivier died off-stage, an ending which displeased Kenneth Tynan.[4] But apart from this one disagreement, Olivier's interpretation of Macbeth met with the kind of consensus of approval among the critics given in earlier years to players like Garrick and Mrs Siddons. Harold Hobson, echoing Hazlitt on Edmund Kean, wrote after hearing Macbeth speak: 'There are tones here like the notes of some divine music, echoes of years of departed happiness...',[5] and T. C. Worsley observed that the black and dominating figure of Sir Laurence had taken his audience to the heart of the dark and the dreadful, discovering there a streak of self-hatred which added yet 'another shade to the sombre palette of remorse'.[6] If Byam Shaw succeeded

[1] 'The Tragic Curve', p. 131.
[2] Reported by G. Byam Shaw in conversation with the writer.
[3] 'The Tragic Curve', p. 125. [4] *Observer* (June 12, 1955).
[5] *Sunday Times* (June 12, 1955). [6] *New Statesman* (June 18, 1955).

in giving Shakespeare's tragedy 'in all its balanced perfection',[1] Olivier certainly made it possible by giving Macbeth his true tragic identity.

Olivier, like some of the great players of the eighteenth and nineteenth centuries before him, created standards by which contemporary actors who attempted to interpret the role of Macbeth were judged. When Richard David saw Paul Rogers play Macbeth at the Old Vic in 1955, he thought the performance lacked the complexity of Olivier's interpretation.

As Michael Benthall directed the play, the emphasis was on the events taking place, not on the poetry. A high value seems to have been placed on speed and pace, and Paul Rogers seems to have been carried along 'post-haste' by the speed of the production. Speeches like 'Now o'er the one half-world Nature seems dead' (II. i. 49–50), or 'Come, seeling night' (III. ii. 46) were interpreted as spurs to action, not as reflections on the terrible implications of action. Paul Rogers appears to have seen Macbeth as a dictator cornered by the forces of law and order, and it was logical that there should be little variety of tone in his speech. Macbeth's speech to the Doctor appears to have resembled 'Hitler attacking an incompetent subordinate', and no distinction was drawn between 'Canst thou not minister to a mind diseas'd' (v. iii. 40) and 'Throw physic to the dogs' (v. iii. 47). The consequence of Paul Rogers's interpretation of Macbeth was that there was little interaction between his dehumanised hero and the other characters in the play. Lady Macbeth was 'necessarily reduced' to using the crudest scorn, and Ann Todd, who seemed uncomfortable in the role, appears to have transformed Shakespeare's poetry into conversational rhetoric which carried little conviction.[2]

In 1957 at 'the people's theatre'—the Theatre Royal, Stratford East—Joan Littlewood's *Macbeth* seems to have been, in spite of noble intentions, of limited value. The reviewers tended to regard it as an unsuccessful attempt to turn *Macbeth* into a melodrama of the rise and fall of a modern dictator.[3] Glynn Edwards as Macbeth butchered his way to power in winter-warm leather leggings and Sam Browne belt.[4] In a programme note Joan Littlewood wrote

[1] 'The Tragic Curve', p. 127.   [2] *Ibid.* pp. 123 ff.
[3] See *Punch* (September 11, 1957).   [4] *Daily Mirror* (September 4, 1957).

that her intention was 'to wipe away the dust of three hundred years' and to 'strip off' the 'poetical interpretations' which 'nineteenth-century sentimentalists' had put upon *Macbeth* and which 'are still current today'. Whereas in Glen Byam Shaw's production of *Macbeth* one senses the presence of a very ancient as well as a very contemporary reality, Joan Littlewood's *Macbeth* seems to have been exclusively contemporary. Laurence Olivier had a tragic dignity, and so to a lesser extent had Vivien Leigh. But at the Theatre Royal, Glynn Edwards and Eileen Kennally seem to have quite consciously set out to strip Macbeth and Lady Macbeth of all dignity. A dramatic critic reports that at the line 'Then be thou jocund' (III. ii. 40), 'Macbeth gave his wife a playful slap on the bottom, to which she responded by rubbing the affected place and biting her underlip as if on the verge of tears'.[1] Joan Littlewood wrote in her programme note that the poetry of Shakespeare's day was 'a muscular, active, forward-moving poetry',[2] but Glynn Edwards does not seem to have been able to capture the real vitality of Shakespeare's verse as Olivier had done.

On February 11, 1958, when *Macbeth* was staged at the Birmingham Repertory Theatre, Albert Finney who played Macbeth had dignity and he could suggest 'soldiership and high command'. He showed in addition, tact and restraint. 'I will not be afraid of death and bane' (V. iii. 59) was not shouted or declaimed but spoken in desperately matter-of-fact tones.[3] J. C. Trewin thought that the interpretation was refreshing in its avoidance of excesses. Yet it was his impression that Finney was a good dramatic actor rather than a speaker of verse. On Finney's lips Shakespeare's verse seemed to lack modulation and variety.[4]

In December 1958, at the Old Vic, Michael Hordern and Beatrix Lehmann, both 'brilliant exponents of the mock-heroic', seemed to the dramatic critic of *The Times* to rely too much on 'tricks of delivery' and 'sonorous rhetoric'.[5] To the dramatic critic of the *Daily Telegraph*, Hordern, as Macbeth, gave 'a distinct impression of artifice rather than nature', though the 'true voice of feeling was heard in the "to-morrow and to-morrow" soliloquy.'[6] The critic of the *Manchester Guardian* quarrelled, however,

---

[1] *The Times* (September 4, 1957). Cf. *Punch* (September 11, 1957).
[2] Quoted in *Punch* (September 11, 1957).
[3] *Birmingham Post* (February 12, 1958).   [4] *Ibid.*
[5] December 19, 1958.   [6] December 19, 1958.

with 'the enormous pause' after 'hereafter' which, 'while being magnificent in its audacity', dissipated rather than intensified the initial emotion.[1] Michael Hordern and Beatrix Lehmann appear to have been most convincing, in fact, during the banquet scene. In this scene Hordern successfully used, with a slight variation, a piece of business first invented by Benson. Their playing subtly disclosed the opposite courses the characters were to take. After the departure of the guests both slumped in exhaustion. When they at last broke the silence, every speech seemed to widen the gulf between them. At the end of the scene, Macbeth emphasised his blood-thirsty resolution by driving his knife into the table, while his wife reached 'a nadir of dumb despair'.[2] In Beatrix Lehmann's hands, the character of Lady Macbeth 'declined from initial hardness to something like sweetness'.[3] The sleep-walking scene was played at unusual speed. Beatrix Lehmann saw Lady Macbeth as mad and Ophelia-like in her last moments. To Miss Lehmann it seemed that Lady Macbeth's eventual suicide could only be explained in terms of the fact that she had lost her reason.[4]

When Beatrix Lehmann and Michael Hordern played at the Old Vic, the nature of the stage and the acoustics of the theatre made it difficult for the player to project Shakespeare's verse naturally and yet be heard.[5] This was probably one reason for the artificial delivery noted by the critics. In 1962, when Eric Porter played Macbeth with Irene Worth as Lady Macbeth at Stratford-upon-Avon, and when John Woodvine played the role opposite Josephine Wilson at the Mermaid in 1964, the players experienced no such difficulty. Yet neither Eric Porter nor John Woodvine succeeded in giving Macbeth tragic stature, the one because he had a limiting conception of Macbeth's character, the other because the complexity of the character seemed beyond his reach.

Eric Porter, who has a wonderfully flexible technique which gives the illusion of spontaneity, displayed at its best when he played the Jew of Malta in 1965, seems to have been hampered in 1962 by a limiting view of Macbeth's character. Porter saw Macbeth as a perfectly reasonable ordinary man driven by a comprehensible ambition. Macbeth is impelled by his own ambition and

[1] December 19, 1958.
[2] *The Times* (December 19, 1958). Cf. above, p. 219.
[3] *Daily Telegraph* (December 19, 1958).
[4] Stated in conversation with the writer.
[5] Stated by Miss Lehmann in conversation with the writer.

by forces outside him towards an object—the crown—which is well within his reach. Having reached the top, however, he finds that it means nothing.[1]

As a result of this conception, Eric Porter delivered the judgement soliloquy with intelligent reasonable logic,[2] though this approach would have suited Davenant's version of *Macbeth* better than Shakespeare's.[3] Shakespeare's soliloquy on judgement reveals the imaginative side of Macbeth—the best part of him. The commonsense approach seemed original and effective at certain points. On being asked why he murdered the king's grooms, Macbeth replied in effect that it was the most reasonable thing to do,[4] and this seems to have been a new and convincing interpretation of the lines. The reasonable approach, while relevant at times, could not however comprehend the variety of feeling and impulse in Macbeth. Seeing Macbeth as an ordinary man who, having reached the top, finds it disillusioning, Eric Porter underplayed the reflective passages in the last act and concentrated on presenting furious desperation. He shouted 'I have liv'd long enough...' (v. iii. 22) and made an angry point of 'There would have been a time for such a word' (v. v. 18). 'A tale / Told by an idiot, full of sound and fury' was delivered 'in large exasperation to "the idiot", some god imagined for a moment above his head.' 'I 'gin to be aweary...' (v. v. 49) was spoken to show how intensely Macbeth repudiated life—'it was another outburst of anger.'[5] 'With sure consistency', writes John Russell Brown, 'his death was that of a tired, angry, disarmed fighter: to make this clear he was killed on stage after he had been encircled by the entire army and lost all his weapons.'[6]

Eric Porter's portrayal of Macbeth was strong, closely observed, but limited. Though the interpretation was logical and lively, it had no tragic complexity. As it seemed to the dramatic critic of the *Observer*, Eric Porter brought intelligence and carefully husbanded resources to a role that demands nothing less than free-spending genius.[7]

[1] This view of the character was expressed by Eric Porter in conversation with the writer.

[2] Stated in conversation with the writer.   [3] See above, pp. 19–20.

[4] *Nottingham Guardian Journal* (June 6, 1962).

[5] See John Russell Brown, 'Acting Shakespeare Today', *Shakespeare Survey* 16 (1963), p. 147.

[6] *Ibid.*   [7] June 10, 1962.

Irene Worth gave at Stratford in 1962 a thoughtful though simple reading of Lady Macbeth's character, 'in keeping with the bias of the whole company'.[1] In Acts I and II she made little of the reactions which conflict with the 'willed ruthlessness' of Lady Macbeth:

> Had he not resembled
> My father as he slept, I had done't   (II. ii. 12–13)

and

> I have given suck, and know
> How tender 'tis to love the babe that milks me—
> (I. vii. 54–5)

were both 'too tense with determination' to suggest, as they did for Mrs Siddons, 'the gentler impulses' that are momentarily resurrected within Lady Macbeth. Irene Worth saw Lady Macbeth as driven by egocentric ambition, which leads to a struggle with guilt and weakness. There were moments when her approach to the part seemed effective. Her terse, low-pitched but strong 'You must leave this' (III. ii. 35) suggested a determination 'to find new ways of confronting danger for herself.' 'Give me the daggers' (II. ii. 53) was said not with obvious drama but with 'rapid, quiet simplicity which spoke eloquently for self-reliance and its limitations.' 'Stand not upon the order of your going, / But go at once' (III. iv. 119) was spoken as two phrases, 'the first a courtesy assumed with difficulty and the second a betrayal of inner tension ...a loud and curt "at once".' In the final moments of the sleep-walking scene:

> To bed, to bed; there's knocking at the gate. Come, come, come, come, give me your hand. What's done cannot be undone. To bed, to bed, to bed.   (v. i. 64–6)

she continued the single line of her interpretation. On leaving, she went towards Duncan's room and not the marriage bed. Realising her mistake, she then turned in horror and ran out. Guilt was the final impression. 'To bed, to bed, to bed' was 'spoken only for fearful haste'.[2]

If Eric Porter and Irene Worth achieved consistency at too great a cost, John Woodvine and Josephine Wilson at the Mer-

---

[1] 'Acting Shakespeare Today', p. 148.
[2] *Ibid.* pp. 149–50.

maid gave the impression that their reach exceeded their grasp. A programme note quoted Aristotle:

> There remains, then, as the only proper subject for Tragedy, the spectacle of a man not absolutely or eminently good or wise, who is brought to disaster not by sheer depravity but by some error or frailty...this man must be highly renowned and prosperous—an Oedipus, a Thyestes, or some other illustrious person.[1]

Yet John Woodvine, alternating between prose and hysteria, could not bring out the complexity of Macbeth's character or suggest his high renown. Josephine Wilson, who with open glazed eyes played an effective sleep-walker, faltered in the great arias composed for Lady Macbeth. The apron at the Mermaid became most effective when the actors used it. The line 'Faith, here's an equivocator...' (II. iii. 8) became immediate when the actor, advancing on to the apron, hurled it at the audience. Yet though the condition of intimacy was there, John Woodvine failed to take advantage of it. Bernard Shaw was probably right when he observed that 'any play performed on a platform amidst the audience gets closer home to its hearers than when it is presented as a picture framed by a proscenium...We are less conscious', wrote Shaw, 'of the artificiality of the stage, when a few well understood conventions adroitly handled, are substituted for attempts at an impossible scenic verisimilitude. All the old fashioned tales,...adventure plays with their frequent changes of scene, and all the new problem plays with their intense intimacies should be done in this way.'[2] But John Woodvine's almost total failure to make his audience imaginatively share Macbeth's tragic fate shows how naive it would be to assume that the apron-stage immediately solves all the Shakespearean actor's problems of interpretation. There is no substitute for a close sensitive encounter with the text.

Though the programme brought out for *Macbeth* at the Mermaid quoted Gordon Craig, the décor, purporting to be Elizabethan, was unimaginative. Its artistic crudity made the play appear tawdry and the characters seemed at times like puppets in a folk tale.

It was Yeats who wrote of the interdependence of all things on the stage. Decorative scene-painting as opposed to natural scene-

---

[1] April 22, 1964.
[2] *Our Theatres in the Nineties*, I, 193–4.

painting, he asserted, should be as inseparable from the movements as from the robes of the players and from the falling of the
light.[1] Yeats made this remark after seeing scenery executed by
Gordon Craig at a Purcell Society performance. He observed on
this occasion that Craig had created an ideal country where everything was possible, even speaking in verse, or speaking in music,
or the expression of the whole of life in a dance. Making a plea
for scenery of this sort for Shakespeare's plays, Yeats relates the
new conception of décor to Shakespeare's characters, observing
that time after time the people in his plays use at some moment of
deep emotion an elaborate or deliberate metaphor which breaks
the naturalistic illusion. Yeats, one feels, would rightly have
rejected both a spurious Elizabethanness as well as any attempt to
make Shakespeare contemporary by sacrificing all the depth and
colour of his verse.

This study has shown that there is some truth in the claim made
for the special insights of the actor. But it has also demonstrated
that the players have frequently obscured the text of *Macbeth*.
Actors like Spranger Barry, who used Davenant's text in the
eighteenth century, tended almost exclusively to provoke pity for
the character and to present Macbeth as a sentimental rather than
a tragic hero. Godfrey Tearle in the twentieth century, even
though he used Shakespeare's text, tended to sentimentalise
Macbeth. On the other hand, there have been players like Edmund Kean in the nineteenth century and Ion Swinley and Ralph
Richardson in the twentieth, who deprived the play of its tragic
content by failing to distinguish sufficiently between Macbeth and
Richard III. In recent years actors like Paul Rogers and Glynn
Edwards have seen the play as a melodrama about the rise and fall
of a Fascist dictator and have tended to confuse Macbeth with
Adolf Hitler. Just as actors have exaggerated certain elements in
Macbeth's character, so actresses have concentrated on this or
that element in Lady Macbeth's character, depriving Shakespeare's creation of its tragic complexity. Ellen Terry made Lady
Macbeth almost exclusively charming, while Fanny Kemble made
her exclusively forbidding. Few could, like Mrs Siddons, who was
both beautiful and terrible, arouse awe and terror as well as pity.
One can make a formidable list of actresses from Mrs Giffard to

[1] *Ideas of Good and Evil*, p. 149.

Ena Burrill and actors from Quin to Michael Redgrave, who have been insufficiently aware of the complexity of the text.

There have been players who achieved consistency at the expense of complexity—Henry Irving and Salvini come to mind —and illuminated this or that facet of the text. But the successful failures of an Irving or a Salvini have another value besides this for the critic. They show how possible it is while interpreting Shakespeare to be quite brilliantly incomplete.

Though some actors have obscured the text of *Macbeth*, or limited its meaning, others have grasped a great deal more of its complexity. At times the instinctive discoveries of the great players resemble the interpretations of modern critics. Garrick, for example, perceived the ambiguity in:

> ...his virtues
> Will plead like angels, trumpet-tongu'd, against
> The deep damnation of his taking-off...   (I. vii. 18–20)

Garrick paused slightly at angels. When he was criticised for doing this, he argued that Shakespeare had conceived of Duncan's virtues (not the angels only) as trumpet tongu'd. At times the players' sensitiveness to the local life of Shakespeare's verse anticipates the sort of criticism described today as 'practical'. Mrs Siddons showed a sensitiveness to the details of Shakespeare's imagery. In her essay on the character of Lady Macbeth she points out that the smell of blood haunts Lady Macbeth's imagination:

> Here's the smell of the blood still. All the perfumes of Arabia will not sweeten this little hand   (v. i. 48–50)

and contrasts these lines with 'the bolder image' used by Macbeth when he expresses similar feelings:

> Will all great Neptune's ocean wash this blood
> Clean from my hand?   (II. ii. 60–1)

Mrs Siddons's interpretation of the changes of tone and rhythm in Shakespeare's verse, demonstrating as it does a sensitive and accurate response to Shakespeare's text, provides an enduring lesson to all critics of Shakespeare. Kemble's re-introduction of the pause after 'well' in

> If it were done when 'tis done, then 'twere well
> It were done quickly   (I. vii. 1–2)

demonstrates a desire to interpret what Shakespeare actually wrote. The pause is suggested by a comma in the First Folio and adds to the depth of meaning in the line. Flora Robson, we know, found a stage direction within the text of the sleep-walking scene—

Come, come, come, come, give me your hand   (v. i. 65–6)

which guided her interpretation both in this scene and in a previous scene between Macbeth and Lady Macbeth after the murder of Duncan. She took Macbeth's hand, clammy with blood, in her own blood-stained hand, first in reality and later on during her sleep, withdrawing her own on each occasion with a shudder.

The last detail suggests that there are certain insights achieved by players which are not normally found in the work of critics and scholars. This sort of insight was achieved by Garrick in the dagger soliloquy. He used a single movement of the hand as he spoke the line,

Come, let me clutch thee.   (II. i. 34)

The single gesture conveyed a great deal. With the satanic look of a man resolved on murder, Garrick, as if snatching the crown itself, clasped the handle of the imaginary dagger. On the stage, more than one interpretation of this line has been possible. We know that Olivier greeted the imaginary dagger with 'sad familiarity' as if it was a part of 'the crooked furniture of his brain'.

There are limits, certainly, to the several possible meanings that players can read into a line—limits sometimes set by the logic of the text. This is clear if one considers the many interpretations of the exchange between Macbeth and Lady Macbeth in I. v. 55–8. In answer to Lady Macbeth's enquiry about the duration of Duncan's stay in Dunsinane—'And when goes hence?'—both Edmund Kean and Donald Wolfit as Macbeth paused after 'To-morrow' and, clearly indicating that murder is in Macbeth's mind, added 'as he purposes', reducing the effectiveness of Lady Macbeth's next line,

O, never
Shall sun that morrow see!   (I. v. 58)

The line when Mrs Siddons played it had an evil grandeur and power.

The most successful interpretations of Macbeth were given by Garrick and Laurence Olivier, who were most alive to the complexity of the character. Kemble achieved his own kind of excellence. Macready came close to conveying the 'mighty opposites' in Macbeth's character, but his performance was weakened at times by his reduction of Shakespeare's poetry to prose. We know that Macready spoke the lines:

> Light thickens, and the crow
> Makes wing to th' rooky wood   (III. ii. 50–1)

as if he was making a note of the time. Olivier, on the other hand, cast an authentic spell over the auditorium and critics remembered what a chill there was in his 'rooky wood'. Yet Macready, in portraying the death of Macbeth, seems to have touched a tragic chord—John Coleman wrote that the 'desperation of his final defiance of fate was appalling to witness. So might the fallen star of morning have confronted the archangel in the last dread conflict'.[1] Macready seems to have successfully brought out a suggestion contained in Malcolm's allusion to Macbeth:

> Angels are bright still, though the brightest fell.   (IV. iii. 22)

The greatest interpreters of Macbeth and Lady Macbeth, one can be sure, would have agreed with W. B. Yeats:

> But actors lacking music
> Do most excite my spleen
> They say it is more human
> To shuffle, grunt and groan
> Not knowing what unearthly stuff
> Rounds a mighty scene.[2]

Players like Olivier, Mrs Siddons and Garrick did not lack music, and they surely had a sense of the unearthly stuff that rounds a mighty scene. They appear to have combined grandeur without pomp and nature without triviality, and they illuminated the text with a rare brilliance.

While other players were less successful, even they at times shed light on Shakespeare's language. One remembers Vivien Leigh's 'Hell is murky' (V. i. 36), which was 'firmly objective', and

---

[1] See above, p. 155.
[2] *Last Poems and Plays* (1940), p. 45.

Irene Worth's 'Stand not upon the order of your going, / But go at once' (III. iv. 119), which was spoken as two phrases, 'the first a courtesy assumed with difficulty, and the second...a loud and curt "at once".' The director Jubal, who had worked with Reinhardt, used to tell his actors that they should read a play with their eyes on the stage and their hearts in the street. Because the players interpreting the roles of Macbeth and Lady Macbeth have often done this, they have illuminated the text in new ways. At times, it is true, they have fatally obscured the text, but on the whole this history proves that the players' insights are unquestionably relevant to the study of *Macbeth*.

The insights of the great players are of value to the critic. It is not merely a case of reading Shakespeare by flashes of lightning, for when Mrs Siddons played Lady Macbeth there were no patches of darkness. Mrs Siddons's performance was an artistic creation of permanent value. In the process of reconstructing it, one is able to enter the tragic world of Macbeth and watch that world come to life upon the stage. Players like Mrs Siddons realised and communicated the quality one finds in certain kinds of myth and in great tragic art, the experience which can be both terrible and joy-bringing, mysterious and yet immediate, 'more distant than the stars and yet nearer than the eye'. Like the Japanese dancer remembered by Yeats, the great players seem to have had the capacity to withdraw into some more powerful life.

APPENDICES

BIBLIOGRAPHY

INDEX

APPENDIX I

This is a list of performances of *Macbeth* mentioned in the text, with, where available, the names of the players who interpreted Macbeth and Lady Macbeth in these performances on the English stage. The following sources were consulted in determining the dates of performances: Gabrielle Enthoven Collection of playbills and cuttings; Frederick Latreille MSS. of newspaper bills; Charles Beecher Hogan, *Shakespeare in the Theatre*; John Genest, *Some Account of the English Stage, 1660 to 1830*; *The London Stage*, parts 1–4, ed. William Van Lennep, Emmet L. Avery, Arthur Scouten and George Winchester Stone.

DATE	PLAYERS	THEATRES
1611, April 20	Burbage?	Globe
1667, April 19	Probably Betterton	Lincoln's Inn Fields
——, October 16	Young	
——, November 6		
1672–73	Betterton and Mrs Betterton	Dorset Garden Theatre
1707, December 29	Betterton and Mrs Barry	Queen's, Haymarket
——, November 28	George Powell	Drury Lane
1709, December 17	Betterton	Queen's, Haymarket
1710, November 18	John Mills	Queen's, Haymarket
1718, November 13	Quin	Lincoln's Inn Fields
1736, November 18	John Mills and Mrs Porter	Drury Lane
——, December 23	Quin and Mrs Porter	Drury Lane
1744, January 7	Garrick and Mrs Giffard	Drury Lane
1752, March 17	Barry and Mrs Cibber	Covent Garden
1754, September 24	Mossop and Mrs Pritchard	Drury Lane
1757, April 16	Mossop and Mrs Pritchard	Drury Lane
1761, April 29	Sheridan and Mrs Pritchard	Drury Lane
1762, January 9	Garrick and Mrs Pritchard	Drury Lane
1764, February 28	Holland and Mrs Pritchard	Drury Lane
1768, January 20	Powell and Mrs Yates	Covent Garden
——, April 25	Garrick and Mrs Pritchard	Drury Lane
1773, October 23	Macklin and Mrs Hartley	Covent Garden
——, October 30	Macklin and Mrs Hartley	Covent Garden
1779, October 18	Henderson and Mrs Hartley	Covent Garden
1781, January 15	Henderson and Mrs Yates	Covent Garden
1785, February 2	Smith and Mrs Siddons	Drury Lane
1794, April 21	J. P. Kemble and Mrs Siddons	Drury Lane
1800, December 5	George F. Cooke	Covent Garden
1803, November 28	J. P. Kemble and Mrs Siddons	Covent Garden
1809, September 18	J. P. Kemble and Mrs Siddons	Covent Garden
——	Charles Kemble and Mrs Siddons	Brighton
1811, September 18	J. P. Kemble and Mrs Siddons	Covent Garden
1814, November 5	Edmund Kean and Mrs Bartley	Drury Lane
1816, June 8	J. P. Kemble and Mrs Siddons	Covent Garden

DATE	PLAYERS	THEATRES
1816, June 16	Charles Young and Mrs Siddons	Covent Garden
1820, June 15	Macready	Covent Garden
1822, April 15	Young	Covent Garden
1827, November 30	Macready	Drury Lane
1831, March 14	Macready and Miss Huddart	Drury Lane
1833, January 2	Macready	Drury Lane
1834, January 15	Macready	Canterbury
——, February 5	Macready	Drury Lane
1835, October 1	Macready and Ellen Tree	Drury Lane
——, October 4	Macready and Ellen Tree	Drury Lane
1836, April 27	Macready and Mrs Bartley	Drury Lane
1837, November 6	Macready and Miss Huddart	Covent Garden
1840, April 26	Macready	Drury Lane
1842, March 28	Macready and Mrs Warner	Drury Lane
1845, August	Phelps and Mrs Warner	Sadler's Wells
1847, September 27	Phelps	Sadler's Wells
1848, February 21	Macready and Fanny Kemble	Prince's Theatre
1850, March 20	Phelps and Isabella Glyn	Sadler's Wells
1851, February 20	Macready and Mrs Warner	Drury Lane
——, March 17	Mr and Mrs W. J. Wallack	Queen's, Haymarket
1852, January 2	Isabella Glyn	Drury Lane
1853, February 14	Mr and Mrs Charles Kean	Prince's Theatre
——, October 18	Brooke	Drury Lane
1857, July 11	Signor Vitaliani and Ristori	Lyceum
1858, February 25	Charles Dillon and Helen Faucit	Lyceum
1866, October 1	Barry Sullivan and Amy Sedgwick	Drury Lane
1869, February 22	Phelps	Drury Lane
——, February 23	Charles Dillon	Drury Lane
1875, September 18	Irving and Mrs Bateman	Lyceum
1876, May 10	E. Rossi and Signora Glech-Pareti	Drury Lane
1884, March	Salvini	Covent Garden
——, July 4	M. Marais and Sarah Bernhardt	Gaiety
1888, December 29	Irving and Ellen Terry	Lyceum
1895, May 25	Lillah McCarthy	St George's Hall
1898, September 17	Forbes-Robertson and Mrs Patrick Campbell	Lyceum
1906, April 26	Mr and Mrs E. R. Benson	Stratford-upon-Avon
——, November 13	Arthur Bourchier and Violet Vanbrugh	Stratford
1908, May 6	Mr and Mrs F. R. Benson	Stratford
1910, July 28	Mr and Mrs. F. R. Benson	Stratford
1911, April 27	Matheson Lang and Hutin Britton	Stratford
——, September 5	Beerbohm Tree and Violet Vanbrugh	His Majesty's
1920, November 2	James Hackett and Mrs Patrick Campbell	Aldwych
1923, May 16	Frank Cellier and Dorothy Green	Stratford
1926, December 24	Henry Ainley and Sybil Thorndike	Prince's Theatre
1928, February 6	Eric Maturin and Mary Merrall	Court Theatre
1930, March 17	John Gielgud and Martita Hunt	Old Vic
1932, November 12	Malcolm Kean and Margaret Webster	Old Vic

DATE	PLAYERS	THEATRES
1933, April 18	George Hayes and Fabia Drake	Stratford
1934, April 2	Charles Laughton and Flora Robson	Old Vic
1935, December 3	Ion Swinley and Vivienne Bennett	Old Vic
1937, November 27	Laurence Olivier and Judith Anderson	Old Vic
——, December 27	Olivier and Judith Anderson	New Theatre
1939, February 21		Arts Theatre, Cambridge
——, May 8	Alec Guinness and Joan Knowles	Sheffield Repertory
1942, July 8	Gielgud and Gwen Ffrangcon-Davies	Piccadilly Theatre
1945, February 12	Donald Wolfit and Patricia Jessel	Winter Garden
1946, April 10	William Devlin and Pamela Brown	Bristol Old Vic
——, June 21	Robert Harris and Rosemary Taylor	Stratford
1947, December 18	Michael Redgrave and Ena Burrill	Aldwych
1949, April 18	Godfrey Tearle and Diana Wynyard	Stratford
1950, June 8	Alec Clunes and Margaret Rawlings	Arts Theatre
1952, June 10	Ralph Richardson and Margaret Leighton	Stratford
1952, September 10	Bernard Miles and Josephine Wilson	Mermaid
1953, March 19	Donald Wolfit and Rosalind Iden	Kings', Hammersmith
1954, September 9	Paul Rogers and Ann Todd	Old Vic
1955, June 7	Laurence Olivier and Vivien Leigh	Stratford
1956, May 22	Paul Rogers and Coral Browne	
1957, September 3	Glynn Edwards and Eileen Kennally	Theatre Royal, Stratford East
1958, February 11	Albert Finney	Birmingham Repertory
——, December 17	Michael Hordern and Beatrix Lehmann	Old Vic
1962, June 6	Eric Porter and Irene Worth	Stratford
1964, April 22	John Woodvine and Josephine Wilson	Mermaid

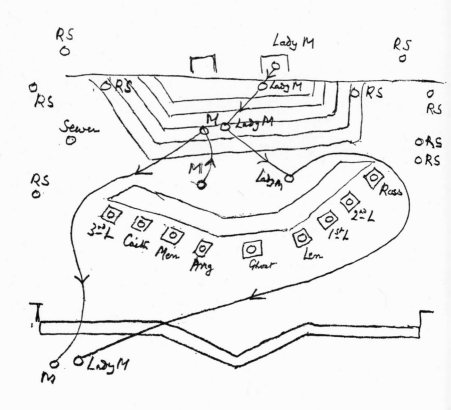

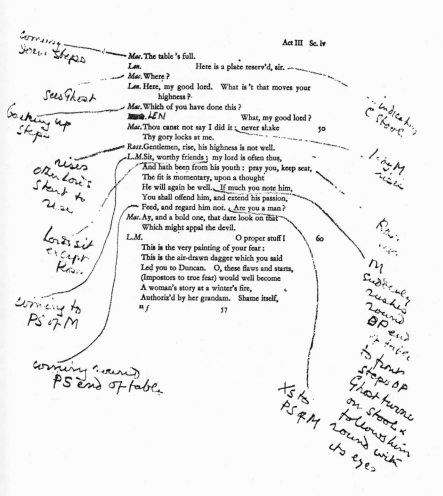

Act III Sc. iv

Mac. The table's full.

Len.　　　　　　Here is a place reserv'd, sir.

Mac. Where?

Len. Here, my good lord. What is 't that moves your
　　　　highness?

Mac. Which of you have done this?

LEN　　　　　　　　What, my good lord?

Mac. Thou canst not say I did it: never shake　　　50
　　　　Thy gory locks at me.

Ross. Gentlemen, rise, his highness is not well.

L.M. Sit, worthy friends; my lord is often thus,
　　　　And hath been from his youth: pray you, keep seat,
　　　　The fit is momentary, upon a thought
　　　　He will again be well. If much you note him,
　　　　You shall offend him, and extend his passion,
　　　　Feed, and regard him not. Are you a man?

Mac. Ay, and a bold one, that dare look on that
　　　　Which might appal the devil.

　　　L.M.　　　　　O proper stuff!　　　60
　　　　This is the very painting of your fear:
　　　　This is the air-drawn dagger which you said
　　　　Led you to Duncan. O, these flaws and starts,
　　　　(Impostors to true fear) would well become
　　　　A woman's story at a winter's fire,
　　　　Authoriz'd by her grandam. Shame itself,

11 f　　　　57

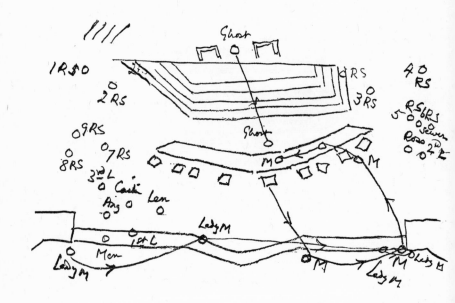

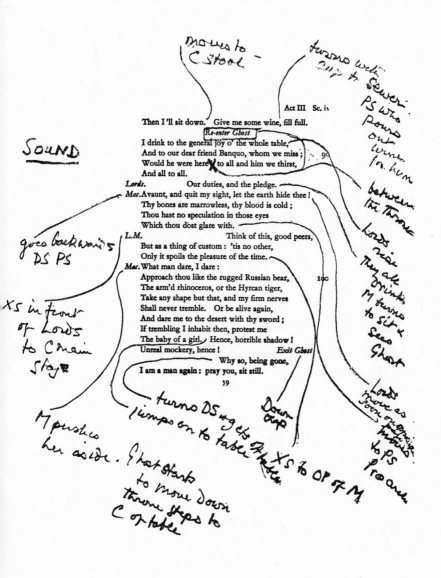

Act III Sc. iv

Then I 'll sit down. Give me some wine, fill full.

Re-enter Ghost

I drink to the general joy o' the whole table,
And to our dear friend Banquo, whom we miss ;
Would he were here ! to all and him we thirst,
And all to all.

Lords.   Our duties, and the pledge.

*Mac.*Avaunt, and quit my sight, let the earth hide thee !
Thy bones are marrowless, thy blood is cold ;
Thou hast no speculation in those eyes
Which thou dost glare with.

L.M.   Think of this, good peers,
But as a thing of custom : 'tis no other,
Only it spoils the pleasure of the time.

*Mac.*What man dare, I dare :
Approach thou like the rugged Russian bear,
The arm'd rhinoceros, or the Hyrcan tiger,
Take any shape but that, and my firm nerves
Shall never tremble. Or be alive again,
And dare me to the desert with thy sword ;
If trembling I inhabit then, protest me
The baby of a girl. Hence, horrible shadow !
Unreal mockery, hence !   *Exit Ghost*
         Why so, being gone,
I am a man again : pray you, sit still.

59

BIBLIOGRAPHY

MSS. AND COLLECTIONS

Burney. Collection of newspapers, 1707. B.M. 1831.

Gabrielle Enthoven. Collection of playbills and cuttings, H.B. Tree Gift, etc. V. and A.M.

Simon Forman. *Boke of Plaies*, 1611. Photostat facsimile, Bodl. Ashm. MS. 208, ff. 200–13.

Frederick Latreille. MSS. of newspaper bills, 1880s. B.M. Add. MSS. 32249–52. 4 vols.

Prompt copies of *Macbeth*. Benson, Byam Shaw and Anthony Quayle: Shakespeare Memorial Library, Stratford. Beerbohm Tree: H.B. Tree Gift, V. and A.M.

G. Byam Shaw. Notebooks and director's copy—in Mr Shaw's possession.

R. J. Smith. *A Collection of Material Towards an History of the English Stage*. B.M. 11826, r.s. 2 vols. n.d.

ARTICLES IN PERIODICALS

Armstrong, W. A. 'Actors and Theatres.' *Shakespeare Survey* 17. Cambridge, 1964.

Bede, Cuthbert. 'Macbeth on the Stage.' *N & Q*, VIII. Seventh series. July 13, 1889.

Brown, John Russell. 'Acting Shakespeare Today.' *Shakespeare Survey* 16. Cambridge, 1963.

Cormican, L. A. 'Medieval Idiom in Shakespeare.' *Scrutiny*, XVII. Cambridge, 1950.

David, Richard. 'The Tragic Curve.' *Shakespeare Survey* 9. Cambridge, 1956.

Donoghue, Denis. 'Macklin's Shylock and Macbeth.' *Studies: An Irish Quarterly Review*, XLIII. Dublin, 1954.

Downer, Alan S. 'Nature to Advantage Dressed.' *PMLA*, LVIII. New York, 1943.

'Macready's Production of Macbeth.' *Quarterly Journal of Speech*. Illinois, April 1947.

Fiske, Roger. 'The Macbeth Music.' *Music and Letters*, XLV. April 1964.

Hunt, R. W., and Wilson, John Dover. 'Authenticity of Simon Forman's Bocke of Plaies.' *RES*, XXIII. Oxford, July 1947.

Klein, David. 'Did Shakespeare Produce his own Plays?' *MLR*, LVII. Cambridge, 1962.

Nosworthy, J. M. 'Macbeth at the Globe.' *The Library*, II. 1947–8.
Rosenberg, Marvin. 'Elizabethan Actors: Men or Marionettes.' *PMLA*, LXIX. New York, 1954.
Shuttleworth, Bertram. 'Irving's Macbeth.' *TN*, V. 1951.
Sprague, Arthur Colby. 'Did Betterton Chant?' *TN*, I. 1946.
Stone, George Winchester. 'Garrick's Handling of Macbeth.' *SP*, XXXVIII. North Carolina, 1941.
  'David Garrick's Significance in the History of Shakespearean Criticism.' *PMLA*, XLV. New York, 1950.
Wain, John. 'Guide to Shakespeare.' *Encounter*, XXII. 1964.
Wilson, John Harold. 'Rant, Cant and Tone on the Restoration Stage.' *SP*, III. North Carolina, 1955.
Wright, Louis B. 'Animal Actors on the English Stage before 1642.' *PMLA*, XLII. New York, 1927.

NEWSPAPERS AND MAGAZINES

Academy: April 15, May 13, 1876.
Athenaeum: March 17, 1838; August 23, 1845; October 2, 1847; March 22, 1851; October 22, 1853; February 15, 1856; October 9, 1880; May 19, 1888; September 24, 1898.
Birmingham Gazette: April 19, 1933; June 11, 1952.
Birmingham Mail: April 19, 1933; April 18, 1949.
Birmingham Post: November 14, 1906; April 19, 1933; April 18, 1949; February 12, 1958; April 17, 1964.
Connoisseur: September 1, September 19, 1754.
Coventry Evening Telegraph: June 11, 1952.
Daily Chronicle: September 6, 1911.
Daily Courant: December 29, 1707.
Daily Mail: June 8, 1955.
Daily Mirror: September 4, 1957.
Daily News: September 21, 1875.
Daily Post: September 27, 1875.
Daily Telegraph: October 3, 1866; September 27, 1875; December 31, 1888; September 6, 1911; April 3, 1934; November 27, 1937; April 18, 1949; June 12, 1952; December 19, 1958.
Drama: or Theatrical Pocket Magazine: IV, 1823; VI, 1824.
English Illustrated Magazine: VI, December 1888.
Evening Standard: September 6, 1911; June 8, 1955.
The Examiner: October 4, 1835; May 2, 1846.
The Figaro: October 2, 1875.
Financial Times: June 9, 1955.
Gazetteer: February 3, 1785.
Gentleman's Magazine: March 1889.

Harper's New Monthly Magazine: December 1862.

Have at You All: Or, The Drury Lane Journal: March 13, 1752.

Herald: April 27, November 18, 1906; August 6, 1910.

Illustrated London News: October 13, 1849; March 23, 1850; August 23, 1851; January 3, 1852; November 1, 1856; March 6, 1869; October 2, 1875.

Lady's Pictorial: January 5, 1889; September 16, 1911.

Listener: April 23, 1964.

Literary Gazette: June 17, 1820.

Liverpool Daily Post: December 31, 1888.

Liverpool Post: April 18, 1949.

London Chronicle: April 14–15, 1757; October 23–6, October 26–8, 1773.

London Magazine: November 1773.

Manchester Guardian: November 27, 1937; June 24, 1946; March 21, 1953; December 19, 1958.

Monthly Mirror: VII, 1799; IV, 1808.

Morning Chronicle: October 25, October 29, October 30, 1773.

Morning Post: February 3, 1785; August 5, 1851; April 28, September 6, 1911; April 19, 1933.

New Monthly Magazine: December 1, 1827.

News Chronicle: March 21, 1953.

New Statesman: June 18, 1955.

New York Mirror: October 14, 1826.

Nottingham Guardian Journal: June 8, 1955; June 6, 1962.

Observer: March 31, 1930; July 12, 1942; December 21, 1947; June 12, 1955; June 10, 1962.

Oracle: April 22, 1794.

Political World: January 5, 1889.

Punch: July 13, 1946; September 11, 1957.

Quarterly Review: XXXIV, 1826.

St. James's Chronicle: January 19–21, 1768; October 28–30, 1773; November 2–4, 1773.

St. James's Gazette: December 31, 1888.

Saturday Review: June 14, 1884.

Sheffield Telegraph: May 9, 1939.

Sketch: January 5, 1927.

Stage: January 4, 1889; June 27, 1946.

Star: December 31, 1888.

Stratford-upon-Avon Herald: April 27, 1906; May 8, 1908; June 8, 1946.

Sunday Times: December 30, 1888; February 18, 1945; April 17, 1949; June 12, 1955.

Theatre: June 17, 1955.

Theatrical Examiner: October 4, 1835.

Theatrical Inquisitor: February 1813; November 1814; August 1819.
Theatrical Journal: I, 1840; III, 1842.
The Times: September 19, 1811; November 7, 1814; September 27,
    1847; February 15, 1853; July 4, 1884; September 19, 1898;
    September 6, 1911; May 17, 1923; May 24, 1923; December 24,
    1926; January 3, January 6, 1927; March 18, 1930; November 22,
    1932; April 3, 1934; November 27, 1937; December 28, 1937;
    February 22, 1939; July 9, 1942; August 1, 1944; June 24, 1946;
    December 19, 1947; March 20, 1953; June 8, 1955; September 4,
    1957; December 19, 1958.
The Times Literary Supplement: August 25, 1927.
Tribune: June 8, 1955.
Universal Museum: April 1768.
Western Daily Press (Bristol): June 9, 1955.

PRINTED BOOKS

Addison, Joseph. *The Spectator*. Ed. G. Gregory Smith. 8 vols. Every-
    man's Library. 1907.
Agate, James. *Brief Chronicles*. 1943.
Alger, W. R. *The Life of Edwin Forrest*. 2 vols. Philadelphia, 1877.
Appleton, William. *Charles Macklin*. Cambridge, Mass., 1962.
Aston, Anthony. 'A Brief Supplement to Colley Cibber Esq.' 1748.
    Rptd in *An Apology for the Life of Mr Colley Cibber, Comedian*. Ed.
    R. W. Lowe. 2 vols. 1889.
Baker, Herschel. *John Philip Kemble*. Cambridge, Mass., 1942.
Baker, H. Barton. *The London Stage*. 2 vols. 1889.
Baldwin, T. W. *The Organization and Personnel of the Shakespearean
    Company*. Princeton, 1927.
Barrault, Jean-Louis. *Nouvelles Réflexions sur le théâtre*. Paris, 1959.
Barton, Margaret. *David Garrick*. 1948.
Beaumont, Francis. *The Knight of the Burning Pestle*. 1613.
Bentley, Eric. *In Search of Theatre*. 1954.
Boaden, James. *Memoirs of the Life of John Philip Kemble*. 2 vols. 1825.
    Memoirs of Mrs Siddons. 2 vols. 1827.
Boswell, James. *The Life of Samuel Johnson, LL.D*. Ed. G. B. Hill. Rev.
    ed. L. F. Powell. 6 vols. Oxford, 1934–40.
    Tour to the Hebrides. Ed. R. W. Chapman. 1933.
Bradley, A. C. *Shakespearean Tragedy*. Rptd 1964.
Brecht, Bertolt. *Brecht on Theatre*. Trans. John Willett. 1964.
Brereton, A. *The Life of Henry Irving*. 2 vols. 1908.
Buck, H. S. *A Study in Smollett*. New Haven, 1925.
Bulwer, John. *Chirologia: Chironomia*. 1644.
Burnim, Kalman. *David Garrick, Director*. Pittsburgh, 1961.

Byrne, M. St Clare. 'The Stage Costuming of Macbeth in the Eighteenth Century.' *Studies in English Theatre History.* 1952.

Byron, George Gordon, Lord. *A Self-portrait: Letters and Diaries, 1798–1824.* Ed. Peter Quennell. 2 vols. 1950.

Campbell, Mrs Patrick. *My Life and Some Letters.* 1922.

Campbell, Thomas. *Life of Mrs Siddons.* 2 vols. 1834. (Vol. II contains the whole of Mrs Siddons's essay, 'Remarks on the Character of Lady Macbeth.')

Casson, Lewis. 'Introduction' to *The Tragedy of Macbeth.* Folio Society Edition. 1951.

Chambers, E. K. *William Shakespeare.* 2 vols. Oxford, 1930.

Chetwood, William Rufus. *A General History of the Stage.* 1749.

Churchill, Charles. *The Rosciad.* 1761.

Cibber, Colley. *An Apology for the Life of Mr Colley Cibber, Comedian.* 1740. Ed. R. W. Lowe. 2 vols. 1889.
　The Laureat: or, the Right Side of Colley Cibber, Esq. 1740.

Cole, J. W. *The Life and Theatrical Times of Charles Kean.* 2 vols. 1859.

Cole, T., and Chinoy, H. K. (eds.). *Actors on Acting.* New York, 1949.

Coleridge, Samuel Taylor. *Table Talk.* Ed. T. Ashe. 1888.

Collier, J. P. *The History of English Dramatic Poetry.* 3 vols. 1831.

Cooke, William. *Memoirs of Charles Macklin, Comedian.* 1804.

Critical Observations on Mr Kemble's Performance. 1811.

Crosse, Gordon. *Shakespearean Playgoing, 1890–1952.* 1953.

Davenant, William. *Gondibert.* 1650.
　Macbeth. 1674.

Davies, Thomas. *Memoirs of the Life of David Garrick, Esq.* 2 vols. 1780.
　Dramatic Miscellanies. 3 vols. Dublin, 1784.

Dent, Alan. *Mrs Patrick Campbell.* 1961.

Dibdin, James. *The Annals of the Edinburgh Stage.* Edinburgh, 1888.

Doran, J. *Annals of the English Stage, from Betterton to Kean.* 2 vols. 1864. Rev. ed. R. W. Lowe. 3 vols. 1888.

Downes, John. *Roscius Anglicanus.* 1708.

Dryden, John. *Albion and Albanius.* 1685.
　The Essays of John Dryden. Ed. W. P. Ker. 2 vols. Oxford, 1926.
　The Works of John Dryden. Ed. E. N. Hooker and H. T. Swedenberg. 2 vols. Berkeley, Cal. 1956–.

Dunbar, Janet. *Flora Robson.* 1960.

Dunlap, William. *Memoirs of George Frederick Cooke.* 2 vols. 1813.

Eliot, T. S. *Murder in the Cathedral.* 1935.
　What is a Classic? 1955.

Ellis, Ruth. *The Shakespeare Memorial Theatre.* 1948.

An Estimate of the Theatrical Merits of the Two Tragedians of Crow Street. 1760.

Farrington, Joseph. *Diary.* 1811.

Faucit, Helen. *Some of Shakespeare's Female Characters.* 1891.

Finlay, John. *Miscellanies.* Dublin, 1835.

Fitzgerald, Percy. *The Life of David Garrick.* 1899.

Flatter, Richard. *Shakespeare's Producing Hand.* 1948.

Flecknoe, Richard. 'A Short Discourse of the English Stage.' *Critical Essays of the Seventeenth Century.* Ed. J. E. Spingarn. 3 vols. Oxford, 1908.

Fletcher, George. *Studies of Shakespeare.* 1847.

French, Yvonne. *Mrs Siddons.* 1936.

Funke, Lewis, and Booth, John E. (eds.). *Actors Talk about Acting.* 1962.

Ganz, Paul. *The Drawings of Henry Fuseli.* 1949.

Garrick, David. 'An Essay on Acting', and 'Supplementary Appendix to "An Essay on Acting".' *Tracts Relating to Shakespeare.* 1779.

The Private Correspondence of David Garrick. Ed. James Boaden. 2 vols. 1831–2.

The Letters of David Garrick. Ed. David M. Little and George M. Karhl. 3 vols. Oxford, 1963.

Genest, John. *Some Account of the English Stage, 1660 to 1830.* 10 vols. Bath, 1832.

Gentleman, Francis. *The Dramatic Censor.* 2 vols. 1770.

Gildon, Charles. *The Life of Mr Thomas Betterton.* 1710.

Gould, G. *Corrigenda and Explanations.* 1884.

Harbage, Alfred. *Theatre for Shakespeare.* Toronto, 1955.

Hazlitt, William. *The Collected Works.* Ed. A. R. Waller and A. Glover. 13 vols. 1902.

Hedgcock, F. A. *David Garrick et ses amis français.* Paris, 1911.

Heywood, Thomas, and Brome, Richard. *Late Lancashire Witches.* 1634.

Hill, Aaron. *The Works of the Late Aaron Hill, Esq.* 4 vols. 1753.

The Prompter: November 12, 1734–July 1736. Rptd *The Gentleman's Magazine.* 1784.

Hill, John. *The Actor.* 1750.

The Actor. 1755.

Hillebrand, H. N. *Edmund Kean.* New York, 1933.

Hogan, Charles Beecher. *Shakespeare in the Theatre.* 2 vols. Oxford, 1951.

Holcroft, Thomas. *The Theatrical Recorder.* 2 vols. 1805.

Hunt, Leigh. *Critical Essays on the Performers of the London Theatres.* 1807.

Dramatic Essays. Ed. W. Archer and R. W. Lowe. 1894.

Dramatic Criticism, 1808–31. Ed. L. H. and C. W. Houtchens. New York, 1949.

Ireland, John. *Letters and Poems by the Late Mr John Henderson, with Anecdotes of his Life.* 1786.

Irving, Henry. *English Actors*. 1886.

Irving, Laurence. *Henry Irving*. 1930.

Isaacs, J. 'Shakespeare as a Man of the Theatre.' *Shakespeare Criticism*, 1919–35. Ed. Anne Bradby. 1936.

James, Henry. *The Scenic Art*. Ed. Allan Wade. New Brunswick, 1948.

Johnson, Samuel. *Miscellaneous Observations on the Tragedy of Macbeth*. 1745.

Johnson's Shakespeare. 1773.

The Works of Samuel Johnson. Ed. Robert Lynam. 6 vols. 1825.

Jonson, Ben. *Ben Jonson. Complete Works*. Ed. C. H. Herford and Percy and Evelyn Simpson. 10 vols. Oxford, 1925–50.

Joseph, Bertram. *The Tragic Actor*. 1959.

Acting Shakespeare. 1960.

Kemble, Fanny. *Records of Later Life*. 3 vols. 1882.

Notes upon some of Shakespeare's Plays. 1882.

Kemble, John Philip. 'Macbeth Reconsidered.' 1786.

'Macbeth and Richard III.' 1817.

Kendal, Dame Madge. *Dame Madge Kendal by Herself*. 1933.

Ketton-Cremer, Robert Wyndham. *Early Life and Diaries of William Windham*. 1930.

Knight, Wilson. *Principles of Shakespearean Stage Productions*. 1936.

Shakespearean Production. 1964.

Knights, L. C. *Drama and Society in the Age of Jonson*. 1937.

Explorations. 1951.

Knowles, James Sheridan. *Lectures on Dramatic Literature: Macbeth*. 1875.

Lamb, Charles. *Works*. 2 vols. 1818.

Laver, J. *Costume in the Theatre*. 1964.

Levey, Michael. *From Giotto to Cézanne*. 1962.

Lewes, George Henry. *On Actors and the Art of Acting*. 1875. Paperback, New York, 1957.

Dramatic Essays. Ed. W. Archer and R. W. Lowe. 1896.

Lichtenberg, Georg Christoph. *Briefe aus England* (1776–8). Ed. W. Grenzmann. 3 vols. 1953. Trans. M. L. Mare and W. H. Quarrell as *Lichtenberg's Visits to England*. 1 vol. 1938.

Lloyd, Robert. *The Actor*. 1760.

The London Stage. Part 1: 1660–1700. Ed. William Van Lennep. Illinois, 1965.

Part 2: 1700–1729. Ed. Emmet L. Avery. Illinois, 1960.

Part 3: 1729–1747. Ed. Arthur Scouten. Illinois, 1961.

Part 4: 1747–1776. Ed. George Winchester Stone. Illinois, 1962.

Macklin, Charles. *An Apology for the Conduct of Mr Charles Macklin, Comedian*. 1773.

Macready, William Charles. *Reminiscences and Selections from his Diaries and Letters.* Ed. Sir Frederick Pollock. 2 vols. 1875.

Mander, R., and Mitchenson, J. *The Theatres of London.* 1961.

Mangin, Edward. *Piozziana.* 1833.
  The Parlour Window. 1841.

Marston, John Westland. *Our Recent Actors.* 2 vols. 1888.

Martin, Theodore. *Helena Faucit.* 1900.

Matthews, Brander (ed.). *Papers on Acting.* New York, 1958.

Matthews, Brander, and Thorndike, Ashley H. (eds.). *Shakespearean Studies.* New York, 1916.

Morley, Henry. *Journal of a London Playgoer.* 1866.

Morozov, A. V. *Shakespeare on the Soviet Stage.* 1947.

Murphy, Arthur. *Life of David Garrick Esq.* 2 vols. 1801.

Muskau, Pückler. *Briefe Eines Verstorbenen.* 4 vols. Stuttgart, 1831. Trans. Sarah Austin as *Tour in England.* 4 vols. 1832.

Nagler, A. M. *Sources of Theatrical History.* New York, 1952.

Nashe, Thomas. *Works.* Ed. R. B. McKerrow. 5 vols. Oxford, 1958.

Nicoll, Allardyce. *A History of Early Nineteenth Century Drama:* 1800–50. 2 vols. Cambridge, 1930.

Noverre, Jean Georges. *Lettres sur la Danse et sur les Ballets.* 1783. Trans. Cyril W. Beaumont as *Letters on Dancing and Ballet.* 1951.

Nungezer, Edwin. *A Dictionary of Actors.* New Haven, 1929.

Odell, G. C. D. *Shakespeare from Betterton to Irving.* 2 vols. New York, 1921.

O'Keeffe, John. *Recollections of the Life of John O'Keeffe.* 1826.

Oulton, W. C. *History of the Theatres of London.* 2 vols. 1796.

Oxberry, W. *Oxberry's Dramatic Biography.* 3 vols. 1825.

Parry, E. A. *Charles Macklin.* 1891.

Pascoe, C. E. *The Dramatic List.* 1880.

Pepys, Samuel. *Diary.* Ed. Richard, Lord Braybrooke. 2 vols. 1825.

Phelps, W. May, and Forbes-Robertson, Johnston. *The Life and Life-work of Samuel Phelps.* 1886.

Planché, J. R. *Recollections and Reflections.* Rev. ed. 1901.

Playfair, Giles. *Kean.* 1950.

Poel, William. *Shakespeare in the Theatre.* 1913.

Pollock, Lady. *Macready as I Knew Him.* 1885.

Pope, Alexander. *The Dunciad.* Ed. James R. Sutherland. 1943.
  Epistles to Several Persons. Ed. F. W. Bateson. 1951.

Purdom, C. B. *Harley Granville-Barker.* 1955.

Puttenham, George. *The Arte of English Poesie.* 1589. Ed. G. D. Willcock and A. Walker. Cambridge, 1936.

Robinson, Henry Crabbe. *The Diary, Reminiscences and Correspondence of Henry Crabbe Robinson.* Ed. T. Sadler. 2 vols. 1872.

Robson, William. *The Old Playgoer.* 1846.

Russell, William Clark. *Representative Actors*. n.d.

Saintsbury, H. A., and Palmer, Cecil. *We Saw Him Act*. 1959.

Scharf, George. *Recollections of the Scenic Effects of Covent Garden Theatre*. n.d.

Shakespeare, William. *First Folio*. Ed. John Heminge and Henry Condell. 1623.

    The Works of Mr William Shakespear. Ed. Nicholas Rowe. 6 vols. 1709.

    The Works of Shakespeare. Ed. Lewis Theobald. 8 vols. 1740.

    Collected Works. Ed. Bell. 1773.

    Collected Works. Ed. Bell. 2nd ed. 1774.

    The Plays of William Shakespeare. Ed. Samuel Johnson and George Steevens. 2nd ed. 10 vols. 1778.

    Macbeth. J. P. Kemble's stage version. 1794.

    Macbeth. Ed. J. Q. Adams. New York, 1931.

    Macbeth (New Cambridge). Ed. John Dover Wilson. Cambridge, 1947.

    Macbeth (New Arden). Ed. Kenneth Muir. 1951.

    Complete Works (Tudor). Ed. Peter Alexander. 1951.

    Macbeth. Ed. Francis Fergusson. New York, 1959.

    Macbeth (New Variorum). Ed. H. H. Furness. New York, 1963.

Shaw, George Bernard. *Our Theatres in the Nineties*. 3 vols. 1931.

    Bernard Shaw and Mrs Patrick Campbell: Their Correspondence. Ed. Alan Dent. 1952.

Siddons, Sarah. 'Remarks on the Character of Lady Macbeth.' (See under Campbell, T.)

    The Reminiscences of Sarah Kemble Siddons. Ed. William Van Lennep. Cambridge, Mass., 1942.

Sillard, R. M. *Barry Sullivan and his Contemporaries*. 2 vols. 1901.

Speaight, Robert. *William Poel and the Elizabethan Revival*. 1954.

Spencer, Hazelton. *Shakespeare Improved*. Cambridge, Mass., 1927.

Sprague, Arthur Colby. *Shakespeare and the Actors*. Cambridge, Mass., 1945.

    The Stage Business in Shakespeare's Plays: A Postscript. The Society for Theatre Research; Pamphlet Series no. 3. 1953.

    Shakespearian Players and Performances. 1954.

Spurgeon, Caroline. 'Leading Motives in the Imagery of Shakespeare's Tragedies.' *Shakespeare Criticism*, 1919–35. Ed. Anne Bradby. 1936.

Stanislavsky, K. *Stanislavsky on the Art of the Stage*. Trans. David Magarshack. 1950.

Taylor, John. *Personal Reminiscences*. Ed. R. H. Stoddard. 1875.

Terry, Ellen. *Ellen Terry and Bernard Shaw: A Correspondence*. Ed. Christopher St John. New York, 1931.

    Memoirs. Ed. Edith Craig and C. St John. 1933.

Thaler, Alwin. *Shakespeare to Sheridan.* 1922.

Thorn-Drury, George (ed.). *More Seventeenth Century Allusions to Shakespeare.* 1924.

Tomkins, F. G. *A Brief View of the English Drama.* 1840.

Trewin, J. C. *The Birmingham Repertory Theatre 1913–1963.* 1963.
Shakespeare on the English Stage 1900–1964. 1964.

Tynan, Kenneth. *He that Plays the King.* 1950.

Walpole, Horace. *Correspondence of Horace Walpole and William Mason.* Ed. J. Mitford. 2 vols. 1851.
The Letters of Horace Walpole. Ed. Paget Toynbee. 16 vols. Oxford, 1903–5.

Webster, Margaret. *Shakespeare Today.* 1957.

Wells, Staring B. *A Comparison between the Two Stages.* Princeton, 1942.

Wilkes, Thomas. *A General View of the Stage.* 1759.

Williamson, Audrey. *Theatre of Two Decades.* 1951.

Williamson, Audrey, and Landstone, Charles. *The Bristol Old Vic.* 1957.

Wilson, John Dover. *Life in Shakespeare's England.* 1944.

Winter, William. *Shakespeare on the Stage.* First Series. New York, 1911.

Woodstock. Ed. A. P. Rossiter. 1946.

Yeats, W. B. *Ideas of Good and Evil.* 1903.
Last Poems and Plays. 1940.

Young, Julian Charles. *A Memoir of Charles Mayne Young.* 1871.

INDEX

action, 9
Adams, J. Q., 8–9
Addison, Joseph, 31
Agate, James, *on* Henry Ainley, 228;
  Vivienne Bennett, 244; Benson, 218;
  Gwen Ffrangcon-Davies, 236; John
  Gielgud, 234–5; Martita Hunt, 235;
  Charles Laughton, 239; Eric Maturin,
  232; Flora Robson, 243; Ion Swinley,
  244; Sybil Thorndike, 227; Donald
  Wolfit, 218, 247–8
Ainley, Henry, 225, 228
Aldwych Theatre, The, 98, 230, 249
Anderson, Judith, 245
apron stage, 12, 24, 44, 222, 226, 254,
  256, 262, 271
Archer, William, 198
Armstrong, W. A., 2
Arts Theatre, The, 251, 252
Arts Theatre, Cambridge, 246
Aston, Anthony, 15, 26, 30
Avery, Emmet L., 25 n., 30, 32

Barrault, Jean-Louis, 28
Barry, Mrs Elizabeth, 16, 26, 29, 36, 48
Barry, Spranger, 82, 93–4, 272
Bartley, Mrs, 145
Barton, Margaret, 35 n., 39 n.
Bateman, Miss, 199–200, 203, 206
Baylis, Lilian, 225, 245
Beaumont, Francis, 1, 8–9, 35
Bell, John, *on* Kemble, 127–9, 130–1;
  Mrs Siddons, 103–22 *passim*
Bennett, Vivienne, 244, 247
Benson, F. R., 217–20, 268
Benson, Mrs, 218–19
Benthall, Michael, 266
Bentley, Eric, 225 n.
Bernhardt, Sarah, 208–9, 212
Betterton, Thomas, xi, 1, 2, 12, 13,
  14–27 *passim*, 29–30, 32, 35–6, 38, 80,
  94, 96, 102, 186, 187, 196, 220, 222
Betterton, Mrs, 25–7, 48, 172
Birmingham Repertory Theatre, The,
  231, 267
Boaden, James, *on* Cooke, 143; Garrick,
  38, 39, 43, 44, 47–8, 52–3, 55, 57–8,
  67, 74, 76; John Kemble, 139; Mrs

Siddons, 102, 104, 105–8 *passim*, 115,
  120; Smith, 122; Shakespeare's use of
  language, 132–3
Bourchier, Arthur, 213
Bradley, A. C., 147, 215–16, 239, 240
Brecht, Bertolt, 21
Bridges-Adams, W., 230–1
Bristol Old Vic, The, 251
Brook, Peter, 98
Brown, Ivor, 235, 249
Brown, Pamela, 251–2
Bullock, Christopher, 16, 18
Bulwer, John, 253
Burbage, Richard, xi, xii, 1, 9–11, 28–9,
  68, 196
Burnim, Kalman, 39, 40 n., 61, 63, 66,
  72, 77, 80
Burrill, Ena, 249, 273
Byrne, Muriel St Clare, 83 n.
Byron, George Gordon, xiii, 103, 139

Campbell, Mrs Patrick, 212, 213, 214,
  230–1
Campbell, Thomas, *on* Kemble, 133;
  Mrs Siddons, 98–101 *passim*
Carrick, Edmund, 250
Carrick, Edward, 237–8
Casson, Lewis, 226–9
Cellier, Frank, 231
Chatham, Earl of, 38, 80
Chetwood, W. R., 36
Churchill, Charles, 92
Cibber, Colley, *on* Betterton, 14–15, 29,
  38, 102; Mrs Betterton, 25–6, 172;
  Drury Lane, 24, 222
Cibber, Mrs, 94, 95
Cicero, 9
Clunes, Alec, 252
Coleman, John, *on* Charles Kean, 180–2;
  Macready, 155, 159, 160, 162–5, 275;
  Phelps, 186; Ristori, 190; Mrs
  Warner, 171
Coleridge, Samuel Taylor, xi, 81, 121,
  146, 147, 148, 157
Comus, 33
concentration, 9, 98
Cooke, G. F., xiii, 103, 139, 142–4, 150,
  206

INDEX

Laughton, Charles, 238, 239–41, 243

Lear, 10, 79, 247

Lehmann, Beatrix, 267–8

Leigh, Vivien, 254, 257–64, 267, 275

Leighton, Margaret, 250–1

Levey, Michael, 62–3

Lewes, G. H., *on* Charles Kean, 181, 183–6, 192; Mrs Charles Kean, 184–5; Edmund Kean, 146; Macready, 154, 164

Lichtenberg, G. C., 72 n.

lighting, 64, 158, 163, 199, 202, 205, 215, 225, 244, 252, 255, 256

Lincoln's Inn Fields Theatre, 16, 24–5, 33

Little, David M., 71, 83

Littlewood, Joan, 266–7

Lloyd, Robert, 62, 133

Lowin, John, 1, 2, 29, 36

Lyceum, The (London), 190, 192, 201, 211

Lyceum, The (New York), 192

Lyric, The, Hammersmith, 247

Lytton, Bulwer, 158, 170

Macbeth, Davenant's version, 15–27 *passim*, 33, 35, 36, 39–59 *passim*, 66, 69–70, 74, 75–6, 81, 90, 93, 94, 125, 159, 216, 220, 269, 272; First Folio, 2, 5–8, 17–24 *passim*, 19 n., 39–60 *passim*, 65–7, 70, 72–4, 76–7, 79, 81, 85, 121, 125, 127, 187, 220–1, 274; Garrick's text (ed. Bell), 39–60 *passim*, 66, 70, 72–4, 75–8, 121, 125, 127, 131, 148, 159; Irving's Part Copy (1875), 198–9, 201–6; Kean's text, 148; Kemble's text, 121, 125, 127, 130, 131, 134, 159; Macready's text, 159, 163 n., 164, 166 n.; Phelps' text, 186–7; Beerbohm Tree's text, 216

Macklin, Charles, 37, 41, 70–1, 82–91, 93, 94, 95, 138; his Notes, 85 n., 87, 88, 90

MacOwan, Michael, 249

Macready, William, xi, 90, 128, 146, 152, 154–71, 175, 176, 177–9, 180, 185, 186, 187, 192, 206, 229, 236, 245, 275; *Reminiscences...*, 124, 135–7, 138, 156–8, 172

Mangin, Edward, 100, 102, 116

Marston, Westland, *on* Charlotte Cushman, 172; Dillon, 195; Charles Kean, 182, 184; Charles Kemble and Van-

denhoff, 152; Macready, 154, 160–1, 164, 165, 167; Wallack, 193; Mrs Warner, 171

Matthews, Brander, xi, 166 n.

Mattingly, Garrett, 243

Maturin, Eric, 232

McCarthy, Lillah, 222–3

Mei-Lan-Fang, 11

Mermaid Theatre, The, 251, 252–3, 268, 270–1

Merrall, Mary, 232

Midsummer Night's Dream, A, 17, 225

Miles, Bernard, 252–3

Mills, John, 16, 30–2 *passim*, 37

Milton, Ernest, 247

Milton, John, 33, 88, 147, 157

Morley, Henry, 175, 188–92

Mossop, Frederick, 63, 82, 91–3, 94

Murphy, Arthur, 47, 55, 60–1, 75, 77, 122

music, *Macbeth* productions, 15, 16–17, 30–1, 66, 70, 83, 135, 158, 161, 163, 165, 186, 207, 230, 232, 259, 265, 272, 275

Nosworthy, J. M., 7

Noverre, Jean Georges, 78

Nungezer, Edwin, 28 n.

Odell, G. C. D., 95 n., 140, 225

Old Vic, The, 225, 226, 233, 236, 237, 238, 244, 246, 266, 267

Olivier, Laurence, 244–5, 246, 248, 251, 254–66, 274, 275

Othello, 10, 150, 152, 156 n., 178, 195, 209, 211, 224

Othello, 17, 194

Oxberry, W., 110 n., 152

Pepys, Samuel, 5, 15, 16, 17, 25

Phelps, Samuel, 152–3, 171, 175, 186–8, 192, 194–5, 220

Planché, J. R., 132

Playfair, Giles, 144

Poel, William, 220–4, 225, 226, 230, 231, 236, 249

Pope, Alexander, 14, 18, 27, 32, 38–9, 43, 121

Porter, Eric, xi, 268–9, 270

Porter, Mrs, 27, 30, 36–7, 38, 48, 96

Powell, George, 30–2 *passim*

Powell, William (the elder), 82, 95

Prince's Theatre, The, 180, 183